LAST YEAR'S issue of ▓▓▓▓▓▓▓ ▓▓▓▓
under Louis ▓▓▓▓▓ ▓▓▓▓▓ ▓▓▓
ceived such an ▓▓▓▓▓▓▓▓▓ ▓▓
one needs to say i▓▓▓▓▓▓▓▓▓ ▓▓▓▓▓▓
that again it is fill▓▓▓▓▓▓▓▓▓ ▓▓▓▓▓▓▓
But there are, in a▓▓▓▓ ▓▓, new features.
The picture sectio▓ ▓▓▓ ▓▓▓n improved, and
through special arrangements with *Life* a much
more dramatic quality of photographic material has been obtained. An entirely new fea-
ture is a section on the "Hit Tunes" of the
year. With a few bars of music, anyone can
now pick out on the piano enough to remind
him of the most popular and distinctive mel-
odies. A new editor is writing of activity on
the whole West Coast rather than just the Los
Angeles area as before.

Most of all, readers will appreciate the ingenious, pithy and very readable summaries,
with excerpts, which make up Louis Kronenberger's ten best plays, and his witty, incisive
review of the season. It has, he says, been an
unusually diversified and promising one —
much more encouraging than many recent
years. His selection of "Outstanding Perform--
ances" and of the best Scenic Designs and Costumes and other new features which he introduced last year, have proved so useful and popular that they are now established parts of
the book, along with all the time-honored
features developed over the years by Burns
Mantle.

THE BEST PLAYS OF 1953–1954

THE BURNS MANTLE YEARBOOK

Illustrated with photographs, and with

Drawings by HIRSCHFELD

from
"The Teahouse
of the August Moon"

THE BEST PLAYS
OF 1953–1954

EDITED BY LOUIS KRONENBERGER

DODD, MEAD AND COMPANY

NEW YORK   1954   TORONTO

EDITOR'S NOTE

IN editing this thirty-seventh volume in the *Best Plays* series, I find myself once again under very pleasant obligations. By far the greatest is once again to my wife, Emmy Plaut, for help that is more fairly called collaboration. For editorial assistance I am much indebted to Helen Winfield and Hollis Mitchell. For the use of photographs I must thank the Editors of *Life* Magazine, and for the use of its tabulation of Hits and Flops, *Variety* and Mr. Abel Green. Particular thanks are due, for their several reports, to Miss Cassidy, Mr. Tynan, M. Josset, Mr. Sherwood and Mr. Nichols; and for kindly granting the use of their sketches, to Boris Aronson, William and Jean Eckart, George Jenkins, Miles White, and Irene Sharaff.

Finally, I must again record my pleasure in being associated in this project with Mr. Hirschfeld.

LOUIS KRONENBERGER

CONTENTS

PHOTOGRAPHS

THE BEST PLAYS OF 1953–1954

THE BEST PLAYS OF 1953–1954

THE SEASON IN NEW YORK

NOT in many years had Broadway known a season boasting such a large number of pretty good plays. The effect was invigorating, for by some weird mental process a lot of slightly better-than-average works seemed to merge into something collectively impressive. In contrast to its predecessor, 1953-54 proved a nice, active, comfortable Broadway season that stimulated gladness and quite annihilated guilt. Hardly a week went by that someone didn't proclaim something or other a masterpiece; and some weeks almost the entire theatrical *corps diplomatique* took to throwing adjectival confetti and tossing metaphorical hats. Moreover, to refer to all this as a Broadway season is a slight misnomer. Much that was liveliest in New York didn't originate on Broadway or even attain to it; and perhaps—in terms of the history books—the prime significance of '53-'54 will be that Broadway, just then, began to be saved (or could it have been doomed?) by Off-Broadway's contributions.

In any case, '53-'54 was not a stereotype. It was the season when surefire things—e.g., *Kind Sir*—exploded in Broadway's face. It was the season when Second Avenue, that a century earlier had rivaled Fifth Avenue for *ton,* came—via the Phoenix Theatre—to rival Broadway in news value. It was the season when virtually none of Broadway's regulars (not Robert Sherwood or Maxwell Anderson or S. N. Behrman or Moss Hart or Lillian Hellman or Clifford Odets or Thornton Wilder or Arthur Miller or Tennessee Williams or Noel Coward or Terence Rattigan or William Inge or Arthur Laurents or George Kelly or Sidney Kingsley or Mary Chase) put in an appearance; and when, conversely, five of the ten Best Plays proved to be their authors' first. During the season, in fact, Mr. Sherwood sang the virtues of the Arts of the Air, of TV and radio, as a stepping-stone or vestibule to Broadway; he cited a number of new playwrights who, so to speak, flew down to the footlights when they might never have got there on foot. His recital made a brave statistic; but, considering what certain of his playwrights had brought with them to Broadway, it was not wholly a paean to TV; it was also an alarm bell. All in all, it was a season for Broadway to feel gratified but not quite complacent about.

3

In any such season it's not easy to choose the "best": next most confusing, where plays are concerned, to an embarrassment of riches is an over-abundance of adequacy. Indeed, though I could choose only ten plays for this book, there were just twice that number to make a final choice from. The reason was not how many of the contenders were outstanding, but how few; for almost every one of the twenty, along with its own special merits, had its particular faults. In the end, something personal as well as strictly critical had to come into play. The older I get, the more readily I accept my own taste, but in the clear knowledge that it's no more than my own taste: something that not just other people will disagree with but that quite possibly—next Saturday or next Summer—I shall disagree with, too. I have not canonized the ten plays that follow without frequently performing the role of devil's advocate. I know very well what is to be said against, for one example, *The Confidential Clerk* —and what can be said, for another example, in favor of *Oh Men, Oh Women*. The author of *Ondine,* again, wrote in a distinguished tradition that I myself find immensely congenial; the author of *The Magic and the Loss,* on the other hand, writes in a tradition that I much less admire or enjoy. Yet the *Ondine* offered on Broadway last season seemed to me, whatever its momentary rewards, essentially lifeless; while *The Magic and the Loss,* though it lacks distinction, is yet impressively honest about something still theatrically topical. It avails little that M. Giraudoux breathes a larger air than Mr. Funt if he offers a play that itself is airless.

If any of this seems apologetic, it's not meant to be; it is only meant to be conversational, to talk over the season's prize entrants as the vulnerable things they are; to suggest that precisely what made the final decision ticklish is what made it interesting. It would have been not only pompous but fatuous to pretend to be guided by some infallible point system or elaborate body of rules. *Tea and Sympathy* has a good deal to be said against it, which shall in due course be said; I've included it because it seems to me a genuine theatre piece, an effective whole. *In the Summer House* seems on the contrary no play at all, and a far better half than whole; it just happens, at its best, to boast the most individual and expressive writing of the season. This having to juggle the merits (or shortcomings) of twenty plays in order to choose ten reveals a great advance over the previous year, when one spent all too much time wondering where on earth ten could be found.

It was generally a more fruitful season for drama than for comedy, though also a season when the two things met at times in the same

Mary Martin and Charles Boyer in "Kind Sir"

play. Such merging can be interpreted for good or bad: for good, in the sense that life is a blend of both; for bad, not only because art rather resists such blending, but also because "comedy-drama" is What the Public Wants. Yet, though in the highest sense this works to the theatre's detriment, in another sense the blending of comedy with drama comes natural to most of our more serious playwriting. Such playwriting is much oftener influenced by life than by art; is, in other words, imitative rather than expressive, photographic rather than imaginative; it is made "true-to-life" by the quantity and precision of its detail. And this working through patient detail rather than by swift bold strokes encourages, indeed often necessitates, comedy-drama: the comedy may itself be dramatic, as in *End as a Man,* or didactic, as in *The Ladies of the Corridor,* or thermostatic, maintaining proportion and perspective, as in *Take a Giant Step.* The point is that without comedy all these plays would, by reason of their methods, be terribly high-pitched and over-intense. (Being— however less expert—more genuinely imaginative, an *In the Summer House* does not so much mate comedy and drama as androgynously contain both within its vision of life.)

On this account, it is understandable why drama last season—in fact, why drama generally—comes off better at any very serious level than comedy does. Unlike light comedy, serious comedy does not merely woo the funnybone; nor does it, like drama, directly assault the emotions or the heart. It would move the mind; or rather (what most people find too difficult and roundabout a journey) the heart by way of the mind. It is at least the *intention* of *The Confidential Clerk* to reach the heart by way of the mind, even though it never fully does. Drama, with its direct attack, its instantaneously felt voltage, comes closer than comedy—as a serious medium—to the genius of the stage.

Drama, last season, quickly went into the lead with three early-autumn exhibits. Characteristically enough, the season's first interesting exhibit, Calder Willingham's *End as a Man,* began life off-Broadway and only later came uptown. It had also begun life as a novel, and its chief over-all weakness was that it never quite managed to end as a play. A brutal picture (with a core of horror imbedded in its varieties of hellraising) of life at a Southern military academy, it offered characters scary to think about as future warriors, or even as future citizens. But however vivid a behavioristic chronicle, its series of scenes never quite became more than a series of scenes. Though something was implied concerning the academy's role in the wrongdoings of its cadets, too much had to be inferred: there was no clear sense of just what the institution was attempting to foster or struggling to prevent. Moved uptown in revised form, *End as a Man* had rather lost than gained and seemed—more than at the out-set—in need of the talented acting it received. But uptown no less than down, it did have the power to shock.

Though also a series of scenes, Broadway's own first interesting exhibit, *Take a Giant Step,* did on the whole come together as a play. It treats very honestly of a young Negro's tragicomic scuffle with adolescence, of growing pains that involve growing awarenesses and dubieties, and of that giant step toward maturity that in moving forward must also turn a corner. One of the play's virtues is that, while primarily about an adolescent, it acquires added significance by being also about a Negro. We get *Seventeen* without a mere Willy Baxter, we get very real humor that is not just one more joke about youth. The fresh humorous smack in much of the writing is the most valuable quality in the play; it provided not merely flavor, but also a sense of proportion. Mr. Peterson has got on top of his subject, or at any rate of his hero; so that his hero is sympathetic without being sentimentalized, and achieves the dignity of a perplexed human being without the portentousness of a "problem." The play is interesting also for being a distinctly middle-class (rather than lower-class) chronicle. But the middle-classness that adds piquancy in terms of a Negro adds familiarity in terms of adolescence itself. Most of Spencer's experiences—whether at home or at school, with sex or with self—are the clichés of adolescent literature; while, worse yet, some of them are clumsily told. The real merit of *Take a Giant Step* is confined to its humor and its hero; but the one, fortunately, pervades the play and the other unifies it.

With the third of the season's early interesting exhibits, with *Tea and Sympathy*, there entered a new note, a sense of something much more professional and artful. *Tea and Sympathy* is a patently well-contrived—as it was also a decidedly well-directed—play. It has a peculiarly contemporary theme of horror—a sensitive schoolboy falsely accused of homosexuality; it has its compensatingly attractive fund of sentiment—the warm sympathy of the housemaster's sensitive and lovely wife. It has its lemon-squeeze of Freud—the lurking homosexuality in the harshly masculine headmaster; it has finally a certain moral force, less for what Tom is branded with than for picturing the thoughtless conformists who apply the branding iron. There is no unevenness, no emotional skimping: *Tea and Sympathy* is a full-fashioned theatre piece, a thoroughly effective matinee drama.

There is no unevenness, but there is hollowness. Doubtless a dramatist must often choose between exploiting and expressing something, between the claims of theatre and those of life; and perhaps one resents it less when, as here, there is a consistent allegiance to theatre rather than a compromise. If *Tea and Sympathy* did not have its precise limitations, it could not have its particular lure. The play is necessarily full of "situations" and, only a little less, of echoes. Yet beyond what it recalls of a *Young Woodley* or of a *Children's Hour* it awakens memories of prep-school books for boys: this is just a little an adolescent yarn recast for adults, the yarn of the wronged, unjustly suspected "hero"—only we encountered him last under suspicion of throwing the big game, or of squealing to the headmaster. As theatre, *Tea and Sympathy* has everything, which is perhaps why as anything better it rings hollow. Can this resemble what William Archer had in mind in contending that the same piece of writing can be bad literature but a good play?

A little later came *The Ladies of the Corridor,* where Dorothy Parker and Arnaud d'Usseau focused on an expressive aspect of upper-middle-class America—the widows who lead pointless, profitless, bustlingly trivial, barrenly lonely lives in apartment hotels. The play offered—beyond fine flashes of the celebrated Parker wit—a recurrent insight into feminine psychology, a sound criticism of a segment of American society. If the play yet, despite its virtues, seemed not theatrically effective or psychologically illuminating enough, it was because of something too restricted in its material and its point of view alike. Unlike the usual hotel, with its vivid cross-section of human types, one that quarters (and caters to) a single breed must tend toward sameness and excess; and this tendency the play could not, in the main, overcome. If anything, it aggravated the tendency by seeing its many ladies in just two lights: either a remorselessly satiric one, which seemed to station the more gossipy and gabbling women not so much in a corridor as in a shooting gallery; or an unabashedly sentimental one, which led the authors to write with their hearts instead of their heads about women who lived that way. Characters thus seemed taken too seriously or not seriously enough; observed from too scornful a height or with no sense of distance at all.

Horton Foote's *The Trip to Bountiful* ran sadly downhill by running out on itself. Its proper theme was that second most ticklish of *ménages à trois*—the husband, the wife, and the husband's mother. In this case, the wife is a giddy, shallow Texas shrew, infinitely the worse for not being married to a good provider; she thus browbeats her long-suffering mother-in-law in the very act of exploiting her; and she so intimidates her husband that he dare not interfere. As domestic drama with an economic base, as a picture of three lives all messed up with no place to go, *The Trip to Bountiful* posits—and for a time portrays—a living situation. But then Mr. Foote abandons his living situation for a soupy story; the mother-in-law runs away, runs back to the town where she had once been happy, and is happy among its ghosts till she is dragged home to reality. Mr. Foote escaped an act too late into mere, pretty escapist fantasy: he had involved us in something harsh and real only to abandon it for something too whimperingly—and too deliberately—pathetic. Hence, at any mature level, his play ended just where he perhaps thought it began.

Where *The Trip to Bountiful* turned away from being a real play,

In the Summer House never truly turned into one. But here there is not the same violation, one might almost call it betrayal, of tone: indeed, *In the Summer House* sustains its tone very much at the expense of its story-telling. Mrs. Bowles possesses, above everything else, a certain style, which is not to be mistaken for mere manner; and this, in the absence of form or movement, crisps and starches the earlier scenes of her play; endows what is neurotic with something attractively atmospheric; and fashions a glass-belled universe of its own. Unhappily, though the play has very much its own style, it has too little of its own substance; once its literary charms are exhausted, a sense of over-literary derivations (and the customary Freudian curse) becomes marked. The trouble is perhaps less that these aren't quite real people than that they seem like other writers' apparitions. The play's beauty is only style-deep: after a time, Mrs. Bowles can not only no longer create, she can no longer contrive. The play, quite incidentally, stresses a rather common failing: many literary playwrights can also, in places, be effectively theatrical; what they fail to be is genuinely dramatic. But, to go no farther, the first ten minutes of *In the Summer House* provide the most electrically personal writing of the season.

In terms of theatre, very nearly everything about *The Caine Mutiny Court-Martial* has virtue, even the play's limitations. With its sharply compressed method and its simple, colorless *mise-en-scène*, it endows literalness with the power of suggestion, it evokes a shipboard drama of events through enacting a courtroom drama of character. Again, by not insisting on being overtly theatrical, Mr. Wouk's piece proves all the tenser theatre; and by sticking to theatre, the play avoids the pitfalls of more ambitious drama. That, to be sure, is its limitation as well as its merit, for nowhere is there the sense of large-dimensioned drama, or of the authentic dramatist. But—with the help of an able cast and of Charles Laughton's brilliant direction—Mr. Wouk does very soundly all that he set out to do. The play possesses, again, that legalistic ingenuity that underlies good theatre, as distinct from the more anarchic sense of fate that overlays life itself. There is the situation of Maryk's lawyer, who would much rather be prosecuting than defending his client, and who wins him an acquittal by not defending him. He attacks others instead, and we thrill to the ingeniousness that slowly walls in, not the accused but the accuser. Courtrooms are not intensely dramatic by accident: about the law of the theatre, as about the law of the land, there is the same inexorableness, the same relentlessly euclidean demonstration.

Opening in January, Jean Anouilh's *Mademoiselle Colombe* was the first of three Broadway offerings from the hands of well-known French writers, the others being *The Immoralist* and *Ondine*. Since I adapted M. Anouilh's play and am therefore an interested party, it seems soundest not to discuss it. *The Immoralist,* which Ruth and Augustus Goetz adapted from André Gide's famous novel, constitutes perhaps the most serious and outspoken treatment of homosexuality that Broadway has seen. The Goetzes combined understanding with detachment; they equally eschewed prissiness and sensationalism, and the result is an honest and clear-sighted study, a soberly effective formulation. If there is a vital weakness, it is that the play is too thorough-going a "study" to come altogether to life on the stage. If it is as accurate, it is also at times as inexpressive as a blueprint. Everyone seems a little too articulate, everything a little too explicit; there is a certain sense of figures carefully placed in the moral landscape. In terms of story, we should be kept guessing more at the beginning, while in terms of theme we should be left guessing less at the end. But what, all in all, seems noteworthy is how much the play achieved rather than fell short of.

Ondine is the play I am unhappiest to omit from the Ten Best—unhappiest though not uneasiest, for the play seems to me theatrically dead. No one can cavil at the justness of the adapter's prose, but wanting to the play—and disastrously in the absence of any continuous drama—are Giraudoux's usual élan and magic. There are moments in the English version that still seem pure Giraudoux; one can still feel too, as it were, a ghostly impression or watery outline of its charm. But how faint—and hence how fatal. My own pleasure in Giraudoux goes back beyond his theatre pieces to his fiction, and it is the pleasure only to be had of a distinguished exponent of a distinguished tradition; of the truest kind of elegant ironist and compassionate worldling, of the man of wit who is never far from being a man of wisdom. Mr. Kenneth Tynan, in his current London report, goes so far as to rank Giraudoux as the finest world playwright between the wars—this in the face of Pirandello and O'Casey and, as some would say, of O'Neill. Such a ranking inevitably raises the point of in what degree distinction may take precedence of stature, or the very best interior decoration be thought superior to architecture. In the end, it perhaps comes down to something more personal than critical; to what one would prefer to have rather than what is "better" worth having.

Ondine, however, even in the ravishing presence of Audrey Hepburn—and how much more in her absence—seems to me flat and often downright dull. A good deal of the trouble may reside in the

*Edna Best, Sam Jaffe, Julie Harris and Eli Wallach in
"Mademoiselle Colombe"*

double change of nationality it underwent—from German into
French, as well as French into English. The shift from German to
French could not but be a spiritually bold one, as though Poulenc
should re-score *Das Rheingold*. Giraudoux could delicately regild
La Motte Fouqué's tale of a sprite who loved and married—and herself became—a mortal, only to flee a dismaying world for the depths
of her lake, her knightly husband dead of her farewell kiss. No
one could savor more than Giraudoux the melancholy turns and implications of Fouqué's romance, its clash between innocence and
worldliness, its contrast between humanity's dreams of perfection
and descents into reality. But all this, when turned into English,
somehow failed of fragrance and the right mournful subaqueous
light: the old magic was lost, uncompensated by new meaning; *Ondine* seemed neither simple enough nor complex enough; it seemed
waxen too, what was pretty about it only stressing what was lifeless.

The Girl on the Via Flaminia, which Alfred Hayes dramatized
from his novel, comes off, after the manner of dramatizations, too

episodic in method and uneven in effect. In an era of really accomplished playwriting, its weaknesses might seem all too glaring; in an era such as ours, they are decidedly pardonable. If there is faultiness in the play's structure, there is a lashing force in much of its writing; more, there is truth—and even a sense of tragic truthfulness—in the character of Mr. Hayes' heroine. The play seizes on one of those moments of national emotion out of which proceeds such an international episode as Mr. Hayes depicts. In a world of "liberation" that actually signifies poverty and defeat, the liberators can hardly not be viewed as selfish coin-jingling conquerors; while, in any such faked marriage of convenience as is chronicled here, though the G.I. may love the Italian girl a little more from being so lonely, the girl will hate the G.I. a great deal more for being so hungry; and will denounce him, at length, with a bitter G.I. bill of wrongs. Add to this the horrifying legal difficulties that ensue and the play runs headlong into tragedy. The girl's dilemma, the girl's emotions, the girl's fate make up for much that elsewhere, and among lesser characters, seems halting and inept. Mr. Hayes' ability, at his best, to be both harsh and compassionate rebukes a Broadway that can seldom do better than be tough and sentimental—*Guys and Dolls,* so to speak, without music.

Mr. Funt's *The Magic and the Loss* perhaps also has virtues that as much rebuke our playwriting as reward our audiences; failing to find in the theatre the expressiveness of the true work of art or the intensity of the essential work of genius, we must be thankful when, moving through the usual liquid ooze, we strike against something firm, even though flattened out, and rocklike, though wanting shape. In fact, to be realistic about it, perhaps the story Mr. Funt has to tell can only be told, just now, by someone sufficiently immersed in it to treat it without imagination, by someone so personally haunted by it as to make a neurotic juggling act of its interrelated problems. What, at any rate, is most central in the play is the particular milieu, the specific way of life it mirrors—that world that has come to be known as "Madison Avenue." It is an aware, aggressive, hucksterish, citified, pedigreed-dog-eat-dog way of life; a careerism with its own satellite Freud-fringed culture; its own guilt-edged liberalism; its cluster of interlocking "problems" based on a cluster of interlocking conflicts. The dilemmas besetting Mr. Funt's heroine—job vs. lover, lover vs. child, inner compulsions vs. outer happiness—are the stigmata of the whole enjittered, high-pressured world that Mr. Funt's heroine inhabits.

The play as conceived—which means, with all that Mr. Funt crams into it—might have fared better in the more spacious world of the novel. Its naturalism, its attempt to achieve impact through accurate abundant detail, proves somewhat self-defeating: too much of it seems foreshortened and ill-timed, hence comes to smack of melodrama and to have too crudely surfaced a morality. The need for haste also stamps the ending (in terms of Grace and her son) as too close to a conventionally happy one, for which the final ironic twist (in terms of Grace and her job) is not countervailing. All the same, Mr. Funt has portrayed something far more real, and has often made it ring far more true, than the vast majority of plays that get praised, or for that matter get prizes.

The season offered comedy of every kind, from the markedly racy to the coyly genteel, from the shamelessly wisecracking to the sporadically witty, from popular playwriting at its best to some choice examples of it at its ghastliest; comedy of United Nations and divided families; comedy of every style and species—sexual farce, satirical farce, psychoanalytical farce; farce-fantasy, comedy of manners, of character, of ideas.

The season's first comedy raised great expectations but fell woefully flat; the season's second became the smash production of the year. *The Little Hut* had the prestige of a three-year London run, plus a naughty reputation, to live up to. Whatever lure it may have had in London (and it presumably derived much more from the production than from the play), *The Little Hut* suffered a sea-change in traveling to Broadway; had the look, in fact, of something that fell in the water. The situation of husband, wife and lover shipwrecked on a tropical isle seemed bright and gay only to start off with, and grew more forced and listless as it ambled on. The play's great weakness is less that it never really expands than that it never really effervesces, never pitches head first into farce or lurches hilariously toward madness. It merely seemed part of that fashionable tradition that slices its amusement as paper-thin as its sandwiches; and since it wasn't served up with a properly tony air, it came to nothing.

A hut having failed, a teahouse next proceeded to triumph. The John Patrick adaptation was to go on to win both the Critics Circle and Pulitzer awards, and indeed *The Teahouse of the August Moon* proved the most attractive sort of popular playwriting. Sticking resolutely to surfaces, it outlawed any need for compromise. It chose a cheerful comedy level and preserved it; aimed at an artificial, fairy-tale mood and achieved it; went in for genial satire and adhered to it. In brilliantly bungling his assignment, in letting the Okinawans mosey toward democracy rather than glumly face it in formation, Captain Fisby demonstrates the superiority of the human heart over the military mind. The demonstration is just enough at the Americans' expense to jab pleasantly at one's complacence, but not enough to afflict one with disturbing thoughts. It being all in the nature of a fairy tale, the natives are uniformly lovable from the outset, and Okinawa, Washington (and New York audiences) are rendered equally satisfied at the end.

One gives *The Teahouse* full marks as entertainment; but one still may wonder by what critical reasoning it should win two seriously intended awards. For though it has its many engaging virtues, it quite lacks the two virtues that might reasonably be associated with an award winner; it has neither real substance nor real distinction. That the writing sometimes falters, sometimes descends to the commonplace and the cute, is less decisive than that it never once rises to actual brilliance. Again, one will settle for uniformly lovable natives and all the rest, on the ground that *The Teahouse* is more fairy tale than satire, brings more sweetness than light. But all the more, then, for lacking significance in what it says, it should display a certain real beauty (rather than tinkly charm) and rueful wit (rather than bustling humor) in how it says it. In any vital sense, *The Teahouse* is no closer to art than to life.

Set beside that other hit and self-styled fairy tale, set beside *The Solid Gold Cadillac, The Teahouse* does rather begin to seem like art. Conceivably *The Solid Gold Cadillac* called itself a fairy tale as a way out of being termed a play; but except for the fairy-story extravagances of the plot, it exchanged one misnomer for another. For it shows not a trace of the poetry or a touch of the wistfulness that a fairy tale implies. Its yarn of an elderly lady stockholder who asks such disquieting questions at a big stockholders' meeting as to create a *richesse d'embarras;* who is then hired by the corporation as a way of being shushed; and who winds up at the head of it—all this, the Messrs. Howard Teichmann and George S. Kaufman have dyed in the loud but fast colors of Broadway. They gave their play a funnybone without a spine, they all but wrote satire without indulging in criticism. But though the farce seems put together with the very pins it sticks in others, it does have a lot of funny lines. Those lines, and the presence of Josephine Hull in the cast, were enough to give the authors a hit and to keep most audiences happy.

Set beside that show with an almost unprecedented build-up, *Kind Sir, The Solid Gold Cadillac* in *its* turn takes on considerable grandeur. It would be misleading to call *Kind Sir* twaddle. Twaddle is sometimes fun; *Kind Sir*—even with Mary Martin and Charles Boyer to adorn it—was not fun, it was almost insolently vapid. It perhaps appealed to Joshua Logan for setting him the greatest challenge a miracle-working director could have. He met the challenge, in any case, full on; and the minutes of the meeting are rather bleak.

Samuel Taylor's *Sabrina Fair* was the nearest to a proper comedy of manners that any American had written in several years; and enhanced as it was by a suave production, it roused the feeling in certain quarters that somehow Congreve had returned from the dead. The play had, certainly, its good points: a decent feeling for tone, a lively eye for manners, a nice ear for dialogue; and if it was pretty remote from Congreve, at least—in writing of the Long Island rich— it wasn't blatantly reminiscent of Philip Barry. But *Sabrina* was, for all that, only fair; only smooth, never really sparkling. The romance was awfully longwinded and awfully thickwitted and awfully thin spun; and Sabrina herself had not character enough, or— what perhaps counts more in drawing-room comedy—not quite enough charm.

Sidney Howard's *Madam, Will You Walk*—the comedy with which the Phoenix Theatre opened its doors—had almost reached Broadway shortly after Howard's death in 1939. Arriving fourteen years later, it proved an agreeable philosophic fantasy, about equidistant between Saroyan and Thornton Wilder, with yet a certain flavor of its own. If slow in getting started and at bottom a trifle commonplace, this latest play to make use of the Devil had at least a touch of novelty and a nice air of lightness and humor. Funnier at its best, but much more fitful in its fun was Liam O'Brien's *The Remarkable Mr. Pennypacker,* an 1890-ish yarn of, as it were, a philosophical bigamist, a high-principled family man with one family in Wilmington and a second in Philadelphia. Hilarious at moments, the play yet indulged in too much joking for its moderate-sized joke, and, when hard pressed, simply substituted commotion for comedy. Edward Chodorov's *Oh Men, Oh Women* is the latest though certainly not the last comic work to have at a psychoanalyst with some of his own weapons; to provide an amorous bed of spikes along with an analytical couch; and to carry the war between the sexes into the analyst's own territory. Before he is finished, Mr. Chodorov has carried the war, or rather the joke, somewhat too far, making it ever broader as it grows thinner. Despite what is fresh and funny, the play cannot maintain a really high level of farce, and the final impression is of something not thoroughbred but mongrel.

Among the better-authored mistakes, Jerome Chodorov and Joseph Fields achieved with *Anniversary Waltz* the season's high in tasteless hackwork; and F. Hugh Herbert, with *A Girl Can Tell,* the season's low in muffled lubricity. More kindly remembered is Nathaniel

Benchley's *The Frogs of Spring*, with its assortment of bubbly moments and its share of the Benchley wit; the one yawning lack was a play to hang them on. In *King of Hearts* Jean Kerr and Eleanor Brooke achieved even more in the way of funny lines and had a megalomaniac's head to wreathe them with; but here, too, there was weakness of plot.

There remains *The Confidential Clerk*, which had enough of Mr. Eliot's easy mastery of verse, exact articulateness of language, and fitful elegance and sharpness, to endow it with a certain distinction; and so much borrowed farcicality, unfleshed symbolism and stiff-jointed spiritual gymnastics as to make the play as a whole disappointing. Mr. Eliot himself, in keeping with the play's trend toward unsuspected parentage, has rooted the play in the *Ion* of Euripides; the less classical-minded might sooner derive it from Gilbert and Sullivan and *The Importance of Being Earnest:* what is clear is that no one, including the author, roots it in real life. Mr. Eliot has industriously spun a web of mistaken identities and mixed-up parentage, with the "Who am I?" of his farce plotting meant suddenly to resound and reverberate on a far deeper level. Beneath the surface lurk very large questions about this world and the next, about human fathers and God the Father, true vocations and paths to happiness. The trouble is, there is no natural bridge between Gilbert and Sullivan and God and salvation; only an intellectualized leap. *The Confidential Clerk* unfortunately pierces to the spirit without cutting through any flesh; even its most momentous questions retain an air of Twenty Questions. It's all too clever by far, without being quite clever enough to achieve its end. And yet (much more in the reading than the playing) there are very touching moments to the final scene. It is noteworthy, too, that despite how much Eliot has borrowed and even bungled, he should stamp the play with something both distinctive and accomplished, something still very much his own.

The season came off worst where the previous one was most to be congratulated: for its revivals. On Broadway, indeed, there literally were no revivals. On Broadway the classics—Shaw, Ibsen, Shakespeare himself—quite failed to exist. At the City Center, however, during a sort of José Ferrer festival *Richard III* did get sandwiched in between *The Shrike* and *Charley's Aunt*. On this score alone, had there been no Phoenix Theatre it might have been necessary to invent one—if only to save the professional theatre of the richest city in the richest country in the world from the stigma of advertising that it had no soul and proclaiming that it had no past. In the circumstances, the Phoenix Theatre can be forgiven its faults of production in a way that Broadway cannot be forgiven for its failure to produce. Moreover, the Phoenix showed courage in its choice of *Coriolanus*—more courage than it realized when it turned out that for many critics *Coriolanus* was mere second-rate Shakespeare. The truth, rather, is that it is simply the least English, in a sense the least "Shakespearean," of his greater plays: there is much that is French about it, that smacks of Corneille and heroic drama; there is also something Roman and even Greek. The great misfortune at the Phoenix was that Robert Ryan could not make the title role seem Roman or French or Greek or even English: only curiously American, a pigheaded prep-school and Wall-Street fellow. In its general staging and movement, however, *Coriolanus* was often vivid. Chekhov's *The Sea Gull*, with which the Phoenix closed its season, was, however, nowhere very satisfying, and least satisfying in the scenes that prove most crucial.

It was no season for thrillers, either. A one-performance English work called *A Pin to See the Peepshow* proved so soporific that first-nighters could hear *A Pin* drop into limbo; another English work, *Gently Does It*, had rather more merit but by no means enough. There was also a *Sherlock Holmes*, written by Mrs. Basil Rathbone so that her husband could play on Broadway the role he made famous in the movies and on the air: rife with crime, *Sherlock Holmes* positively swirled with inaction and perished after the third performance.

The season, in its first weeks, suggested that with a little encouragement it might consist principally of one-man (or all but one-man) shows. First came Anna Russell, an English mimic whose diligent, intelligent, mirthless performing was like a perfume with every merit but fragrance. Then came *At Home with Ethel Waters*, who was personally pleasing as always, but not sufficiently at home with her material. Then (it was still very early Fall) came Victor Borge, and he was so good that no one else dared come after. He all but demonstrated that, in terms of entertainment, two's a crowd: a fine showman, a winning zany, above all a highly accomplished pianist, his various selves constantly offset and enhanced one another. Four months later, another solo performer did indeed dare follow him, secure in the knowledge that where Ruth Draper stands, there is the head of the procession. The lady who, as girl and amateur, long ago delighted two such fastidious hearers as Henry James and Henry Adams, remains not only—in ability—one of the theatre's few real geniuses, but also—in method—one of its few real aristocrats.

It was also, in a somewhat different sense, a season of single performances. Elsewhere in this volume you will find the best performers crowned with laurel; but it remains to be said here that it was an outstanding season for feminine skill and feminine oomph—whether Audrey Hepburn in *Ondine* or Deborah Kerr in *Tea and Sympathy* or Ina Claire in *The Confidential Clerk* or Julie Harris in *Mademoiselle Colombe* or Josephine Hull in *The Solid Gold Cadillac* or Uta Hagen in *The Magic and the Loss* or Edna Best in *The Ladies of the Corridor* or Betsy von Furstenberg in *Oh Men, Oh Women* or Shirley Booth in *By the Beautiful Sea* or Renée Jeanmaire in *The Girl in Pink Tights* or Dolores Gray in *Carnival in Flanders* or Carol Haney in *The Pajama Game*. The ladies, particularly when they were not too ladylike, had much to do with effecting the success, or slowing down the failure, of a number of musicals. Mademoiselle Jeanmaire, for example, could say with little exaggeration: *"The Girl in Pink Tights, c'est moi,"* with Miss Booth chiming in, where her show was concerned, "moi aussi."

Musically, however, the season wound up better than the previous one, though it could not easily have started off worse. The first entry, *Carnival in Flanders,* had spent $300,000 and almost a year getting itself in shape; and was still so shapeless that even a very engaging Miss Gray couldn't make it last beyond a week. The second entry, *Kismet,* had spent $400,000 rigging up a sort of *Carnival in Baghdad;* but cleverly came to New York while the newspaper strike had disposed of the critics and the critics had no chance to dispose of the show. The public, left to their own sovereign devices, ate the show up. Public favorite or not, *Kismet* is as resplendently banal and elaborately absurd as Hollywood at its most supercolossal; its plot requires virtually the entire population of Baghdad, including Omar Khayyam; and its hero is successively rich man, poor man, beggar man and thief, not to mention prisoner, poet, magician and emir. Far more pertinently, its hero is Alfred Drake, and the one sane reason for seeing the show.

The aforementioned *Girl in Pink Tights* was a period piece of the 1870s, presumably an account of how the American musical was born, though it seemed, everything considered, a better account of how it died. Thanks to nothing but Jeanmaire, it ran for three months. *By the Beautiful Sea* was also a period piece—and also about stage folk—laid in Coney Island during the 1900s. Its first act is diverting enough, but all that it is or ever hopes to be it owes to its star Shirley Booth.

The season's only revue, *John Murray Anderson's Almanac,* insisted on being a big, lavish, dress-up affair, with stage-wide but still very commonplace production numbers. This was the more misguided in that the *Almanac* had all the makings, in the way of sketches, spoofs and comedians, of a bright sassy intimate revue; and whenever it flung its ostrich plumes and tiaras and stomachers into the wings, it got much more amusing. By spending only half the money, the show might well have proved twice the fun.

The season's decidedly most individual musical began off Broadway, though it ended on. *The Golden Apple* was, indeed, the Phoenix's most rewarding production; and demonstrated, among other things, how with enough ingenuity on its creators' part, and at least a little on its producers', a crisp-looking musical can be achieved for $75,000. Thanks to William and Jean Eckart's sets, no recent musical has looked fresher, and not for a while back had there been anything more generally unhackneyed. In transferring, quite without reverence, the Trojan War set to small-town America around 1900, the Messrs. Latouche and Moross have contrived a kind of mock-domestic—stripping Homer of all poetic lure and epic stature, making Paris a traveling salesman, awarding the apple of discord to the best local baker of pies, letting the face that launched a thousand ships now set perhaps eight hundred tongues a-wagging; and equally, thereafter, converting the adventures of Ulysses into waterfront hotcha at a neighboring seaport. Doubtless *The Private Life of Helen of Troy* had, in its different way, got there first; but the trick of diminishing (rather than debunking) history, of making Babbitts of the men who strove with gods, has always a comforting and malicious appeal. It was wise also in Mr. Latouche and Mr. Moross to rule out the spoken word, for by using a completely musical framework *The Golden Apple* can court a certain commonplaceness and yet keep a certain charm. If the show seemed a little fancy at moments—or at others, a little cute—it was much oftener livelier, and in general witty and fresh.

It was not till the very last production of the season that Broadway itself proved up to snuff in the musical field; nor is *The Pajama Game* very notable for its music, or for its lyrics or its libretto either. But it is enough—such are the excellences of the production—that these things are competent. The excellences of the production are precisely those that have given Broadway its world primacy in straightforward musical comedy, and earned for George Abbott his undiminishing prestige. Never more than in this tale of a sitdown strike in a midwest pajama factory has Mr. Abbott achieved—or rather, achieved and uninterruptedly maintained—such spanking pace and explosive zest. So high are the show's jinks, they all but offset the primitiveness of its jesting; so lively are its spirits, they half-conceal the virtual absence of all satire. The whole thing is so

George Abbotty that even the workers' slowdown gives the impression of a speed-up; that every dancer has the exuberance of a cheerleader and every ditty the strong beat of a marching song. With a very attractive cast for a final virtue, *The Pajama Game* brought the season to a close on a hightide of froth and on a perhaps just mildly insane note of cheer.

THE SEASON IN CHICAGO

By Claudia Cassidy

Drama Critic, the Chicago *Tribune*

TO look back over an apprehensive shoulder at Chicago's alleged theatre season is to covet the politician's "No comment," which at least leaves a twinge of doubt. The facts are not just depressing, but dangerous. Suppose a managing editor saw them, decided that his drama critic had become an anachronistic case in clinical point, and set him to watching television?

For in a season when the Chicago Symphony Orchestra rescued itself by engaging Fritz Reiner as conductor, when the Lyric Theatre decided that the town had dallied long enough in the restoration of provocative resident opera, when the concert, opera and ballet talent of the world poured in a stream of boxoffice enticement, Chicago slipped to 19 shows. A handful were worth seeing, some were commonplace, some were a horror in the night.

Just one, "The Caine Mutiny Court-Martial," had the whetted edge of fresh brilliance to get the town excited. It stopped over for two nights on its way east, played the 3,587-capacity Civic Opera house through a barrage of microphones, and jammed the place to the tune of $20,363.69. What might have happened had it opened for a run in a theatre of average size? Why speculate? It did no such thing. Paul Gregory considered rushing in a Chicago company, but preferred to wait and bring the original back, without Henry Fonda. When and if the show returns, it may find lingering sparks in the ashes. It may not.

So when producers contend that Chicago is difficult, Chicago may be forgiven a tilted eyebrow or a shoulder twitch. A second season duplicate of "The Seven Year Itch," starring Eddie Bracken, had the season's longest run, 35 weeks. "Time Out for Ginger" is runner-up, with 20 weeks, so far. A shining company of "The Teahouse of the August Moon" might have been a gold mine, but none was cast. For London, yes. For Chicago, no. True, "Wish You Were Here" trundled its swimming pool to town and died to regret it, but it was a terrible show. "Me and Juliet" gave its all, the first Rodgers and Hammerstein musical in which all was not enough. "The Children's Hour" came 20 years late and withdrew just as it was beginning to

21

Gig Young, Larry Blyden, Franchot Tone and Betsy von Furstenberg in "Oh, Men! Oh, Women!"

prosper, because the budget had been exhausted on the way to Chicago, and it had to catch on overnight or close.

Walter Slezak was about all that remained of "My 3 Angels," but we cherished him until he had to tear himself away, Europebound. "An Evening with Beatrice Lillie" was sleek and shipshape when it started, but toward the end of the run it either got out of hand or played to an unreasonable number of cantankerous people. "Misalliance" extended the slapstick arc. "Porgy and Bess" returned. "New Faces" held over from the previous season for a run of 28 weeks, "Pal Joey" for 15. The premature visit of the American Savoyards displayed a Pooh-Bah who resembled an outraged dragon fly, and an "orchestra" inviting that Gilbertian venom,

> "He never would be missed,
> The piano organist."

In the cut-rate bracket, things took a whimsical turn. One producer told the critics, "This is a second-rate show for second-rate people. I wish you wouldn't come." Another said, "Thank you for not coming." Still another, beaming and bow-tied, bought sizable space in the dailies to hold forth as columnist, discussing on a lofty plane such theatrical personalities as Shakespeare, the Lunts, and Katharine Cornell.

Meanwhile, "Maid in the Ozarks" completed 16 weeks begun in the previous season, Barbara Payton and Tom Neal miscalculated their luck in "The Postman Always Rings Twice," and there were return engagements of a hoarser and hairier "Stalag 17" and a still sniggering "Good Night Ladies." When "Twin Beds" arrived with a stage manager named George Spelvin, the *Tribune* files confided that 40 years before Percy Hammond had labeled it "a farce of venerable genre."

Theatre Guild subscribers, a hardy crew, were left wistfully contemplating such pre-season bait as "Picnic," "The Love of Four Colonels," "The Time of the Cuckoo" and "The Crucible," none of which arrived.

Outside the Loop, our elastic equivalent of off-Broadway, "The World of Sholom Aleichem" was happily received with Jacob Ben-Ami. Lillian Gish dismayed us with the sudsy woes of "The Trip to Bountiful." The Equity Library Theatre made an interesting start with "Summer and Smoke," then subsided. The Playwrights Theatre Club ran a vociferous upstairs rendezvous with ungrateful plays, and just as blithely promised a Summer Shakespeare festival. On the highways, many a restaurant discovered that an adjacent tent with actors could be alluring, so Summer theatre in the round, square and oblong flourished and multiplied. Odd if eventually it should work its way back into town.

Here is the record for the 1953-54 season:

Shubert Theatre: 39½ weeks—"Pal Joey," 13½ weeks this season, 15 in all; "Oklahoma!", 8; "Wish You Were Here," 10; "Me and Juliet," 8.

Great Northern Theatre: 35½ weeks—"New Faces," 23½ weeks this season, 28 in all; "Stalag 17," 2; "Good Night Ladies," 10.

Erlanger Theatre: 35 weeks—"The Seven Year Itch."

Harris Theatre: 26 weeks—"The Postman Always Rings Twice," 1; "The Children's Hour," 4; The American Savoyards, 1; "Time Out for Ginger," 20 so far.

Selwyn Theatre: 19 weeks—"Maid in the Ozarks," 12 weeks this season, 16 in all; "Misalliance," 3; "My 3 Angels," 4.

Blackstone Theatre: 9 weeks—"An Evening with Beatrice Lillie," 8; "Twin Beds," 1 so far.

Civic Opera House: 4 weeks—"Porgy and Bess," 4; "The Caine Mutiny Court-Martial," 2 performances.

THE SEASON IN CALIFORNIA

By LUTHER NICHOLS

Drama Critic, San Francisco *Chronicle*

ONCE again professional theatre on the West Coast played a sort of muted obbligato, for the most part, to Broadway's tune. The only trouble was that Broadway finished the tune a season or more ago. We were still playing it, a year or so behind the beat, in 1953-54— or a few of its high notes, anyway, as they drifted out to these shores in the form of road companies.

If there were disappointingly few original dramatic blossoms in fertile California during the past season, at least there were a good many seeds; if there was little payment, there is yet much promise. For the theatre may be assuming a new shape out here; a shape those with their eyes fixed on Broadway don't as yet see; an indigenous shape that is still frail and dependent, but appears to be gaining strength.

However, let's deal with the hard realities of the season before we dabble in prophecy.

The hardest reality is that the Coast is still largely reliant on "the road" for its professional stage supply. And the road rivals the one to Tibet for unpredictability.

I counted twenty-one professional stage companies of various description that passed through San Francisco from May to May. This is about par for post-World War II years. Of the plays offered in San Francisco and, usually, in Los Angeles, three were revivals and about a dozen were worth remembering. To run through them briskly—

"John Brown's Body" returned for a second run, with Tyrone Power and Raymond Massey still in their virtuoso roles, but with Anne Baxter a bit roomy in Judith Anderson's shoes. Though a retread, this platform play was still impressive. In a time of drably realistic prose, emotional detachment, and national cynicism, it dared to stand on heights of poetic eloquence, breathe passion, and shout its patriotic fervor. "An Evening with Beatrice Lillie" raised parlor exhibitionism to perhaps its highest level, with Miss Lillie being assisted by Reginald Gardiner. The Dublin Players, from the Abbey and Gate theatres of that city, were well received in "Pygmalion" and "Shadow and Substance," and drove home the advantages of a balanced, no-star repertory company. All agreed that "Dial 'M' for Murder," with Maurice Evans and Margaret Phillips, was by far the best detective play seen here in years. But "Sabrina Fair," with Wendell Corey, Diana Lynn, and Estelle Winwood in a Russell Lewis-Howard Young production out of Hollywood, seemed only a pale pastiche of ideas and characters borrowed from Barry, Shaw, and Congreve.

The fourteenth annual San Francisco-Los Angeles Civic Light Opera season lost money on its four summer shows. And, for the first time in years, Director Edwin Lester had to call on the Los Angeles guarantors to make up a deficit. Its festival started off with a brilliant restaging of "Carousel" by Rouben Mamoulian that shot William Johnson to stardom; sagged with a ho-hum revival of "The Great Waltz," starring a pair of truants from grand opera, Dorothy Kirsten and John Charles Thomas; and floundered with a Michael Sloane-Paula Stone production of "Carnival in Flanders" that managed to obscure even the bright talents of Dolores Gray as too many cooks, including Herb Fields and Preston Sturges, tried to make something savory out of a mangled version of a French movie. The series partially revived with a Civic Light Opera original, "Kismet," though by then it was too late. "Kismet," a musicalized Arabian Night based on Edward Knoblock's old melodrama, had the most versatile performer of the season in Alfred Drake, making his first appearance here; the comeliest in Doretta Morrow—and went on to become a hit in New York. Peering through its veils, you could see it was a long step backward in its gaudy plot banalities and perversion of Aleksandr Borodin's music, but a lot of people seemed to enjoy it, and who cares about art in the face of that?

Other musicals during the theatre year were "Top Banana," with Phil Silvers carrying on as a television Napoleon; "Pal Joey," in which San Francisco's Harold Lang showed the niftiest pair of dancing feet to be seen here on a leading man in ages; another company of "Guys and Dolls," with Pamela Britton and Charles Fredericks; and "New Faces of 1952," in which Eartha Kitt, Ronny Graham and company had the same fresh, vital appeal here that they once had in New York, though their material, such as the Oliviers skit, had somewhat dated.

Let's skip the dregs of the season—including the umpteenth return of "Harvey," "Bagels and Yox," Spike Jones' "Musical Insanities," Olsen and Johnson's "Oh, Whatta Nite!", and something for the boys in the back room called "Good Night, Ladies"—and turn to more important matters.

As you can deduce from the above-mentioned plays, it was a fairish season for those who desired no more than to lose themselves in light entertainment. For those who wanted to find themselves, in plays that work out important living issues, it was a season of near starvation at the commercial cupboard. Not a single play from Broadway required the least exertion of one's gray matter.

Is this rout of the consequential by the superficial something that spread from other media to infect the stage? Is it so uneconomical to put a show of some topicality and substance on the road that such plays are now ruled out altogether? What has become of playwrights of real wit and conscience? These are questions many West Coasters asked themselves as the season unfolded in all its cheerful mindlessness.

There was some hope, however. For most of it, Californians turned to a meteoric young producer, Paul Gregory, and to the directorial gyrocompass behind his productions, Charles Laughton. Gregory-Laughton, who habitually build their shows in Los Angeles, try

Scene from
"Kismet"

them out in Santa Barbara, and give them their first big metropolitan test in San Francisco, did so in October with their most ambitious production to date, "The Caine Mutiny Court-Martial." Herman Wouk performed a most skillful operation as he cut the heart out of his book without injuring it, and Lloyd Nolan was shatteringly effective as the pitiable, neurotic, self-betraying Queeg. Here was drama as naked and robust as a Finn in his steam bath. Literary drama, if you please, with a minimum of sets or props to distract the viewer from the actors and their wrenching revelation of the rights and wrongs of a U. S. Naval mutiny at sea. In every town it played on brief tour of the state, it drew praise and full houses, proving once again the existence of a vast, almost untapped audience for good theatre in secondary cities.

About Gregory. He seems to be one of the few producers with the money, brains, and energy to solve the tough road situation. His formula—a good literary work, a few well-known actors, and no baggage that can't be packed into a single large Trailmobile—is so beautifully simple it would take the Attic Greeks to think of it, as indeed they substantially did. Everyone looks forward eagerly to his future productions.

There were a number of miscellaneous theatre events during the 1953-54 year, some for the good, some for the bad.

Henry Duffy's hopeful attempt to keep shows going at the Carthay Circle in Los Angeles folded. And Randolph Hale's plans for making the historic Alcazar a third, full-time, legitimate house in San Francisco have been suspended. The Equity Theatre Project in Los Angeles, an equivalent of New York's Equity Library, is, I understand, undergoing reorganization after three productions, including "Saint Joan" and "The Male Animal." And the ANTA-Monterey Drama Festival, a Monterey Peninsula showcase for top dramatic groups of Northern California for two summers, was abandoned because it put too much strain on the funds and energies of its sponsors.

Countercurrents to this flow of mishaps are Huntington Hartford's splendid new theatre near Hollywood and Vine, scheduled to open in the fall; the establishment of the Ebony Theatre in Los Angeles, which has done good work in putting on original Negro plays in the past six months; and the continued productivity of such comparatively new ventures as Lewis and Young's Summer Music Circus in Sacramento, which played everything from "Hit the Deck" to "Song of Norway" and "Carmen" in a tent theatre; and the Players' Ring Theatre and Circle Theatre.

Playgoers here have become pretty hard-crusted about the commercial theatre. Too often they've felt bamboozled by the difference between what the Theatre Guild announces and what actually materializes. Too often shows grown legendary since their New York raves haven't lived up to expectations. "How could they possibly?" said Maurice Evans. Too often they've been the victims of weary or second-rate road companies whose players had their minds on a Summer's rest or their next job.

As a result of this general disenchantment, which you hear on every side, it's my sanguine belief that a reaction is setting in.

Glenn Hughes said 'way back in 1931, when he was setting up the University of Washington's fine theatre, that if people can't get good drama consistently from other sources, they'll make it themselves. Hence it's not surprising that community, independent, and university theatres are flourishing as never before on the West Coast. There are increasing signs that this part of the country is becoming more self-sufficient, though our regional drama could hardly be called a vigorous native art that expresses the real concerns of its people as yet.

Most of California's own producing groups must admit to *Theatre Arts'* charges that the regional theatre slavishly apes Broadway. The famed Pasadena Playhouse in its season, for instance, included "Point of No Return," with Dana Andrews; "Gigi," with Betta St. John, and "The Male Animal," with William Schallert. The La Jolla Playhouse stood in Broadway's debt with "I Am a Camera," Dorothy McGuire, Don Taylor; "Stalag 17," Aldo Ray and Robert Strauss; "Dial 'M' for Murder," Leora Dana, Douglas Montgomery; and "My Three Angels." The same Broadway-derived tone applied to the plays given at the fine Wharf Theatre at Monterey, which included "The Love of Four Colonels," "Mr. Roberts," and "A Streetcar Named Desire." I chide no one for this heavy reliance on New York hits. Directors argue it's demonstrably necessary to a healthy box office. But it does nothing to advance the cause of local creativity.

There were, however, some notable exceptions to this follow-the-leader. The Hillbarn Theatre of San Mateo, for example, put on a season that included "Pelleas and Melisande," a highly experimental production of Goldini's "The Fan"; and an original modern work that won top honors in Stanford's annual Dramatists' Alliance play contest, "Uncertain Voyage," by Crane Haussamen.

Around San Francisco, a hive of little-theatre activity, such plays were given as "Miss Julia," "The Sea Gull," "Ring Round the Moon," "Nathan the Wise," "The Great God Brown," "Oedipus Rex," "The Miser," "The Climate of Eden," and "When We Dead Awaken"—to take a small sampling. This was hardly what you would call imitative of Broadway. Yet the Bay Area's groups could meet Broadway on its own terms, too. One of them in San Francisco, the Actor's Workshop, has twice within recent memory done productions of New York hits superior to those the touring companies brought here. Its "Death of a Salesman," which emphasized the fighting, rather than the defeated and resigned, qualities of Willy Loman, and thus gave the play a heightened tragic stature, was the bombshell of the past local season.

Such theatres have every reason to thrive. For the playgoing potential of this rich and ever more populous state is woefully underdeveloped. Neither Los Angeles, with one of the world's greatest pools of dramatic talent, nor the San Francisco Bay Area, which has a population of three million and less aversion to things intellectual than most communities, has a fully professional theatre company of its own. Which is, to say the least, absurd.

But it's not incomprehensible. Official support for a civic professional theatre as a cultural need can hardly be expected if the commercial theatre, as seen here, so persistently refuses to take itself seriously. Nor can audience support for a theatre of ideas be expected if no plays appear to whet the public's appetite for them.

It is in the university theatres, where fiscal problems are reduced and experimentation is not so risky, that I see the most hope for the growth of West Coast drama.

Without too much chauvinism, it can be said that this state boasts some excellent drama schools, among them those at the University of California at Los Angeles, the University of Southern California, Stanford, San Jose State College, and San Francisco State College. All were furiously active during the past year. In March, S. F. State opened one of the best theatre plants in the country on its new campus. Three fine auditoriums permit every form of staging, and are equipped with everything from the latest Izenour electronic control board to a soundproof glass booth in which students may watch and comment during actual performances. Here, and in other university drama departments, we may expect our desperately needed playwrights to learn their craft. U.C.L.A., in its six-play season, offers two "originals," and also produces nearly forty one-act student manuscripts a year. The other schools, too, offer valuable training for dramatists.

Moreover, university theatres prove the existence of large audiences for plays that are not Broadway hits. At Stanford and U.C.L.A., subscribers by the thousands, most of them in the 30 to 60 age group, buy their tickets before the complete programs are even announced.

The business of developing playwrights is, of course, central to the West Coast's chances of ever releasing itself from Broadway's apron strings. Another problem is to hold talent once it begins to develop. This is the job of postgraduate community groups. But many a promising group has just begun to jell, when its leading man or ace director is abruptly whisked off by the magnetism of Hollywood, New York, or television.

How are you going to keep 'em down on the farm? Only a strong, permanent, well-subsidized theatre that pays respectable salaries can hope to do it. And since high costs and uncertain profits offer little incentive to private enterprise in this field, most persons are convinced that if we are to have professional theatre companies out here—repertory or otherwise—they will have to be city-sponsored.

To establish such bastions of the drama is the hope, and to neglect them is the tragedy, of West Coast theatre at this time.

THE SEASON IN LONDON

By Kenneth Tynan

Dramatic Critic, London *Observer*

The New Plays

DOES sap-rise stir the theatre? Until Spring arrived, the West End slumbered. Suddenly, around March, life quickened; and the drama, like St. Joan in the last scene of Anouilh's "L'Alouette," skipped down from the stake and gave us a happy ending. Or happyish: for the social range of most English dramaturgy remained as limited as ever. At one point in the season, twenty-two out of twenty-six straight plays in London were concerned with life in the upper or upper-middle class: and the other four were broad farces. It was the depression which forced American playwrights to face the bleaker facts of contemporary life: today we are the poor country, but you would never guess it from the plays we write.

Three works of exceptional and lasting power emerged, none of them English: one was Welsh, one Irish, and the third French. It is, I admit, stretching a point to include Dylan Thomas' "Under Milk Wood," since it was written for radio; but two Sunday-night performances at the Old Vic, with a cast headed by Sybil Thorndike, Richard Burton, and Emlyn Williams, left no doubt that Thomas' death had robbed the theatre of an epic talent. Written in prose occasionally reminiscent of Hopkins' poetry, the play unfolds, in the talk and thoughts of its inhabitants, a day in the life of a Welsh coastal village: the soil, the people, the sea and wind of Wales have been seldom so gloriously, and never so wickedly, celebrated. One echoes, at curtain-fall, the line of Polly Garter, the local tart: "Isn't life a terrible thing—thank God!" Historically, Thomas' play may prove to have been one of the last outposts of the ear in a period increasingly ruled by the eye; a memory of the time when a phrase was a concrete thing, and people could converse in the dark without courting boredom. As Philip Hope-Wallace wrote: "Not since 'Juno and the Paycock' have we heard in a theatre words coming up thus, not chosen, but compelled: a fountain from the heart."

The Irish challenger was Bridget Boland's "The Prisoner." Set in a castle behind the iron curtain, it traced with rigid economy (only three speaking parts) the process by which interrogation unaided by

33

drugs or torture can force an enemy of the state, in this case a lean, proud cardinal, to make a public confession. The interrogator, lynx-eyed but not unlikeable, embarks on a rush job of psychoanalysis, finally pricking the cardinal's raw spot, shame at having never loved his sluttish mother, and planting in his mind the notion that his subsequent piety has been nothing but an act of neurotic atonement. One thinks, conversely, of Koestler's "Arrival and Departure," in which the Communist hero is analyzed into a state of self-destructive inertia; one thinks, too, of Orwell's "1984." "The Prisoner" isn't always on this level; Miss Boland's writing fails frequently to provide an emotional as well as a logical spur to the action; but her theme—a human being driven inexorably to desperation—is the fundamental business of drama, and it gave an unique opportunity to Alec Guinness, who played the cardinal quite unsentimentally as an unlovable man on the rack, trying stiffly to swallow his screams. The production, clear as a chessboard, was by Peter Glenville.

Several other plays about Middle-European states, named and nameless, rolled last year out of English typewriters. One was "Marching Song" by John Whiting, a young author whose fault is a tendency to fall over backwards in his effort to avoid making concessions to the frailty of his audience. This hostility to direct emotional appeal gave "Marching Song" an aura of refrigeration. A wartime military leader, released from prison to face trial, returns to the home of his mistress, whom he no longer loves. The government, anxious to keep national scandals out of open court, implores him to commit suicide, and the action covers the twenty-four hours within which he must make up his mind. His decision is forced on him (the desperation theme again) by contact with an adolescent girl disenchanted by long acquaintance with war, who convinces him that modern life has no room for heroes, but simply for gestures of self-abnegation. The play's impressiveness was impaired by a cluster of semisymbolic characters, including a priest, a doctor, and a drunken movie director—and by the lack of warmth in the writing: on this showing, Whiting is the most determined antiromantic in England. The setting, a vast UFA interior by Reece Pemberton, was superb, but Robert Flemyng, a whimsical comedian, was grossly miscast as the general, a part conceived in terms of Erich von Stroheim.

A more disappointing Ruritanian excursion was Christopher Fry's "Winter story," "The Dark Is Light Enough." Possibly Fry has lived too long with the play, grown too familiar with its intricacies; its situations, vivid in themselves, are never allowed to flower naturally. We are in a mansion near the Austro-Hungarian border, and

Montgomery Clift and Judith Evelyn in "The Sea Gull"

the Hungarian revolt of 1848 has just begun; our chatelaine, the Countess Rosmarin, astounds her salon by sheltering Gettner, an Austrian deserter from the Hungarian army. He is not only a traitor: he has married and abandoned her daughter, he wounds her son in a duel, and his philosophy is one of violent nihilism. Yet, such is her charity, she continues to shield him: and when she dies, peacefully in her great chair, he inherits her spirit of compassion. Beneath its surface meaning, the play is an exposition of the circuitous love of God, radiating through the Countess and infecting all who come within her orbit. Its drawback, dramatically, is that the Countess, being perfect, is entirely insusceptible of development. Just as Gettner is all sneers and bitterness, she is all tolerance and forgiveness. Their union is a misalliance of Dostoevsky and Mary Baker Eddy; one wishes, passionately, that she could but slam a door or curse, this crinolined soup kitchen. Fry's style has certainly been pruned and pared to the bone, but (except in the eventful second act) it seldom strikes to the heart. It has acquired the compressed texture of diatomite, a substance used in the manufacture of pipes which contains thousands of fossils to the cubic inch. The characters, uniformly articulate, *tell* us what kind of people they are instead of letting us find out for ourselves, which gives them the air of puppets hopping in slow motion while the author's voice reads the lines from the wings. The verse too often lapses into jingle: "for my sake, if my sake is worthy," "a coward, if a coward is what you are," "splendidly sleeping," "precariously promising," "inconsolable inclination." This is not to say that there aren't some wonderful arias; but the best speech, that in which the Countess describes Gettner as a plucked goose shivering on the water's edge, embodies the germ of the play's weakness—it is descriptive, not dynamic. Gettner (James Donald) scowls effectively, and Edith Evans, as the Countess, looks magnificent in her Winterhalter costumes. It is not their fault if we are ultimately unmoved.

In the category of *drame*, there was Wynyard Browne's "A Question of Fact," which makes great play with a single off-stage effect, a skeleton rattling in a cupboard. The hero, a young classical scholar, learns from his foster mother that his father was hanged for murder; oppressed by the news, he sets out to discover what manner of man the murderer was. The upshot smacks of compromise: father wasn't a monster, but a raffish fraud who, faced with exposure, panicked and pulled a trigger. And the hero's long-lost mother turns out to be Gladys Cooper, whose presence in a play all but implies a happy ending. For a dramatic treatment of heredity which does not evade the issue, one must still go to "Ghosts," which could easily have been a matinee success (like "A Question of Fact") if the disease afflicting Oswald's father had been mumps. Miss Cooper is dashingly sure, and Paul Scofield's display as her son, as disturbing in its power as an electric storm, proclaims him decisively the best young actor of his generation.

Charles Morgan's "The Burning Glass" was something of a sermon, something of an ultimatum, and not very much of a play. There is a whiff of the bone yard about Morgan's prose; I suspect that he chips his dialogue on a tombstone with a chisel. His latest was a *démodé* treatment of an urgent subject, the destructive power of science. A young meteorologist stumbles by chance on "The Burning Glass," a device for focusing the sun's rays down to an annihilating pinpoint: shall he make his discovery public or keep it to himself? A few brisk moments of melodrama, when the scientist is kidnaped by "The Enemy," failed to expunge my dislike both of what Morgan was saying and the way in which he was saying it. The hero consents to the use of his weapon in wartime, but refuses to let it be employed for peaceful purposes: like many puritans, Morgan smells sin in any attempt to improve the human condition. Militantly, he drags God and Lucifer into every argument. Because the Western allies are vaguely good, it follows that their adversaries must, by definition, be diabolically inspired. Acting, amid these great dead Edwardian certainties, was mostly a matter of resonance, which nobody in the cast, except Laurence Naismith as the Prime Minister, supplied.

N. C. Hunter, who wrote "Waters of the Moon" for Edith Evans, Wendy Hiller, and Sybil Thorndike, has again cornered the star market with "A Day by the Sea," in which Dame Sybil is joined by John Gielgud and Ralph Richardson. The play, an achievement of unexampled triviality, unwinds in a cliffside country house; we are invited to observe the relationships, mostly motionless, of its inhabitants. Dame Sybil, at her wit's exquisite end, copes with a decrepit brother; if that palls, consider the plight of Sir John, as a prim diplomat engaged in recapturing his youth by proposing to a pretty widow. Or contrast his idealism with the rococo escapism of Richardson, rejoicing in the role of a red-necked, gin-drenched doctor. Nobody marries, nobody dies; life, somewhere or other, goes on; and the action, in fact, does not take place. Mr. Hunter's method derives from Chekhov and his material from any unpublished collection of short stories by a woman novelist of uncertain health. He writes on the free association principle, assembling irrelevancies in the prayer that two of them may coalesce into a poetic image. One knows the *genre:* a spinster crosses the stage, bearing an invalid duck, someone recalls that two years ago a bat flew into the garage, someone else retaliates with a line and a half of Keats, while in the distance, wanly, a mouth organ pipes its lament. None of this happens in Mr. Hunter's play; but it might, all too easily. The acting, especially that of Dame Sybil and Sir Ralph, is a delight.

Comedy had an uneven season, beginning with T. S. Eliot's "The Confidential Clerk," a conjuring trick with no rabbit in the hat, a play of "the wrong shape," such as one might expect if one's reverend uncle set about playing with a model railway set. To illustrate the problems of paternity, Eliot took fragments of Wilde, Pirandello, Euripides, and Gilbert and Sullivan, and slapped them together as farce. The words were physically unexciting to listen to; verse in aspic, you might say, very tasteful, without slang or colloquial elisions. Eliot's gift as a dramatist is not to raise but to lower the temperature, as spooks are said to do when they enter a room; by the use of an odd, hieratic word he can induce a chill mystery. In "The Confidential Clerk" he stooped to the creation of one stock character, the old retainer Eggerson (perfectly played by Alan Webb); the women, Margaret Leighton and Isobel Jeans, were both enslaved to that most potent of influences, the vocal style of Edith Evans. I found the play puzzling in retrospect but fascinating in performance.

The most prosperous comedy was Terence Rattigan's "The Sleep-

José Ferrer in "The Shrike," "Cyrano de Bergerac,"

ing Prince," a Cinderella story set in London on the eve of George V's coronation. Its stock in trade was charm, fatally bordering on ingratiation. The Prince Regent of Carpathia, a monocled roué, is preoccupied partly by a Balkan crisis but mostly by a pretty American actress who comes to supper and demands gypsy violins and dramatic protestations of love rather than casual seduction. Olivier, neighing gutturally in an impeccable Slavic accent, attacked a part which must be regarded as a holiday for him, though it was heartening to see again those gorgeous trademark gestures—the outflung arms and the finger wagged in emphasis, as if bidding us hearken to bird song. Vivien Leigh, looking very healthy in a strawberry-blonde wig, was beautiful without being particularly attractive; and the play was swept off its feet by Martita Hunt as a jubilantly batty Grand Duch-

"Richard III" and "Charley's Aunt"

ess. Miss Hunt (in by far the best-written part) conducted her three scenes as if they were orchestral compositions, exiting from each of them like a troop of horse, distributing the joy of her lines like largesse to a downtrodden peasantry.

If a play's stature can be measured by the disparity between its pretensions and its achievement, Peter Ustinov's "No Sign of the Dove" (a quick flop) was one of the worst imaginable. It was an allegory designed to show how God would take revenge on the idle intellectuals; but to satirize the clerisy one must meet them with their own weapons, grace, wit, and a sense of proportion. Mr. Ustinov, mocking without insight and preaching without eloquence, made something of a clown of himself. "Hippo Dancing," adapted by Robert Morley from André Roussin's "Les Œufs de l'Autruche," was—to borrow a phrase from George Kaufman—a bad play saved by a bad performance. Morley, on stage almost throughout, plays a suburban householder reduced to apoplexy by the knowledge that one of his sons has taken up *haute couture,* while the other is being kept by an Italian princess. Unfortunately Roussin's principal joke —the homosexuality of the dressmaking son—has been removed by the Lord Chamberlain. Morley's peculiar achievement, therefore, is to have taken a sixty-minute vaudeville, extracted its point, and then expanded it into a flabby three-act play.

The season's most vivacious comedies were both previewed on Broadway. John Patrick's nimble "Teahouse of the August Moon," with Eli Wallach as the amoral *compère* Sakini, made an immediate success at Her Majesty's Theatre; and Jean Giraudoux's "The Enchanted" (in Maurice Valency's translation), rejected by New York, drew the town in a limited season at the Arts Theatre Club. Giraudoux, with his prankish, humane irony, stood revealed as the finest playwright of the period between the wars. "The Enchanted," a fable about a young girl enamored of a ghost, rippled throughout with that combination of sophistication and innocence which is the great delight of French drama. The heroine is finally dissuaded from her death wish by the local doctor, who organizes for her ears a symphony of the petty noises of everyday life; she revives an adult, reconciled to the tumult of reality. The play was atmospherically directed by John Fernald.

Three American importations fared well. Dorothy Tutin, incandescent in "The Living Room," extended her range as Sally Bowles in John van Druten's "I Am a Camera": idly suspended from a cigarette holder, like a negligee on a hook, she almost equaled the limpid lostness of Julie Harris. The rest of the company (above all Michael Gwynn as Isherwood) materially improved on the American cast. Sylvia Regan's garment-trade comedy, "The Fifth Season," was rescued by Joseph Buloff in the Menasha Skulnik part: squat, low-slung, with the resignation of a tree thrice-struck by lightning, Mr. Buloff belongs in the line of great American Jewish comedians. Finally, there was Clifford Odets' "The Big Knife," ably directed by Sam Wanamaker, who also played (less ably) the part of Charley Castle, an idealistic Hollywood actor chained to the studios by a crime he committed years before. The play, an anatomy of desperation, seemed even more topical than the day it was written: agreed, it goes overboard, but this is a virtue in a country whose playwrights seldom set sail.

Two murdering-pieces round out the list. "Someone Waiting," by Emlyn Williams, was clammy and undercharacterized. The author, playing a tutor bent on revenging the death of his framed son, made a characteristic entrance, edging in like the thirteenth guest at a Borgia banquet, and bringing with him an atmosphere of dust and dead doves. A much neater detective play was embedded in Agatha Christie's "Witness for the Prosecution," to which I bow as the most ingenious crime play I have ever seen. The double-reverse-backhand-spin-twist of the last two minutes represents a more consummate piece of triple bluffing than Mrs. Christie or anyone else has ever brought off in a theatre.

The Musicals

Drury Lane welcomed "The King and I," probably because it came closer than any of the other Rodgers and Hammerstein shows to the sentimental-genteel spirit of our sick friend, English musical comedy. Apart from the "Uncle Thomas" ballet, it reminded me of something James Agate said of a performance given by Mrs. Patrick Campbell: that it was like the Lord Mayor's coach with nobody inside it. Valerie Hobson coolly re-created the Gertrude Lawrence part, and Herbert Lom rivaled the knockdown triumph of Yul Brynner as the king. "Wish You Were Here" thrived on the strength of its rowdy lubricity. And, late in the season, "Pal Joey" blew into town: this decadent anecdote, which shocked several London critics, seemed to me the cream of Rodgers and Hart. And though Harold Lang lacked the sleazy charm for Joey, Carol Bruce had all of Vivienne Segal's suavity and more.

Two intimate revues found large audiences. "At the Lyric," written by Alan Melville, owed much to the briskness of Dora Bryan and the buoyancy of Ian Carmichael, but much more to the majesty of Hermione Baddeley. Miss Baddeley, a stubby bundle of womanhood on toothpick calves, is a very great comedienne. Her voice is a bronchial gurgle; she addresses most of her lines directly to her bust, wearing an expression of fixed distaste; and, although she is barely middle-aged, she affects an aspect of grandiose dilapidation suggestive of a wrecked Christmas pudding.

"Intimacy at 8:30," a bitchy, raucous revue by Peter Myers, Alec Grahame, and David Climie (all in their twenties), advanced from a suburban club theatre to the West End. This success for youth came hard on the heels of another: Sandy Wilson's "The Boy Friend," a musical-comedy pastiche of the 1920's. Mr. Wilson, aged twenty-nine, has the same amused affection for the jazz age that some people have for eighteenth century grottoes: and his show (devoutly directed by Vida Hope) strikes the mind as a marvelously sustained satire and the heart as a labor of love. Each night, enraptured matrons sneak into the theatre and snuffle into their cambric as they watch a mirage of their lost girlhood, with a finishing school on the Riviera and tunes like the whiplash tango and "A Little Room in Bloomsbury." The cast, led by a wonder of ingenuous tact named Anne Rogers, contains no stars. Since "Oklahoma!" no musical has struck London with such a reverberating storm.

The Revivals

John Gielgud directed a speedy new production of "Charley's Aunt" with John Mills as Fancourt Babberley, which he first played in 1930. Motley's settings, glowing with solidity, evoked Oxford more effectively than the old farce itself: Mills' performance was as clever as clockwork, though it was a clock which failed to strike twelve. I liked best Philip Stainton, as the girls' amorous guardian, tipsily whispering the last enchantments of the middle-aged.

John Clements and Kay Hammond revived "Pygmalion" with Edwardian aplomb: meanwhile, the Old Vic embarked on a five-year Shakespeare program, in which all the plays in the First Folio will be presented. The company, led by Richard Burton, Claire Bloom, Fay Compton, and Michael Hordern, had six plays before them and an overpowering permanent set of Renaissance arches behind them. Michael Benthall, the new director of productions, struck off with Richard Burton in "Hamlet." One hoped for a tough, attacking display which should be a corrective to Gielgud's finger-tip delicacies, a trumpet instead of a flute. Pale and haunted, Burton looked splendors, but the range, vocally, wasn't there. He jerked from strangled sobs to harsh roars, lacking a middle register for contemplation. The real absentee was finesse, which Burton can convey only "with much forcing of his disposition." Claire Bloom's Ophelia was fine: the mad scenes were treated as cadenzas, the voice flying and plunging, the hair everywhere, the body restless as a Van Gogh cypress, and the whole performance a terrible premonition of the jester's grave to which, ironically, Ophelia is finally committed. Next came "All's Well That Ends Well," in which Michael Hordern, at forty-two the pedigree war horse of the English classical theatre, made a gorgeous fantastic out of Parolles; and then "King John," an inchoate production of an inchoate play. Burton (Faulconbridge) gave a slack performance, at once cautious and careless, and Hordern played the title part for much more than it was worth. Similarly, he ran away with "Twelfth Night," quivering with pride (as Malvolio) like a snake standing on its tail.

The last two productions showed great improvement. Benthall gave vigorous life to that disturbingly modern play, "Coriolanus"; I especially applauded his decision to bring the curtain down on the stabbing of the hero, like a pathetic footnote to a purple page. "Action is eloquence" says Volumnia; and Burton, in this sense, was riotously eloquent, tearing the rages to tatters and giving us, in the middle acts, a thumping demonstration of power.

"The Tempest" closed the season, imaginatively staged by Robert Helpmann. Claire Bloom's Miranda, a comic child dazzled by her first man, was a highly original piece of acting: and Michael Hordern's Prospero, a tyrant touched with sweetness, set the seal on a reputation which, twelve months before, would not have extended far beyond that of "actors' actor." Richard Burton, who will try anything, tried Caliban, and found everything in the part save its vital lyricism. The difference between Hordern and Burton is that which the Spanish recognize between the "long" bullfighter, who knows every pass in the book, and the "short" one, who can perform a few difficult passes supremely well.

My quarrel with the Vic, as with the West End in general, boils down to the uninventiveness of its directors. There is no one of the stature of Kazan in New York or Barrault in Paris. Perhaps the era of the "creative" director is over. If so, I shall mourn precipitately.

THE SEASON IN PARIS

By André Josset

Playwright; and Secretary-General of the International Theatre Institute, UNESCO

OF the hundred and thirty-one plays presented in Paris during the season of 1953-54, only twenty-three were successes.

Everywhere a general drop in receipts was noted. A distrustful public is administering sharp punishment to the theatre in the form of staying away. Already last year such a crisis was imminent. Indeed it had begun long before, and it seems to reflect a widespread judgment by the public, which wants something different from what is offered it. What are offered are overwhelmingly light, so-called commercial plays. The competition of cinema, television, and variety shows has made the public more demanding, for these different art forms frequently offer performances that are extremely original and diversified. Hence if plays continue to be little more than frivolous, we must foresee a continuing crisis in receipts. Quite possibly this crisis may finally oblige the leaders of the theatre in France to rediscover that taste for risks which was the glory of the theatres of the "Cartel," those directed by Louis Jouvet, Charles Dullin, Pitoeff, Gaston Baty, and René Rocher. Modern dramatic art has come from these great men of the theatre, but the lessons of the past are on the way to being forgotten.

The Théâtre National Populaire of Jean Vilar does continue, however, as if to prove by its success that a form of theatre which puts quality foremost is precisely the form that the public wants.

I must go back into the past for a moment, in order to say a few words about the creation at the Théâtre National Populaire (in a small suburb of Paris) of Shakespeare's *Richard II*. The same enthusiastic and discerning crowd which supports Jean Vilar's efforts was present as always, and the play then left with the rest of the program to tour the provinces. It was presented again later during the season, with a moving and anguished portrayal by Gérard Philippe.

Then came the Summer vacation, and the Paris season began once more on the first of October, 1953, at the Théâtre Edouard VII, with a play adapted from Axelrod's *Demeure Chaste et Pure* (Remain Chaste and Pure), starring the whimsical Jean Richard. This play, ably done, kept the principal actor continually on the stage: the required hard work had its reward, since the play is still on the boards.

On October 3rd, to the Théâtre Marigny, came a very much anticipated event, Paul Claudel's *Christophe Colomb* (Christopher Columbus), directed by Jean-Louis Barrault and performed by Madeleine Renaud and their whole company. That remarkable animator Jean-Louis Barrault gave us, in the first part of the play, a production that was pervasive, filled with pathos, and extremely brilliant and varied, the power of which overwhelmed the audience, which followed the action with growing excitement. Then came the second part with less brilliance, something perhaps due to the play itself. There were moments of poetry, however, not yet forgotten: I recall, for example, the extraordinary impression of solitude made by a great sail slapping in the wind, among the shadows and foam of an imaginary sea. It is here that the theatre shows that when it knows how to exploit its own weaknesses, it can easily rival the most enchanting effects of the cinema.

At the Théâtre de la Renaissance, on October 5th, was presented *La Corde* (Rope). This play, adapted from the English, remarkably produced and very well performed, did not entirely fulfill its promise, but was yet a success from certain points of view. I feel some difficulty in speaking of the following play, *Frère Jacques* (October 6th at the Théâtre des Variétés), starring Fernand Gravey and Gisèle Pascal. Good passages floated through this well-constructed comedy, which was above all fortunate in its spectacular cast.

I did not have the opportunity in my last chronicle to speak of an extraordinary play presented last season at the Petit Théâtre de Babylone and revived this year after a very long success—*En Attendant Godot* (While Waiting for Godot), by an Irish playwright who lives in France and writes in French. Unforgettable tragic clowning in a deserted set, lit by an eclipsing moon. It showed us in a subtle and indirect manner the vain waiting of men, their unconquerable hope for the advent of a divinity who is always announced and never comes. On this metaphysical theme Samuel Beckett has written a small masterpiece of excruciating humor, which moves the heart and the imagination without ever exceeding the limits of patience. This Théâtre de Babylone is a little nest that should be watched, and from which, perhaps, a few other birds equally bizarre, curious, and moving will be seen to soar.

Next, on October 14th, those who had the right to opening-night seats rushed to the Théâtre Montparnasse to see the first performance of *L'Alouette* (The Lark) by Jean Anouilh. It is the story of Joan of Arc, of her life as told by a penetrating, sharply precise playwright, whose preceding works gave us no reason to suppose he would write such a play. There is no sickness of body or spirit, no despairing vision of souls and loves, or of life in general, in *L'Alouette*. This marvelous, ardent creature, drunk with the brightest genius, particularly enchanted us in the first part of the play. The role was played by Suzanne Flon, who showed that she was literally capable of everything, that is, of breathing life into the simplest roles, and enriching the poetry of the most difficult ones. The success of this play was considerable, and continues even now.

The following day, one's relentless love for the stage carried one into the Théâtre Hébertot almost without allowing one time to draw breath. In this theatre, which is one of the prettiest, oldest, and technically best in Paris, was given *La Maison de la Nuit* (The House of the Night). It is about a house, situated on the boundary of the Iron curtain, which is used as headquarters by a man whose work is to help fugitives escape over the frontier. The central theme is pity, which finally subdues the hardest hearts and even leads them to death, when they become incapable of any longer accepting a stifling cruelty of spirit. Remarkably directed and performed by Michel Vitold, this play lasted 150 nights.

There was one evening which caused me great emotion: not that the evening was of the same quality from beginning to end. I will only speak, therefore, of the extraordinary moment and not of the rest. The subject was a poem by Federigo Garcia Lorca, a long plaint entitled *Chant funebre pour Ignacio Sanchez Mejias, Torero* (Funeral Dirge for Ignacio Sanchez Mejias, *Torero*). The *torero*, a friend of Garcia Lorca, met death in the afternoon, and all who loved and admired him came to weep over his body. The producer had the moving idea of emphasizing, by a guitar accompaniment, the recitation of the poem by an invisible actor. At the same time, against a severely bare background, the body of the *torero* was carried, as if on a great shield, by a small troup of friends. The friends, pressed against each other, seemed slowly and tenderly to be carrying the great bullfighter, already stiffened under his great, blood-colored shroud, to his tomb. The mood continued for a long time, then the guitar, together with the reciting voice, fell silent. Thus during many evenings there was carried to his grave, before a deeply moved audience, Sanchez Mejias, *torero*.

The *Chemin de Crête* (The Road over the Crest), presented at the Vieux Colombier on November 3rd, had only an unfortunate and brief career. The same happened at the Théâtre de la Bruyère to the extremely rich, brilliant, and audacious play by Audiberti, directed by Georges Vitaly, *Les Naturels de Bordelais* (The Natives of Bordeaux), a title difficult to translate, which, besides, did not cover the subject, since the play was a very daring satire of the human heart, public opinion, and public complexes. A powerful, fascinating play, which got criticisms remarkable for their severity, and, to speak truly, most ferociously unjust. It is true that frankness is sometimes thought by certain people to be a provocation, but it is equally untrue that the author has much talent, that the theatre could not long hold out against such a storm, and received a heavy blow that it felt for several months.

On November 7th, the Comédie des Champs Elysées presented *Le Desir sous les Ormes* (Desire Under the Elms) by Eugene O'Neill. It is difficult to pass judgment on this work, which we know only through translation. The violence of the situation must have reached us in quite attenuated form for the audience not to have been carried away by the drama.

On November 13th, at the same Théâtre de Babylone where *En Attendant Godot* had been such a success, Mr. Charles Spaak, brother of the Foreign Secretary of Belgium, gave us his *La Rose des Vents* (Windrose) but this play, as its title indicated, quite soon was gone with the wind.

Finally, at the Théâtre Marigny on November 16th, Jean-Louis Barrault and Madeleine Renaud brought us Giraudoux's posthumous *Pour Lucrece* (For Lucretia). The critics' reviews were brilliant. There was a first act as lovely as any to be found in the greatest successes of the late author; a cruel, but no less fine second act; a bitter and despairing third. Marvelous production by Barrault, marvelous performances by Madeleine Renaud and Edwige Feuillère.

The Comédie Française entered the lists on November 18th with Philippe Hériat's play *Noces de Deuil* (Marriage in Mourning). A lovely title (in French), but the drama met with what one might politely call a mixed reception. The opening night was the scene of one of the greatest tumults of late years. The audience felt that it was unnecessary to present a new play written in nineteenth-century style, and that enough of this type of theatre existed without being added to in deliberately outmoded language: this judgment was rather a summary one, but a house that has got out of hand is very much amused by its own noise. French art of the romantic nineteenth century had, on the other hand, simultaneously inspired another undertaking at the Théâtre Sarah Bernhardt, where the actor Pierre Brasseur played Alexandre Dumas' *Kean.* The actor's strik-

Ben Astar, Felix Aylmer, Katharine Cornell, Roger Dann and Minoo Daver in "The Prescott Proposals"

ing silhouette, his thundering voice, his enormous wig, his frizzy power—that is my memory of a performance that for several months drew the public to this large theatre.

Georges Vitaly, whose pride had been so roughly wounded but who did not lose courage, brought us on November 20th *La Danseuse et le Collegien* (The Dancer and the Student), a play by a new, unknown playwright. Alas, the dancer soon went home to mother and the student back to school.

At the Salle Luxembourg of the Comédie Française, on November 26th, opened *La Vérité est Morte* (The Truth is Dead). The author, Emmanuel Roblès, had had considerable success with his first play.

His second play, as it happens very often with young playwrights, was concerned with almost the same subject, but treated it less persuasively, and the work did not have a happy career.

I come now to an important and thrilling evening, one which, perhaps together with *Pour Lucrece*, was the most interesting of the season—Molière's *Don Juan*, presented and played by Jean Vilar at the T.N.P. In the past I had seen the extraordinary *Don Juan* of Louis Jouvet, which remains in my memory an almost perfect accomplishment. Listening to Jean Vilar, I understood how much the personality of Louis Jouvet had stood between Molière's work and the spectator—how much this powerful personality had closed off the avenues through which the imagination penetrates to the heart of a work. Jean Vilar's performance, which was absolutely transparent, led us for the first time into the character of Don Juan, allowed us to participate in it, to follow it through all its twists and turns. In the same fashion, the difficult scenes in which the peasants speak in naïve patois, the scene in which M. Dimanche comes to dun Don Juan for a bill, have never in my opinion been clarified and respected with a sharper psychological and comic sense. The whole performance was for all these reasons a feast of the spirit, a veritable triumph of intelligence and of sensitive regard for great masterpieces. For the first time I really made the acquaintance of Molière's Don Juan.

Then on December 17th in the small and illustrious Théâtre de l'Œuvre, founded long ago by Lugné Poe and where he introduced the great Scandinavian playwrights to Paris, a play by Tennessee Williams, *Été et Fumée* (Summer and Smoke), with a gigantic and poetic set filling the whole stage and leaving little room for the actors to speak the text. The play did not last long.

Similarly, in the Salle Luxembourg on December 20th, a revival of the famous *Crainquebille* of Anatole France, and a revival of *Dardanelle* tumbled together and were unable to get back on their feet again.

Georges Vitaly, already mentioned twice here, a very example of obstinacy, but made prudent by two successive failures that half ruined him, then presented in association with the Théâtre National Belge, a theatre-in-the-round revival of Priestley's *An Inspector Calls*. This time he had a success, and the spectators, drawn by curiosity, came for quite a few weeks to lean from all sides over the luminous little circus.

On January 23rd, to the Théâtre de la Renaissance came an adaptation of Guy de Maupassant's *Bel Ami* (Handsome Friend), the ferocious history of a young man who tries to get on through contacts with women. A remarkable production whose artistry brought us back to an epoch comparable to that of Toulouse-Lautrec.

We went once again on February 4th to the Salle Luxembourg, where the Comédie Française was doing a revival of Jacques Deval's *Etienne* (Stephen), and where on February 18th there was a new play by Simone, *En Attendant L'Aurore* (Waiting for the Dawn). Despite the author's great talent, it was met with extreme reserve.

On the very next day, February 19th, our exhausted band went on to the Théâtre des Ambassadeurs, a delightful theatre at the end of the Champs Elysées, in the midst of groves of chestnut trees. We went to see André Roussin's new play, *Le Mari, la Femme, et la*

Mort (The Husband, the Wife, and Death). Roussin, as you no doubt know, is the playwright whose work has been most frequently performed in Paris for many years. I am getting ready to go, this very evening, to a charming restaurant to celebrate the thousandth performance of his play, *Lorsque l'Enfant Parait* (When the Child Appears). Roussin's new play met with great favor, which was justified insofar as the play improved from act to act, to conclude in three scenes of irresistible drollery. It is still playing.

Then on March 3rd, we went to the Théâtre des Bouffes Parisiens to see the new play by Julien Green, the Franco-American author, entitled *L'Ennemi* (The Enemy). I recall having already spoken of this author last year, in reference to his play *Sud* (South). Once again we found ourselves in the presence of a technique which does not seem to be made for the theatre, even though the quality of the text was very beautiful. It concerned a theme familiar to Green: the effective presence of the devil in certain beings with whom we are on familiar terms. A door is opened, and there in the half-darkness stands the silhouette of a handsome young man whose great charm lies in a frightful hardness. In like fashion, a woman who has fallen into sin lifts herself above it. By a cruelly bizarre fact, the woman's husband is incapable of defending her by human means since long ago he had been grievously wounded in a vital part of his person. The whole play takes place in a château in the country, during the period of the French Revolution. If I recall aright, the demonical young man is killed at the end, but his presence remains so deeply imbedded in the souls of those around him that the door of the room in which he had lived must be walled up. In spite of its faults, I retain a strong impression of this strange story, though in my opinion, Green, however remarkable a writer, is not yet a playwright. What is more, his subjects and characters are of an exaggerated singularity, though this would matter less if they were not also so remote, so enclosed inside something that creates a sense of glacial cold. Julien Green writes desperate plays, and he writes as from some far-distant exile, all this forming a complex of attraction-repulsion which until now has not permitted his plays to enjoy the real favor of the public.

On March 13th, the Comédie Caumartin brought us Husson's new play, *Les Paves du Ciel* (Heaven's Cobblestones). Two years ago this playwright had written a comedy which had enormous success, called *La Cuisine des Anges* (My Three Angels). Unfortunately, *Les Paves du Ciel*, despite Jean-Pierre Aumont's performance, had only a half-hearted success. The Summer did not fulfill the promise of springtime.

Exactly six days later, the Théâtre Grammont offered us *N'Import Quoi pour Elle* (Anything for Her), a new play by Steve Passeur. After a very fine career, this author remained silent for quite a while, and reappeared with a seventeenth-century costume-play of unbridled passions, modeled on another of his works which had had considerable success, *I Shall Live a Great Love Story*. But alas, the play was found to be complicated, with a style at once ardent and formal. Even though the second act was very good, the play only lasted a very few weeks. Since the author is a remarkably lucid man, it was curious to hear this work of frenzied love developed by a coldly incisive brain. This, in French cooking, is what we call a "hot and cold": the hot things are mixed with the cold, leaving the sensation that one has held an icicle in one's mouth.

By way of concluding, let me refer to theatre news of a more general nature. At present in Paris there is taking place a very important International Theatre Festival, in the vast and admirable Théâtre Sarah Bernhardt, with twelve countries participating or about to participate: Italy, Norway, Denmark, Yugoslavia, Ireland, Germany (East Berlin), Spain, Belgium, Poland, Germany (West), Great Britain, and naturally, France.

The Italian company has already presented *Cyrano de Bergerac* in an Italian version, with the Italian star, Gino Cervi, in the leading part. This Italian masterpiece was a triumph. Then Norway brought us Ibsen's *Ghosts,* produced by Axel-Otto Normann, one of the honorary presidents of the International Theatre Institute. We are now awaiting Corneille's *Le Cid* in Danish, *Uncle Maroje* in Yugoslav, Bertold Brecht's *Mother Courage* in German, *Life is a Dream* by Calderón de la Barca in Spanish, *Built on Sand* by the Théâtre Royal du Parc of Brussels, another version of *Le Cid* (this time in Polish), Kafka's *The Castle* in German, T. S. Eliot's *The Confidential Clerk,* and *The Golem* by the Habimah Theatre of Tel Aviv.

The festival was organized in record time (two months) by Mr. A. M. Julien, director of the Théâtre Sarah Bernhardt, and represents an extremely interesting endeavor to create an International Festival where the best companies from several countries can regularly offer their best work. It is to be hoped that the United States will participate in future Festivals of Paris. These encounters can only help to increase knowledge of dramatic art throughout the world.

The theatre crisis I spoke of at the beginning of this chronicle is due in part to the burden of taxes and the cost of stage materials. But, at the risk of having myself assassinated by my colleagues the playwrights, I must add that the absence of true creators of dramatic works is the basic cause of this grave situation. What is called for are works that are powerful and poetic, fantastic and satiric, joyous and tragic. Then the lighter plays can continue to live as much as they choose, but at least they will not invade the entire theatre, and thus risk sinking a ship overladen with a ballast of trifles.

THE CAINE MUTINY COURT-MARTIAL *

A Play in Two Acts

BY HERMAN WOUK

(Adapted from Mr. Wouk's novel *The Caine Mutiny*)

[HERMAN WOUK, *though only 39 years old, has had a career crowded with activity. His major works include three novels, two motion pictures, and a play. Born in New York City, he went to Columbia, worked for five years on Fred Allen radio scripts, and during World War II worked for the U. S. Treasury on radio shows to promote the sale of bonds. After Pearl Harbor he served in the Navy. His novels include "Zane," "City Boy" (also a film), "The Caine Mutiny." In 1949 he wrote a melodrama "The Traitor" in which Lee Tracy and Walter Hampden appeared.*]

"THE CAINE MUTINY COURT-MARTIAL" takes place in February, 1945, in the General Court-Martial Room of the Twelfth Naval District, San Francisco. "The Caine Mutiny Court-Martial" has three Navy Regulation Articles as its basis: Articles 184, 185, and 186; but the U.S.S. *Caine* never existed, nor do the U. S. naval records show an instance of a captain being relieved at sea under these articles.

The first part is the PROSECUTION, the second is the DEFENSE. On an empty stage, barren except for the chairs, tables, and witness box, stands the big, raised, curved judges' bench. The start of the play is marked by the dimming of the house lights and the brightening of the stage, for the curtain is up when the audience enters the theatre.

The Orderly and Stenographer, two sailors in blue, come on, carry Greenwald's desk and chairs down to the left of the stage, and roll the witness stand into place down center. Greenwald, a lanky lieutenant in a green flier's uniform with wings and campaign ribbons, puts his brief case on his desk and, as the sailors leave, strolls to the witness stand, his face stern and abstracted. The defendant, Lieutenant Stephen Maryk, his hair cropped, big and powerfully built, in navy blues, comes to the other side of the witness stand. Maryk is upset and confused about the way the trial is proceeding, with nothing to show for the time spent. He doesn't care, either, for the way Greenwald is handling his case.

GREENWALD—Good. That makes us even.
MARYK—How's that?
GREENWALD—I don't like handling you.
MARYK—What? Well, then, maybe I'd better—
GREENWALD (*crossing to desk and taking papers from brief case*) —Maryk, I'd rather be prosecuting you than defending you. I told you that the first time we met. Nevertheless, I'm defending you. If it's humanly possible to win an acquittal in this case I'm going to win you an acquittal. If you want a prediction, I believe I'm going to get you off. But you can't help me. So just leave me be.

Maryk is hurt and nervous at Greenwald's remark about prosecuting rather than defending him. He wonders if he should get another lawyer. Once again he asks Greenwald: "Do you think I was right to relieve Captain Queeg?"

GREENWALD—I can't say that.
MARYK—After everything I told you, you still don't think he was nuts?
GREENWALD—No, I don't.
MARYK—Then I get hung.

Greenwald doesn't find that necessarily so. No matter how many legal officers have advised Maryk to plead guilty, he thinks he'll get him off. But Greenwald is bothered for a different reason. While he knows he's a damn good lawyer, he found out he was a pretty poor flyer. He took a shellacking at flight school from young ensign instructors, and daydreamed of the day he'd get a court-martial case in which he could personally twist the Navy's arm. Now that he has the opportunity he lacks all enthusiasm; he has too much respect for the way the Navy has turned hopelessly raw recruits into real fighting machines. "A lot of guys take it in stride. Me, it's sort of turned all my old ideas wrong side out. And this is a war that sure needs winning, for my dough." Maryk's ideas of the Navy aren't quite that. "There's still a big pile of foolishness connected with the Navy. In fact—I sometimes think the Navy is a master plan designed by geniuses for execution by idiots."

GREENWALD—Where'd you hear that?

MARYK (*injured*)—Couldn't I just have made it up?

GREENWALD—You could just have made up the Gettysburg Address, too. Where'd you hear it?

MARYK (*grins reluctantly*)—Well, matter of fact, it's one of Tom Keefer's favorite cracks.

GREENWALD (*nods*)—Ah, yes. You echo your novelist friend quite a bit, don't you?

MARYK—Tom's got the keenest mind on the ship. About the keenest I've ever run into.

GREENWALD—He's keen, all right.

MARYK—I'm sure glad Tom is going to testify.

GREENWALD—You are?

MARYK—Hell! He knows everything Captain Queeg did. He knows psychiatry. I'm a stoop about those things. I'll foul myself up. Tom Keefer can tell the thing straight.

If Greenwald had his way, Tom Keefer would never testify; he's going to do Maryk no good. He's one man Greenwald would really enjoy prosecuting. Maryk indignantly warns him not to pin anything on Keefer: "It was my responsibility." "That's right," says Greenwald. "You did what you did."

The six court members enter, followed by a stenographer and the Judge Advocate, Lt. Comdr. Challee, who puts his brief case down and calls everyone to attention. Captain Blakely enters, takes his place on the bench, immediately rings his desk bell, and addresses himself to Challee. He advises him to get on with the case, keeping technicalities to a minimum. He then holds out a paper to Challee: "Court finds the charge and specification in due form and technically correct. Is the accused ready for trial?" Maryk, at Greenwald's prompting, rises and says he's ready. With that Challee, on a signal from Blakely, reads the charges. "Charge. Conduct to the prejudice of good order and discipline. Specification. In that Lieutenant Stephen Maryk, U.S.N.R., on or about 18 December, 1944, aboard the U.S.S. *Caine*, willfully, without proper authority, and without justifiable cause, did relieve from his duty as commanding officer Lieutenant Commander Philip Francis Queeg, U.S.N., the duly assigned commanding officer of said ship, who was then and there in lawful exercise of his command, the United States then being in a state of war. . . . Stephen Maryk, Lieutenant, United States Naval Reserve, you have heard the charge and specification preferred against you; how say you, guilty or not guilty?" "Not guilty," says Maryk, while Greenwald rises and states: "Accused admits he is Lieutenant Stephen Maryk, U.S.N.R., and that he was the executive officer of the U.S.S. *Caine* on December 18, 1944."

Directed by the bench to present his case, Challee first calls Lt. Comdr. Queeg. The Orderly ushers in the natty, erect naval officer. Queeg is sworn in by Blakely. Challee asks him to state his name, rank, and present position, which he does: "Philip Francis Queeg, Lieutenant Commander, United States Navy, temporarily assigned to Commandant, Twelfth Naval District, awaiting reassignment by Bu Pers." Challee has him next identify the defendant, and then assert that on December 18, 1944, he was in command of the U.S.S. *Caine*. Told to describe his ship, Queeg responds in an easy manner: "Her official designation is high-speed minesweeper. What she is, is a four-piper, one of those flush-deck, twelve-hundred-ton destroyers from World War I, fixed up with minesweeping gear . . . about the oldest type still doing combatant duty."

CHALLEE—What is her primary mission?

QUEEG (*smiling*)—That's a hard one. These old buckets are regarded as pretty expendable. By and large we were doing the usual destroyer duty—antisubmarine screening—also ran the mail, transported marines, carried aviation gas and torpedoes, gave fire support in minor landings, or what have you? Also swept mines now and then.

CHALLEE—Commander, on December 18, 1944, were you relieved of command of the *Caine?*

He was, answers Queeg—by the accused, and it was totally irregular. "The most charitable description would be that it was an incident, a regrettable incident of temporary and total collapse of military discipline." Told to relate all the facts that bear on this unauthorized relief, Queeg gives the date they sortied from Ulithi Atoll as the 15th or 16th of December. They went along as a screening vessel for a group of fleet oilers, to a rendezvous with Admiral Hal-

sey's fast carrier force in the Philippine Sea. They made the rendezvous. Then on the morning of the 18th, the typhoon came along,
the fueling was broken off and the fleet began maneuvering to escape
the storm, which was moving due west. Admiral Halsey set his
course due south, and they began to make a run for "the safe semi-
circle." The storm was bad at this point, visibility was almost zero:
"We were just steaming blindly through rain and spray. And of
course with the wind and sea and all, we had to maneuver pretty
smartly with engines and rudder to hold fleet course and speed. But
we were doing fine. My executive officer, however, pretty early in
the game began to show unusual symptoms of nervousness. And I
had to—"

CHALLEE—What were these symptoms of nervousness?
QUEEG—Well, for instance, he began talking very early—oh, it
couldn't have been half an hour after the fleet started to run south—
that we should operate independently and come around north. . . .
(*With illustrative gestures.*) Well, to give you the picture on that—
you see the typhoon was coming at us from the east. We were on
the western edge of it. Now as you know these blows spin counter-
clockwise above the equator. That means where we were the wind
was from due north. Admiral Halsey, of course, was running south
with the wind, to get out of the storm's path. Now that's in accord-
ance with all existing storm doctrine from Bowditch on up. But my
exec insisted that the ship was on the verge of foundering and we'd
better come around and head into the wind—that is, north—if we
were to survive. Of course we weren't in any such bad shape at all.
That's what I mean by nervousness.

To Queeg that was the worst of ideas—his ship was in no danger,
and functioning normally. To head into the heart of the typhoon
would have been suicidal and against orders given. He had since
checked his decision against that of the finest ship-handlers he knew,
and they had all agreed with him.
Challee politely calls the Commander's attention to his last remark, since hearsay evidence is not acceptable to the court. He also
feels he has to call this to the attention of Greenwald, who all
through Queeg's testimony has been doodling. To Blakely and
Challee, Greenwald's manner is so casual they feel they must remind
him of his duty to his client. Challee points out that a ship-handler
expert will be called to testify, so Queeg proceeds with his testimony
about Maryk's behavior, culminating in his relieving Queeg of his
command.

He felt that Maryk, with his constant insistence on going north, had simply panicked. The barometer was as low as it ever had been in U. S. naval history; they had taken one really bad roll, when Maryk suddenly informed Queeg that he was on the sick list and being relieved of his command. Challee inquires if the *Caine* was in grave danger. Queeg felt it wasn't, having righted nicely from the roll. Although Maryk repeatedly ordered him off the bridge, Queeg remained, giving orders only when it seemed necessary, bringing his ship through the storm despite his executive officer's running amuck.

CHALLEE—Did Maryk cite any authority at all when he relieved you?

QUEEG—He mumbled something about Article 184. I didn't even catch it at the time. Later he said his authority was Articles 184, 185, and 186 of the Naval Regulations.

CHALLEE—Are you familiar with those articles?

As Queeg understands it: "They make it possible for an executive officer to take over in an emergency, a highly unusual emergency where the captain is—well, frankly, where the captain's gone absolutely and hopelessly loony." Asked whether those articles were properly invoked in this situation, Queeg wryly replies that they needn't take his word; there were over 130 witnesses. He smilingly stands corrected when once again Challee remonstrates against offering, as testimony, the conclusions of others. Blakely for the second time shows his annoyance with the still-doodling Greenwald (who again hadn't caught this hearsay evidence) and asks that it be stricken from the record.

Queeg testifies that he warned Maryk he was performing a mutinous act: Maryk was determined to retain command, even knowing it would end in a court-martial. And, Queeg continues, his officer of the deck, Lt. (j.g.) Keith, in a state of panic, backed up Maryk— as did Stilwell, the emotionally unbalanced helmsman, a devoted friend of Mister Keith's: ". . . a competent officer of the deck would have repudiated Maryk's orders and a normal sailor at the helm would have disregarded both officers and obeyed me. It was just bad luck that those three men—Maryk, Keith, and Stilwell— were combined against me at a crucial time. Bad luck for me, and I'm afraid, worse luck for them."

Blakely questions Queeg on his fitness. He replies that he has passed all examinations, physical and mental, prescribed by the Navy. Queeg says he even carries a letter of commendation in his jacket. Then, Blakely inquires, how could Queeg explain Maryk's opinion that he was mentally ill? Queeg makes an effort to clear this up: "Well, sir, I'll have to say that I assumed command of an extremely disorganized and dirty ship. Now that's no reflection on the officer I relieved. The *Caine* had had a year and a half of the most arduous combat duty, and it was understandable. Still, the safety of the ship and its crew demanded its being brought up to snuff. I took many stern measures. Lieutenant Maryk, I may say, from the first didn't see eye to eye with me at all on this idea of making the *Caine* a taut ship again. Maybe he thought I was crazy to keep trying. I guess that's the picture, sir."

Challee having no more questions retires to his desk, leaving the field to Greenwald. The latter rises: "Commander Queeg, I should like to ask you whether you have ever heard the expression, 'Old Yellowstain.'" Queeg looks genuinely puzzled. Greenwald prods him: "You aren't aware, then, that all the officers of the *Caine* habitually referred to you as Old Yellowstain?" Challee jumps to his feet protesting: "I object to the question! It is impertinent badgering of the witness." Blakely frostily adds: "How does the defense counsel Greenwald justify this line of questioning?" Greenwald offers: "If the court please, the nickname, 'Old Yellowstain,' used by the officers of the *Caine* will be relevant to the issue of mental competence." Blakely stares hard at Greenwald: "Before ruling, the court wishes to caution defense counsel. This is a most unusual and delicate case. The honor and career of an officer with an unblemished military record of fourteen years' standing is involved. The defense counsel will have to bear full responsibility for the conduct of his case." The question is allowed to stand, and Queeg's answer that he was unaware of being called such a name is on the record. At which point, to the court's surprise, Greenwald forgoes any further cross-examination of the captain, saying that he will call Commander Queeg later on for the *defense*. Challee and Blakely wonder at Greenwald's competence; but Queeg is excused and leaves the room.

Lt. Thomas Keefer is next sworn in. The tall, clever-looking officer takes the witness stand, identifies the accused, gives his civilian occupation as "writer," and admits that beyond having published a number of stories, he has sold a half-finished war novel to a publisher. Challee asks him the title of his novel. Keefer says *Multitudes, Multitudes* and then repeats it for Blakely. Challee asks for Keefer's background in an effort to establish his reliability as an observer of personalities. He asks him how he found out about the relief of Captain Queeg. "Well," says Keefer, "Mister Maryk passed the word over the loudspeakers for all officers to lay up to the wheelhouse. When we got there he told us that the Captain was sick and he had assumed command." He then testifies that Queeg looked no worse than Keith, or Maryk. "We were all tired, dripping, and knocked out." He took no "remedial action," in spite of recognizing the seriousness of the situation, because by then the whole ship was obeying Maryk's orders, and for the safety of the ship he did the same. Keefer, having been aboard all during Captain Queeg's command, Challee asks if he had ever observed any evidences of insanity in the captain. This Keefer hesitates to affirm, not being a psychiatrist. On further questioning, Keefer admits to at least an elementary knowledge of psychiatry. And on the basis of this admission, Challee asks whether Captain Queeg ever exhibited deranged behavior. Keefer saw nothing like that. Challee then puts it to him directly: "Did you ever think he might be insane?" To which Greenwald promptly objects, matters of opinion not being admissible evidence.

Keefer, however, reports his objections to Maryk's using a "medical log" on Queeg's behavior as a means to relieve Captain Queeg of his command. In his opinion, it would not justify such action. At the time, he persuaded Maryk to give up the idea and return with the log from the flagship to the *Caine*. When two weeks later, Maryk relieved the Captain, Keefer was not only "flabbergasted," but thoroughly disturbed over what his friend Maryk had let himself in for. Listening to his friend testify, Maryk is disturbed himself.

Challee, having finished with the witness, nods to Greenwald. But Greenwald says: "No questions," and he has no intention of recalling the witness at a later time, either. Whereupon, the court questions Keefer in an effort to ascertain whether he judged Queeg—on the evidence of the medical log—to have been a normal and competent officer. Keefer answers: "Sir, speaking from ignorance, it's always seemed to me that mental disability was a relative thing. Captain Queeg was a very strict disciplinarian and extremely meticulous in hunting down the smallest matters. He was not the easiest person in the world to reason with. There were several occasions when I thought he bore down too hard and spent excessive time on small matters. Those were the things that were recorded in the medical log. They were very unpleasant. But to jump from them to a conclusion that the Captain was a maniac—no—I was compelled in all honesty to warn Maryk against doing that." And he is excused, warned not to discuss his testimony outside the courtroom. Maryk can't understand why Greenwald didn't cross-examine Keefer, can no better understand Greenwald's explanation: "It would have made things worse for you. You'll get your chance on the stand." But Maryk swears he'd never say a word about Tom Keefer. ". . . Not

me. God damn it, he should have talked himself." Greenwald
agrees: "You don't understand, do you?" he adds. "Not about
Keefer. Not even about yourself."

Twenty-year-old Signalman Junius Hannaford Urban is next
sworn in. He proves the sort of witness who will barely state the
names of those who were in the wheelhouse at the time Captain
Queeg was relieved. Each bit of information has to be dragged out
of him, each question has to be repeated several different ways.
Asked to describe what happened in the ten minutes before Captain
Queeg was relieved, he answers: "Well, like I says, the ship was rolling very bad," and then stops. Under further questioning, he does
admit to having heard the Captain say he wanted to come north,
and the exec wanting to come south—or the other way around—or
something. But he didn't know why.

> CHALLEE—Did the captain act crazy?
> URBAN—No, sir.
> CHALLEE—Did the exec seem scared?
> URBAN—No, sir.
> CHALLEE—Did the captain?
> URBAN—No, sir.
> CHALLEE—Did anyone?
> URBAN—I was goddamn scared, sir.

And to more questions as to whether the Captain acted queer or
crazy, or sane, he finally answers: "He was sane, sir, so far as I
know." That's as far as his one-year-of-high-school education will
take him. At this point Blakely would like to know: "Have you been
telling the whole truth here, or haven't you?" Urban explains: "Sir,
a signalman isn't supposed to listen to arguments between the captain and the exec." To Blakely's: "Did you like the Captain?" he
miserably answers, *"Sure* I liked him, sir." Challee is through questioning him, but Greenwald is ready: "Urban, were you aboard when
the *Caine* cut her own tow cable the time she was towing targets
outside Pearl Harbor?" Urban was. "What were you doing at the
time it happened?" Urban starts to say: "I was—that is, the captain
was eating my—" when he catches himself just short of an obscenity,
with a glance of horror at Blakely, "bawling me out—on the bridge,
sir." Asked why, he answers: "My shirttail was out," and what's
more: "Sir, he was a nut on—yes, sir. He was very strict on shirttails, sir . . ." Greenwald concludes: "And while the Captain was
discussing your shirttail the ship went right around in a circle and
steamed over its own towline? Is that the way it hap—" Here

Challee jumps to his feet, objecting to such a line of questioning, which introduces a material point not touched upon in direct examination. He is upheld by the court, but Greenwald reasons: "Please the court, the witness stated he had never seen the Captain do anything crazy. I am attempting to refute this." But his cross-examination is stricken from the record. Greenwald now directly asks: "Urban, what is a paranoid personality?" Urban is baffled: "Sir?" And to: "Could you recognize a psychotic person?" Urban blurts out: "Me?" This concludes Greenwald's cross-examination.

The prosecution intends to call a dozen more members of the *Caine*'s crew to confirm Urban's testimony that the captain was never seen to do a crazy thing. Greenwald is willing to concede: ". . . that the testimony of all these witnesses will corroborate Urban's . . . if the Judge Advocate will concede that these twelve men don't know any more about a paranoid personality than Urban." Challee is more than willing; Blakely remarks that this is a weighty concession on Greenwald's part. Blakely then asks Greenwald whether he thinks he has had ample time to prepare his case, and whether he took it willingly. Challee rises and addresses the court: "If it please the court. Lieutenant Greenwald accepted the assignment at my earnest request." Blakely expresses doubts as to Greenwald's competence, and asks Maryk whether Greenwald's handling of the defense meets with his approval. Maryk hesitates; Greenwald asks for a delay, not a recess—that he may speak with his client—which is granted.

Maryk is hurt and feels sunk. He doesn't understand why Greenwald didn't obtain more favorable testimony from Keefer, why he wouldn't cross-examine him. He doesn't understand why Greenwald wants to fight this case; moreover, if he does, why did he say he'd rather prosecute than defend him? Greenwald, with time running short, makes Maryk listen to him: "Implicating Keefer harms you. . . . Two disgruntled bastards instead of one heroic exec." Still Maryk stares uncomprehending. "I've got a chance with a lone heroic exec," Greenwald explains. "Making that picture stick is my only chance to win for you. Please try to let that sink in." As Maryk slowly begins to see what Greenwald is about, Blakely is inquiring about him from Challee. He too finds Greenwald hard to understand. Challee assures him Greenwald was a successful young Washington lawyer, whom he personally knew—one of the most successful in Washington. Blakely finds: "He's putting up a damned queer show . . ." Learning that Greenwald is Jewish, Blakely can only say: "Well, maybe he's a hell of a lot smarter than he seems."

When handsome young Lieutenant Keith takes the stand, he doesn't hide his antagonism for Captain Queeg. In describing what he considered the captain's persecution of Gunner's Mate Second Class Stilwell—his restricting him to the ship for six months for reading on watch—he reveals that Maryk deliberately violated Queeg's order and gave Stilwell a pass to see his wife.

CHALLEE (*pleased and surprised*)—Are you testifying, Mister Keith, that Maryk deliberately violated his captain's orders?

KEITH (*rattled*)—Well, I mean it was my fault actually, I begged him to. I was morale officer, and I thought the man's morale—I mean—

CHALLEE—Mister Keith, we now have your testimony that you and Maryk and Stilwell connived to circumvent an express order of your commanding officer, a whole year before the typhoon of 18 December . . . Now please tell the court any other instances of maltreatment that occur to you.

Keith tells of Queeg's cutting off movies for six months, but he can't say Queeg ever did anything that violated regulations. And in spite of thinking Queeg a tyrant, he didn't regard him as insane until the day of the typhoon. "Very well, come to the day of the typhoon. Was your decision to obey Maryk based on your judgment that the captain had gone mad, or was it based on your hatred of Captain Queeg?" Keith, after a betraying pause and a glance at Maryk says miserably: "I just don't remember my state of mind that long ago." Challee contemptuously dismisses him. But Greenwald brings out—as bearing directly on the mental fitness of Captain Queeg to command a naval vessel—further reasons for Keith's dislike of his commanding officer. Keith is permitted to tell his story of the so-called extortion the captain practiced on him.

The captain was sneaking in a big case of tax-free whiskey from Pearl Harbor. Keith was appointed to supervise its loading into a gig. Through the captain's excitable and contradictory orders, the sailors dropped the crate into the water. Keith was to go on leave the next day, so—to get Queeg to sign his leave papers—he paid him the cost of the drowned liquor. Keith, mustering his nerve, goes on: "My chief reason for disliking Captain Queeg was his cowardice in battle."

GREENWALD—What cowardice?

KEITH—He repeatedly ran from shore batteries—

CHALLEE (*infuriated*)—Objection! Counsel is originating evidence beyond the scope of direct examination. He is leading the witness into irresponsible libels of an officer of the Navy! (BLAKELY *starts looking through "Naval Regulations."*)

GREENWALD—Please the court, the witness's dislike of Queeg was not only in the scope of direct examination, it was the key fact brought out. The witness has confessed ignorance of psychiatry. Things Queeg did, which caused the witness in his ignorance to dislike him, may in fact have been the helpless acts of a sick man.

Blakely, for the benefit of all parties, reads from the "Articles for the Government of the Navy," on cowardice. He warns the defense counsel and witness they are on the most dangerous possible ground —in charging an officer with an offense punishable by death. Since Greenwald does not withdraw his question, nor Keith his answer, Blakely icily tells them to proceed.

Keith relates Captain Queeg's running from shore batteries.

KEITH—Practically every time we heard gunfire from the beach. I guess the worst time was at Kwajalein. That's where he got the nickname, "Old Yellowstain."

GREENWALD—What did this nickname, "Old Yellowstain," imply?

KEITH—Well, cowardice, of course. It referred to a yellow dye-marker he dumped over the side.

GREENWALD—Describe this Yellow Stain incident.

KEITH—Well, I wasn't on the bridge, so I only heard about it afterwards. What happened was that Captain Queeg—

CHALLEE—Objection. Does the defense counsel seriously expect to enter these hearsay libels on the record?

GREENWALD—I withdraw the question. Defense will introduce direct evidence on the Yellow Stain incident.

The question and answer are stricken from the record. Greenwald then asks Keith for an incident of cowardice he eyewitnessed. Keith offers: "Well, in any combat situation Captain Queeg was always found on the side of the bridge away from the firing. I saw that a dozen times when I was OOD." But on Challee's cross-examination, Keith cannot give anything in the way of records to substantiate his charge of cowardice. Nor has he evidence or a witness to the fact that Queeg's crates actually contained liquor. To Challee's final question: "Mister Keith, on the morning when the captain was relieved, did you really think he had gone crazy?" Keith, losing assurance, answers: "I said before I can't say for sure what my state of mind was." Challee is quickly done with him.

An expert ship-handler, Captain Southard of the Regular Navy, is the next witness. A competent old-hand, he gives his answers to Challee's hypothetical ship-handling problem without a moment's hesitation, and his facts and opinions are those of Captain Queeg. Then Greenwald has a go at this witness.

GREENWALD—Captain, have you ever conned a ship through the center of a typhoon?

SOUTHARD—Negative. Been on the fringes often but always managed to avoid the center.

GREENWALD—Have you ever commanded a destroyer-minesweeper, sir?

SOUTHARD—Negative.

GREENWALD—This case, sir, concerns a destroyer-minesweeper at the center of a typhoon—

SOUTHARD (*frostily*)—I'm aware of that. I've had DMS's under my command in screens, and I've read the book on 'em. They don't differ from destroyers except in details of topside weight characteristics.

GREENWALD—I ask these questions, Captain, because you are the only expert witness on ship-handling, and the extent of your expert knowledge should be clear to the court.

SOUTHARD—That's all right. I've handled destroyer types in almost every conceivable situation for ten years. Haven't handled a DMS at the center of a typhoon, no, but I don't know who has besides the skipper of the *Caine*. It's a thousand-to-one shot.

GREENWALD—Will you state without reservation that the rules of destroyer handling would hold for a DMS in the center of a typhoon?

SOUTHARD—Well, at the center of a typhoon there are no hard and fast rules. That's one situation where it's all up to the commanding officer. Too many strange things happen too fast.

GREENWALD—Sir, you remember the hypothetical question of the Judge Advocate about the typhoon?

SOUTHARD—I do.

GREENWALD—Now in that situation, I ask you to assume that the winds and seas become worse than any you've ever experienced. Your ship is wallowing broadside. You actually believe your ship is foundering. You're in the last extremity. Would you bring your ship north, into the wind, or continue on south, stern to wind?

SOUTHARD—You're getting mighty hypothetical.

GREENWALD—Yes, sir. You prefer not to answer that question, Captain?

SOUTHARD—I'll answer it. In the last extremity I'd come around to north and head into the wind, if I could. But *only* in the last extremity.

Challee has one more question for Captain Southard: Who is the judge of whether a ship is in its last extremity? Southard unhesitatingly says the Captain, whose experience and training make him the only qualified judge. ". . . Panic is a common hazard at sea. The highest function of command is to override it and listen to nothing but the voice of his own professional judgment." And he is excused.

Dr. Lundeen, the psychiatrist head of the Naval Hospital, San Francisco, is the next witness. Examined by Challee, he tells of the findings on Captain Queeg, whom they had had under observation, and then discharged with a clean bill of health. He further testifies that Queeg could not have been psychotic two months ago when relieved of his command. The board didn't find him a perfect officer, but his relief was completely unjustified. Challee shows his pleasure by a thin cold grin in Greenwald's direction, as he yields him the floor.

Greenwald is almost apologetic as he shuffles forward to have Dr. Lundeen clear up some technical terms for him. Lundeen is delighted to act the professor: he explains to Greenwald that "normality" is a fiction in psychiatry. There is no adult except a happy imbecile without problems. Captain Queeg has his, but he's adjusted: "His identity as a naval officer is the essential balancing factor. It's the key to his personal security. Therefore he has a fixed anxiety about protecting his standing. That would account for the harshness and ill temper." Lundeen agrees that Queeg would be disinclined to make mistakes, that his personality would make him a perfectionist. ". . . any mistake of a subordinate is intolerable because it might endanger him." The commander's weakness, Lundeen continues, lies in his distortion of reality, so that he comes out blameless: "Other people have other weaknesses. It's definitely not disabling." Under Greenwald's questioning, Lundeen concedes that: ". . . you'll have a certain rigidity of personality in such an individual. The inner security checks him from admitting those who differ with him may be right." Suddenly, Greenwald clicks out: "Doctor, you've testified that the following symptoms exist in the commander's behavior: rigidity of personality, feelings of persecution, unreasonable suspi-

Scene from "The Caine Mutiny Court-Martial"

cion, withdrawal from reality, perfectionist anxiety, an unreal basic premise, and an obsessive sense of self-righteousness."

LUNDEEN (*looking startled, then appreciatively amused*)—All mild, sir, all well compensated.

GREENWALD—Yes, Doctor. Is there an inclusive psychiatric term —one label for this syndrome?

LUNDEEN—Syndrome? Who said anything about a syndrome? You're misusing a term. There's no syndrome, because there's no disease.

But Lundeen knows what Greenwald is driving at: "It's a paranoid personality, but that is not a disabling affliction." Greenwald asks: "What kind of personality, Doctor?" "Paranoid," says Dr. Lundeen. "Paranoid, Doctor?" Greenwald makes it clear for the record. "Yes, paranoid," answers Lundeen. It is Greenwald's turn to catch Challee's eye, but not Challee's turn to cross-examine. Greenwald questions, this time to Lundeen's annoyance, whether a paranoid personality like Commander Queeg, though not disabled for minor duties, might not be disabled for command? Lundeen finds that conceivable; the disabling factor would show up in an interview with a skilled psychiatrist. "Why is a psychiatrist needed, Doctor? Can't an educated, intelligent person, like myself, or the Judge Advocate, or the court, detect a paranoid?" Lundeen is quite sarcastic: "You evidently are not too well acquainted with the pattern. The distinguishing mark of this neurosis is extreme plausability and a most convincing normal manner on the surface. Particularly in self-justification." That answers it for Greenwald, who thanks the doctor, and says nothing more. The court shows its interest and its uneasiness in the doctor's testimony.

Next, young Dr. Bird, an intellectual naval doctor, takes the stand. He is to be Challee's last witness. He at once testifies that the board has found Commander Queeg mentally fit for command, and never previously unfit. Challee, after an understandable pause, asks Bird whether there was any indication of Queeg's being a paranoid personality. Bird prefers, ". . . to call it an obsessive personality with paranoid features, but this does not indicate mental unfitness." The medical board was unanimous in considering Queeg to be fit. Challee has no further questions.

Greenwald appraises Bird with a cold eye, and right off the bat gets him to agree that the Freudian usage of "disturbed" and "adjusted" corresponds roughly to the layman's "sick" and "well." Greenwald has Bird explain the difference between "compensated"

and "adjusted," when Bird says Queeg's feelings of inferiority are
well compensated. Bird smilingly obliges: "Well—let's say a man
has some deep-seated psychological disturbance. He can compensate
by finding outlets for his peculiar drives. He can never adjust without undergoing psychoanalysis."

GREENWALD—Has Commander Queeg ever been psychoanalyzed?
BIRD—No.
GREENWALD—He is, then, a disturbed person.
BIRD—Yes, he is. Not disabled, however, by the disturbance.

Bird says Queeg has compensated in two ways: "The paranoid
pattern, which is useless and not desirable; and his naval career,
which is extremely useful and desirable." His military career is a
result of his disturbance, as Bird comments: "Most military careers
are." At Greenwald's request, Bird goes into Queeg's habit of rolling
the steel balls in his hands, the incessant rolling of these small balls
in either hand to conceal their trembling. "Why do his hands trem-
ble?" Greenwald inquires. "The inner tension," Bird explains. "It's
one of the surface symptoms." Challee asks the court to limit these
irrelevant details, but Greenwald forges ahead, leading the way for
Bird. "Doctor, you have testified that the commander is a disturbed,
not an adjusted person." Bird agrees, but smiles with assurance as
he catches Greenwald playing with words again, and repeats: "We
found no disability." But, Greenwald asks him to suppose, if the
requirements of command were particularly severe, wouldn't this
mild sickness disable Queeg? Bird begins to bridle, and when asked
if he has ever *been* to sea, his assurance quickly fades. Bird has not
been to sea, his navy experience is limited to five or six months on
shore, and this is the first ship's captain he has had to deal with.
From his general knowledge, he doesn't feel that the command of a
ship requires a highly gifted person. Greenwald eggs him on. "Not
highly gifted, no," opines Bird. "Adequate responses, fairly good
intelligence, and sufficient training and experience, but—" Greenwald says it for him: "In other words, it takes more ability to be a
psychiatrist than the captain of a naval vessel?" Greenwald is not
unaware of Blakely's reaction to such a line of reasoning. Bird now
takes umbrage at the implication that because he knows little about
the requirements of command, he may err, and should perhaps have
disqualified himself from serving on the board.
    Bird is quivering with indignation when Challee thinks to win him
over by saying sympathetically: "Doctor Bird, the defense counsel
manages to put words into your mouth that I'm certain you don't

mean, and I'd like to—" Bird stands on what is left of his dignity, and pompously asserts: "I'm not aware that he succeeded in putting any words into my mouth." Challee tries to explain that Greenwald drew the implication from him that Queeg was sick. "Sir," states Bird, "I'm careful in my use of terminology. I did not introduce the term 'sick.' I don't regard it as a precise term. Nevertheless, if you're going to use such a loose term—Captain Queeg, like a vast number of seemingly healthy people, is sick. However, he is definitely not disabled for command, which is the only issue here." Challee tries to point out a contradiction that he feels sure Bird never intended, but Bird is so wound up that he'd go on and on rather than retract anything. Challee rather hastily decides there are no more questions. Blakely, on the verge of questioning Bird, thinks better of it, too. The Prosecution rests.

The Defense is ready to present its case, and since Greenwald will be calling only two witnesses, Blakely is sure that: ". . . . we can button it all up tomorrow morning." He recesses the court till 0900. The court rises, Blakely leaves, followed by the court members and entourage. Challee, gathering his papers together, comments on Greenwald's handling of Bird, but says it won't do any good with a man of Blakely's experience. He leaves Greenwald, who is weary and morose over all he must do to win the case. On the other hand, Maryk is suddenly sanguine about his chances, and admiring of Greenwald's skill. Maryk watches Greenwald pacing around, and listens to him on why he doesn't like Tom Keefer: "I look at Keefer and I see my own self a couple of years ago. Only like in a crazy-house mirror, all distorted and upside down. I'm not amused. Maybe Keefer didn't enjoy sailing under Queeg for half a year. Maybe he'd enjoy it less if the Nazis and the Japs were shaking hands right now at the Mississippi River. I guess what I've found out, Maryk, is that there's a time for everything, including rebellious youth. Possibly you and Mr. Keefer were dead wrong in your timing. In which case the next question is, who is the real victim in this courtroom? You? Or Captain Queeg?" And, knowing exactly what he has to do in court tomorrow, Greenwald plans to get drunk tonight.

ACT II

The Defense

The lights brighten on the empty stage—the court reassembles for Maryk's defense.

Greenwald calls Maryk to the stand, where before being sworn in, Blakely informs him he needn't take the stand. If he does, however, he may be subjected to a vigorous cross-examination. Maryk understands, so Blakely says: "Court stenographers will affirmatively record that the statutory request was made," and swears Maryk in.

Greenwald first asks Maryk what his occupation as a civilian had been. Maryk answers: "Helping out in my father's fishing business. . . ." He had been on his father's boats since he was fourteen. Maryk next states he relieved the commanding officer of the *Caine* on December 18, 1944. The *Caine*, he asserts, was in the last extremity—they were unable to hold course, and broached to three times in an hour. "Yes. Wind and sea took charge and tossed us sideways for ten minutes at a time. We were rolling too steeply for the inclinometer to record. We were shipping solid green water in the wheelhouse. The generators were cutting out. The ship wasn't answering to emergency rudder and engine settings. We were lost and out of control." Queeg's only response to Maryk's repeatedly pointing this out was, ". . . mostly a glazed look and no answer, or a repetition of his own desires," which were, Maryk supposed, to hold fleet course until they went down.

Greenwald then asks Maryk when and why he started his medical log on Captain Queeg. After the dye-marker incident before the invasion of Kwajalein, Maryk answers. Maryk testifies he was navigator and witness to the *Caine*'s leaving far behind the assault boats it was to lead to within a thousand yards of the beach. The boats were so low in the choppy water that they had to depend on the *Caine*'s navigation. The *Caine* was ringing up ten knots, whereas the assault boats at most could manage five or six. "They began to fall way behind. Naturally they signaled for us to slow down. But the captain just ignored them. We pulled further and further ahead until we could hardly see them. Then, when we were about twenty-five-hundred yards from the beach, we heard some gunfire. The captain suddenly yelled, 'We're running up on the beach! Reverse course! Make thirty knots!' And while we were turning, he threw over one of those yellow dye-markers you use to mark water where there's a floating mine or something. So we went barreling out of there. The attack boats were just a lot of specks way off in the distance. All you could see behind us was this big spread of yellow, all over the water." The court bell rings, and Blakely wishes to know how Maryk knew he was twenty-five-hundred yards from the beach when they turned.

MARYK—Sir, I was navigating. There wasn't a doubt in the world where we were, by visual plot. And our radar range to the beach was also twenty-five hundred when we turned.

BLAKELY—Did you inform your captain that he was turning fifteen-hundred yards short?

MARYK—Sir, I shouted it at him, over and over. He just stood there smiling.

Blakely makes some notes as Maryk tells him that the boats signaled to them to slow down, and that he himself reported this to Captain Queeg, who was looking right at them. "I pointed out," testifies Maryk, "that if we got too far ahead, the boats wouldn't know where the line of departure was. That's when he said, 'Well, we'll throw over a dye-marker, then.'" Blakely nods to Greenwald to proceed. Maryk is asked why he hadn't gone to a higher authority to report on his Captain's mental health. Maryk decided the medical log would put him in a stronger position, and if he was wrong, he could always burn the record. He testifies that he recorded in the log any incident that seemed strange or abnormal—like the Silex business. This concerned an inquiry over which messboy had burnt out the Silex coffeepot. The captain had the entire body of ship's officers sit as a court for thirty-six hours, with all other work suspended. Finally, no one having confessed, the weary officers offered to take cuts in their fitness reports for being inadequate investigators if the captain would call off the inquiry.

Maryk touches on the water business (the captain turning off the water for two days at the equator) and then mentions the strawberry business. Here Challee objects: "The so-called medical log was introduced in evidence at the start of these proceedings. All this is just repeating a lot of trivial, disloyal gripes." Blakely would agree, only he feels there's some confusion over the strawberry business that somehow turned into a search for a key. According to Maryk, it was the messboys again, but the captain was sure that someone had made a duplicate key to the refrigerator. After describing the frenzied search for the key Maryk goes on: "Well, when I saw Captain Queeg sitting by the icebox, taking those keys one by one out of the barrels and trying them on the [refrigerator's] padlock, hours on end, with a gleam in his eye, I gave up. That was when I showed the medical log to Lieutenant Keefer."

Under Blakely's questioning, Maryk assumes full responsibility and absolves Keefer of all blame. Greenwald then asks him: "Mister Maryk, when the typhoon was over, did Captain Queeg make any effort to regain command?"

MARYK—Yes, on the morning of the nineteenth. The storm had blown out. We'd just sighted the fleet.

GREENWALD—Describe what happened.

MARYK—Well, I was in the charthouse writing up a despatch to report the relief to Admiral Halsey. The captain came in and said, "Do you mind coming to my cabin and having a talk before you send that?" I went below and we talked. It was the same thing at first— about how I'd be court-martialed for mutiny. He said, "You've applied for transfer to the Regular Navy. You know this means the end of all that, don't you?" Then he went into a long thing about how he loved the Navy and had no other interest in life, and even if he was cleared, this would ruin his record. I said I felt sorry for him, and I really did. Finally he came out with his proposal. He said he'd forget the whole thing and never report me. He would resume command, and the whole matter would be forgotten and written off—

Maryk tells how amazed he was at such a proposal. "I said, 'Captain, the whole ship knows about it. It's written up in the quartermaster's log and the OOD's log.' Well, he hemmed and hawed, and finally said it wouldn't be the first time a penciled rough log had been corrected and fixed after the fact." Greenwald then asks Maryk if he had reminded the captain of the rule against erasures, which he had. The interview went from the captain's cajoling him, to the captain's pleading with him and at one point to the captain's weeping. It finished with the captain's sudden burst of anger and his ordering Maryk out of his quarters. So twenty-four hours after the relief, Maryk had the chance (and wouldn't take it) of erasing the whole event from the official record.

Greenwald asks if Maryk was at all panicky during the typhoon. No, he answered, he knew what he was doing. "Did you relieve without authority?" Greenwald asks him. "No," Maryk replies. "My authority was 184, 185, and 186." Did he relieve Captain Queeg without justifiable cause? Again Maryk answers: "No, my justifiable cause was the captain's mental breakdown at a time when the ship was in danger."

Greenwald is through with Maryk, and Challee approaches him. Challee starts his cross-examination by asking if there were any witnesses to his amazing interview with the captain. Had anyone seen the chart showing the ship turned away too soon at the Kwajalein beach? Has Maryk any documentary evidence of it? Maryk has neither witnesses nor written evidence: the radar men who called ranges called so many they wouldn't remember, the marines fought so hard they would only remember the fighting. Challee asks whether Maryk considers himself a loyal officer—after admitting disloyalty in issuing Stilwell a pass in defiance of Queeg's express instructions. Maryk admits that this was not a loyal act.

Challee next concentrates on the nature of Maryk's education. It turns out to have been poor. Maryk had just scraped by in college, was below average as a student. As for any knowledge of psychiatry, Maryk proves himself puzzled over the simplest facts. "In fact," says Challee, "you don't know what you're talking about when you discuss mental illness, is that right?" Maryk flounders about. Challee points out that Maryk, with his own ignorance of all things psychiatric, has heard qualified psychiatrists state that Queeg was not crazy, has heard Keefer, a man of superior intelligence, say the same thing; yet despite all this, Maryk insists that his diagnosis of Queeg is the right one? Maryk says weakly: "Only about Queeg on the morning of the typhoon." Challee is done with him; Greenwald has no further questions; Blakely orders Maryk to step down. Stunned, Maryk goes back to his seat.

Blakely waits for Greenwald to call his next witness, Captain Queeg. The captain enters debonair and assured as ever. Since the oath he previously took is still binding, he immediately takes the witness chair. Greenwald wants first to hear about the interview Queeg had with Maryk the day after the typhoon. Queeg gives his version of it: "Well, as I say, I felt sorry for him. I hated to see him ruining his life with one panicky mistake. Particularly as I knew his ambition was to make the Navy his career. I tried as hard as I could to show him what a mistake he had made. I recommended that he relinquish command to me, and I offered to be as lenient as I could in reporting what had happened." "You never offered not to report the incident?" Greenwald asks. Queeg states the utter impossibility of such a course: it was all in the logs. But, Greenwald asks, were the logs in pencil? After a little thought, Queeg says they probably weren't yet typed into smooth copies. But he asserts when questioned further that it's against the rules to make erasures. When told of Maryk's version of the interview, Queeg answers calmly that it's not a true one, then qualifies this by saying that it's, ". . . a distortion of what I told you. My version is the exact truth." He denies completely everything about erasures and hushing up the story, or his weeping and pleading. Greenwald asks: "You are accusing Mister Maryk of perjury?" Queeg retorts: "I'm not accusing him. He's accused of enough as it stands. You're likely to hear a lot of strange things from Mister Maryk about me, that's all." When Greenwald points out that somebody is obviously not telling the truth, and what proof has Queeg that it's not he, all Queeg can do is to cite: ". . . a clean record of over fourteen years as a naval officer, against the word of a man on trial for a mutinous act."

Greenwald then asks Queeg about the $110 Keith gave him. At first, Queeg doesn't recall ever receiving such a sum, but he suddenly recollects it when the loss of the crate is mentioned, and goes on: "It was over a year ago—December or thereabouts. He was responsible for the loss and insisted on paying and so he did."

Queeg's testimony isn't quite so direct concerning the contents of the lost crate. At first, in fact, it's his impression that it held clothes. When Greenwald doubts whether a crate full of clothes would sink, Queeg thinks maybe it held some souvenir rocks. Greenwald draws a complete denial from Queeg that the crate held liquor. But when Greenwald offers to bring to the stand under subpoena the carpenter who made the crate, and when Challee's objection that the crate is irrelevant is overruled by Blakely, Queeg offers a new explanation: he had two crates at the time. Greenwald courteously points out that so much of this trial depends on the credibility of witnesses, that Queeg can have a recess if he chooses, to clear his mind. Queeg finds that unnecessary, just wants a moment to think. After a moment's thought, Queeg remembers that one of the crates contained clothes, while the other (that sank) contained liquor. Reminded about liquor regulations in his ship, Queeg breaks in: "I'm aware of regulations. The crate was sealed prior to getting under way. I gave it the same locked stowage I gave the medicinal brandy. Liquor was damned scarce and expensive in the States. I'd had three years of steady combat duty. I gave myself this leeway as captain of the *Caine* and it was a common practice and I believe rank has its privileges, as they say. I had no intentions of concealing it from the court and I'm not ashamed of it. I simply mixed up the two crates in my mind." He denies Keith's testimony that he gave contradictory orders, denies Keith's testimony that he held up Keith's leave until Keith paid for the loss. Again it is his word against Keith's. "You'll hear nothing but lies about me from Keith," Queeg tells the court. "He has an insane hatred of me." Greenwald wonders: "Do you know why, sir?"

Queeg can't say: "Unless it's his resentment against fancied injuries to his crony, this sailor Stilwell. Those two were mighty affectionate." Greenwald draws this insinuation out in the open, asking if Queeg meant to suggest abnormal relations between the men. Greenwald then asking the court if it wishes to caution the witness about the gravity of such an insinuation, Queeg breaks in: "I'm not insinuating a thing, sir! I don't know of anything improper between those two men and I deny insinuating anything. All I said was that Keith was always taking Stilwell's part and it's the easiest thing in the world to prove and that's all I said or meant. I resent the twisting of my words."

Greenwald abandons this topic to pursue the charge that at Pearl Harbor the *Caine* steamed over its own towline and cut it. This brings Challee to his feet: "Objection! This towline business is the last straw. The tactics of the defense counsel are an outrage on the dignity of these proceedings. He's systematically turning this trial into a court-martial of Commander Queeg." Greenwald addresses the court and explains: "Sir, the Judge Advocate has made it perfectly clear that he thinks he has a prima-facie case in the report of the two psychiatrists. But I say it's up to the court, not to shore-bound doctors, however brilliant, to decide whether the captain of the *Caine* was mentally well enough to retain his self-control and his post during a typhoon." Blakely overrules Challee's objection, and the Judge Advocate, apparently stunned, slowly sits down.

Greenwald proceeds to the question whether Queeg was repri-manding Urban, the signalman, for having his shirttail out, when the *Caine* was turning 360 degrees. Queeg calls this another malicious lie. But in answering each of Greenwald's questions on the shirttail incident, Queeg gives the impression that most of Urban's own testi-mony was true; and he doesn't help himself by lashing out at Keith. "When I took over the ship it was like the Chinese Navy. And I bore down on Keith to watch those shirttails, and for all I know that's another reason he hated me and circulated all this about my cutting the towline." Greenwald now proceeds to the yellow dye-marker business. Queeg at first can't recall whether he dropped one in the invasion of Kwajalein. He recalls that his mission was to lead a group of attack boats to the line of departure. If he fulfilled his mission, Greenwald asks, why did he drop the marker? Queeg isn't sure that he did drop one, but if he did it was perhaps to mark the line more plainly—a thousand yards from the beach.

GREENWALD—Commander, didn't you run a mile ahead of the attack boats, drop your dye-marker more than half a mile short, and retire at high speed, leaving the boats to grope their way to the line of departure as best they could?

CHALLEE (*rises*)—The question is abusive and flagrantly leading.

GREENWALD (*wearily*)—I am willing to withdraw the question, in view of the commander's dim memory, and proceed to more recent events.

BLAKELY—Court desires to question the witness. (GREENWALD *crosses to his desk.*) Commander Queeg, in view of the implications of this line of testimony, I urge you to search your memory for correct answers.

QUEEG—I am certainly trying to do that, sir. But these are very small points. I've been through several campaigns since Kwajalein and the typhoon, and now all this business—

Blakely appreciates that but would like to have him give a few definite answers on points of fact. First, he would like to know whether those boats were at point of departure when the *Caine* turned away. Queeg says that as near as he could calculate, yes. Then why the dye-marker? Queeg hesitates: "Well, you might say a safety factor. Just another added mark. Now—maybe I erred in being overcautious and making sure they knew where they were, but then again, sir, I've always believed you can't err on the side of safety." Blakely now asks with a slight, acrid impatience, "Did you have the conn?"

Queeg recalls that Maryk had the conn, and Queeg had to caution him against there being too much open water between the *Caine* and the assault boats. Admitting that the *Caine* was too far ahead, Queeg shifts the blame for it to Maryk. And when Greenwald questions him again about his position on the bridge during combat, Queeg claims he had to be on all sides of the ship at once, because his officers were always scurrying toward the safe side.

Queeg takes the two steel balls out of his pocket, and Challee quickly requests a breather for him. Just as Bird did with Challee, Queeg grandly refuses help and insists on answering any and all questions. He insists that he didn't make a single mistake in fifteen months aboard the *Caine* and that he can prove it. Blakely asks why, if these officers were so unspeakably bad, Queeg had tolerated them. Queeg sanctimoniously says he was softhearted.

Greenwald asks: "Commander, on the morning of 18 December, at the moment you were relieved, was the *Caine* in the last extremity?" This Queeg emphatically denies. He had the ship under complete control—at which point he puts away his steel balls. Then if the ship wasn't in danger, Greenwald asks, why did he think to change course and come north? After a long pause, Queeg finds no inconsistency in saying that the ship wasn't in danger, but a typhoon was a typhoon. He might have come around and he might not. Then, concludes Greenwald, Maryk's decision wasn't a panicky blunder?

Queeg is asked, since he found them to be lies and distortions, to give his version of the episodes in Maryk's medical log. Queeg cockily goes into the strawberry business, then lunges into the water conservation matter, veers back again to the strawberries, then lurches off to the Silex story. There is talk of discipline, then of lack of respect for officers.

Greenwald listens respectfully to this diatribe, while leaning against his desk. Challee slouches in his chair biting his nails, and the members of the court eye one another, and after a while eye their wrist watches.

When the interminable outpouring is over, Greenwald courteously thanks Captain Queeg, hands him a photostat of the fitness report Queeg had written for Maryk the previous July, and asks him to read it aloud. Queeg, recognizing that this letter was written after all the medical log incidents had taken place, chokes and mumbles over the laudatory phrases which end with: "He [Maryk] cannot be too highly commended. He is recommended for transfer to the Regular Navy."

Greenwald has no further questions. Challee refuses to cross-examine, and Blakely excuses Captain Queeg. The Defense rests.

Challee waives his argument, but in the strongest words possible condemns counsel's manner of conducting this case as if it were a court-martial of Queeg rather than of Maryk. He denounces Greenwald for dragging up malicious criticisms of the commander and for making Queeg defend himself against them on the spur of the moment—and without advice of counsel, or with any of the safeguards provided under naval law. Challee further asks the court if it can permit such a precedent as a captain being deposed by his underlings for not pleasing them. He considers this a blank check to mutiny. Therefore, knowing the court won't be impressed by Greenwald's shyster tactics, he formally recommends, whatever the verdict, ". . . that defense counsel Greenwald be reprimanded by this court for conduct unbecoming an officer of the Navy—and that this reprimand be made part of his service record."

Blakely asks for Greenwald's closing argument. He rises and tells the court that he took this case with the greatest reluctance, at Challee's behest. Greenwald was aware that the only defense was to show the mental incompetence of a naval officer. He did what he could for an acquittal, as representing the duty of a defense counsel appointed by the Navy, and as a member of the bar.

One thing Greenwald is most anxious to make clear: the defense never contended that the commander was a coward. "The entire case of the defense rests on the assumption that no man who rises to command of a United States naval ship can possibly be a coward. And that therefore if he commits questionable acts under fire, the explanation must lie elsewhere. The court saw the bearing of Captain Queeg on the stand. The court can picture what his bearing must have been at the height of a typhoon. On that basis the court will decide the fate of the accused."

Before the court recesses, Blakely has the court rule on the recommendation to reprimand. Greenwald rises, and comes to attention, at the center of the stage. Blakely addresses Greenwald: "Lieutenant, this has been a strange and tragic trial. You have conducted your case with striking ingenuity. The Judge Advocate's remark about 'shyster tactics' was an unfortunate personal slur. But your conduct has been puzzling, and it does raise questions. With talent goes responsibility. Has your conduct here been responsible, Lieutenant Greenwald?" When the votes come in Blakely coldly announces that any reprimand will have to come from Greenwald's own conscience. The recommendation to reprimand is denied.

The court is recessed, and as at the beginning, the Orderly and Stenographer push the witness stand and Greenwald's desk to their original positions. Maryk, alone now with Greenwald, wants to know his chances. Greenwald advises him moodily that it will be safe to stick around for an hour or two. Maryk says with admiration: "You murdered Queeg." Greenwald answers: "Yes, I murdered him." He accepts Maryk's thanks without enthusiasm.

When Maryk tells him that Tom Keefer is throwing a party that night to celebrate his getting a $1000 check in the mail as an advance on his novel, Greenwald couldn't be bitterer. He hears that they are both invited to the party and that Maryk, in spite of everything, is going.

MARYK—Well, I know what you probably think. But hell, one way or another it's all over. I don't know what I'd have done in Tom's place.

GREENWALD—You'd go to Keefer's party?

MARYK—Tom's always called me a good-natured slob. I'll go if you will. If you think we should.

GREENWALD (*staring at him*)—All right. Maybe we'll both go and help Mr. Keefer celebrate.

There is a blackout, and then drunken voices in the darkness, singing "I've got Sixpence."

SCENE II

At the Fairmont Hotel that night, a long, garland-draped table stretches across a private dining room. It is stacked with champagne bottles and glasses, and with a huge cake in the form of a book. Seven maudlinly drunken officers, including Maryk, Keith, and Keefer, are singing and bellowing. Greenwald comes in unnoticed and silently watches the group at the table. Keefer is the first to see him, and with everyone egging him on, toasts Greenwald in doggerel, ending with: "And gave us all the Fifth Freedom—Freedom from Old Yellowstain!"

Greenwald won't make a speech: "No, no, no. I'm drunker'n any of you. I've been out drinking with the Judge Advocate—trying to get him to take back some of the dirty names he called me—finally got him to shake hands on the ninth whiskey sour—maybe the tenth—" Greenwald assumes that Keefer's war novel will give the Navy quite a pasting, and that the hero will be Keefer? Keefer demurs: "Well, any resemblance, you know, is purely accidental . . ."

Greenwald thinks that if he wrote a war novel he'd make Old Yellowstain his hero, on account of his mother, a little, fat, gray-haired Jewish lady. "Well, sure you guys all have mothers, but they wouldn't be in the same bad shape mine would if we'd of lost this war. See, the Germans aren't kidding about the Jews. They're cooking us down to soap over there. . . ." He comes back to Old Yellowstain. While little Willie was playing at Princeton, and he was studying law, Old Yellowstain was standing guard. When the Germans started to march, Greenwald couldn't have stopped them with his law book, so he went to learn how to fly. Keefer went to communication school, Willie Keith to midshipman school. And who protected his Mama at the time? "Old Yellowstain, maybe? Why, yes, even poor sad Queeg. And most of them not sad at all, fellows, a lot of them sharper boys than any of us, don't kid yourself; you can't be good in the Army or Navy unless you're goddam good. Though maybe not up on Proust, 'n' *Finnegans Wake*'n all." Maryk urges him to forget it and enjoy the dinner.

Greenwald declares: "Steve, this dinner's a phony. You're guilty. Course you're only half guilty. There's another guy who's stayed very neatly out of the picture. The guy who started the whole idea that Queeg was a dangerous paranoiac—who argued you into it for half a year—who invented the name Old Yellowstain—who kept feeding you those psychiatry books—who pointed out Article 184 and kept hammering it at you—" Here Keefer starts to protest, but Greenwald lets him have chapter and verse: "If you hadn't filled Steve Maryk's thick head full of paranoia and Article 184, why he'd have got Queeg to come north, or he'd have helped the poor bastard pull through to the south, and the *Caine* wouldn't have been yanked out of action in the hottest part of the war. That's your contribution to the good old U.S.S., my friend. Pulling a minesweeper out of the South Pacific when it was most needed. That, and *Multitudes, Multitudes.*" Keefer tries to shut him up; Greenwald says he's finished, he's come to the toast. It's to Keefer, who has kept his own skirts clean, who will make a million off his novel that proves the Navy stinks, so he won't mind, ". . . a li'l verbal reprimand from me, what does it mean? I defended Steve because I found out the wrong guy was on trial. Only way I could defend him was to murder Queeg for you. I'm sore that I was pushed into that spot, and ashamed of what I did, and thass why I'm drunk. Queeg deserved better at my hands. I owed him a favor, don't you see? He stopped Hermann Goering from washing his fat behind with my mother. So I'm not going to eat your dinner, Mister Keefer, or drink your wine, but simply make my toast and go. Here's to you, Mister, *Caine*'s favorite author, and here's to your book." Greenwald throws his wine in Keefer's face: "You can wipe for the rest of your life, Mister. You'll never wipe off that yellow stain."

Maryk calls out: "Barney . . ." Greenwald smiles wryly, brushes his hand across Maryk's head, says: "See you in Tokyo, you mutineer," and staggers out.

IN THE SUMMER HOUSE *

A Play in Two Acts

By Jane Bowles

[Jane Bowles *is the author of novels and short stories but "In the Summer House" is her first play. The first act of this play— developed from her story "Two Serious Ladies"—appeared eleven years ago in "Harper's." Mrs. Bowles is married to composer Paul Bowles who did the incidental music for his wife's play as he has for many another. "In the Summer House" had several tryouts before reaching New York and Mrs. Bowles revised it many times before it emerged in its present form.*]

GERTRUDE EASTMAN-CUEVAS' garden (somewhere on the coast of Southern California) is a mess. Nothing will grow in it except the vines that cover the round summer house. The garden has a low hedge separating it from a dirt lane. Beyond the lane is the beach and sea.

Overlooking the garden is a low balcony of Miss Eastman-Cuevas' house. The balcony provides a fine spot from which Gertrude can survey everything, whether the sea or (as now) what her daughter is doing.

Gertrude Eastman-Cuevas is a beautiful, middle-aged woman, with sharply defined features, good carriage, bright red hair, and a resonant voice. Her tacky dress fits the disorder of her garden. As she sits on the balcony she calls down in a clipped yet tense tone: "Are you in the summer house?" At first her daughter doesn't answer. Molly, an eighteen-year-old with a strangely somnolent and passive face, simply doesn't hear. When her mother repeats the question, Molly answers: "Yes, I am."

Gertrude—If I believed in acts of violence, I would burn the summer house down. You love to get in there and loll about hour after hour. You can't even see out because those vines hide the view.

* Copyright as an unpublished work 1948 by Jane Auer Bowles. Copyright 1954 by Jane Bowles. Reprinted by permission of Random House, Inc.

Why don't you find a good, flat rock overlooking the ocean and sit
on it? (MOLLY *fingers the vine.*) As long as you're so indifferent
to the beauties of nature, I should think you would interest yourself
in political affairs, or in music or painting or at least in the future.
But I've said this to you at least a thousand times before. You admit
you relax too much?

MOLLY—I guess I do.

Gertrude continues that she feels temperamentally unsuited to
taking in boarders although they are needed to make ends meet: "I
simply hate gossiping with strangers and I don't want to listen to
their business. I never have and I never will. It disgusts me. Even
my own flesh and blood saps my vitality—particularly you. You
seem to have developed such a slow and gloomy way of walking
lately . . . not at all becoming to a girl. Don't you think you could
correct your walk?" Molly murmurs that she is trying to correct it.
But now Gertrude is off an another subject. She is seriously considering marrying Mr. Solares to free herself of financial worry:
". . . and I'm sure I could gradually ease his sister, Mrs. Lopez, out
of the house because she certainly gets on my nerves. He's a man-
ageable man and Spanish men aren't around the house much, which
is a blessing. They're almost always out . . . not getting intoxi-
cated or having a wild time . . . just out . . . sitting around with
bunches of other men . . . Spanish men . . . Cubans, Mexicans
. . . I don't know. . . . They're all alike, drinking little cups of
coffee and jabbering away to each other for hours on end. That
was your father's life, anyway. I minded then. I minded terribly,
not so much because he left me alone, but he wasn't in his office for
more than a few hours a day . . . and he wasn't rich enough, not
like Mr. Solares. I lectured him in the beginning. I lectured him
on ambition, on making contacts, on developing his personality.
Often at night I was quite hoarse. I worked on him steadily, trying
to make him worry about sugar. I warned him he was letting his
his father's interests go to pot. Nothing helped. He refused to
worry about sugar; he refused to worry about anything." She knits
a moment in silence, then continues: "I lost interest in sugar . . . in
him. I lost interest in our life together. I wanted to give it all up
. . . start out fresh, but I couldn't. I was carrying you. I had no
choice. All my hopes were wrapped up in you then—all of them.
You were my reason for going on, my one and only hope . . . my
love."

Gertrude knits furiously for a moment, then abruptly gets up and goes to the balcony rail, trying to see into the summer house. Has Molly gone to sleep, or is she at her comics? Molly isn't asleep.

GERTRUDE—Sometimes I have the strangest feeling about you. It frightens me. . . . I feel that you are plotting something. Especially when you get inside the summer house. I think your black hair helps me to feel that way. Whenever I think of a woman going wild, I always picture her with black hair—never blond or red. I know that what I'm saying has no connection with a scientific truth. It's very personal. They say red-haired women go wild a lot but I never picture it that way. Do you?

Molly remarks: "I've never seen a wild woman."

Music starts, as Gertrude tells of another feeling that sometimes comes over her at night—a feeling of isolation, a loss of all personal identity. When this shadow passes over her, she puts her wrapper on: ". . . and I go down into the kitchen. I open the ice chest and take out some fizzy water. Then I sit at the table with the light switched on and by and by I feel all right again." As the music fades, Gertrude thinks matter-of-factly of Mr. Solares arriving with one of his hot picnic lunches, and her seventeen-year-old boarder who will be arriving pretty soon. The manners involved in allowing Mr. Solares to bring the lunch to her home, she admits, are dubious. But then his tribe is so large, and there are only two of them. And she may well marry him.

Gertrude finds Molly no conversationalist. She never expresses an opinion. "What on earth is your outlook?" Gertrude cries. Molly uncertainly offers: "Democracy . . ." This does not satisfy Gertrude. "I don't think you feel very strongly about it," she says. "You don't listen to the various commentators, nor do you ever glance at the newspapers. It's very easy to say that one is democratic, but that doesn't prevent one from being a slob if one is a slob. I've never permitted myself to become a slob, even though I sit at home all the time and avoid the outside world as much as possible." Her father avoided the outside world as much as possible too, and he is the model she sets herself. She admired him more than anyone on earth: "He admired me, of course. I was so much like him—ambitious, defiant, a fighting cock always. I worshiped him. But I was never meek, not like Ellen my sister. She was very frail and delicate. My father used to put his arms around her and play with her hair—long golden curls. . . . Ellen was the weak one. That's why he spoiled her. He pitied Ellen . . ." The music fades after she says: "He pitied Ellen, but he was proud of me. I was his true love. He never showed it. . . . He was frightened Ellen would guess. He didn't want her to be jealous, but I knew the truth. . . . He didn't have to show it. He didn't have to say anything. . . ." And back Gertrude comes again to matters at hand—getting Molly out of her summer house to clean up and change her dress. Molly obediently comes out of the summer house and sniffs the blossoms on the vine: "The honeysuckle's beginning to smell real good. I can never remember when you planted this vine, but it's sure getting thick. It makes the summer house so nice and shady inside." Gertrude stiffens with anger. The vine was there when they bought the house, as her daughter well knows. She considers it ". . . an underhanded Spanish trait of yours you inherit from your father. You love to mock me." Molly would clearly never do such a thing. But now Gertrude whips herself up into a rage over Molly's shortcomings: her fear of the water, so she'll never swim; her constant retreat to the summer house. Gertrude threatens to marry Mr. Solares and send Molly off to business school. She threatens no more than that, because from her vantage place on the balcony she sees Mr. Solares and his retinue moving up her lane, carrying the covered pots of the hot lunch she loathes.

She shoos Molly off to change her dress, pats her hair into place, then, feeling ready to receive, leans over the rail to hulloo to her guests. The Spanish people—they are actually Mexicans—Mr. Solares, Mrs. Lopez, his sister, and her daughter Frederica, file in, followed by three servants. The servants, two hags and a brilliantly dressed half-caste, carry the pots wrapped in bright bandannas; the gaiety of the bandannas contrasts with the dark clothes of Mr. Solares and Mrs. Lopez. Pushing Mrs. Lopez against the gate in his haste to greet Gertrude, Mr. Solares asks her to come down into the garden for their picnic. Gertrude is most perfunctory: "I think I'll stay here on the balcony, thank you. Just spread yourselves on the lawn and we'll talk back and forth this way. It's all the same." She tells the maids, "You can hand me up my food by stepping on that little stump and I'll lean over and get it."

Mrs. Lopez, all smiles and accent, asks "Miss Eastman-Cuevas" to come down, but Mr. Solares pokes her sharply and tells her in Spanish what's what. The next few minutes are full of music as the servants spread themselves and the bandannas and pots on the ground, raucously singing while they busy themselves. They dish out enormous plates of spaghetti, which Mr. Solares announces is: "Italian spaghetti with meat balls!" He directs Esperanza, the half-caste, to serve a big plate to Miss Eastman-Cuevas up on her porch, and indicates the stump she's to stand on. Esperanza disagreeably does only half the job: she hands the plate to Gertrude, but doesn't bother to wait till Gertrude gets a firm grip on it. The spaghetti swarms down all over Mrs. Lopez' hat and bosom, a sight that causes the servants to burst into hilarious laughter. It only gradually occurs to them to help clean up the mess, and to serve Gertrude over again.

As they settle down to eating the spaghetti, Mr. Solares inquires of Gertrude whether she likes chop suey. She has no idea. When Mr. Solares thinks it would be fine to try some at a restaurant, where a little dancing is thrown in, Gertrude coolly declines: "That's very nice of you but I've told you before that I don't care for the type of excitement you get when you go out. . . . You know what I mean —entertainment, dancing, etc. Why don't you describe chop suey to me and I'll try and imagine it?" Mrs. Lopez whoops with laughter for a reason apparent to no one. Gertrude doesn't care for this levity. She states her preference for her porch with its ocean view to any restaurant, only causing Mrs. Lopez to declaim her loathing for the ocean. This time, Gertrude perceptibly freezes, so Mr. Solares takes over, scowling all the while at Mrs. Lopez: "Oh, she loves the ocean. I don't know what the hell is the matter with her today." Gertrude winces at such language, but Mr. Solares goes on unaware: "Myself, I like ocean, land, mountain, all kinds of food, chop suey, chili, eel, turtle steak . . . Everything. Solares likes everything." And in a hideous French accent, announces: "Joie de vivre!" and snaps his fingers.

Gertrude, between forkfuls of spaghetti and with growing irritation, quizzes Mr. Solares on his attitude towards business. Mrs. Lopez bursts out: "He don't like no business . . ." and Mr. Solares' attitude towards her becomes furious. There is, however, no holding her back.

GERTRUDE—If Molly doesn't come out soon she will simply have to miss her lunch. It's very tiring to have to keep reminding her of the time and the other realities of life. Molly is a dreamer.

MRS. LOPEZ—That's right.

GERTRUDE (*watching* FREDERICA *serve herself*)—Do you people always eat such a big midday meal? Molly and I are in the habit of eating simple salads at noon.

MRS. LOPEZ (*wiping her mouth roughly with her napkin, then without pausing, and with gusto*)—For breakfast: chocolate and sugar bread; for lunch: soup, beans, eggs, rice, roast pork with potatoes and guava paste. . . . (*Pulls on a different finger for each separate item.*) Next day: soup, eggs, beans, rice, chicken with rice and guava paste—other day: soup, eggs, beans, rice, stew meat, roasted baby pig and guava paste. Other day: soup, rice, beans, grilled red snapper, roasted goat meat and guava paste.

FREDERICA (*speaking for the first time, rapidly, in a scarcely audible voice*)—Soup, rice, beans, eggs, ground-up meat and guava paste.

GERTRUDE (*wearily*)—We usually have a simple salad.

Mr. Solares puts an end to this by saying he doesn't like a big lunch either, but he is interested in marrying her: ". . . I've told you so before. You remember?" Mrs. Lopez, laughing and whispering to Frederica, plots to give Gertrude something that she's bound to have if she has a wedding. With that she pulls a bag of rice from her shopping bag and hurls it at Gertrude's head. The rice goes all over Gertrude, and everyone roars with laughter. Gertrude, thoroughly upset, stands up to brush the rice off herself, demanding that they stop this racket.

As she stands on the balcony she is puzzled by what she can see coming up her road. It looks like a king; it turns out to be a cardboard figure of Neptune, held on high by a young man. Neptune is followed by the figures of a channel swimmer and a mermaid. Lionel, the carrier of Neptune, dangles a toy lobster from a fishing line. The procession arrives to music, which dies down as Lionel explains that these figures are advertisements for the Lobster Bowl, and could he have a drink of water? Gertrude calls loudly to Molly to come out. She then addresses Lionel directly: "Excuse me but I think your figures are really awful. I don't like advertising schemes anyway." Lionel is sorry: "I have nothing to do with them. I just have to carry them around a few more days and after that I'll be working at the Bowl. I'm sorry you don't like them." Says Gertrude: "I've always hated everything larger than life."

Lionel and the other figure-bearers enter the garden, lending added congestion to the already crowded place. The Mexicans nearly swoon with delight over the figures, and Molly, coming out of the house, stops short in wonder. She approaches the figures slowly and touches Neptune: "It's beautiful." Lionel dangles the toy lobster in Molly's hand, and then presents her with one for herself. Mrs. Lopez shoves an unwilling Frederica forward, calling to Lionel: "Give my girl a little fish, please!" He reluctantly complies.

Gertrude, from her lookout, sees her boarder's car approaching. Casting a thoroughly disgusted look over her grounds, she orders Mr. Solares to have his people put things in order at once, and Lionel to remove his figures. All this is for Vivian, the boarder—a painfully thin girl of seventeen, wearing high heels and a bright dress. She comes from the lane, her eyes about to pop out of her head with excitement, peers for a moment at the house, and remarks: "The house is heavenly." And the garden is heavenly too. Gertrude disagrees: "The garden is a wreck at the moment." "Oh, no!" insists Vivian. "It's fascinating." Gertrude for her part maintains: "You can't possibly tell yet." Vivian is equally insistent that she can: "I decide everything the first minute. It's a fascinating garden." Mrs. Lopez would like to give Vivian some spaghetti, but she feels too excited to eat. Gertrude requests the still-munching Mr. Solares to show Vivian and the men carrying her bags into the house; she will meet them at the top of the stairs.

Mrs. Constable, Vivian's mother, trails into the garden. A frail, colorless woman, she is immaculately dressed in city clothes, even to a veil and gloves.

VIVIAN (*spying her mother, her expression immediately hardens*) —Why did you get out of the taxi? You promised at the hotel that you wouldn't get out if I allowed you to ride over with me. You promised me once in the room and then again on the porch. Now you've gotten out. You're dying to spoil the magic. Go back. . . . Don't stand there looking at the house. (MRS. CONSTABLE *puts her fingers to her lips, entreating silence, shakes her head at* VIVIAN *and later scurries off stage, nodding distractedly to the people on the lawn.*) She can't keep a promise.

GERTRUDE (*coming out onto the balcony again and spotting* MR. SOLARES, *still eating on the grass*)—What is the matter with you, Mr. Solares? I asked you to show Miss Constable and the chauffeur into the house and you haven't budged an inch. I've been waiting at the top of the stairs like an idiot. (MR. SOLARES *scrambles to his feet and goes into the house, followed by* VIVIAN *and the chauffeur. Enter* MRS. CONSTABLE *again.*)

MRS. CONSTABLE (*coming up to the hedge and leaning over. To* MRS. LOPEZ)—Forgive me, but I would like you to tell Mrs. Eastman-Cuevas that I am at the Herons Hotel. (MRS. LOPEZ *nods absently.* MRS. CONSTABLE *continues in a scarcely audible voice.*) You see, Mrs. Eastman-Cuevas comes from the same town that I come from and through mutual friends I heard that she took in boarders these days, so I wrote her that Vivian, my daughter, was coming.

MRS. LOPEZ—Thank you very much.

MRS. CONSTABLE—My daughter likes her freedom, so we have a little system worked out when we go on vacations. I stay some-

where nearby but not in the same place. Even so, I am the nervous
type and I would like Mrs. Eastman-Cuevas to know that I'm at the
Herons. . . . You see, my daughter is unusually high-spirited. She
feels everything so strongly that she's apt to tire herself out. I want
to be available just in case she collapses.

Mrs. Lopez knows about this; her Frederica tires easily too. Mrs.
Constable, afraid that her daughter may see her, effusively thanks
Mrs. Lopez, murmurs: "You'll notice right away what fun she gets
out of life," and vanishes.

Mrs. Lopez makes up her mind to leave too. Mr. Solares sullenly
obeys her orders, and in turn bawls at the servants to get ready.
While the servants go through the process of ineffectually cleaning
up, Vivian comes from the house, talking her head off to a comparatively attentive Gertrude.

VIVIAN (*to* GERTRUDE, *continuing a conversation*)—I'm going to
be sky-high by dinnertime. Then I won't sleep all night. I know
myself.

GERTRUDE—Don't you use controls?

VIVIAN—No, I never do. When I feel myself going up I just
go on up until I hit the ceiling. I'm like that. The world is ten
times more exciting for me than it is for others.

GERTRUDE—Still, I believe in using controls. It's a part of the
law of civilization. Otherwise we would be like wild beasts. (*Sighs.*)
We're bad enough as it is, controls and all.

VIVIAN (*hugging* GERTRUDE *impulsively*)—You've got the prettiest hair I've ever seen, and I'm going to love it here. (GERTRUDE
backs away a little embarrassed. VIVIAN *spots the summer house.*)
What a darling little house! It's like the home of a bird or a poet.
(*She approaches the summer house and enters it.*)

As the hags do their sloppy job of cleaning up, music begins, and
Vivian calls out from the summer house: "I can imagine all sorts of
things in here, Miss Eastman-Cuevas. I could make plans for hours
on end in here. It's so darling and little." Gertrude coldly replies:
"Molly usually sits in there. But I can't say that she plans much.
Just dozes or reads trash. Comic strips. It will do no harm if
someone else sits in there for a change." Vivian immediatey wants
to meet Molly.

Raising his Neptune, while the other boys hoist their figures, Lionel
says he doesn't want to bother Molly for the water: "I'll come back

if I may. I'd like to see you all again . . . and your daughter. She disappeared so quickly." Gertrude tells him to stay right where he is, and screams to Molly: "Come out here immediately! Molly!" Vivian, like a shrill echo, trills: "Molly! Come on out! . . . I'm in your little house . . . Molly!" Again Gertrude furiously calls: "Molly!!", but no one appears.

SCENE II

A month later, everyone is at the beach. The Solares tribe and servants sprawl about precisely as they did in the garden. This time, however, there is a beautiful backdrop of the sea, and sad and disturbing music.

Vivian—while a Spanish song is sung—lies adoringly at Gertrude's feet. Lionel and Molly are sitting a little apart from the group; Molly balefully watches Vivian make up to her mother. The Spanish song comes to an end. Vivian's attentions becoming too pronounced, Gertrude jumps up to put a halt to them. She abruptly urges the Solares entourage to take a stroll up the beach. The Mexicans groan, wanting to sleep off their meal, but they haven't a chance. In drill-master tones, Gertrude orders the girls to stay behind, although they seem to be the only ones who want to go. Then, marshaling the sleepy, draggy Mexicans, Gertrude leads the way.

Molly, sad that she is not allowed to be with her mother, returns to Lionel's side only to find Vivian in possession. She retires to a rock some distance away, and sits brooding.

Vivian babbles about the make-up of her life, "When I have a plan in my head I get so excited I can't sleep," interesting Lionel briefly. But Lionel, who is always pulled different ways, has nothing but conflicts: "For instance, one day I think I ought to give up the world and be a religious leader, and the next day I'll turn right around and think I ought to throw myself deep into politics." This leaves Vivian uninterested, and when he goes on to tell about his gloomy family, she is off again, deciding it would be better to swim. Lionel finds an audience in Molly; she half listens to him.

LIONEL (*goes over and sits next to her*)—Doesn't the ocean make you feel gloomy when the sky is gray or when it starts getting dark out?

MOLLY—I don't guess it does.

LIONEL—Well, in the daytime, if it's sunny out and the ocean's blue, it puts you in a lighter mood, doesn't it?

MOLLY—When it's blue . . .

LIONEL—Yes, when it's blue and dazzling. Don't you feel happier when it's like that?

MOLLY—I don't guess I emphasize that kind of thing.

LIONEL—I see. (*Thoughtfully.*) Well, how do you feel about the future? Are you afraid of the future in the back of your mind?

MOLLY—I don't guess I emphasize that much either.

LIONEL—Maybe you're one of the lucky ones who looks forward to the future. Have you got some kind of ambition?

MOLLY—Not so far. Have you?

Lionel tells her much of what he had told Vivian, about his dread of being a minister, and his yet feeling that he may have a message for people. He dreads being a political leader too: "That should cheer me up more, but it doesn't. You think I really like working at the Lobster Bowl?" Molly asks: "Don't you?"

LIONEL—Yes, I do, but of course that isn't life. I have fun too, in between worrying . . . fun, dancing, and eating, and swimming . . . and being with you. I like to be with you because you seem to only half hear me. I think I could say just the opposite and it wouldn't sound any different to you. Now why do I like that? Because it makes me feel very peaceful. Usually if I tell my feeling to a person I don't want to see them any more. That's another peculiar quirk of mine. Also there's something very familiar about you, even though I never met you before two months ago. I don't know what it is quite . . . your face . . . your voice . . . (*Taking her hand.*) or maybe just your hand. (*Holds her hand for a moment, deep in thought.*) I hope I'm not going to dread it all for too long. Because it doesn't feel right to me, just working at the Lobster Bowl. It's nice though really . . . Inez is always around if you want company. She can set up oyster cocktails faster than anyone on the coast. That's what she claims, anyway. She has some way of checking. You'd like Inez.

MOLLY—I don't like girls.

LIONEL—Inez is a grown-up woman. A kind of sturdy rock-of-Gibraltar type but very high-strung and nervous too. Every now and then she blows up.

Lionel, cheered by the Lobster Bowl decorations, liking it as a place to work, feels in his bones that he shouldn't remain there too long. He tries to change the subject when Molly wanders away from him. "Now I'm getting too deep in. I suppose you live mainly from day to day. That's the way girls live mainly, isn't it?" Molly isn't sure. Her difficulty is keeping from getting mad after she sees through people: "Most people can't, like I do. I'd emphasize that all right. The rest of the stuff doesn't bother me much. A lot of people want to yank you out and get in themselves. Girls do, anyway. I haven't got anything against men. They don't scheme the way girls do. . . ." She has solved this difficulty by keeping to herself as much as she can. Lionel has another solution—if her mother marries Mr. Solares, why doesn't Molly plan to marry him?

MOLLY—I won't think of it until it happens. I can't picture anything being any different than it is. I feel I might just plain die if everything changes, but I don't imagine it will.
LIONEL—You should look forward to change.
MOLLY—I don't want anything different.
LIONEL—Then you *are* afraid of the future just like me.

But Molly won't even think of the future.
Vivian, on the other hand, comes rushing back from her swim with wild, exotic ideas for the future. She has concocted an idea of starting an odd kind of restaurant, one inspired half by Turkey, half by the silent movies. Lionel is to be her partner and, as an afterthought, Molly is included: "She has to escape from her mother too."
Molly starts to shake so noticeably that Lionel goes off to get her a wrap. Vivian needs nothing to keep her warm; she is too excited about her restaurant plan. As the girls are left together, Molly starts climbing the rocks to get away from Vivian, warning her not to follow. Vivian, continually chattering, follows anyway.

MOLLY—The day you came I was standing on the porch watching you. I heard everything you said. You put your arm around my mother, and you told her she had beautiful hair, then you saw my summer house and you told her how much you loved it. You went and sat in it and you yelled, Come out, Molly. I'm in your little house. You've tried in every way since you came to push me out. She hates you.
VIVIAN—What?
MOLLY—My mother hates you! She hates you!
VIVIAN (*after recovering from her shock, starts out after her in a rage*)—That's a lie, a rotten lie. . . . She doesn't hate me. . . .

She's ashamed of *you* . . . ashamed of you. (*Exits, then repeating
several times off stage.*)   She's ashamed of you . . . ashamed of
you. . . .

As the girls disappear over the rocks, the procession returns. The
servants, in the lead, are singing and chattering, while Mr. Solares
and Frederica, carrying a tremendous, purple-spotted, pink rubber
horse, bring up the rear. Mrs. Lopez is delighted with the animal,
and is proud that it cost so much money. Gertrude considers it a
ridiculous thing to spend money on. Pinned down to what would
be a wiser purchase, she says clothing for one thing. Mr. Solares is
proud to announce that Mrs. Lopez has fifty-nine dresses, every one
of which he had bought for her.
Up the beach wanders Mrs. Constable. She is dressed to the teeth
in an immaculate summer outfit, large hat, and black glasses, together
with a fishing rod and creel. Mr. Solares is delighted when she
proposes to join them. "I think I might sit down for a few minutes
and wait for my bird to come back," Mrs. Constable tells them. "I
call Vivian my bird. Don't you think it suits her, Mrs. Eastman-
Cuevas?" Gertrude, already bored, says: "Yes."

Mrs. Constable—I miss her very badly already. It's partly
because she has so much life in her. She finds so many things of
interest to do and think about. (*Speaks with wonder in her voice.*)
I myself can't work up very much interest. I guess that's normal
at my age. I can't think of much to do really, not being either a
movie-goer or a card player or a walker. Don't you think that makes
me miss her more?

Gertrude listens to Mrs. Constable in icy boredom. When she has
finished her narrative of day-long nothingness, Gertrude asks: "Don't
you read?" Mrs. Constable is regretful: "I would love to read but
I have trouble with concentration."
Mr. Solares, full of Latin feelings for this new lady, seats himself
admiringly next to her. He inquires whether she likes turtle steak.
Her startled "Oh, yes" compels Gertrude to tell him: "Perhaps I
might try chop suey with you, after all. Did it originate in China
or is it actually an American dish?" Mr. Solares' mind is on Mrs.
Constable. But Mrs. Lopez raps out: "Now you want to go eat
chop suey because he's talkin' to the other lady. You be careful,
Señora Eastman-Cuevas, or you gonna lose him." This makes Gertrude so furious that she offers herself up to a chop suey date for
that very night. Mr. Solares is briefly deflected from his new in-

terest, but turns back to Mrs. Constable with the suggestion that they share a turtle steak. Before she can answer, Gertrude sees a shaken Molly standing alone on the rocks.

GERTRUDE—Molly, we met Lionel. He's bringing the coats. (*Sees* MOLLY'S *stricken face and questions her.*) Molly, what's happened? (MOLLY *doesn't answer.*) What is it, Molly? What's happened to you . . . Molly . . . what happened? What is it, Molly? (*Looking around for* VIVIAN.) Where's Vivian? (MOLLY *still does not answer.*) Molly . . . Where is she? Where's Vivian?

MOLLY (*in a quavering voice*)—She's gathering shells. . . . (MRS. CONSTABLE *rises and starts looking vaguely for* VIVIAN. *Then she sits down again.*)

GERTRUDE (*gathers her composure after a moment and speaks to* MR. SOLARES)—Mr. Solares, I'm going home. It's windy and cold. . . . The clouds are getting thicker every minute. . . . The sun's not coming out again. I'm going back to the house.

Meeting Lionel as she starts off, she repeats that Vivian is gathering shells. Everyone gets ready to leave. Molly comes face to face with Mrs. Constable; they look at each other for a moment before Molly rushes off after her mother. Mr. Solares asks Mrs. Constable to come with them, but she prefers to stay and wait for "her bird."

LIONEL—But she might climb up the cliffs and go home around the other way. It's getting colder, Mrs. Constable. . . . I could wait with you. . . .

MRS. CONSTABLE—I don't want to talk. No, I'll just sit here and wait a little while.

LIONEL (*going off*)—Don't worry, Mrs. Constable. She'll be all right.

MRS. CONSTABLE (*left alone on the stage*)—I get so frightened, I never know where's she's going to end up.

SCENE III

There has been a double wedding in the sunlit Cuevas garden. The Solares servants are lying in the shade of the festooned table: hot dogs and the remains of a wedding cake above, three pairs of feet protruding below. Molly has removed her wedding veil and stands by the table contentedly chewing a hot dog. Gertrude, in her own bridal outfit, is sitting bolt upright on a straight-backed chair in the middle of the garden. She has made only one concession to comfort: she has put bedroom slippers on her pinched feet. She also has to cope with Mrs. Constable weaving about in flowing, funereal black. The lady, champagne glass in hand, has but one idea: to be with Gertrude, Mr. Solares, Mrs. Lopez, and Molly forever. Mrs. Constable puts this idea across by wildly embracing Gertrude, who extricates herself, saying: "Now you must stop brooding. Can't you occupy yourself with something?"

MRS. CONSTABLE—I'm not brooding. I can think about it without feeling a thing, because if you must know it's just not real to me. I can't believe it. Now what does seem real is that you and Mr. Solares are going away and deserting me and Mrs. Lopez and Molly and Lionel too. And I don't want to be anywhere except in this garden with all of you. Isn't it funny? Not that I'm enjoying myself, but it's all that I want to do, just hang around in this garden. (*She goes over to the stand rather unsteadily and pours some champagne into her glass out of a bottle. She takes a few sips, then bitterly, in a changed tone.*) I want to stay right here, by this stand.

GERTRUDE (*looking over her shoulder at* MRS. CONSTABLE)— Drinking's not the answer to anything.

MRS. CONSTABLE—Answer? Who said anything about answers? I don't want any answers. It's too late for answers. Not that I ever asked much anyway. (*Angrily.*) I never cared for answers. You can take your answers and flush them down the toilet. I *want* to be able to stay here. Right here where I am, and never leave this garden. Why don't you have a drink, or one of these lousy hot dogs? (*Brushes a few hot dogs off the stand, onto the grass.* MOLLY *stoops down and picks them up.*) Let's stay here, Gertrude Eastman-Cuevas, please.

GERTRUDE—You're being silly, Mrs. Constable. I know you're upset, but I hope you realize that I've sold the house and that Molly and I are going on honeymoons.

MRS. CONSTABLE (*vaguely*)—What about Mrs. Lopez?

GERTRUDE—Well, now, I guess she has her own affairs to attend to, and Frederica. Mrs. Constable, I think a sanatorium would be the best solution for you until you are ready to face the world again.

MRS. CONSTABLE (*thickly*)—What world?

GERTRUDE—Come now, Mrs. Constable, you know what I mean.

MRS. CONSTABLE—I know you're trying to be a bitch!

GERTRUDE—Mrs. Constable . . . I . . . (*Turns to* MOLLY, *who has come to her side.*) Molly, go inside. At once . . . (MOLLY *runs into the house.*) Mrs. Constable, you ought to be ashamed. I won't tolerate such . . .

MRS. CONSTABLE—You have no understanding or feeling. Mrs. Lopez is much nicer than you are. You're very coarse. I know that, even if I do hate to read. You're coarse, coarse, and selfish. Two awful things to be. But I'm stuck here anyway, so what difference does it make?

Gertrude refuses to listen to any more of her ramblings; refuses to put up with this: "What would Vivian think?" According to Mrs. Constable, Vivian was an all-understanding bird, who was far too delicate to show her feelings as Gertrude and she would. This riles Gertrude even more. She lets it be known that never in her life has she shown her feelings. But anything she has to say is lost on Mrs. Constable, who waves champagne and offers hot dogs as Gertrude starts for the house.

MRS. CONSTABLE—We were kept far away from tragedy, weren't we?

GERTRUDE—No, Mrs. Constable. None of us have been kept from it.

MRS. CONSTABLE—Yes, well, now it's close to me, because Vivian hopped off a cliff—just like a cricket.

GERTRUDE—Life is tragic, Mrs. Constable.

MRS. CONSTABLE—I don't want tragic.

Gertrude advises her to lie down, and Mrs. Constable amiably complies, collapsing all in a heap just where she was standing.

Up pop the hags from under the table, and start grabbing hot dogs, only to be interrupted by Molly's going to her summer house. A moment later Gertrude calls out last-minute orders for Molly and Lionel when she and Mr. Solares shall have left. Molly refuses pointblank. She pleads with her mother not to go: "No, I wont let you go!" Gertrude is tired: "Please, Molly, no mysteries. It's very hard getting everyone started and I'm worn out. And I can't find my pocketbook. I think I left it in the garden. I'm coming down to look."

Molly comes out of the summer house and waits for her mother, a small bunch of honeysuckle in her hand. Gertrude sees her crying and goes to her: "What on earth is wrong, Molly? Why are you crying? Are you nervous? You've been so contented all day, stuffing yourself right along with the others. What has happened now?" Molly simply hadn't pictured what it would be like after the wedding. She had thought as long as they were here, they would always remain here. No one would leave: "So I just ate along with the others, like you say." Molly places her flowers in Gertrude's hand. Gertrude tries to push them back, saying they belong on her wedding dress. But Molly says they're from the vine and they're for her, and she loves her, and she mustn't leave her. Molly repeats this protestation of love, and Gertrude is startled and incapable of knowing what to do at this strange moment.

GERTRUDE (*shocked and white*)—Molly, stop. You can't go on like this!

MOLLY—I love you. You can't go!

GERTRUDE—I didn't think you cared this much. If you really feel this way, why have you tormented me so . . .

She lists all the things she feels Molly did to disturb her: the talk about the vine, the unnatural fear of the ocean . . . Molly, in a frenzy of despair, in an effort to prove her love, starts to claw at the buttons on her dress, and to pull open her dress so as to go into the water she hates. Gertrude tells her to button up, and instead of acknowledging all this as a gesture of love, decries it as a symptom of violence: ". . . I didn't want to be sure. But I was right, there's something heavy and dangerous inside you, like some terrible rock that's ready to explode. . . . And it's getting worse all the time. I can't bear it any more. I've got to get away out of this garden. That's why I married. That's why I'm going away. I'm frightened of staying here with you any more. I can't breathe. Even on bright days the garden seems like a dark place without any air. I'm stifling!" And she goes towards the front door.

As Gertrude passes under the balcony she becomes a perfect target for Mrs. Lopez, who happily dumps rice on her head and urges her daughter to do likewise. Mrs. Lopez then alerts everyone for the farewell procession. The servants crawl out of their hiding place, pulling themselves together. Mrs. Lopez calls for music, then comes out of the house with rice for "bride number two" in the summer house. She energetically hurls handfuls at the summer house; it catches in the vines. She closes in on the door for one good shot at Molly. As the band plays in a gay, naïve style, Mr. Solares and Lionel bring out the bags, and Mrs. Lopez goes into the summer house to mother the weeping bride.

For one quick moment, as Molly comes out and encounters Gertrude crossing the garden, they look at each other without speaking. Gertrude then continues on her way to the road, and Molly goes back

to the summer house. The wedding party files out to the music, and
Molly is left alone as the music fades away.

Lionel returns and draws Molly out of her house. He leads her
to the balcony to look at the sunset. But Molly, looking down into
the garden, can only say in a very small voice: "It looks different."

LIONEL (*after gazing off into the distance very thoughtfully for a
minute*)—I've always liked it when something that I've looked at
every day suddenly seems strange and unfamiliar. Maybe not always, but when I was home I used to like looking out my window
after certain storms that left a special kind of light in the sky.

MOLLY (*in a whisper*)—It looks different. . . .

LIONEL—A very brilliant light that illuminated only the most
distant places, the places nearest to the horizon. Then I could see
little round hills, and clumps of trees, and pastures that I didn't
remember ever seeing before, very, very close to the sky. It always
gave me a lift, as if everything might change around me but in a
wonderful way that I wouldn't have guessed was possible. Do you
understand what I mean?

MOLLY (*shakes her head negatively. He looks at her for a moment, a little sadly. Anguished, she turns away from him*)—I don't
know. I don't know. It looks so different. . . .

ACT II

Molly and Lionel have been living at the Lobster Bowl next to the
sea for the past ten months. As they sit playing cards into the dawn,
the breaking of the waves can be heard through the open, oyster-
shell door.

The card players sit in a pool of light, while the rest of the room,
including the bench where Mrs. Constable lies, is in complete darkness.

As usual Lionel and Molly have been talking, and talking at cross
purposes. Lionel has been telling Molly of his brother in St. Louis
who wants them to live with him, and has been urging this on her
as a wise thing to do. Molly thinks of her mother, and her mother's
cure for dark thoughts—she would go downstairs and drink fizzy
water: ". . . Once I went down when I was twelve years old. I
waited until she was asleep and I sneaked down into the kitchen very
quietly. Then I switched the light on and I opened the ice chest
and I took out a bottle of fizzy water just like she did. Then I went
over to the table and I sat down." Lionel messes up the cards; he's
disappointed and defeated: "I was trying to tell you something. It

meant a lot to me. . . . I wanted you to listen." Molly doesn't understand: "I was listening."

LIONEL—You told me about fizzy water . . . and your mother. (MOLLY automatically passes her hand over her own cards and messes them up.) I wanted you to listen. I don't want you to half hear me any more. I used to like it but . . .

MOLLY (*pathetic, bewildered*)—I listen to you. We had a nice time yesterday . . . when . . . when we were digging for clams.

LIONEL (*looking back at her, unable to be angry, now with compassion*)—Yes, Molly, we did. We had a very good time . . . yesterday. I like digging clams. . . . (*They hold, looking at each other for a moment.*) I'm going upstairs. I'm tired. I'm going to bed.

He goes up to their little room, leaving Molly alone, unhappy that he wouldn't play cards with her.

Mrs. Constable, though she was supposed to have been asleep, has heard everything. She now emerges from the darkness: "I was waiting because I wanted to tell you something . . . a secret. . . . I always tell you my secrets. . . . But there's one I haven't told you. . . . I've known it all along . . . but I've never said anything to you . . . never before. . . . But now I'm going to . . . I must.

MOLLY (*wide-eyed, thinking she is referring to* VIVIAN)—It wasn't my fault! I didn't mean to . . .

MRS. CONSTABLE—My husband never loved me . . . Vivian?

MOLLY—Vivian! It wasn't my fault. . . . I didn't . . . She . . . I didn't . . . (*Starts to sob.*)

MRS. CONSTABLE (*clapping her hand over* MOLLY'S *mouth*)— Shhhhh . . . They belonged to each other, my husband and Vivian. They never belonged to me . . . ever. . . . But I couldn't admit it. I hung on hard to the bitter end. When they died . . . nothing was left . . . no memories . . . Everything vanished . . . all the panic . . . and the strain. . . . I hardly remember my life. They never loved me. . . . I didn't really love them. . . . My heart had fake roots . . . when the strain was over, they dried up . . . they shriveled and snapped, and my heart was left empty. There was no blood left in my heart at all. . . . They never loved me! Molly . . . your mother . . . It's not too late. . . . She doesn't . . .

Molly interrupts before she has to hear the awful thing Mrs. Constable might say, and tells her she has had a letter from her mother, who hates Mexico. But Mrs. Constable persists: "Molly, if you went away from here, I'd miss you very much. If you went away there wouldn't be anyone here I loved. . . . Molly, go away . . . go away with Lionel. . . . Don't stay here in the Lobster Bowl." Molly can only think of her mother, and reads from the letter. The climate, and the large, noisy Solares family don't suit her mother at all: "Things are getting more and more unbearable. . . ." Gertrude hopes Molly is occupying herself in a sensible fashion and not dreaming. Mrs. Constable interrupts: "Why shouldn't you dream?" Molly answers that she probably wasted too much time daydreaming, and: "Because she wanted me to grow up to be wonderful and strong like she is. Will she come back soon, Mrs. Constable? Will she make them all leave there? Will she?" she asks longingly. "I don't know, dear," Mrs. Constable comforts her. "I don't know. . . . I suppose she will. . . . If she needs you, she'll come back. If she needs you, I'm sure she will." And Mrs. Constable gets up, planning to walk home over the wet beach: "I love the waves breaking in this early light. . . . I run after them. I run after the waves. . . . I scoop up the foam and I rub it on my face. All along the way I think it's beginning . . ."

MOLLY—What?
MRS. CONSTABLE—My life. I think it's beginning, and then . . .
MOLLY—And then?
MRS. CONSTABLE—I see the hotel. (MRS. CONSTABLE *exits through the oyster-shell door.*)
MOLLY (*reads again part of her mother's letter*)—"Two days ago, Fula Lopez went into the city and came back with a hideous white dog. She bought it in the street. The dog's bark is high and sharp. It hasn't stopped yapping since it came. I haven't slept at all for two nights. Now I'm beginning a cold. . . ."

SCENE II

Another two months have gone by at the Lobster Bowl.

Big, full-bosomed Inez is cleaning up noisily behind the bar while talking across the room to Molly, tucked away in a booth. Inez berates her for reading comics all day long. Molly isn't. She's reading and re-reading the letter she received a week ago from her mother: "She's coming back today. She's coming back from Mexico." Inez hopes she'll pep things up a little.

INEZ—I hear she's got more personality than you. (*Shifts some oysters.*) You didn't model yourself after her, did you?

MOLLY—No.

INEZ—Ever try modeling yourself after anyone?

MOLLY—No.

INEZ—Well, if you don't feel like you've got much personality yourself, it's an easy way to do. You just pick the right model and you watch how they act. I never modeled myself after anyone, but there were two or three who modeled after me. And they weren't even relatives—just ordinary girls. It's an easy way to do. (*Shifts some oysters.*) Anyway, I don't see poring over comic books. I'd rather have someone tell me a good joke any day. What's really nice is to go out—eight or nine—to an Italian dinner, and sit around afterwards listening to the different jokes. You get a better selection that way! Ever try that?

MOLLY—I don't like big bunches of people.

INEZ—You could at least live in a regular home if you don't like crowds, and do cooking for your husband. You don't even have a hot plate in your room! (*Crash of stool to floor, followed by some high giggles.*) There goes Mrs. Constable again. You'd think she'd drink home, at her hotel, where no one could see her. She's got a whole suite to herself there. It's been over a year since her daughter's accident, so I could say her drinking permit had expired. I think she's just on a plain drunk now. Right? (MOLLY *nods*.)

Inez fears that Mrs. Constable is headed that way, and her conversation will once more be on death. Mrs. Constable arrives, and it is very obvious that she has been drinking.

INEZ—I'm kind of rushing, Mrs. Constable. I've got to have three hundred oyster cocktails ready by tonight and I haven't even prepared the hot sauce yet.

MRS. CONSTABLE—Rushing? I didn't know that people still rushed. . . .

INEZ—Here we go, boys!

MRS. CONSTABLE—Then you must be one of the fortunate ones who has not yet stood on the edge of the black pit. There is no rushing after that, only waiting. It seems hardly worth while even keeping oneself clean after one has stood on the edge of the black pit.

INEZ—If you're clean by nature, you're clean.

MRS. CONSTABLE—Oh, really? How very interesting!

And the lines are drawn, in spite of Inez' determination to ignore Mrs. Constable's drunken taunts and hoity-toityness, and get on with her oysters. She can't, though. Mrs. Constable takes her glass of liquor and airily pours some on the floor. Inez blows up. With three hundred cocktails, and three hundred hookers of hot sauce, she hasn't time to talk, and certainly hasn't time to mop up after Mrs. Constable. Mrs. Constable is full of condescending comments, and exits, accusing Inez of being plain bossy. Inez has had more than she can take. She decides to go upstairs to get herself in hand: ". . . I guess I'll give myself a fresh apron while I'm up there. Then I'll be ready when they come for their oysters." Vaguely touching her head, she says, "I don't like to eat oysters any more. I suppose I've seen too much of them, like everything else in life." She pulls the chain to the big light over the bar, leaving the room in darkness.

Molly's booth, covered with artificial leaves and flowers, is lit up by a small light. The summer-house music plays as she daydreams over her mother's letter.

Lionel, his mind made up because of a wire from his brother, comes in to speak to Molly.

LIONEL—To me this place is a fake. I chose it for protection, and it doesn't work out.

MOLLY—It doesn't work out?

LIONEL—Molly, you know that. I've been saying it to you in a thousand different ways. You know it's not easy for me to leave. Places that don't work out are ten times tougher to leave than any other places in the world.

Mrs. Constable breaks in and talks with Molly, but Lionel tries doubly hard to have Molly think about what he is saying, but she won't, so he leaves.

Mrs. Constable tries to have Molly leave with Lionel, but she will only think of dressing for her mother's birthday party, and goes upstairs. Says Mrs. Constable as she stumbles to the bar: "You're hanging on just like me. If she brought you her love you wouldn't know her. You wouldn't know who she was." And she sinks out of sight in a chair behind the bar.

Gertrude Eastman-Cuevas arrives. She appears somewhat distraught, and becomes progressively more so when Mrs. Constable avoids saying where Molly is, and Lionel announces he didn't even know that Gertrude had written to Molly. Lionel further upsets her by saying he's quitting his job and getting out of here. He leaves before Gertrude can find out what he's planning to do.

Mrs. Constable drags a decidedly unwilling woman to a table, and instead of letting her hear about Molly, peppers her with questions about Mexico. She doesn't make Gertrude feel any better by inspecting her and pronouncing her sickish-looking. Gertrude can only say: "I'm not sick. . . . I'm just tired, exhausted; that's all. They've worn me out in a thousand different ways. Even today . . . I wanted to see Molly the second we arrived, but I had to wait. I tried to rest. I had a bad dream. It's hanging over me still. But I'll be all right in a little bit. I'll be fine as soon as I see Molly. I'm just tired, that's all." Mexico was one continual racket. Mrs. Lopez, whom Mrs. Constable admires extravagantly, was much to blame for the larger share of the confusion. Mrs. Constable ingenuously keeps her on what happened in Mexico, and won't tell Gertrude anything she wants to know. In fact, she tells her only disturbing news: "Lionel is sick of the Lobster Bowl. I'm not. Molly likes it too, more than Lionel." Gertrude refuses to believe Molly could like a place like this after their life in the ocean house. Mrs. Constable tries to worry Gertrude some more: "They take long walks down the beach or go digging for clams. They're very polite. They invite me along. But I never accept. I know," she says pointedly, "they'd rather go off together all by themselves." "All by themselves!" Gertrude cries in alarm, and as she gets out of her seat and paces up and down, Mrs. Constable suggests that she go back to Mexico. If she doesn't want to do that, she should settle for a drink. Gertrude doesn't drink, and she feels like crying. Everything is upsetting, and the bad dream she had earlier hangs on.

GERTRUDE (*picking up one of the two boxes she brought with her and brooding over it*)—It was a senseless dream, a nightmare.
MRS. CONSTABLE—What's in the box?
GERTRUDE—Little macaroons. I bought them for Molly on the way up. I thought she'd like them. Some of them are orange and some are bright pink. (*Shakes the box and broods again, troubled, haunted by the dream.*) They were so pretty. . . .
MRS. CONSTABLE—Aren't they pretty any more?
GERTRUDE—I had a dream about them just now, before I came. I was running very fast through the night trying to get to Molly, but I couldn't find the way. I kept losing all her presents. Everything I'd bought her I kept scattering on the ground. Then I was in a cold room with my father and she was there too. I asked him for a gift. I said, "I want something to give to my child," and he handed me this box. . . . (*Fingering the actual box.*) I opened it up, and took out a macaroon and I gave it to Molly. (*Long pause—she looks haunted, deeply troubled.*) When she began to eat it, I saw that it was hollow—just a shell filled with dust. Molly's lips were gray with dust. Then I heard him . . . I heard my father.

(*Excited.*) He was laughing. He was laughing at *me!* (*She goes away from* MRS. CONSTABLE *to collect herself.*) I've loved him so. I don't know what's happening to me. I've never been this way. I've always thrown things off, but now even foolish dreams hang over me. I can't shake anything off. I'm not myself . . . I . . . (*Stiffening against the weakness.*) When I was in the ocean house . . . (*Covering her face with her hands and shaking her head—very softly, almost to herself.*) Oh, I miss it so . . . I miss it so.

Now that Gertrude hasn't her ocean house, she remembers a beautiful life there; now that she hasn't Molly, she recalls what a full life she had with her daughter. She is miserable, her life has no meaning. She means to take Molly, whom she'd lost, back with her tonight.

When Lionel comes into the bar, Gertrude turns on him, demanding what he meant earlier about leaving, then taunts him with having no backbone, with running home to his family. Lionel is unafraid.

LIONEL—I've got to get Molly out of here, far away from everything she's ever known. It's her only chance.

GERTRUDE—You're taking her away from *me.* That's what you're doing.

LIONEL—You're like a wall around Molly, some kind of a shadow between us. She lives . . .

GERTRUDE (*interrupting, vehement*)—I'm not a shadow any more. I've come back and I'm staying here, where I belong, with Molly! (LIONEL *looks at her with an expression of bitterness and revulsion.*) What is it? Why do you look at me that way?

LIONEL—What way?

GERTRUDE—As if I was some terrible witch. . . . That's it, some terrible witch!

LIONEL—You're using her. You need Molly. You don't love her. You're using her. . . .

Lionel calls to Molly her mother is here. And Molly, wearing her wedding dress in her mother's honor, comes slowly down the stairs. Almost as if she were under a spell, she says: "I knew you'd come back." They sit together at a table, while Gertrude starts to woo her away from Lionel. He hears the tone she is using, and firmly announces he has made his arrangements for the trip to St. Louis tomorrow; in a few minutes Molly will have to make up her mind what she will do. He leaves the two together. Molly, with her dreams of the past, finds Gertrude in her new pleading, promising role a stranger. Gertrude has another house for them, with a surprise for Molly, of a new summer house. Molly looks at her so oddly that Gertrude becomes apologetic about her appearance, saying she's been sick. But to Molly she simply appears different. Gertrude blames it all on the Mexicans and their way of life. And with that Mrs. Lopez and Frederica come in loaded with paper bags. There is much excitement as Inez calls out: "Something tells me I hear Fula Lopez, the girl I love . . ." Mrs. Lopez includes Molly in the hugging and kissing that follows. Gertrude, worried about Molly's new remoteness, becomes almost enraged over the chicken Mrs. Lopez has bought for the dinner. As Mrs. Lopez dangles it in front of her, Gertrude inquires: "The chicken. Why is he here?" Mrs. Lopez explains: "The chicken? He go home. We put him now with his rice and peas." In a fury, Gertrude asks: "But *what* rice and peas? You know what we're having . . . I ordered it myself. . . . It was going to be a light meal . . . something *I* liked . . . for once . . . we're having jellied consommé and little African lobster tails." Ever so pleasantly, Mrs. Lopez agrees: "That's right, jelly and Africa and this one too." Mrs. Constable, now wandering in, gives her opinion: "A chicken. I hate chickens. I'd rather have a dog." With which Frederica pulls out a toy horn and tootles on it. Gertrude orders them to stop the racket and start for home.

When Molly and she are finally alone, Gertrude uses all her powers of persuasion on Molly. She literally imprisons Molly at her side as Lionel comes downstairs and informs him that Molly will be leaving with her. Lionel, seeing his wife stand there silent and overpowered by her mother, accepts this pattern as hopeless: "Good-by, Molly. Have a nice time at the birthday supper. . . ." And he adds bitterly, before leaving through the oyster-shell door: "You look very pretty in that dress."

Molly doesn't want to go with her mother; she wants to go out; she suddenly tries rather hard to get by her mother, who now blocks her path.

GERTRUDE (*blocking the way*)—I'll make it all up to you. I'll give you everything you wanted, everything you've dreamed about.

MOLLY—You told me not to dream. You're all changed. . . . You're not like you used to be.

GERTRUDE—I will be, darling. You'll see . . . when we're together. It's going to be the same, just the way it was. Tomorrow

we'll go back and look at the vines, thicker and more beautiful . . .
MOLLY—I'm going . . . Lionel!

Gertrude turns into a fiend, first full of accusations against Lionel,
then, when Molly still calls desperately for him, she turns on her.

GERTRUDE—I know what you did. . . . I didn't want to . . . I
was frightened, but I knew. . . . You hated Vivian. I'm the only
one in the world who knows you. (MOLLY, *aghast, ceases to strug-
gle. They hold for a moment before* GERTRUDE *releases her grip on*
MOLLY. *Confident now that she has broken her daughter's will forever.*) Molly, we're going. . . . We're going home."

But Molly backs away from her in horror and refuses to go, re-
treating as her mother advances on her. Gertrude, grabbing at
Molly, shakes her and calls wildly for Mrs. Constable so she can tell
her about Vivian's death. But Mrs. Constable breathes quiet defiance and insists: "Nothing happened . . . Nothing!" Gertrude
hangs onto Molly, who is straining to go: "It *had* to happen. I
know Molly. . . . I know her jealousy. . . . I was her whole world,
the only one she loved. . . . She wanted me all to herself. . . . I
know that kind of jealousy and what it can do to you. . . . I know
what it feels like to wish someone dead. When I was a little girl . . .
I . . ." She stops dead as if a knife had been thrust in her heart
now. The hand holding Molly's in its hard, iron grip slowly relaxes.
There is a long pause. Then she murmurs, under her breath,
"Go. . . ." Molly slips through the oyster-shell door and disappears. Mrs. Constable, listening to the Mexican band, compassion-
ately urges Gertrude to go away, then leaves herself.

Gertrude stands motionless and white, oblivious of Frederica's
hulloo that they're all waiting for her. Frederica falters at the sight
of Gertrude's white face: "Qué pasa? Qué tiene? Miss Eastman-
Cuevas, you don't feel happy?" She unpins a simple bouquet of
red flowers and puts it into Gertrude's hand. "For your birthday,
Miss Eastman-Cuevas . . . your birthday . . ." Not knowing what
to do next, the girl backs away into the shadows. And Gertrude,
the bouquet stuck in her hand, whispers: "When I was a little
girl . . ."

THE CONFIDENTIAL CLERK *

A Comedy in Three Acts

By T. S. Eliot

[T. S. Eliot *is regarded by many as the greatest living English poet and critic. In 1948 he won the Nobel Prize for Literature. Besides being a writer, he is a partner in the publishing firm of Faber & Faber, Ltd., London. His other verse dramas are "Family Reunion," "Murder in the Cathedral," and "The Cocktail Party." He was born in St. Louis, Mo., of New England stock. He got his A.B. from Harvard in three years and his M.A. in his fourth. In 1914 he won a traveling fellowship and went to Germany and England. When World War I came he remained in England, became a British subject, and went on to write "The Waste Land," "The Hollow Men," "Sweeney Agonistes," "Four Quartettes," and much other poetry; to edit "The Criterion" and write many critical essays.*]

IN the Business Room of his London house—a kind of library— Sir Claude Mulhammer is giving instructions to his retiring confidential clerk. He has had the clerk, Mr. Eggerson, come all the way to London, from his home in Joshua Park, so as to meet Lady Elizabeth Mulhammer's plane. Eggerson is to acquaint her with the facts about the new confidential clerk, Colby Simpkins.

Sir Claude
Well, of course, Eggerson, you're irreplaceable . . .

Eggerson
Oh, Sir Claude, you shouldn't say that!
Mr. Simpkins is far better qualified than I was
To be your confidential clerk.
He was finding his feet, very quickly,

During the time we worked together.
All he needs is confidence.

"And experience," Sir Claude adds.   Simpkins seems to be taking
a keen interest in business affairs.

EGGERSON
And getting over his disappointment?
Of course, I never mentioned that:
It's only what you told me.

SIR CLAUDE
About his music.
Yes, I think so.   I understand his feelings.
He's like me, Eggerson.   The same disappointment
In a different form.   He won't forget
That his great ambition was to be an organist,
Just as I can't forget . . . no matter. . . .

So far Simpkins has been left to his own devices.   His quarters in
the mews are almost ready for furnishing.   Sir Claude says: "I'm
trying to find him a really good piano."   Eggerson suggests window
boxes, too: Simpkins had shown such an interest in Eggerson's
garden.   Now as to what is to be said to Lady Elizabeth: she knows,
says Sir Claude, that Eggerson wished to retire, but because of her
high regard for him, the choice of successor is doubly difficult.   "She
thinks she ought to have a hand in the choosing; and besides, she
is convinced that she, of all people, is a better judge of character
than I am."

EGGERSON
Oh, I wouldn't say that, Sir Claude!
She has too much respect for your business genius.
But it's true she believes she has what she calls "guidance."

SIR CLAUDE
Guidance.   That's worse than believing in her judgment:
We could argue about that.   You can't argue about guidance. . . .

The excuses Eggerson should have ready are doctor's orders for his
retirement, high recommendations for Simpkins, and a rival offer to
the young man so that they had to snatch him up.   "And," adds
Sir Claude, "I rather hope that she will take to him at once: if so,

she is certain to come to believe that she chose him herself.   By
the way, don't forget to let her know that he's very musical.   She
can take him to concerts.   But don't overdo it!"

Also: has Eggerson prepared Simpkins for Lady Elizabeth?   He
could prepare him better than Sir Claude, being more at ease with
him.   Eggerson confesses he hasn't told Simpkins much, except about
Lady Elizabeth's interest in "Light from the East" and a word or so
about her other interests . . . the Book of Revelation and the Wisdom of Atlantis.   But, Eggerson wonders, how will Sir Claude explain Simpkins to Lady Elizabeth?   Sir Claude says: "When—or
indeed whether—I reveal his identity depends on how she takes to
him.   This afternoon she will only learn that you have finally retired
and that you have a young successor, a Mr. Colby Simpkins. . . .
The reason for meeting him as merely Mr. Simpkins," Sir Claude
explains, "is, that she has a strong maternal instinct . . ."

EGGERSON
I realize that.

SIR CLAUDE
Which has always been thwarted.

EGGERSON
I'm sure it's been a grief to both of you
That you've never had children.

SIR CLAUDE
                         No worse, Eggerson,
Than for you and your wife, to have had a son
Lost in action, and his grave unknown.

EGGERSON
And you're thinking no doubt that Lady Elizabeth
Would be put in mind of the child *she* lost.

SIR CLAUDE
In a very different way, yes.   You might say, *mislaid,*
Since the father is dead, and there's no way of tracing it. . . .

Sir Claude has hopes that if she comes to like Simpkins, Lady
Elizabeth may wish to adopt him.   Eggerson's support of the plan
would be helpful: Lady Elizabeth thinks the world of his opinion.
Except, as Eggerson points out, in matters to do with Miss Angel:

"She becomes abstracted, whenever I mention her." "But she knew about Lucasta—Miss Angel, from the start," explains Sir Claude. "That was one difficulty. And there are others. For one, they're both of them women." "True," agrees Eggerson. And Miss Angel will soon be getting married, which, Eggerson agrees further, is a most suitable arrangement. But should Lady Elizabeth consider adopting Simpkins—Eggerson would like to know—will Sir Claude let her know he is actually Sir Claude's son? Sir Claude admits: "That's where I'm in the dark. I simply can't guess what her reaction would be."

Colby Simpkins, clerk's brief case in hand, arrives in the Business Room. Sir Claude leaves until the time he will come back to greet Lady Elizabeth. Colby Simpkins is somewhat nervous at the prospect of meeting her. The little he knows of her, Colby tells Eggerson, he has heard from B. Kaghan, and that little was rather alarming. Eggerson is quick to reassure him: B. Kaghan, being a rough diamond, didn't get on too well with Lady Elizabeth. She never cared for him. But it will be different with Mr. Simpkins.

COLBY

I don't know why it should be so different.
I like B. Kaghan. I found him very helpful
And very good company apart from business.

EGGERSON

Oh yes, Mr. Kaghan is very good company.
He makes me laugh sometimes. I don't laugh easily.
Quite a humorist, he is. In fact, Mrs. E.
Sometimes says to me: "Eggerson, why can't you make me laugh
The way B. Kaghan did? She's only met him once;
But do you know, he began addressing her as Muriel—
Within the first ten minutes! I was horrified.
But she actually liked it. Muriel *is* her name.
He has a way with the ladies, you know.
But with Lady Elizabeth he wasn't so successful.
She once referred to him as "undistinguished";
But with you, as I said, it will be very different.
She'll see at once that you're a man of culture;
And besides, she's very musical.

B. Kaghan, after a loud knock, brings in Lucasta Angel. She is out of a job again, and wants money of Eggerson. He, however, is

no longer clerk, nor is Colby Simpkins taking over that part of his
job that keeps Lucasta in funds. All Lucasta can do is bubble and
prattle over Colby Simpkins, whom she would be pleased to dine
with in public in the near future, since he is unmarried, and she is
to be one of his duties.

Lucasta asks Eggerson: "You're going to meet Lizzie?" He is.
"Well, I don't propose to be on the scene when *she* comes."

KAGHAN
And I don't propose to leave you with Colby.
He's had enough for one day. Take my advice, Colby.
Never allow Lucasta the slightest advantage
Or she'll exploit it. You have to be tough with her;
She's hard as nails. Now I'll take her off your hands.
I'll show you how it's done. Come along, Lucasta,
I'm going to make a day of it, and take you out to tea.

LUCASTA
I'm dying for my tea. The strain of this crisis
Has been too much for me. Another time, Colby.
I'll ring you up, and let you take me out to lunch.
                    (*Exit* LUCASTA.)

KAGHAN
Take it easy, Colby. You'll get used to her.

After they leave, a gasping Colby wonders about Lucasta's sanity.
"But you never warned me about Miss Angel. What about *her?*"
Peaceful Eggerson ticks her off as "flighty" but "of good heart."
Colby is astonished at Lucasta's use of first names. Eggerson assures
him he'll soon get used to it. Colby admits her influence is fright-
ening. . . . "But tell me about Lu . . . Miss Angel: What's her
connection with this household?"

EGGERSON
Well. A kind of fiduciary relationship.
No, I don't think that's quite the right term.
She's no money of her own, as you may have gathered;
But I think her father was a friend of Sir Claude's,
And he's made himself responsible for her. . . .

Colby is not to worry, for she'll marry Mr. Kaghan in the end.
She won't be a nuisance unless encouraged. Eggerson has never

encouraged her. "But you," Colby tells him, "have Mrs. Eggerson."
"Yes," replies Eggerson, "She's a great protection. And I have my
garden to protect me against Mrs. E. That's my joke."

Colby feels sure that Lady Elizabeth can't be so unusual. "Oh
yes, Mr. Simpkins," Eggerson tells him, "much more unusual."

COLBY

Oh!

EGGERSON
Well, as I told you, she really is a lady,
Rather a *grande dame,* as the French say.
That's what Sir Claude admires about her.
He said to me once, in a moment of confidence—
He'd just come back from a public luncheon—
"Eggerson," he said, "I wanted a lady,
And I'm perfectly satisfied with the bargain. . . ."

Eggerson finds her unusual for more than being a real lady. One
trait in particular stands out: she is very absent-minded. Colby
worriedly asks: "I hope you don't mean, she has lapses of memory?"
Eggerson didn't mean that, for she hasn't much memory to lose,
though more at times than you'd expect. . . . "But she does forget
things. . . ." And since she travels, mainly for her health, Eggerson has been granted "some rare adventures! . . . It's been a very
unusual privilege to see as much of Europe as I have, getting Lady
Elizabeth out of her difficulties." And it is entirely possible, as
Colby suggests, that she won't arrive by this plane. But just as
Eggerson is setting off for the airport, Lady Elizabeth's voice is
heard downstairs.

Sir Claude hears her, too, and can't imagine what happened to her,
or how they can impress her properly when she enters. Colby is
ordered to sit at the desk and look businesslike.

EGGERSON & SIR CLAUDE
(*Simultaneously.*)
Lady Elizabeth!
Elizabeth!

SIR CLAUDE
What on earth has happened?

EGGERSON

Lady Elizabeth! This is most surprising.

LADY ELIZABETH

What's surprising, Eggerson? I've arrived, that's all.

EGGERSON

I was just starting for Northolt to meet you.

LADY ELIZABETH

That was very thoughtful of you, Eggerson,
But quite unnecessary. And besides,
I didn't come by air. I arrived at Victoria.

SIR CLAUDE

Do you mean to say that you changed your ticket?

EGGERSON

Yes, how did you manage to change your ticket?

LADY ELIZABETH

I went to the agency and got them to change it.
I can't understand why you're both so surprised.
You know I'm a very experienced traveler.

She wished to come with a friend who had taken the treatment with
her, so she took the night train and the Channel crossing. "But who
is this young man? His face is familiar." Sir Claude tells her:
"This young man is Eggerson's successor. You know that Eggerson's been meaning to retire . . ." And before Lady Elizabeth can
say anything the two men air all their rehearsed reasons. Eggerson
gets to: "And Mr. Simpkins is much more highly qualified than I
am, to be a confidential clerk. Besides, he's very musical."

LADY ELIZABETH

Musical?
Isn't this the young man I interviewed
And recommended to Sir Claude? Of course it is.
I remember saying: "He has a good aura."
I remember people's auras, almost better than their faces.
What did you say his name was?

SIR CLAUDE
Colby Simpkins.

LADY ELIZABETH
(*Counting on her fingers.*)
Thirteen letters. That's very auspicious—
Contrary to what most people think.
You should be artistic. But you look rather frail.
I must give you lessons in the art of health.
Where is your home, Mr. Colby?

COLBY
Simpkins.

EGGERSON
Mr. Colby Simpkins.

LADY ELIZABETH
I prefer Colby.
Where are you living?

Sir Claude tells her that he's having the mews done over for Colby,
because he lives so far away. In all the wrong colors, Lady Elizabeth feels sure. Men don't understand the importance of color for
the spiritual life. "What color have you chosen, between you?" "I
thought primrose yellow would be cheerful," Sir Claude tells her.

LADY ELIZABETH
Just what I expected. A primrose yellow
Would be absolutely baneful to Mr. Colby.
He needs a light mauve. I shall see about that.
But not today. I shall go and rest now.
In a sleeping-car it is quite impossible
To get one's quiet hour. A quiet hour a day
Is most essential, Dr. Rebmann says.

SIR CLAUDE
Rebmann? I thought it was a Dr. Leroux.

LADY ELIZABETH
Dr. Leroux is in Lausanne.
I have been in Zurich, under Dr. Rebmann.

SIR CLAUDE

But you were going out to Dr. Leroux
In Lausanne. What made you go to Zurich?

LADY ELIZABETH

Why, I'd no sooner got to Lausanne
Than whom should I meet but Mildred Deverell.
She was going on to Zurich. So she said: "Come to Zurich!
There's a wonderful doctor who teaches mind control."
So on I went to Zurich.

SIR CLAUDE

So on you went to Zurich.
But I thought that the doctor in Lausanne taught mind control?

LADY ELIZABETH

No, Claude, he only teaches *thought* control.
Mind control is a different matter:
It's more advanced. But I wrote you all about it.

SIR CLAUDE

It's true, you did send me postcards from Zurich;
But you know that I can't decipher your writing.
I like to have the cards, just to know where you are
By reading the postmark.

LADY ELIZABETH

But Claude, I'm glad to find
That you've taken my advice.

Sir Claude wonders about what? Lady Elizabeth is astonished and
distressed at his not remembering her advice about Mr. Colby.
"Don't you remember, I said before I left: 'Trust my guidance
for once, and engage that young man'? Well, that was Mr. Colby."
And saying to Colby Simpkins that he is to have tea with her tomorrow, she departs, leaving behind her some thoroughly astounded
gentlemen. "If this is what the doctor in Zurich has done for her,
I give him full marks . . ." Sir Claude exclaims, at the same time
apologizing for bringing Eggerson to town for nothing. Eggerson
says he wouldn't have missed it for the world; and offering his services whenever Simpkins needs them, he goes home.
   Sir Claude, on the whole, was rather pleased with the young man's

unplanned meeting with Lady Elizabeth. "It's very obvious that she took to you at once." "Did she really think that she had seen me before?" Colby asks.

SIR CLAUDE
Impossible to tell.
The point is that she's taken a fancy to you
And so she lays claim to you. That's very satisfactory.
She's taken it for granted that you should have the flat—
By tomorrow she'll be sure it was she who proposed it.
So I feel pretty confident that, before long,
We can put matters onto a permanent basis.

Colby up to now has not relished the idea of building his life on a deception. "Do you really believe that Lady Elizabeth can ever accept me as if I was her son?"

SIR CLAUDE
As if you were her son? If she comes to think of you
As the kind of man that her son would have been—
And I believe she will: though I'm perfectly convinced
That *her* son would have been a different type of person—
Then you *will* become her son, in her eyes. She's like that.
Why, it wouldn't surprise me if she came to believe
That you really are her son, instead of being mine.
She has always lived in a world of make-believe,
And the best one can do is to guide her delusions
In the right direction.

COLBY
It doesn't seem quite honest.
If we all have to live in a world of make-believe,
Is that good for us? Or a kindness to her?

SIR CLAUDE
If you haven't the strength to impose your own terms
Upon life, you must accept the terms it offers you. . . .

Sir Claude would like to alter the formal relationship he has had with Colby. They hardly know each other: When Colby was a child, Sir Claude felt he belonged to his aunt, and could never see him alone. And then during the war he sent them both to Canada thinking—perhaps wrongly—it was best. After that, there was Colby's schooling, his military service, and then his music. As for Colby, he finds this work with Sir Claude "In a way, exhilarating. To find there is something that I can do so remote from my previous interests. It gives me, in a way, a kind of self-confidence I've never had before. Yet at the same time it's rather disturbing. I don't mean the work: I mean, about myself. As if I was becoming a different person. . . ." But he's not sure he likes this new person (though he's fascinated by him). When now and then the old person takes over for a moment: "And I am again the disappointed organist, and for a moment the thing I cannot do, the art that I could never excel in, seems the one thing worth doing, the one thing that I want to do. I have to fight that person."

This is entirely understandable to Sir Claude: it duplicates his own experience. Sir Claude had wanted to be a potter. To him china and porcelain are beyond most people's ideas of "decoration" and "use." To Sir Claude "they are life itself. To be among such things, if it is an escape, it is escape into living, escape from a sordid world to a pure one. . . ." Sir Claude wants a world "where the form is the reality, of which the substantial is only a shadow. It's strange. I have never talked of this to anyone. Never until now. Do you feel at all like that when you are alone with your music?"

This is just how Colby feels, but if this is Sir Claude's passion, why did he not make it his profession?

Family pressure turned Sir Claude to business: "My father—your grandfather—built up this business starting from nothing. It was *his* passion. He loved it with the same devotion that I gave to clay, and what could be done with it—what I hoped I could do with it. . . ." Sir Claude loathed his work until he began to feel his power in it: "The life changed me, as it is changing you: it begins as a kind of make-believe and the make-believing makes it real." His father knew he hated it, but after his father's death, Sir Claude came to see that he had been right: ever since, Sir Claude has tried to atone for not understanding his father. Colby would like to know why Sir Claude feels that his father had been right. "Because I came to see," Sir Claude tells him, "that I should never have become a first-rate potter. I didn't have it in me. It's strange, isn't it, that a man should have a consuming passion to do something for which he lacks the capacity? Could a man be said to have a vocation to be a second-rate potter? . . ."

Colby, listening to Sir Claude tell of the moments when other men's creations have transported him, knows exactly what he means: "Indeed, I have felt, while you've been talking, that it's my own feelings you have expressed, although the medium is different. I know I should never have become a great organist, as I aspired to be. I'm not an executant; I'm only a shadow of the great composers. Always, when I play to myself, I hear the music I should like to have written, as the composer heard it when it came to him; but when I played before other people I was always conscious that what *they* heard was not what I hear when I play to myself. What I hear is a great musician's music, what they hear is an inferior rendering. So I've given up trying to play to other people: I am only happy when I play to myself."

Sir Claude has his private room for his pieces of pottery, where sometimes he too finds that sense of creative identification and ecstasy which makes life bearable. His wife's explorations into the life of the spirit are her substitute, he supposes, for true religion. Truly religious people and men of genius can contrive a unity; others must live as best as they can in two kinds of make-believe worlds.

Once again Colby understands Sir Claude, for his recognizing the conditions that life has imposed; yet something in himself can't accept such conditions: "It would be so much simpler if you *weren't* my father! I was struck by what you said, a little while ago, when you spoke of never having understood your father until it was too late. And you spoke of atonement. Even your failure to understand him, of which you spoke—that was a relationship of father and son. It must often happen. And the reconcilement, after his death, that perfects the relation. You have always been his son and he is still your father. I only wish that I had something to atone for!" Colby feels this lack in their relationship—Sir Claude, instead of being a father, has been a kind benefactor and patron. There was no father in those empty years of childhood. That is why he rebels against life's terms.

It's all his fault, says Sir Claude—trying to avoid his own father's mistake, he has apparently made a greater one. Colby hates to hurt him in any way; he is very grateful for all Sir Claude's kindness, and would like to justify that kindness: "I don't want my position to be, in any way, a make-believe." Then, turning businesslike, he reminds Sir Claude to have a look at some figures, when Sir Claude had planned to go look at his china.

ACT II

A few weeks later, Colby is entertaining Lucasta in his new flat. Rather surprisingly, he has been playing for her.

LUCASTA

Did you find it a strain, then, playing to me?

COLBY

As a matter of fact, I think I played better.
I can't bring myself to play to other people,
And when I'm alone I can't forget
That it's only myself to whom I'm playing.
But with you, it was neither solitude nor . . . people.

LUCASTA

I'm glad I'm not people. Will you play to me again
And teach me about music?

Lucasta, now very comfortable with Colby, hopes he will take her
to concerts he would like to hear, not to American musicals: "Because you don't like them—American musicals. Do you think it's
any compliment to invite a woman to something she would like
when she knows *you* wouldn't like it? That's not a compliment:
that's just being—patronizing. But if you invite me to something
you like—that *is* a compliment. It shows you want to educate me."

   After listening to Lucasta's theories, Colby suspects it is he who's
being educated. He confesses that at first he was bewildered by
her and B.: "Only afterwards, when I had seen you a number of
times, I decided that was only your kind of self-defense."

LUCASTA

What made you think it was self-defense?

COLBY

Because you couldn't wait to see what happened.
You're afraid of what would happen if you left things to themselves.
You jump—because you're afraid of being pushed.
I think that you're brave—and I think that you're frightened.
Perhaps you've been very badly hurt, at some time.
Or at least, there may have been something in your life
To rob you of any sense of security.

LUCASTA

And I'm sure you have *that*—the sense of security.

COLBY

No, I haven't either.

LUCASTA

There, I don't believe you.
What did I think till now? Oh, it's strange, isn't it,
That as one gets to know a person better
One finds them in some ways very like oneself,
In unexpected ways. And then you begin
To discover differences inside the likeness.
You may *feel* insecure, in some ways—
But your insecurity is nothing like mine.

COLBY

In what way is it different?

When Lucasta heard from him of his disastrous discovery that
he'd never be a good musician, so that he had decided to go into
business and be like Claude or B., she felt sorry for him, but also
envious. For he may have lost his outer world, but he still had an
inner world that the rest of them didn't—a "secret garden." Her
secret garden, if she could find it, would only be a "dirty public
square in a shabby part of London—like the one where I lived for
a time, with my mother. . . ." Colby admits she may be right, still
his garden isn't real to him, though it's as real as this world is: "But
that's just the trouble. They seem so unrelated. I turn the key,
and walk through the gate, and there I am . . . alone, in my 'garden.' Alone, that's the thing. That's why it's not real. You know,
I think that Eggerson's garden is more real than mine."

Lucasta wonders if he's laughing at her, but he's altogether serious:
"What I mean is, my garden's no less unreal to me than the world
outside it. If you have two lives which have nothing whatever to
do with each other—well, they're both unreal. But for Eggerson his
garden is a part of one single world." He explains further: "It's
simply the fact of being alone there that makes it unreal." As they
talk, Lucasta gradually feels so understood, almost secure, in knowing that Colby completely accepts her for what she is that she insists on telling him "who" she is.

B., she says, has been a wise friend to her: he has known that
what some men supposed of her wasn't true.

COLBY

What wasn't true?

LUCASTA

That I was Claude's mistress—
Or had been his mistress, palmed off on B.

COLBY

I never thought of such a thing!

LUCASTA
                You never thought of such a thing!
There are not many men who wouldn't have thought it.
I don't know about B. He's very generous.
I don't think he'd have minded. But he's very clever too;
And he guessed the truth from the very first moment.

COLBY

But what is there to know?

LUCASTA
                You'll laugh when I tell you:
I'm only Claude's daughter.

COLBY
His daughter!

LUCASTA
His daughter. Oh, it's a sordid story. . . .

She tells how her mother would squander Sir Claude's money before
the end of each quarter, probably on gin and betting; even as an
eight-year-old child, she knew how her mother supplemented her income. When the mother she hated died of an "accidental dose" Sir
Claude took over.

Colby's reaction to this story is so marked that Lucasta thinks he
is shocked at her being illegitimate. She is deeply disappointed in
him. She had expected complete understanding: "Why, I'd actually
thought of telling you before, and I postponed telling you, just for
the fun of it: I thought, when I tell him, it will be so wonderful
all in a moment. And now there's nothing, nothing at all. It's far
worse than ever. Just when you think you're on the point of release
from loneliness, then loneliness swoops down upon you; when you
think you're getting out, you're getting further in, and you know
at last that there's no escape. Well, I'll be going." Colby begs
her to wait: to explain his own position to her, he will even break
his promise to Sir Claude. But B. Kaghan's blithe entrance prevents him.

B. has come to pick up his charge, take a look at the new flat,
and drink a toast to Colby. Even though Lucasta protests she

doesn't like sherry, B. insists: "You've got to drink it, to Colby, and a happy bachelor life! Which depends, of course, on preventing Lizzie from always interfering. Be firm with her, Colby; assert your right to a little privacy. Now's the moment for firmness. Don't let her cross the threshold."

LUCASTA

As if you weren't as afraid of her as anybody!

KAGHAN

Well, at least, I've always managed to escape her.

LUCASTA

Only because she's never wanted to pursue you.

KAGHAN

Yes, I made a bad impression at the start:
I saw that it was necessary. I'm afraid Colby
Has made a good impression; which he'll have to live down. . . .

Kaghan admires the apartment until he hears that Lady Elizabeth decorated it. Then he's not so sure. But he is sure he's a good judge of character, and to prove this, he points out the difference between Lucasta and himself and Colby: "You and me—the one thing *we* want is security and respectability! Now Colby doesn't really care about being respectable—he was born and bred to it. I wasn't, Colby. Do you know, I was a foundling? You didn't know that! Never had any parents. Just adopted, from nowhere. That's why I want to be a power in the City, on the boards of all the solidest companies: because I've no background—no background at all. That's one thing I like about Lucasta: she doesn't despise me."

LUCASTA

Nobody could despise you.
And what's more important, you don't despise *me*.

KAGHAN

Nobody could despise *you*, Lucasta;
And we want the same things. But as for Colby,
He's the sort of fellow who might chuck it all
And go to live on a desert island.
But we hope you won't do that. We need you where you are.

COLBY

I'm beginning to believe you've a pretty shrewd insight
Into things that have nothing to do with business.

Lady Elizabeth sweeps in, glances at the company, doesn't relish
it, and says: "Have you just arrived, or are you just leaving?" She
sees to it that B. and Lucasta leave immediately, under orders to
go to the Herbal Restaurant. Lucasta's weak reaction is: "I'm so
hungry, I could even eat a herbal salad." "That's right," urges Lady
Elizabeth. "Just mention my name, Mr. Kaghan, and ask for the
table in the left hand corner: it has the best waitress. Good night."
Thus having rid herself (and Colby) of Lucasta and B. Kaghan,
whom she considers "worldly and materialistic, and . . . well, rather
vulgar" and not Colby's sort at all, she tells Colby what his sort
should be: "In the first place, you ought to mix with people of
breeding. I said to myself, when I first saw you, 'He is very well
bred.' I knew nothing about you, but one doesn't need to know, if
one knows what breeding is. And, second, you need intellectual
society. Now, that already limits your acquaintance: because, what's
surprising, well-bred people are sometimes far from intellectual; and
—what's less surprising—intellectual people are often ill-bred. But
that's not all. You need intellectual, well-bred people of spirituality
—and that's the rarest." Lady Elizabeth is equally definite in other
matters. She approves of the flat, at least of the part that she did.
She announces that if she still believed in re-incarnation, she and
Colby would have known each other in some previous incarnation.
She is convinced, in spite of all contrary evidence, that she and Colby
must have had similar backgrounds. He is less convinced; he had
no relatives at all, and simply lived with his widowed aunt, where
Lady Elizabeth's childhood swarmed with titled relatives and gov-
ernesses. Lady Elizabeth confides: "Do you know, Colby, when I
was a child I had three obsessions, and I never told anyone. I
wonder if *you* had the same obsessions." Colby groggily asks what
they were. "The first," recites Lady Elizabeth, "was, that I was
very ugly and didn't know it. Then, that I was feeble-minded and
didn't know it. Finally, that I was a foundling, and didn't know it."
This last appealed to her because she hated being the daughter of an
ordinary earl. When she gets through with how different she felt
herself to be, she pauses for breath, and lets Colby tell about his
childhood home and his aunt. She finds the name of his aunt, Mrs.
Guzzard, and of his home, Teddington, very familiar. "What became of your father?" she next inquires. Colby hesitates: "Well
. . . I didn't have a father. You see . . . I was an illegitimate

child." Lady Elizabeth accepts this matter-of-factly. She is now on Mrs. Guzzard's trail. "And are you quite sure that Mrs. Guzzard's sister—who you say was your mother—really was your mother?"

COLBY

Why, Lady Elizabeth! Why should I doubt it?
That is not the kind of story my aunt would invent.

LADY ELIZABETH

Not if she *is* your aunt. Did Mrs. Guzzard
And Mr. Guzzard—have any children?

They had a child who died when Colby was very young; he can't remember him. Colby can't help wondering why Lady Elizabeth should show such interest in his uninteresting background. "It may be more interesting than you are aware of," she tells him portentously, but says no more because of Sir Claude's sudden entrance.

Sir Claude, well knowing that Lady Elizabeth was here, came to give Colby some notes for a speech he is to make at a dinner of the Potters' Company. Suddenly Lady Elizabeth, who has been unusually silent, bursts out: "I've just made a startling discovery! All through a name—and intuition. But it shall be proved. The truth has come out. It's Colby. Colby is my lost child!"

Sir Claude asks quietly why she thinks so. It is Mrs. Guzzard's name: "It's the name I've been hunting for all these years—that, and the other name, *Teddington:* Mrs. Guzzard of Teddington. That was all I knew. Then Tony was killed, as you know, in Africa, and I had lost the name. Mrs. Guzzard." She wants Mrs. Guzzard to come and tell everything. Sir Claude is sorry, but he fears that when Mrs. Guzzard does come, her confession will be quite different. He had hoped that Lady Elizabeth would grow fond of Colby "and that he might come to take the place of your own child, if you got to know him first—and that you'd want to adopt him."

LADY ELIZABETH

But of course I want to adopt him, Claude!
That is, if one's allowed to adopt one's own child.

SIR CLAUDE

That's not what I meant, Elizabeth,
Colby is *my* son.

LADY ELIZABETH
Quite impossible, Claude!
You have a daughter. Now you want a son.

Lady Elizabeth refuses to give up so easily, and proceeds to grill Sir
Claude: Where was he when the baby was born; how does he know
Mrs. Guzzard's sister had a child? At the end, she still feels sure
she is Colby's mother.

Colby, during all this wrangling over his parentage, has become
"numb": "If there's agony, it's part of a total agony which I can't
begin to feel yet. I'm simply indifferent. And all the time that
you've been talking I've only been thinking: 'What does it matter
whose son I am?' You don't understand that when one has lived
without parents, as a child, there's a gap that never can be filled.
Never. I like you both, I could even come to love you—but as
friends . . . older friends. Neither, as a parent. I am sorry. But
that's why I say it doesn't matter to me, which of you should be
my parent." Lady Elizabeth, at the time of his birth, chose not to
be his mother. Now it's too late. "I never wanted a parent till
now—I never thought about it. Now, you have made me think, and
I wish that I could have had a father and a mother."

Lady Elizabeth has an inspiration: Colby should be *their* son,
and they can all be happy together. Sir Claude likes the idea, it is
close to what his own had been. But Colby finds: "It would be
easier, I think, to accept you both in the place of parents if neither
of you could be. If it was pure fiction—one can live on a fiction—
but not on such a mixture of fiction and fact. . . ." Tonight he
wants to know the fact of his parentage. Sir Claude decides to send
for Mrs. Guzzard. Lady Elizabeth rather wisely suggests they send
for Eggerson, too.

In the meantime, Colby is determined to concentrate on his work
and write Sir Claude's speech, though what does Sir Claude want him
to do with the note "Reminiscent mood"?

SIR CLAUDE
Reminiscent of what? Reminiscent of what?
"Tonight I feel in a reminiscent mood"—
Oh yes. To say something of my early ambitions
To be a potter. Not that the Members
Of the Potters' Company know anything at all
About ceramics . . . or any other art.
No, I don't think I shall be in a reminiscent mood.
Cross that out. It would only remind me

Of things that would surprise the Potters' Company
If I told them what I was really remembering.
Come, Elizabeth.

LADY ELIZABETH
My poor Claude!

ACT III

Several mornings later, Sir Claude is in the Business Room, arranging chairs for the "investigation." Eggerson, he has decided, should sit at his desk as chairman. He, Lady Elizabeth, and Colby will be less conspicuously placed, while Mrs. Guzzard will sit with the light full on her.

After a sleepless night, Lady Elizabeth has decided it would be fairer if Colby were Sir Claude's son; she actually has had one, whereas Sir Claude has not: "So I hope Mrs. Guzzard will say he is your son and I needn't believe her. I don't believe in facts. You do. That is the difference between us." Sir Claude admits to always acting as though he believed in facts. But he's not so sure he has. He felt sure his father believed in power and wealth, when actually what his father sought to instill in him "was that idea, that inspiration which to him was life. To me, it was a burden. You can't communicate an inspiration, like that, by force of will. He was a great financier—and I am merely a successful one. I might have been truer to my father's inspiration if I had done what I wanted to do."

And what was that? Lady Elizabeth asks. When he tells her, she cries: "But I should have loved you to be a potter!" Sir Claude had assumed she was only interested in a "husband of importance." And she had assumed he was only interested in finance, and needed her chiefly as "a hostess." Lady Elizabeth says: "It's a great mistake, I do believe, for married people to take anything for granted." What Lady Elizabeth had wanted above all was to inspire an artist. "Or to inspire a poet. I thought Tony was a poet. Because he wrote me poems. And he was so beautiful. I know now that poets don't look like poets: and financiers, it seems, don't look like potters— Is that what I mean? I'm getting confused. I thought I was escaping from a world that I loathed in Tony—and then, too late, I discovered he belonged to the world I wanted to escape from. He was so commonplace! I wanted to forget him, and so, I suppose, I wanted to forget Colby. But Colby is an artist.

SIR CLAUDE
A musician.
I am a disappointed craftsman,
And Colby is a disappointed composer.
I should have been a second-rate potter,
And he would have been a second-rate organist.
We have both chosen . . . obedience to the facts.

This is the first time, Lady Elizabeth says, they have ever talked understandingly together. And now she doesn't care what Mrs. Guzzard reveals, so long as Colby is satisfied.

Eggerson arrives. Sir Claude offers apologies for bringing him to town and asks after Mrs. Eggerson's health. "Pretty well," says Eggerson. "She's always low-spirited around this season, when we're getting near the anniversary."

SIR CLAUDE
The anniversary? Of your son's death?

EGGERSON
Of the day we got the news. We don't often speak of it;
Yet I know what's on her mind, for days beforehand.
But here I am, talking about ourselves!
And we've more important business, I imagine.

Sir Claude explains, while Eggerson listens carefully, that they have sent for Mrs. Guzzard, since Lady Elizabeth is convinced it was she who was given the care of her child.

Eggerson suggests that Mrs. Guzzard may have made a profession of looking after people's children, or at least had taken in another child besides Colby. Lady Elizabeth apparently accepts this, for an odd reason: "That seems to be what happened. And now we must find out what became of your child, Claude." Sir Claude is exasperated: it is *her* child they must trace. Whereupon Lucasta barges in with the announcement: she has decided to marry B. But for Colby, she explains, she never would have come to appreciate B. Sir Claude is startled: "But Colby! Lucasta, if I'd suspected this I would have explained. Colby is your brother."

Eggerson corrects him: "Half-brother, Miss Angel." Lady Elizabeth wishes to make a further correction, but Claude insists that he do the explaining to Lucasta, and clears up the misunderstanding of the day at Colby's flat. Today Lucasta finds she doesn't dare to understand him so well: "What's so difficult is to recognize the limits

Aline MacMahon, Ina Claire, Joan Greenwood,

of one's understanding." Colby is delighted that she is to marry B. whom he is very fond of. "I shall need you, both of you, Lucasta!" Again Lucasta is not so sure: "We'll mean something to you. But you don't *need* anybody," and she goes downstairs.

Formidable Mrs. Guzzard, a woman who plainly brooks no nonsense, is shown in. Eggerson opens the investigation with a reference to Lady Elizabeth's "mislaid son" . . ."Who was taken charge of by the father. That is to say, placed out to be cared for till further notice by a foster-mother. Unfortunately, the father died suddenly . . ." Lady Elizabeth adds: "He was run over. By a rhinoceros in Tanganyika." Eggerson goes on: Lady Elizabeth never knew the name of this lady, or at any rate has forgotten it. Mrs. Guzzard musters sympathy. She too had a son, and lost him,

Newton Blick and Claude Rains in "The Confidential Clerk"

not, however, the way Lady Elizabeth had. "Let us hope," she says stuffily, "that her son may be restored to her." That is why they are here, Eggerson explains: "We have a clue—or what appears to be a clue." Had Mrs. Guzzard ever taken in a child whose parents were unknown to her? "Yes, I did take in a child," she answers. "My husband and I were childless . . . at the time, and very poor. . . ." This child, Eggerson finds, was Lady Elizabeth's, but it wasn't Colby. Mrs. Guzzard waxes indignant at the very idea: "Your son, Lady Elizabeth? Are you suggesting that I kept a child of yours and deceived Sir Claude by pretending it was his?"

Eggerson keeps the ruffled ladies from getting out of hand by asking what became of the child who might have been Lady Elizabeth's. Mrs. Guzzard confesses that when the payments ended, she reluctantly parted with the "dear little boy"; some childless neighbors had taken a fancy to him and adopted him. Their name was an unusual one: Kaghan. The boy had been baptized Barnabas. Lady Elizabeth is indignant: "Barnabas? There's never been such a name in my family. Or, I'm sure in his father's. But how did he come to be called Colby?" Characteristically, Lady Elizabeth ignores facts, is all at sea: "What with Colby being Barnabas—I mean, not Barnabas. And Mr. Kaghan being Barnabas. I suppose I'll get used to it." She gets the chance at once, when Colby goes after the engaged couple. Sir Claude says: "I believe, Elizabeth, that you have found your son." Eggerson adds: "Subject to confirmation." Lady Elizabeth adds further: "And to my being able to adjust myself to it."

Mrs. Guzzard quizzes B. about his parents, then, satisfied, pronounces him Lady Elizabeth's son. B. is startled, to say the least, and Lady Elizabeth controls her joy. She will permit B. to address her hereafter as Aunt Elizabeth, and immediately orders him and Lucasta to have a church wedding instead of a quiet one at a registry office. At this point, Mrs. Guzzard asks Lady Elizabeth if she is satisfied: "Are you contented to have him as your son?" Sir Claude finds the question strange. Says Mrs. Guzzard: "I have been asked here to answer strange questions; and now it is my turn to ask them. I should like to gratify everyone's wishes."

Lady Elizabeth tries to be game, and B. is gallant: "It's very much better than being a foundling—if I can live up to it. And . . . yes, of course, if I can make it right with my parents. I'm fond of them, you know." Lady Elizabeth says graciously: "I shall see to that."

Mrs. Guzzard asks Colby, rather ominously, if he's had his wish. Colby would like a father: "whom I could get to know only by report, by documents; the story of his life, of his success or failure . . . perhaps his failure more than his success . . . by objects that belonged to him and faded photographs in which I should try to decipher a likeness; whose image I could create in my own mind, to live with that image. An ordinary man whose life I could in some way perpetuate by being the person he would have liked to be, and by doing the things he had wanted to do. . . . A dead, obscure man," he tells Mrs. Guzzard, who immediately grants his wish. His father was Herbert Guzzard, a disappointed musician. The registration of his birth will confirm this: "To Herbert and Sarah Guzzard a son."

EGGERSON
And what about your sister and her child?

MRS. GUZZARD

Registration of death.   The child was never born.

Sir Claude won't believe this: it's something Mrs. Guzzard invented in response to Colby's wish.   Eggerson calms him, saying he will check the records.   Mrs. Guzzard agrees that it's the thing to do.

Mrs. Guzzard never meant to deceive Sir Claude, but at the first meeting he was so sure the boy was his, and so pleased, she shrank from disillusioning him.   Then she thought: "Why not?"   She had been widowed, she was poor, and if she let Sir Claude continue to think the child was his, the child's future would be assured.   Mrs. Guzzard overrules Sir Claude's denials: "Consider, Sir Claude. Would I tell you all this unless it was true?   In telling you the truth I am sacrificing my ambitions for Colby.   I am sacrificing also my previous sacrifice. . . ."   Colby believes her.   "I must believe you: This gives me freedom."   Sir Claude tells him if this is his wish, he should believe Mrs. Guzzard, but it won't alter their relations, except for the better.   Colby thinks otherwise.   His one idea is to follow after his own father; he hates to hurt Sir Claude, but must refuse his terms.   "But you would still think of me as your son. There can be no relation of father and son unless it works both ways. For you to regard me as you would—as your son, when I could not think of you as my father: if I accepted that I should be guilty towards you.   I like you too much.   You've become a man without illusions about himself, and without ambitions.   Now, that I've abandoned *my* illusions and ambitions all that's left is love.   But not on false pretenses: that's why I must leave you."

Sir Claude and Lady Elizabeth plead with Eggerson to help.   But Eggerson won't interfere.   Instead he offers a delighted Colby the position of organist in his parish church at Joshua Park.   He is sure the Church Council will only be too pleased to have him.

EGGERSON

The stipend is small—
Very small, I'm afraid.   Not enough to live on.
We'll have to think of other ways
Of making up an income.   Piano lessons?
As a temporary measure; because, Mr. Simpkins—
I hope you won't take this as an impertinence—
I don't see you spending a lifetime as an organist.
I think you'll come to find you've another vocation.
We worked together every day, you know,

For quite a little time, and I've watched you pretty closely.
Mr. Simpkins!   You'll be thinking of reading for orders.
And you'll still have your music.   Why Mr. Simpkins,
Joshua Park may be only a stepping-stone
To a precentorship!   And a canonry!"

In the meantime, Mrs. Eggerson has a spare room and nothing
would please her more than for Colby to use it.   Mrs. Guzzard, having been the wife of an organist, can't see eye to eye with Mr.
Eggerson's plans.   But she tells him: "You too, I think, have had
a wish realized."   And goes on: "Then I will say good-by.   You
have all had your wish in one form or another.   You and I, Sir
Claude, had *our* wishes twenty-five years ago; but we failed to
observe, when we had our wishes, that there was a time-limit clause
in the contract."   Colby has gone to get Mrs. Guzzard a taxi, and
she now follows.

Sir Claude, bewildered and desolate, sits with the ruins of his carefully planned life around him.   Lady Elizabeth tries to console him.
Lucasta sits at his feet.   And B. realistically takes over.   "We
should like to understand *you* . . . I mean, I'm including both of
you, Claude . . . and Aunt Elizabeth.   You know, Claude, both
Lucasta and I would like to mean something to you . . . if you'd
let us; and we'd take the responsibility of meaning it."   Lucasta
embraces Sir Claude who tells her: "Don't leave me, Lucasta.   Eggerson!   Do *you* really believe her?"   (EGGERSON *nods.*)

TAKE A GIANT STEP *

A Play in Six Scenes

By Louis Peterson

[Louis Peterson *grew up in Hartford, Conn., in just such an environment as is described in "Take a Giant Step." In fact the play is partly autobiographical. He went to Morehouse, a Negro college in Atlanta, Ga. He first studied music, but acting in school productions turned his mind toward the theatre, and after graduation he went for a year to the Yale School of Drama and then went to N.Y.U. for his M.A. He has acted for The Blackfriars and the Henry Street Settlement, and was assistant stage manager of "The Member of the Wedding." During that period he attended Clifford Odets' playwriting class; it is to Odets that he gives credit for learning "how to sit down and really write a play."*]

ALTHOUGH it's the Fall of the year, you can still hear the sounds from a boy's baseball game across the street, as the seventeen-year-old Negro boy enters his own back yard. Spence Scott's house might be on any middle-class street in any New England town. It's a rather ordinary house but has been well kept up, and shows it.

You can see a cross section of part of the house: back entrance hall, kitchen-dining room, living room—with the suggestion of a hall. There is a staircase near the center of the back wall, and at the very top of the stairs is a very small chair. Spence's piano stands near the front door.

Spence comes into the house by the back door, lugging his school-books and whacking himself on the thigh with a croquet stake he's yanked from the yard. His grandmother, hearing him slam the door, starts calling to him before he has time to throw down his books on the living-room couch. While he sits down to pull off his shoes he parries Grandma's questions—he's in no mood to tell why he's late

---

135

coming home from school. But his grandmother isn't so easily put off, and announces she can't hear and is coming downstairs.

Spence—If you do—I'll tell Mom that you've been horsing around again today.

Grandma—Just you be quiet and come up and help me.

Spence (*gets up, and goes upstairs*)—You know you haven't got any business coming downstairs. Mom told you to stay up. Not only am I going to tell Mom, but when the doctor comes, I'm going to tell him, too.

Grandma—Tell him. You think I care? Now come up and help me. (*He goes all the way upstairs and helps her.*)

Spence—Just lean on me, and hold tight to the railing, and I think we'll make it.

Grandma—I don't know why I can't come downstairs if I want to. (*Pauses as she labors down the stairs.*) And you keep your mouth shut about it, too.

Spence (*both coming downstairs*)—I've already told you what I'm going to do. I'm going to spill the beans all over the house.

Grandma—You do and I'll tell your mother you were late coming home from school and that you haven't practiced yet.

Spence—You'd better put all your concentration on getting down the steps, Gram, or you're gonna fall and break your behind.

Grandma—Now you stop that kind of talk—you hear me?

Spence—Now be careful, Gram—and don't get excited.

Grandma—Well then—you stop it—you hear me?

Spence—All right, Gram. All right. Just stop hopping around like a sparrow.

Grandma—I never thought I'd live to see the day when my own daughter's child was cursing like a trooper.

Spence—Haven't said anything yet, Gram. All I said was that if you weren't careful you'd fall down and break your behind. And you will, too.

Grandma—Take your hands off me. I can do the rest myself. (*Crosses to kitchen; she notices the stake.*) What are you doing with that dirty thing in the house?

Spence—I wanted it. Something to bang around.

Grandma—You're banging dirt all over the rug. (*She is going into the kitchen. Spence is going toward the living room.*) Where are you going?

Spence—I'm going in and practice. (*Crosses to piano.*)

Grandma—Wouldn't you like something to eat first?

SPENCE—No. I wouldn't. You think you can trick me—don't you? I'm going in and practice, and then you won't have a thing to tell Mom when she gets home. (*Sits at piano.*)

GRANDMA (*going into kitchen*)—Suit yourself. (*She sits down at the table: he begins practicing scales. There is a pause.*) Spencer, would you get me a glass of water? I'm so out of breath.

SPENCE (*still practicing*)—You mooched down all those stairs without batting an eye. You can get your own water. (*Piano continues.*)

With that his grandmother accuses him of being downright mean. Spence remains unruffled. His grandmother now has to coax him and to promise that if he'll join her in the kitchen, she won't squeal on him for not practicing. Spence coolly continues to pound away. "I took your word the day before yesterday," he tells her. "And as a result I had to practice two hours in the morning." After some stalling, Grandma agrees to take the oath that Spence exacts of her: "I swear and promise that—no matter what happens—I will not tell anybody that Spencer Scott did not practice this afternoon—and if asked I will lie and say that he did." Even this isn't completely satisfactory to Spence; he makes her swear that she won't write notes either. "And," says Spence, "I swear and promise under fear of death." "I swear and promise under fear of death," repeats Grandma. But she starts to balk again when Spence wants her to kiss the book: "I'll do no such thing; it's dirty." He makes her kiss it, whereupon she discovers it's not the Bible. "It's *Crime and Punishment.*" In the next breath he wants to know what they're going to eat.

As they settle themselves cozily at the kitchen table with their crackers and cheese, Spence begins putting pressure on his grandmother for something else. He's all for striking a bargain, but she isn't. He wants some of his father's beer, but she'll be a party to no such thing. "All right, Gram," says Spence. "Fine. When you're taking twice as many of those ugly, nasty-tasting pills—don't say I didn't try to be a good sport."

GRANDMA—One glass.

SPENCE (*opens the icebox*)—It's a deal. One glass. (*Crosses the kitchen.*) What shall I do with the rest of the bottle? (*His grandmother continues to look out of the window.*) If he sees half a bottle he'll know right away.

GRANDMA—Pour it down the sink.

SPENCE—Good idea. (*He opens the bottle and pours a glass.*)
GRANDMA (*as he starts to pour the rest out*)—How much is left?
SPENCE—Not much.
GRANDMA—Well, bring it here. Shame to let it go to waste.

Spence tells her she ought to be in politics—she sure knows how
to strike a hard bargain. But he is willing to agree with her that
this being together is nice. But soon, however, he is using the croquet stake to hit himself again; and again his grandmother is asking
questions of him. Spence decides he might as well tell her, because
his mother will hear about it on the way home, anyway. So Spence
asks what would she think the very worst thing that could happen
to him.

GRANDMA—You haven't gotten any little girls in trouble—have
you?
SPENCE—Nothing like that, Gram. Worse.
GRANDMA—What have you done? Will you stop hitting yourself
with that thing!
SPENCE—Well, Gram, I just went and got my ass kicked out of
school today.
GRANDMA—Spencer Scott! What were you doing?
SPENCE—Nothing much. Just smoking in the john.
GRANDMA—Smoking! Where?
SPENCE—In the john—the can, Gram. The Men's Room.
GRANDMA—Well, that's a pretty nasty place to be smoking if you
ask me. What were you smoking?
He was smoking a cigar—one of his father's cigars. "Well, I sure
loused myself up proper this time," admits Spence.
With that he's off to look if there's any mail, even though his
grandmother tells him there's nothing for him. So he now lets loose
at his brother, who's away at college and hasn't answered Spence's
letters. "He'll answer soon enough," Spence prophesies, "when he
finds out they've shoved me into some loony bin." His grandmother
wants to know what's wrong with him, and tells him to stop hitting
himself with that "thing." Spence answers: "Will you leave me
alone? Don't you understand that when a guy's upset he's got to
hit himself with something? You gotta do something like that."
But his grandmother persists. "What's the matter, Spence?" she
asks softly. This time Spence can't tell her because her sympathy
is bound to make him feel sorry for himself and start him bawling.

He figures, though, if she'll just eat—and not look at him—he can tell her all about this mess.

SPENCE—Well—from the very beginning of school I could've told you that that Miss Crowley and I weren't going to see eye to eye.

GRANDMA—Who's Miss Crowley?

SPENCE—The history teacher, Gram. The one that thinks she's cute. She's always giving the guys a preview of the latest fashions in underwear.

GRANDMA—Nasty little hussy!

SPENCE—That's the one. Well, today they started talking about the Civil War and one of the smart little skirts at the back of the room wanted to know why the Negroes in the South didn't rebel against slavery. Why did they wait for the Northerners to come down and help them? And this Miss Crowley went on to explain how they were stupid and didn't have sense enough to help themselves. (*Crosses and sits at table.*) Well, anyway, Gram, when she got through talking they sounded like the worst morons that ever lived, and I began to wonder how they've managed to live a few thousand years all by themselves in Africa with nobody's help. I would have let that pass, see, except that the whole class was looking at me—so I got up and just stood next to my desk looking at her. She looked at me for a couple of minutes and asked me if perhaps I had something to say in the discussion. I said I might have a lot of things to say if I didn't have to say them in the company of such dumb jerks. Then I asked her frankly what college she went to.

GRANDMA—What did she say?

SPENCE—She told me I was being impudent. I told her it was not my intention to be impudent but I would honestly like to know. So she puts one hand on her hip—kinda throwing the other hip out of joint at the same time—and like she wants to spit on me she says "Scoville." Then I says, "And they didn't teach you nothing about the uprising of the slaves during the Civil War—or Frederick Douglas?" She says, "No—they didn't." "In that case," I said, "I don't want to be in your crummy history class." And I walk out of the room. When I get out in the hall, Gram, I'm shaking, I'm so mad. And I had this cigar I was going to sell for a sundae. I knew I couldn't eat a sundae now 'cause it would just make me sick, so— I just had to do something, so I went into the Men's Room and smoked the cigar. I just had about two drags on the thing when in comes the janitor and hauls me down to old Hasbrook's office—

and when I get down there—there's Miss Crowley and old Hasbrook talking me over in low tones—and in five short minutes he'd thrown me out of school.

Grandma's idea that the principal should have given him another chance collapses when Spence admits to being a chronic offender. After a week's expulsion he has to go back, accompanied by his father. And will his father be mad! Spence is getting angry himself, when his grandmother says his mother won't like his story, either. Grandma is frank: "I'm afraid that you're going to get what you rightfully deserve." Spence considers it thoroughly nasty of his grandmother not to back him up. She lets him know she's tired of his language and his beating himself to a pulp with the croquet stake. Spence, now thoroughly aroused, throws the stake down, and asks: "Listen—are you my friend, or not?" "No—I'm not—not when you talk like that," Grandma snaps back. "Well—thanks for that," answers Spence. "Thanks. You're a real good Joe. You're a psalm singer—just like the rest of them, Gram. Love me when I'm good—hate me when I'm bad. Thanks."

Grandma spiritedly gets in her two cents, but the bickering is interrupted when a boy calls to Spence to come outside. Spence is ready to let him keep on calling, let him wait forever. Let him holler now, since he certainly didn't speak up for Spence at school. But Grandma insists that he ask Tony in. Spence lets the young Italian boy come into the kitchen, but he's not going to hide his feelings. He lets Tony know how he felt about being thrown out of school, and about no one's coming to his aid. "I caught their sympathy when Miss Crowley was bitching me out." Grandma immediately says: "I'm going to tell your mother."

Tony protests that Spence has it all wrong, but Spence reminds him of the job he did for Tony when someone called him a Wop. His grandmother takes in this account of both boys' deviltry, then says: "I think I should warn you both now—that everything you're saying is going to be used against you—because I'm going to tell all of it." But Spence is reminding Tony of this past escapade, to point up his loyalty toward his friends, either in school or out. And he has another grievance against his gang. "I dunno—maybe I'm getting deaf and need a hearing aid or something, but I don't hear you guys calling me for school any more in the morning."

Tony—Ah, Spence—how many times do I have to tell you? I'm taking Marguerite to school in the morning.

SPENCE—And where are you taking her at night when you mosey past the house with her curled around your arm like a snake?

TONY—We're doing our homework together.

SPENCE—It's a little dark up in the park for homework.

TONY—Spence—cut it out—your grandmother.

SPENCE—My grandmother knows what the score is. She's been knowing it an awful long time now. She's going on eighty-three years old. You can talk freely in front of her.

When Tony does, his excuse is that Marguerite's father, being an intolerant man, doesn't like colored people. Grandma proves equally intolerant: "Well, I don't like Polish people either. Never have—never will. They come over here—haven't been over, mind you, long enough to know 'and' from 'but'—and that's the first thing they learn. Sometime I think Hitler was right—" Spence, being more reasonable than his elders, tries to quiet her down, but she repeats: "I don't care—I don't like them. Never have—never will."

SPENCE—You say "them" as though it was some kind of bug or something. Will you do me a favor like a real pal, Gram? Quit trying to mix in things that you don't understand. (*To* TONY.) Okay, friend—you've said your piece—what did you come over for?

TONY—Nothing—I didn't want nothing.

SPENCE—Aw—cut the bull, Tony. You must've come over here for something. You just don't come over here for nothing any more. What do you want? (TONY *crosses to TV set.* SPENCE *crosses to a chair.*) You feel uncultured—you want to hear a little Bach or something? You want to see a little television—borrow a book? I just read a good one—all about the causes and prevention of syphilis.

GRANDMA—Spencer Scott!

SPENCE (*turns to* GRANDMA)—That's what the book said, Gram. Bring it out in the open—so I'm bringing it out.

But Spence now comes right to the point. He knows why Tony's come over: the boys are playing baseball on the lot, and finding they needed Spence's equipment, they've appointed Tony to get it for them. Tony is embarrassed, and mutters he hadn't wanted to come. "Aw," says Spence, "why didn't you want to? You're my friend, aren't you? Just because I'm sore at you? Damn sore at you?" Tony protests: "Cut it out now, Spence. I did the best I could." Admitting that Tony has, Spence impulsively but deliberately loads Tony down with all his baseball paraphernalia, causing his grandmother to wonder if he's drunk. Tony at least has the grace to ask if he'll be wanting them back—even though Spence has made clear that it's his present to the gang.

SPENCE—Geez—the things you can't understand. I'm giving them to you because you've been such good friends to me—one and all.

TONY (*starts to pick up equipment; starting to go*)—Well, thanks, Spence—thanks.

SPENCE—Think nothing of it. But there's just one more thing I want you to know. If I couldn't do any better than Marguerite Wandalowski and her old man I'd cram my head into a bucket of horse manure.

GRANDMA—Now see here—

TONY (*crosses to* SPENCE)—See—that's the way you are. You can't do one nice thing without a dirty dig at the end. I ought to throw these things in your puss—

SPENCE—You won't, though—will you?

GRANDMA—Take them back, Spence. Take them right back.

TONY—Somebody—someday is going to take a poke at you.

GRANDMA (*takes a swing*)—If he hits you, Spence—hit him right back.

SPENCE—He's not going to hit anyone, Gram. He's just talking to be sure he hasn't lost his mouth some damned place. (*Throws* TONY *to door.*) Now scram the hell out of this house before I beat you and your whole team over the head. Get out! (TONY *exits quickly.*) Well, I sure went and milked myself in public that time.

GRANDMA—What are you talking about now?

Spence is mad at himself for letting Tony know he was hurt. Grandma—not grasping the fact—says if he won't watch television with her, she's going back upstairs: "I don't understand what's wrong with you. You're just no fun to be with any more—cussing and ripping and tearing. Won't even watch a little television with me!" Spence pettishly answers that she should just watch it herself: "Spend the rest of your life with your head stuck in front of an old light bulb."

But then he confesses what's really bothering him: he's an outcast. "They don't want me around any more, Gram. I cramp their style with the broads." Gram still won't understand. So Spence spells it out for her, "Because I'm black—that's why."

GRANDMA—Well, it's a good thing if they don't want you around. (*Turns to window.*) I told your mother years and years ago, "May —stay out of the South End, 'cause mark my words, there's nothing down there, nothing—but Wops and Germans and Lord knows what else they'll get in the future." And what did they get? More Wops and Germans and a few Polacks thrown in for good measure, and not one self-respecting colored family in the whole lot.

SPENCE—Cut out that kind of talk. Sometimes, Gram—you're no help at all. I tell you my troubles and you tell me how we shouldn't have moved here in the first place. But we're here, Gram —right here—and I was born here—and they're all the friends I've got—and it makes me damned unhappy, Gram.

He's ready to cry. But Grandma now knows how to take care of him, as she has done with so many of her boys through the years. She persuades him to get his hairbrush, and she'll brush his hair, comfort him, and listen to his troubles. Spence brightens up a little under Grandma's touch, and ever so casually asks directions for reaching the colored section of the town. Grandma hasn't been there in many years. But after finding out what he wants to know, Spence gets her to lend him five dollars, ostensibly to take the curse off the evening ahead when his parents will give him hell: "In other words, Gram," he explains, "if you'd lend me five dollars I could go out and get some flowers for Mom and some cigars for Pop and begin by telling them how sorry I am, and it might take the edge off what is going to be at best a hell of an evening." Spence helps Grandma up the steps, then quickly runs to the back hall for suitcase and clothes. The doorbell brings him up short. "Dear, dear God," Spence prays, "if that's my mother, just kill me as I open the door." He hides the suitcase, and opens the door.

It's his friend Iggy, who has really come over to trade stamps after finishing all his vacation homework.

SPENCE—You know, Iggy—you're going to be out of school for a week. You didn't have to get your homework done so soon. That's the most disgusting thing I ever heard.

IGGY—Now look, if I want to get my homework done—that's my business. I don't tell you it's disgusting when you don't get yours done at all, do I?

Spence had thought that he'd really come over after hearing that Spence had been bounced out of school. But Iggy hadn't known, and now broods at the news: "I was just thinking that if I got kicked out of school, I guess I'd just as soon I dropped dead right there on the floor in the principal's office." Spence tells him to drop the subject as long as he can't help. Iggy tries to be helpful: "I didn't mean that business about dropping dead. I probably wouldn't drop dead anyway. There's nothing wrong with my heart." Spence manages to shut him up, but in the process realizes he's hurt Iggy's feelings. "I know how sensitive you are and all that, and I just mow into you like crazy. I wish someone would tell me to shut my mouth." He goes over to the stairs and yells to his grandmother for the money, then turns around and takes his treasured stamp album from the top of the piano. He gives it to Iggy, for his own, giving his reason as: "Hell, Iggy—because I'm growing up. I'm becoming a man, Iggy. And since I'm going out in just a few minutes with my girl friend—you know it's time for me to quit fooling around with stuff like that." What's more, he may be getting married and have to forget about school, and think about a job instead.

He urges Iggy to take the album and go, because he has packing to do. Iggy takes it gratefully; Spence is suddenly torn—and calls out: "Hey, Iggy! You won't mind if just once in a while—I come over and see how you're doing with it?"

Iggy—I hope you will. Good-by.
Spence—Geez—I don't know what's wrong with me. I think maybe my brains are molding or something. (*Gets suitcase, shoves clothes inside, and runs upstairs.*) Hey, Gram—will you hurry up with that five bucks so I can get the hell out of here before I really do something desperate!

Scene II

In a small, tawdry, bar-restaurant—mainly bar and very noisy—a woman is standing at a wall phone, two women are seated at a table, a man is arguing with the bartender, and at the far side of the barroom, a girl is sitting by herself. She is the only quiet figure in the room.

Violet, at the telephone, is finding it hard to get through to her customers because of the noise. Her sister prostitutes, Rose and Poppy, are ready to fight with the bartender, only they need his pay phone for their business, and his bar for a home base. They're short on rent money, and are going through their address books after likely names for blackmail. They've just reached the end of their lists, and have got nowhere. Frank, the bartender, is getting nasty, too, and making them pay for their setups. "The ice will cost you a dime," he tells them as he crosses to serve the girl, Carol, on the other side of the room. Poppy is getting angry: "Damn—let's get the hell out of here before he begins charging for sitting down." Violet tells

her to pay the man. Poppy obediently tells Frank: "Well, bring it
on over, you chinchy skunk."

Spence, carrying some books, had drifted in unnoticed from the
street and is staring at the girl in the corner. When Frank sees him
he orders him out. Spence leaves, in a rather embarrassing fashion,
but with a backward glance at Carol. By this time the three beat-up
tramps are down to the last name in Violet's book. It's Poppy's
turn to make the call, and she calls her number and gets her man.

POPPY—Hello, Sidney. This is Poppy. One and the same.
Haven't seen you lately. Well, that's too bad. (*Pause.*) Sugar,
we're in a bad spot 'cause tomorrow the rent man is coming around,
an— (VIOLET *crosses to phone.*) Well now, Sugar, Violet is sitting
right here and she's upset about the rent, too. Do you remember
that time you took Violet down to New York and registered in that
hotel as Mr. and Mrs.? (ROSE *crosses to bar above* POPPY.) Well
now—Honey—to get down to New York, you has to cross a state
line. Now have you ever heard of the Mann Act? Well, Violet has.
Well—I don't know all the details of it, but it seems you can get
into about ten or fifteen years' worth of trouble for carting girls over
state lines for the kind of purposes you had in mind. Now all Violet
is asking for is about ten dollars—that roughly comes out to sev-
enty-five cents a year, and she wants it tonight—at Carter's drugstore—or else the F.B.I. Now have you got all that, Sugar? Fine—
we'll be looking for you, hear? (*She hangs up and crosses back to
chair.*) Well, Sidney suddenly decided he had ten loose dollars
around someplace. We're supposed to meet him in Carter's in fifteen
minutes.

Rose admires Poppy's skill in handling Sidney, Violet figures they
only have to get fifteen more dollars, but Frank is mad. "Coming
in here—blackmailing people on my telephone."

POPPY—We ain't blackmailing anybody. We're just keeping ourselves available. There's no telling—next week sometime—one of
those boys might be glad we're still here.
MAN (*at the bar*)—I can't see why.
ROSE—Why don't you shut up?
MAN—This is a place of business. Man comes in here to have a
quiet drink. If it ain't a bunch of whores, it's a television set.

The girls don't like being called whores, and Violet snaps: "Coming in here for a quiet drink—he calls it. I seen you lamping the

little girl over in the corner. You ought to be ashamed of yourself. Baby," she says, crossing to Carol, "if he bothers you—just come over and tell me and I'll knock his brains out. Hear?"

Just then Spence reappears at the door. Rose tells Violet to get her little black book out again, saying: "We ain't got all night." Poppy is pessimistic: "I don't know why we ain't got all night. We haven't got anything else to do." They all look at her. "Well— have we?" "No," replies Violet, "we haven't, stupid. But you don't have to say it in here—do you? Hell—you have to keep up some pretenses, Poppy."

Spence enters and sits at the bar, putting his books in front of him. This time he has decided to be a customer. When the bartender balks at serving him because of his youth, Spence cockily says he's twenty-one, and by way of proof, unblinkingly states his birthday as January 20th, 1932. Frank takes a pencil and paper to check this: then, finding it jibes, he tries to foist some of his "special" whiskey on Spence, rather than the beer he ordered. Spence insists on the beer, not needing Poppy's: "That's right, Sugar— Don't drink none of that man's whiskey. He ferments it himself." Poppy invites Spence to their table with his book by Freud; Violet tells him to sit down. Poppy asks, "Does that book say anything about umbrellas? I keep having the damndest dreams with umbrellas in them."

While Poppy digs through *The Interpretation of Dreams,* Spence tries to find out about the girl sitting by herself, and Rose gets orders to take her turn at the phone. Poppy can't find anything in the book about umbrellas, but Spence finds a nasty case history of a woman who dreams about a man carrying canes. Poppy doesn't like this: "Well, I didn't say I dreamed of canes, did I? Don't be trying to push her dreams off on me. Look for umbrellas—and don't be looking in those crazy people's dreams either. Look for some nice person that dreams of umbrellas."

Just then Rose reaches her man, Homer, on the phone: "Well, Sugar, I was calling you because we are kind of in a jam. Violet, Poppy, and me. That's right—the three flowers. We need money for the rent. I don't know—I guess everyone is trying to save money, what with Christmas coming and all, and they must be cutting down on the little luxuries. Oh! Homer—you say the most terrible things." Rose puts her hand over the mouthpiece and remarks: "The son of a bitch—" As Spence listens to all this phone talk, he asks apologetically: "Hey! Pardon me, are you girls prostitutes or something?" "Honey, we try to be," answers Poppy.

Spence is fascinated, and he'd like very much to ask them a lot of questions, but Violet orders Poppy and Rose to their rendezvous at Carter's drugstore. When they come back, they'll answer all his questions. "In the meantime," she suggests, "why don't you go over and talk to the little girl over there until we come back?" Rose objects to their all going for a paltry ten dollars, but Poppy knows why: "Because in union there is strength," and she leads the way out of the room.

Spence now finds the courage to approach Carol, sitting by herself at the side table. "Do you mind if I sit down?" The girl shakes her head, so Spence sits beside her. Still he's not sure. "You're sure I'm not bothering you or anything, 'cause if I am, I can get the hell up and go someplace else." Carol stiffly tells him, "These tables aren't reserved," which succeeds, as intended, in scaring him off. But then Carol relents and lets him sit with her. Spence appreciates her coolness towards him, remarking that nice girls have to be careful. Carol is surprised: "What makes you think I'm such a nice girl?" Spence is positive he can spot such things, but Carol persists: "What makes you think I'm not like Violet, Rose, and Poppy?" She herself isn't so sure—except in one or two respects. Spence is visibly relieved to find there is that much difference, promptly introduces himself, and starts in on his life history, including his right age. Carol is only half listening; her mind is really on the man at the bar who's been staring at her all night. Spence however is encouraged.

When Spence finds out Carol's name, he tells her it reminds him of a book he loved as a kid, *The Birds' Christmas Carol*. He used to cry over it regularly, until he finally gave it away to Iggy. This mention of Iggy makes Spence deliver his theory of Iggy's shyness. He asks Carol if she would like to hear it. Carol numbly answers: "I can hardly wait." "Well—it's like this," states Spence. "My theory is that everybody needs somebody else." Carol agrees. Spence is once more encouraged: "I kind of thought that you'd think so." After a pause he continues, "I need somebody, too, I guess. I know you wouldn't believe it to look at me, but you're looking at one of the most friendless persons in the whole United States." Carol faintly protests, so Spence concedes: "Well, I guess that that wasn't exactly the truth—because you see there's my gram. She's the only real pal I got left—I guess." Carol tries to show some interest, but seems restless and vague. She gets up to put money in a juke box that doesn't work.

Spence then tells her his troubles with the neighborhood white boys. When sex entered their lives, he went out of theirs. At first he thought it was his personality: "You see—I'm a real guy. I play the piano—but not enough for the boys to think I'm a sissy. I'm a little thin but I got a build that would knock you out, to be perfectly honest with you—" Carol finishes the picture for him, telling Spence that all he's been saying is an old story, which has the old ending of running away to find: "happiness—a nice girl, maybe." Spence says, "Yes, I guess that's it. But all the kids my age are interested in the broads now. So I was passing by here—saw you in the window—and decided to give it a whirl." He makes Carol laugh, but he tries to give her statistics in his favor: "Well, I'm honestly not one to boast—but it says in that book—the Kinsey report— that boys my age are usually pretty sexy. In fact they're sexier at my age than they ever will be again in their whole goddamn lives. And what with my other qualification that I told you about, I should be a pretty good boyfriend to have." "You know," says Carol, "I'd almost bet that was the truth." Spence feels he's getting somewhere in spite of his technique, and bravely offers to pass up college, so that they can get married—if things work out right between them.

Carol tells him he's a sweet kid and thanks him for the proposal. Then, as Spence admits to being queasy, she takes away his beer glass and urges him to go home to his grandmother. But that's as far as her sympathy will go. She can't be burdened with his little-boy problems when she has so many of her own—a husband who works day and night to support her and still can't manage to. Carol wants a good time for a change, and she is ready to let the man at the bar give it to her. Spence is outraged as she gets up to leave him. Her answer is to kiss the boy squarely on the mouth, and to approach the waiting figure at the bar. The man settles her check, and they leave together.

The three flowers, having been stood up by their intended victim, return empty-handed. Used to such experiences, they pull themselves together and call Spence to their table. At first he won't answer, then suddenly he gets up and asks Violet whether there's lipstick on his mouth. When Violet assures him there is, Spence revives.

Poppy—What're you doing smearing lipstick all over your mouth like that? You queer or something?

Spence—Cut the comedy. Did you see that girl over there in the corner?

Rose—You mean she kissed you?

Spence—Yeh. I guess I'm what you call a pretty fast worker, huh?

This gives Violet an idea, and she suggests that he come with her to a quiet place where they can be alone. Spence is willing, except for his headache. "Well, come on, Sugar," urges Violet. "You got enough money to buy me a sandwich or something?" "Sure," Spence tells her. "I got two dollars and thirty-nine cents." Violet winces. "That sounds like the price of something in a fire sale, doesn't it? Well, Hell—" And she follows Spence out the door.

Scene III

Violet brings Spence into her sleazy room and locks the door behind them. Spence, who had hoped to go to a restaurant, finds this decidedly unpleasant; he wants something to eat. When Violet disappears behind a curtain to get undressed, Spence pesters her till she says there are some crackers on the dresser. Spence takes them gratefully. Then he discovers her short-wave radio. Violet explains it's for police calls. "Why would anyone want the crumby police calls?" he wants to know. "For a number of reasons," she answers. But Spence continues: "What ever happens in this crumby town that would interest anybody?" Violet comes out and tells him, "Sugar— that radio is like a husband to me. Now why don't you stop worrying about the radio and take off your tie and get comfortable so we can talk." Spence balks: "I can talk with my tie on. That's never been one of my difficulties." Violet then suggests that she get a little music on the radio, which meets with more approval. She then goes back behind her curtain to get changed. Spence now rummages around for some cheese, but finds none.

Violet comes out in a bronze satin negligee, and is very critically received. Spence refuses to sit beside her on the bed, and tells her from his chair: "I should think that it would tickle the back of your neck something awful." Violet doesn't want to talk, but Spence is hungry and thoroughly unco-operative. Violet has to drag him down beside her, while he protests: "I honestly don't see how a kiss is going to do anything for my hunger." She grabs him and kisses him, and after some time Spence manages to break away, full of lame excuses. Safe again in a chair, he confesses to being afraid: "Well— to be perfectly honest with you, I guess I am kind of scared. I guess I just want to go and get my books, if you don't mind." Violet straightens him out: "Look, kid—I most certainly do mind." Spence sits down again. "Let me tell you how this mess works."

Violet—You've taken me out of circulation for roughly fifteen minutes, now—fifteen minutes in which anything could happen—and if you think you're just going to put your coat on and walk out of here—you've got another think coming. I want my two dollars and thirty-nine cents.

SPENCE—But that's all the money I have.

VIOLET—I know it's all the money you have. You think if you had more I'd be asking for two dollars and thirty-nine cents? What do you take me for anyway? It ain't that I don't understand, Sugar; it's just that business is business.

Violet won't let him deduct supper money, either. She lets him keep the crackers and that's all. But that isn't the only thing that worries him—if he returns to the bar for those books, too soon—Violet's co-workers will know that he's a "bust"! Spence begs Violet not to tell on him; she agrees if he doesn't publicize that her take for the night was two dollars and thirty-nine cents. He also gets permission to stay in her room for a little while longer, only he has to talk to her. The one thing she can't stand is silence. And she becomes indignant when Spence offers to read to her: "Do I look like an old lady to you?" Spence admits she doesn't. "Well," Violet puts him straight, "I can see to read myself, thank you very much."

Violet gives up when Spence asks for carfare to the South End: "Well, that's what I get for playing around with kids. Just reach in my bag and take a dime—and only a dime." With carfare in hand, Spence is finally about to leave, when he begins feeling sick again. But he acquires the strength to say to Violet: "I think that's one of the ugliest bathrobes I've ever seen in my life!" and departs.

SCENE IV

Later that night, Spence's father, Lem, has dozed off in his living-room armchair while lying in wait for the boy. A street noise abruptly wakes him, and he shouts upstairs to ask the time. When his wife's answer annoys him, he calls: "Well, how can you be up there asleep—when for all you know he could be dead someplace?"

MAY—If he's dead, Daddy—there's nothing we can do about it until we know. I'm not asleep.

LEM—Is that mother of yours asleep?

MAY—I don't see how she could be.

LEM—I think she knows more than she's letting on.

MAY—Well, there's a five-hundred-watt light downstairs in the pantry. Why don't you bring it up along with your rubber hose and give her the third degree?

LEM—Why don't you cut out being so smart? That's the trouble
with your whole family—they think they're smart. (*Kicks stool.*)

May tells him to go look at television or his paper. This only
causes Lem to blow up and rail against his son, calling Spence a
"bastard." With that, both of the womenfolk upstairs really let fly
at Lem. Grandma comes out of her room onto the upstairs landing
in a fighting mood, telling her son-in-law that if there are any bastards
in the family it's he who sired them. Gram demands that her daughter fire away, too; all May can get in is: "I'd speak up, Mama, if
you'd give me half a chance." Now Grandma is on the warpath:
"Calling your husband 'Daddy' all the time. If that isn't the silliest
thing I ever heard." Grandma is so furious with Spence's parents,
and so worried about the boy, that she lets slip that he's in trouble,
then pulls herself together and won't tell his worried parents another
thing. She goes up to her room, leaving Lem and May in a stew.
May wants to call the police, but Lem wants no police involvement.
Just then, Spence comes up the porch steps with his bag.

Grandma hears the door close and quickly calls to him to fetch
the eyeglasses she has dropped. But she can't save him so easily
from his parents' wrath, and she next calls down to him that she
hasn't told them a thing, adding: "If they say I have they're lying."

May realizes the boy is hungry and goes to the kitchen to fix him
something hot, leaving Spence to Lem's persistent and sarcastic questioning. Where was he? How could he have been this long at the
library? Did he think Lem didn't know when the library closed?
At Spence's "What time does the library close, Pop?" Lem in frustrated anger calls for his wife: "You'd better come in here and talk
to this little bastard before I break his neck." Grandma, listening
to every word from upstairs, calls down: "There he goes again. It's
disgraceful." May comes in and quickly gets Spence to confess he's
been drinking beer. "Well, I'll be damned," says Lem. May tries
to quiet him with: "Daddy—please." Whereupon Grandma calls
down: "Don't be calling that man 'Daddy.' He's no husband of
mine."

Although Spence refuses to tell his parents who he's been drinking
with, May lets it pass for the moment, mentions that his grandmother
spoke of his being in some kind of trouble. Spence tells her, "I—
got kicked out of school." All his father can do is be "damned"
once again. His mother wants to know what happened, but Spence
doesn't feel like telling the whole thing over again, so he gives a
quick summary of his teacher's remark about Negroes; tells how
they had both flared up in consequence; and how he had stalked

out of her room into the Men's Room where he was caught smoking a cigar. So he was hauled up before the principal and thrown out of school for a week. "And that's all there was to it," finishes Spence. His father is furious, and becomes, if possible, even more so when he finds the cigar had been taken from his own private stock.

May breaks in and flatly orders her son to go back to school and apologize to his teacher. Spence just as flatly refuses. "I suppose you can make me go up there with you—but I won't apologize to anyone." "Stop talking back to your mother," snaps his father. "I'm not talking back to her," Spence insists. "I just want her to know how I feel."

LEM—We don't care how you feel. Now, what do you think of that? You talk about what you'll do and what you won't do. We do things we don't like to do every day of our lives. I hear those crumbs at the bank talking about niggers and making jokes about niggers every day—and I stay on—because I need the job—so that you can have the things that you need. And what do you do? You get your silly little behind kicked out of school. And now you're too proud to go back.

GRANDMA—Will you listen to him running his big mouth.

MAY—Mama! (*To* SPENCE.) We've given you boys everything that you could possibly want. You've never been deprived of anything, Spence. I don't need to tell you how hard we both work, and the fact that I'm in pain now doesn't seem to make any difference to you. I have arthritis in my wrist now so badly that I can barely stand it, and it certainly doesn't help it to hear you talk like this.

SPENCE—I'm sorry that your wrist hurts, Mom.

MAY—You're not sorry at all. If you were, you'd do something about it. We've bent every effort to see that you were raised in a decent neighborhood and wouldn't have to live in the slums, because we always wanted the best for you. But now I'm not so sure we haven't made a terrible mistake—because you seem not to realize what you are. You're a little colored boy—that's what you are—and you have no business talking back to white women, no matter what they say or what they do. If you were in the South you could be lynched for that, and your father and I couldn't do anything about it. So from now on my advice to you is to try and remember your place.

SPENCE—You'll pardon me for saying so—but that's the biggest hunk of bull I've heard in my whole life.

Lem becomes increasingly angry, and when Spence upbraids his parents for the way they talk to him, Lem slaps his face and orders him upstairs. Spence agrees to go, but refuses to apologize. Grandma yells down encouragement to Spence, and after he goes to his room, she comes out of hers and gets in the fight. May forbids her to come downstairs, to which the old lady snaps: "Oh, tell him, smell him, knock him down and sell him. What do you think I care? All this slapping and going on." And down she comes.

Grandma settles herself on the sofa and tells Spence's parents all the things they should know, starting with: "Now in the first place— that nasty little hussy that's teaching history in that school deserves exactly what she got—and the only thing that I think is that Spence didn't tell her enough." May protests that he can't go around talking that way to people, but her mother asks her if she ever considered that something like this was bound to happen sooner or later, and that: "the most important thing might be just having your love and company? You did not. You kept right on working—and instead of your company, they got a book or a bicycle or an electric train. Mercy—the stuff that came in this house was ridiculous."

This time Lem protests, but Grandma wants to finish, and she does. "Well, I don't agree with that kind of raising one bit—and allow me to be the first one to tell you both. You got away with it with Mack because Mack had Spence. But do you know that that boy is absolutely alone? He hasn't a friend in the world. You didn't know, did you, that all his little pals around here have taken to the girls, and the little girls' mothers don't want their little daughters going around with a colored boy. Did you know that there was a dance up at school last week and Spence couldn't go because he didn't have anybody to take? Well, whether you know it or not, he's alone. And now you want to desert him completely by not backing him up. You moved out of a slum and taught him to think of himself as something to be respected—and now you get mad when he does the things that you made it possible for him to do. That bull—as he called it—about staying in his place. I'm ashamed of you both and I want you to know it." And Grandma finishes them off by saying they've always been much too careful. Lem wishes to help her upstairs but she insists on going herself. Behind her, Spence's parents stand demolished.

They try to blame one another. When Spence comes down at his grandmother's bidding, May disappears into the kitchen, forcing Lem to meet him alone. Lem makes a huge effort to be understanding; he's both gauche and touching as he gives advice to Spence. He reminds Spence the reason Mack hasn't been heard from is that he's busy at college, and college is where Spence is heading. "Now you go on and forget these little bastards around here. Don't pay any attention to them. You've got bigger things to think about—and if they won't play with you—you just tell them to go to hell—because you're better than any ten of them put together. All right. Now— you've got your books and you've got your music—and if there's anything you want—you just tell me about it and I'll get it for you. Understand?" And Lem gruffly tells Spence not to mind what those lousy teachers say. The main thing is to graduate and get to college. "And," he adds, "you can't afford to get your butt thrown out of school too often. You understand?" Spence says he does, so Lem with enormous relief feels he's settled everything, and tells the boy to run along and get fed by his mother. But Spence doesn't feel like eating. Lem can't help saying: "Now—that's what I'm talking about. It's silly to go around moping." But Spence can't help it, any more than Lem can help laying it on the line; and he starts upstairs.

Suddenly terrifying calls for Spence come from Grandma's room. The boy races up, followed by his parents; a moment later he hurries down to phone the doctor. May comes out at the head of the stairs as the boy is talking to the doctor, and tells him there's no hurry now. His grandmother is dead.

Spence is beside himself; he wants to go out of the house and be alone. His father tries to prevent him, and tells him he should be in bed. May tells Spence he doesn't have to leave the house to cry, he can cry in front of them. Spence starts to sob on his father's shoulder, then breaks away and runs out the door. His father sees him standing in the empty lot.

Scene V

For the past two weeks Spence has been lying in his darkened room. He has been sick, and in mourning for his grandmother. He hasn't wanted to get well: in fact, he is quite a problem to the house-keeper his mother had to hire. She climbs the stairs to Spence's room with his food and medicine, and knows he will refuse them.

The trim, good-humored Christine has no luck with her jokes and cajolery: "Spence, won't you please sit up and eat something? Any-thing? Crust of bread? You know it kills me when folks won't eat." No answer from Spence. "I never knew anybody who could pick out just the right way to worry somebody. Won't you just eat a little bit?" He still refuses. Christine puts the tray down, but doesn't give up. She tells Spence to get up and walk around while she makes his bed. He won't do that either till she splashes him with cold water. This time, Spence laughs in spite of himself and hops out of bed: "All right— All right. I'm getting up now," adding as he sits in a chair: "You make me sick."

CHRISTINE—The feeling is, oh, so mutual. (*She begins to make the bed.*) I've seen a mess of mourning in my day, but if the mourning you do don't beat anything I've ever seen yet, I don't want a nickel. But at the rate you're going, you're not going to have much longer to mourn. You're going to be joining them that you're mourning for, if you don't watch your step.

SPENCE—What do you say to my making a little bargain with you?

CHRISTINE—What is it?

SPENCE—I'll eat that slop that you brought up here if, as soon as that bed is made, you get the hell out of here and leave me alone.

CHRISTINE—There ain't no call to be rude and nasty. All I'm saying is that you look like a bag of bones, and you do.

SPENCE—I've always been skinny.

CHRISTINE—It's humanly impossible for somebody to be as skinny as you are and live. Consumption is chasing you in one direction and pneumonia is chasing you in the other—and when they meet with you in the middle, it's sure going to be a mess.

SPENCE (*in a real pet, picks up his tray, and settles down to poke at the food. He doesn't like it*)—You sure are a lousy cook; no wonder you can't keep a husband.

CHRISTINE—I'll have you know that I've only had one husband— and he died.

SPENCE—I'm not surprised.

CHRISTINE—I'm not speaking to you again today. And that's final.

SPENCE—You're not really mad, are you, Christine? (*Pause.*) Christine, I was just kidding. Aw! Come on, Christine. You know I don't really think you killed your husband.

Christine laughs at Spence and hands him a line that holds a few left-handed compliments. Her rough kindness reminds Spence of his grandmother, and the reminder stops him from eating. When Christine tells him not to go on that way—that there are doors one just keeps shut—Spence feels it's impossible. In fact, one of the things that have occurred to him is that his friends haven't come over to see him at all. He excuses their not coming the first week because of the funeral, but this past week is something else. Christine answers that she is not surprised.

Then she changes the subject by feeling the boy's forehead to see if he has fever. He seems all right, and the touch of her hand suddenly makes him want to know all about her own life down South, and her reasons for coming north. He learns about the doors in her heart that she has firmly locked: behind one is the memory of her dead husband; beyond the other the memory of a dead child.

Spence realizes that other people also have sorrows and surmount them; he apologizes for acting towards Christine the way he has. And begging her to stay with him a little longer, he embarks on a list of all the things he must do, beginning with getting well. He's full of ideas; he will cut out drinking and smoking, and do something about the guys and Gram: "I'm going to be honest with you about Gram—it's going to be hard. I miss her a hell of a lot. But she's dead, Christine. She's dead—and you can tell yourself that and you can accept it, and maybe I'm a little selfish about it, but you know that on other living soul is talking with her or having fun with her. She didn't ditch you. She died. But the guys are different, Christine. They're not dead. They're over in the lot playing baseball. They're still horsing around up in the park. I don't suppose they can really help what's happened because that's the way it is. I've said some pretty lousy things to them, Christine, and I don't want it to be that way." Spence pauses, near to tears. "God damn it— I hate being black, Christine. I hate it. I hate it. I hate the hell out of it."

Christine holds him and comforts him. He knows she understands—so much so he's able to get something else off his chest, knowing she won't tell. He wants to sleep with a girl. When, controlling her laughter, Christine asks, "Who's the lucky girl?" Spence can only say: "Aw! Christine. You know I haven't got any girl in mind. I think about it quite often, but I can't think of anybody. I suppose you think that sounds pretty horny to be thinking of it all the time?" Christine wouldn't say that.

Spence finds her not only understanding, but very interesting. He's very much interested, too, in the experience she's had. She gets him off that side of her life, only to hear about his own: "Hell, I'm practically a virgin. And you know, I was thinking when I was sick, supposing I died. Supposing I just passed out now and died. Why, I'd regret that I hadn't slept with anybody, for the rest of my life practically." Spence's talk becomes guileless, but it seems now to have an anything but innocent goal. Asking Christine to turn her back—he wouldn't like to see her laugh at him—he asks first if she likes him. Reassured on that score, he gets on with his program. He realizes liking isn't loving, but since Christine is very lonely, he has a loneliness to match hers. And what he lacks in age he makes up for in loneliness. He suggests: "So maybe—if you stayed, Christine—since things are like I said they were—we might find a little happiness together. I don't mean forever or anything like that—but could you call and say you couldn't make it?" Christine tells him he is very young, and she could be very foolish to listen to him. But he has moved her. She agrees to phone her afternoon job and try to get out of it.

SPENCE—You know where the phone is. If you can't come back, Christine, you don't need to come up and tell me. Just go. But if you can, there's a bell downstairs on the table that mother uses to call us to meals. Would you ring it—if you can?

CHRISTINE—I'll try. (*She exits, taking the tray. There is a long pause.*)

SPENCE—Why in hell is she taking so long? (*The bell rings, and he slowly goes over to the window to lower the shade.*)

SCENE VI

The next day is Saturday. May comes out of the kitchen and crosses the living room to call Spence to lunch. Spence lopes downstairs, making an elaborate basketball shot with his bunched-up sweater. He's in a fine, sassy, argumentative mood. May fusses with him because he's been sloppy about getting his school clothes ready for the tailor. Spence breezily wants to leave such chores for Chris on Monday.

MAY—Chris? Christine won't be back on Monday or any other day.

SPENCE—What are you talking about?

MAY—Christine will not be back. You're no longer ill. There's no need for Christine any longer.

SPENCE—But I thought you said—

MAY—I changed my mind. I called her and told her this morning.

SPENCE—What did you tell her?

MAY—I told her that her services were no longer needed by me. I decided that there was no need to spend that money since I could do the things myself. I've been doing them myself anyway.

And May lets Spence know that she was on to what he'd been thinking; she had eyes in her head. "Besides," May adds, "all that pampering and coddling she did with you makes me sick to my

stomach." "Will you please explain what you mean by that?"
Spence demands. May can't exactly. "I don't know. What should
I mean by that? Maybe you can tell me. Well, I've heard those
stories about maids being left alone in houses with boys before. I'm
not saying it's gone that far yet. But an ounce of prevention is
worth a pound of anybody's cure." Spence blurts out: "You know
you sure have got a dirty mind," and insists that she is dirty, too,
taking away Christine's job. And to show his indignation, he refuses
to eat the lunch May has prepared, and starts upstairs. He is going
to the tailor's with his clothes.

It's too late. May has asked his entire gang in for ice cream and
cake. Spence completely loses his temper at this. "You can call
them up and tell them to stay home. What right did you have to
do that? It's none of your business. It's my business and you stay
out of it. I'm not bribing those kids with ice cream, cake, or pink
punch. I'm never going to bribe anyone to be my friend." And he
won't stay for the party. May follows him to the front door and
tells him: "Go ahead—and see how far you get acting the way you
act. Your father's right about you. You're too proud. You think
you can go through life being proud, don't you? Well, you're wrong.
You're a little black boy—and you don't seem to understand it. But
that's what you are. You think this is bad; well, it'll be worse.
You'll serve them pink punch and ice cream—and you'll do a lot
worse. You'll smile when you feel like crying." And May begins to
cry. "You'll laugh at them when you could put knives right into
their backs without giving it a second thought—and you'll never do
what you've done and let them know that they've hurt you. They
never forgive you for that. So go on out and learn the lesson. Now
get out of here. Get out of here and don't ever come back." May
sits on the sofa, and after a moment continues: "You think it's easy
for me to tell my son to crawl when I know he can walk, and walk
well? I'm sorry I ever had children. I'm sorry you didn't die when
you were a baby. Do you hear that? I'm sorry you didn't die."
She breaks down completely.

Spence apologizes and begs her not to cry. "I'm sorry. It seems
to me that for the past two weeks all I've done is apologize to people.
I seem to be apologizing for trying to be a human being." He hasn't
time to say more, because someone of the gang is ringing the bell.
Spence quickly tells his mother that as long as the food is ready, she
needn't feel she has to stay around. May decides to do some shopping, and goes for her hat, as Tony and Gussie make their awkward
entrances. Tony finds it difficult to make his tardy condolences, and
Gussie clumsily tries to avoid telling Spence of the gang's activities

these last weeks. It is very clear that the boys have drifted apart. As May leaves, Iggy and the Reynolds boys arrive. Iggy at least helps things a little by saying to Spence: "I didn't come to see you, because I thought maybe you wouldn't want any visitors, but I kept asking your mother about you." Spence is grateful, but the strain is so great that even the ice cream and cake can only momentarily relieve it. Tony sees to that: "Hey, Iggy, will you get your ass out of my ice cream?" Iggy apologizes; Tony graciously tells him: "Nothing to be sorry about—just get out of it is all." Gussie, wanting to liven things up, tells of a wild foray the boys, including Spence, made on a grocery store a couple of Summers back. But he makes things worse by calling the proprietor of the store a "Jew bastard." After Gussie apologizes to Iggy, he starts in again on the gang's exploits, in those days when Spence was a friend and a leader.

GUSSIE (*enthusiastically*)—Those sure were the good old days. (*Pause.*) As a matter of fact we're going up to the park tonight. We're going on a hay ride. You're all better, ain't you, Spence?

SPENCE—Yes.

GUSSIE—Well, why in hell don't you come along?

TONY (*puts down his plate sharply on the table, and rises. Everyone reacts to the slip*)—You did say you were coming back to school Monday, didn't you, Spence?

SPENCE—Yes, Tony. Monday I'm coming back to school.

TONY—Well, I guess we gotta be going.

As the others follow him, he suggests that the gang call for Spence on the way to school Monday. It's now Spence's turn to draw the line: he can't go with them on Monday because his father is driving him to school, but there was a reason for this party: "You know, I've been doing a hell of a lot of fooling around and I've been neglecting my lessons, not practicing, and all manner of things like that. And if you're going to college you got to be a little more serious about things than I've been. So from now on I've got to buckle down to the old books and concentrate on the things of the mind. So I've got a little schedule made out for myself. In the morning before school I've got to practice. And in the afternoon after school I've got my homework to do. So you see I'm going to be pretty busy." Gussie tells him: "Geez, Spence. You sure do play the piano damn good. You know that? Are you going to be a musician or something?" Spence says he hasn't given it much thought; but he does let on that this was a farewell party, because he won't have much time to play around. " 'Course, it's going to be a little hard at first 'cause I'm not used to it, so all you guys could help me if you just kind of let me alone and let me get my work done." They're all pals and make very pleasant good-bys. Spence says good-by to everyone but Iggy, whom he asks to wait a minute. Then Spence says he wants to apologize for Gussie's talk. Iggy understands, and Spence thanks him for coming to his party, but also can't help asking him: "Look, I know you're busy and all that, but would you mind if I came over and looked at the old stamp collection?"

IGGY—Do you want it back, Spencer?
SPENCE—No. I don't want it back. I'd just like to see what you've added to it—that's all.
IGGY—Come over any time.

Spence clears away the party mess. May returns and is startled that no one is there, and feels something has happened. As his mother puts her bag down on the dining table, Spence assures her: "Nothing—nothing. I just told them that I didn't want to see them any more. That's all. I just said it to them before they said it to me.

MAY—You'll never learn, will you?
SPENCE—Mom, you've just got to believe that I'm trying to learn. I'm trying as hard as I know how. I might be wrong, but if I am, I think I'd like to find that out for myself.
MAY—What are you going to do?
SPENCE—I don't know, Mom. I don't know.
MAY—Spence, look at me— You're not running away, are you?
SPENCE—No, Mom. I'm not running away—and if you don't mind, Mom, let's not talk about it any more—I did the right thing. So let's just both try to forget it happened and go on to something else. Okay?

And Spence goes to the piano, then to the front door to shut out the baseball noises. As he starts to play "Praeludium," his mother tells him: "Spence—I love you very much."

THE TEAHOUSE OF THE AUGUST MOON *

A Comedy in Three Acts

By John Patrick

(Based on the novel by Vern Sneider)

[John Patrick *was born in Louisville, Ky., and educated at various Southern boarding schools and at Columbia University. His Broadway plays include "The Willow and I," "The Hasty Heart," "The Story of Mary Surratt," "The Curious Savage," and "Lo and Behold." One of his first writing jobs was providing radio scripts for Helen Hayes. He has also done considerable screen writing, having most recently adapted Irving Stone's "The President's Lady" and John Secondari's "Coins in the Fountain."*]

THE scene throughout is the island of Okinawa. A bamboo curtain, divided into four panels that can individually be raised or lowered at will, hides the stage. The bamboo, the oriental strains from stringed instruments, and the interpreter, Sakini, immediately provide the island atmosphere.

A pool of light picks up Sakini, framed against the bamboo panels. His shorts and shirt are tattered, his GI shoes are too large, and his socks hang in wrinkles over his ankles. His age is somewhere between twenty and sixty, but his smile is that of a child. He walks to the footlights, all formality and solemnity; he holds his hands in prayerlike supplication. He bows right, he bows left, then straightens up to examine the audience with great curiosity. When the music stops, Sakini's jaws start to work. He announces his choice of chewing gum is "tootie-fruitie—most generous gift of American sergeant." He then carefully removes the gum from his mouth, and as carefully wraps it in paper, puts it in a match box, and pockets the box. Then, assuming his former dignified pose, Sakini introduces himself and the play:

* Copyright 1952 by John Patrick. Courtesy of G. P. Putnam's Sons.

SAKINI—
Lovely ladies—kind gentlemen.
Please to introduce myself.
Sakini by name.
Interpreter by profession.
Education by ancient dictionary.
Okinawan by whim of gods. (*Kneels.*)
History of Okinawa reveal distinguished record of conquerors.
We have honor to be subjugated in fourteenth century by Chinese pirates.
In sixteenth century by English missionaries.
In eighteenth century by Japanese war lords.
And in twentieth century by American marines.
Okinawa very fortunate.
Culture brought to us—not have to leave home for it.
Learn many things.
Most important that rest of world not like Okinawa. . . .

Sakini then gives pointers on the differences in manners and customs between America and Okinawa, then claps his hands. In succession each bamboo panel rises; a backdrop reveals the destruction done to the island. There is also a clothesline strung from one tree stump to another, hung with the laundry of "Colonel Purdy, III." This laundry has a sign showing that it is "OFFICERS' LAUNDRY ONLY," to make sure that it isn't contaminated by "enlisted men's" laundry.

Sakini points this all out to the audience, particularly Colonel Purdy, III's specialty: the sign. When the last bamboo panel rises, it reveals the inside of a hut. This is the colonel's office, with another sign posted, admonishing visitors to "THINK!" Frozen at one of the two desks, near a bulletin board for "DAILY ORDERS," is Sergeant Gregovich. He is waiting to be introduced into the play's action. Sakini crosses down center to explain: "This gentleman honorable Sergeant Gregovich—assistant to Colonel Purdy. Not son of a son of a son. Play has begun, Sergeant."

Thus brought to life, the sergeant loudly snaps his gum, crosses to Colonel Purdy's desk, gets down on all fours, and reaches under it. Sakini explains that the sergeant is on the trail of Colonel Purdy's *Adventure Magazine.* The colonel's wife sends him this every month, and he tries to hide it from his overeager men. But as Gregovich rises in triumph Sakini informs the audience: "Sergeant always find. Smart mouse."

As the sergeant buries his head in the magazine, large, bulky

Colonel Purdy, III appears outside the office. He surveys the laundry line, then makes a note in his little black book. Sakini introduces him, although his own presence hasn't yet been acknowledged by the colonel: "This gentleman exalted boss—Colonel Purdy Three. Subject of Sovereign American city of Pottawatomie, Michigan." The colonel hiccups, taps his chest, then, hands on hips, he looks at the sky and makes his daily prediction: "It's not going to rain today." "And you know what?" Sakini adds: "Not rain. Of course, not rain here this time of year in whole history of Okinawa. But Colonel not make mistake." Purdy sets about reviewing the laundry on the line: he buttons the top button of a pair of shorts, and so draws comment from Sakini: "Colonel Purdy gentleman of propriety." Then the colonel starts counting the laundry in French. Sakini explains this, too: "Army teach Colonel French for invasion of Europe. Then send to Okinawa instead." The colonel's French figures don't lie: another pair of shorts is missing in Okinawa.

Sakini knows this is the time to hide, but he is quickly routed out, his explanation ready: "Very simple. Boy takes laundry to top of mountain stream and throws in water. Then run down hill fast as dickens to catch laundry at bottom. Sometimes not run fast enough." Colonel Purdy heaves a martyr's sigh: "No wonder you people were subjugated by the Japanese. If you're not sleeping you're running away from work. Where is your 'get-up-and-go'?" And he orders Sakini over to the mess to check on Captain Fisby's arrival and see that he reports at once.

First, however, he bellows at Sakini as a civilian employee of the United States Army to pull up his socks. Sakini obliges without noticeable improvement, leaving the frustrated colonel counting up to ten in French.

Sakini re-enters downstage, gives a signal for the bamboo panel to shut out the colonel, and orders Gregovich into action. The sergeant comes to life, quickly hides the magazine, and stands at attention for the colonel's entrance. The latter has a lot on his mind; not least, how to rid himself of Sakini. His irritation is blended with pride and pleasure over being sent a new officer straight from "Psychological Warfare"—that home of army geniuses. But the colonel is also thinking of a new sign to be made for the canteen. He has observed the men dancing together. Gregovich writes down for the sign-maker: "No Dancing Allowed." The colonel is annoyed. That's not what he meant: the sign must read, "Sergeants Are Forbidden to Dance with Privates." And Gregovich goes off to the busy sign-maker.

Sakini brings in Captain Fisby, whom the colonel greets extravagantly. Fisby, a nice, rather earnest-looking young man, immediately lets the colonel down. He confesses that his transfer has been put through because his propaganda to undermine the enemy morale had undermined Psychological Warfare's instead. Under Purdy's startled questioning, Fisby further reveals that he had arrived at that cradle of genius only because the Paymaster General's office wished to get rid of him.

PURDY—What was your duty there?

FISBY—I was in charge of the Payroll Computation machine until —until— (*He flounders unhappily.*)

PURDY—Until *what?*

FISBY—Well, sir, machines have always been my mortal enemies. I don't think they're inanimate at all. I think they're full of malice and ill will. They—

PURDY—I *asked* you what happened, Captain.

FISBY—Well, this computation machine made a mistake of a quarter of a million dollars on the payroll. Unfortunately, the men were paid before—the mistake was discovered.

PURDY—What did they do to you?

FISBY—For a while I was given a job licking envelopes.

PURDY—Then you asked for a transfer?

FISBY—No, sir—I developed an allergy to glue.

PURDY—How many outfits in this man's army have you been in, Captain?

FISBY—How many are there, sir?

PURDY—Never mind. I admit disappointment but not defeat. I'd thought you were given to me in recognition of my work here. Frankly, I expect to be made a general soon, and I want that star for my wife's crown. Naturally, that's very hush-hush.

FISBY (*nods*)—Naturally. Maybe I just wasn't cut out to be a soldier.

PURDY—Captain—none of us was cut out to be a soldier. But we do the job. We adjust. We adapt. We roll with punch and bring victory home in our teeth. Do you know what *I* was before the war?

FISBY (*hesitates unhappily*)—A football coach?

PURDY—I was the Purdy Paper Box Company of Pottawatomie. What did I know about foreigners? But my job is to teach these natives the meaning of Democracy and they're going to learn Democracy if I have to shoot every one of them.

FISBY—I'm sure your wife wouldn't want her star that way, sir.

When Purdy finds out that before the war Fisby was an associate professor of humanities, his hopes rise slightly, for the captain's job is to teach the natives of Tobiki democracy. He is to make them self-supporting by creating some sort of industry in their village. Purdy now brings forth an enormous document the size of a telephone book: "Washington has drawn up full instructions pertaining to the Welfare and Recovery of these native villages. This is Plan 'B.' Consider it your *Bible*, Captain." Fisby would like to study it carefully in case he might have some questions, but Purdy quickly quashes such an idea: "Washington has anticipated all your questions." Still Fisby can't help thinking, but that's not permitted: "You don't even have to think, Captain. This document relieves you of the responsibility." "But in dealing with the natives, sir—" Fisby persists. Purdy interrupts, "It's all covered in Section Four, 'Orienting the Oriental.' "

Fisby knows nothing of the native dialect, so Colonel Purdy finds a perfect excuse to unload Sakini on him. Fisby is grateful for an interpreter, and Sakini in his turn is delighted to return to his village, Tobiki, and goes outside to await their departure. Purdy now takes, the opportunity for some last-minute instruction.

PURDY—Well! To get back to Tobiki. Your first job when you get there will be to establish a municipal government and build a school.

FISBY—A school?

PURDY—It's all in Plan "B." I'll see that cement and lumber are sent down to you. Plan "B" calls for the schoolhouse to be pentagon shaped.

FISBY—If you say so, sir.

PURDY—When the school is built—you will organize a Women's League for Democratic Action. You will deliver a series of lectures on Democracy, as outlined in the outline. Captain, this is a chance for you to make a name for yourself.

FISBY—I will, sir. You see, I feel that I've personally delayed victory at least a year and I have to vindicate myself.

PURDY—That's the kind of talk I like to hear from my officers. Well, I won't detain you then. My only order to you is—put that village on the map.

And he asks, too, that Fisby send him bimonthly Progress Reports, imbue the natives with the Spirit of Occupation, and keep in mind: "The eyes of Washington are on our Occupation Teams. And the eyes of the world are on Washington." Fisby salutes smartly and leaves the colonel to his solemn thoughts. But a moment later, the colonel is loudly demanding: "Where in Hell is my *Adventure Magazine.*"

Scene II

A few minutes later, Captain Fisby and Sakini are crossing in front of the bamboo curtain on their way to the jeep. Fisby bids Sakini wish him luck, which Sakini deems totally unnecessary: "You already lucky, boss—you got me." Fisby inquires about the road to Tobiki —whether a jeep will make it.

Sakini—We find out, boss.
Fisby—Naturally. How long will it take us?
Sakini—Oh, not know until we arrive, boss.

Fisby finds this natural, too.

When Sakini claps his hands, the panels rise to disclose a jeep piled to the sky with bundles, with at the very peak of the pyramid— an ancient, wrinkled Okinawan woman. She is tied on for the ride to Tobiki, and proves to the indignant Fisby that she is the most aloof hitchhiker imaginable. Sakini advises against her being taken off the jeep: "Her grandson mayor of Tobiki village. You make him lose face if you kick old grandmother off jeep." Fisby sees the point: "Well, tell her to yell out if she sees any low branches coming. Let's get started." But that is not so easy. The old lady's daughter wheels up her belongings in a wheelbarrow, intending to come along. And that's not all—she goes back after her children. Fisby is getting desperate: "Come here, Sakini. Now look—this sort of thing is always happening to me and I have to put a stop to it some place. This time I'm determined to succeed. It's not that I don't want to take them. But you can see for yourself *there's no room left for kids!*" Sakini is reasonable: "But daughter not go without children and old lady not go without daughter. And if old lady not go— mayor of Tobiki be mad at you."

The daughter hurries back with three polite children, whom she piles on the hood of the jeep. Fisby can't figure out how he'll see to drive. Sakini says they'll use the high-seated old woman as lookout. Even so, the jeep still can't start—now one of the children dashes off it. The mother contentedly climbing to the top of the pyramid, explains in Luchuan that the child has gone back for his goat. This for Fisby is the end. It's not that *he* doesn't like goats, but he's

sure the colonel wouldn't. Sakini reminds him of the mayor of Tobiki, so the goat is installed beside the children on the hood. Fisby
yells out: "We've got to get started or we'll never get off the ground."
Sakini for once agrees: "All ready to go, boss. You get in now.
Nobody else going." But now a very old, unidentified man insists
on riding on the back of the jeep. Sakini interprets: "He say why
you not take him—you take goat. He say maybe you think he not
as good as goat? Fisby pleads that the eyes of Washington are on
him, only to find that the eyes of Colonel Purdy are on him also:
"Captain Fisby!"

FISBY—Yes, sir.
PURDY—What in the name of Occupation do you think you're
doing?
FISBY—It's hard to explain, sir—I—ah— (*As he founders, the*
OLD LADY *on top of the jeep comes to life.*)
OLD LADY (*looks down and screams shrilly*)—Yakamashii oyaji-
jana, hayo *iko, iko!*
PURDY—What is *she* saying?
SAKINI—She say—tell fat old man to shut up so we can get
started!

SCENE III

Ten days later, Sakini tells about the trip to Tobiki. It should
have taken no time at all, but the children wanted to see the ocean,
their mother wanted to visit in Awasi. Each time he asked to be
taken to Tobiki, Captain Fisby was voted down. The old man even
got to see a cousin in Yatoda. And so it went: "Damn fool old lady
not know one road from another. Now we arrive in Tobiki. Tobiki
welcome rice and Democracy."
Sakini signals the panels to rise, and Tobiki village, its huts sag-
ging, its villagers ragged—appears in all its dejection. The natives
are assembled in the square outside Captain Fisby's office. The captain is inside, concentrating on Plan "B." His office is very make-
shift, merely a desk with field telephone, and a cot.
Fisby wants to be sure that Sakini will make clear to the village
that he has come as a "friend of the people," that the U. S. Army
means to lift " 'the yoke of oppression' from their shoulders." Sakini
is delighted: "Oh, they like that, boss—this their favorite speech,"
and explains that the Japanese said just that and took everything.
Fisby righteously corrects him: "Well—we're not here to *take* anything." Sakini smiles: "They got nothing left to take away, boss."

Still annoyed, Fisby explains that the Americans are here to give them something. "Oh—not get angry, boss," Sakini placates him. "We not mind. After eight centuries—we get used to it. When friends come now—we hide things quick as the dickens."

Fisby is persuaded, as he goes out to speak, to wait first for the presentation of the natives' gifts. Otherwise, "You make them lose face if you refuse, boss. They not accept Democracy from you."

The procession of gift-bringers begins. First Mr. Hokaida, in tattered clothing, comes forth, cricketless, with a "cricket cage." Sakini explains, "Bad luck to give cricket. You must catch your own fortune. No one can get it for you." Fisby voices appropriate thanks. Next, a very ancient native, Mr. Omura, offers him chopsticks. Then handsome Mr. Seiko presents a pair of wooden sandals. By now Fisby is warming up: "I shall walk in the—the cool—meadow—of— of pleasant memories. . . ." Sakini's translation makes them all beam. Even the homely, aggressive woman who follows with her present of eggs is pleased with Fisby's style. After he graciously accepts a few more gifts Sakini compliments him, but Fisby modestly dismisses this with: "It's all in getting the hang of it."

Then after old Mr. Oshira gives Fisby a fine lacquered cup, Fisby, to his astonishment, finds his thanks acknowledged in English. Mr. Oshira had, it seems, worked in Manila in President McKinley's day; indicating the cup, he wishes: "May August moon fill your cup."

FISBY—May I ask—why an August moon?

OSHIRA—All moons good, but August moon little older—little wiser.

FISBY—Did Sakini say you made this cup yourself?

OSHIRA—Oh, yes. I learned from my father before me who learned from his father before him. It is our heritage.

Fisby is inspired to visualize a whole industry of this lost art. Mr. Oshira points out rather sadly: "I take pride in painting one cup at time, Captain. How can I take pride in work of machine?" Although momentarily deflated, Fisby is determined to put Tobiki in the souvenir business. He is sure that if they make enough sandals and cricket cages, he can guarantee the village's recovery.

Now it's his government's turn, so Fisby, following Plan "B"'s advice, directly asks the villagers: "Do you want to be ignorant?"

SAKINI—They say "yes."

FISBY—What do you mean, "yes"? They *want* to be ignorant?

SAKINI—No, boss. But in Luchuan, "yes" means "no." They say "yes" they *not* want to be ignorant.

And to Fisby's question do they want their children to be ignorant, Sakini confuses him further: "They say 'no.' " Fisby puzzles: " 'No' they do or 'no' they don't?" Sakini simply says, "Yes, they not want no ignorant children."

Fisby tells them about the rice stations and the pentagon-shaped schoolhouse where everyone will learn about democracy.

SAKINI—They say—explain what is Democracy. They *know* what rice is.

FISBY—Oh. (*Scratches his head.*) Well—it's a system of self-determination. It's—it's the right to make the wrong choice.

SAKINI—Machigattemo iindayo. (Well, you can make mistakes.) (*They look up blankly—silently.*)

FISBY—I don't think we're getting the point over. Explain that if I don't like the way Uncle Sam treats me—I can write the President himself and tell him so.

At this incredulous point, what they really want to know, according to Sakini, is: "Do you *send* the letters?"

Fisby proceeds to the organization of the village and, following Sakini's advice, keeping the present mayor, Mr. Omura—because he has the only white coat in the village. Sakini's other advice, which Fisby refuses to take: "You just look over gifts and see who gave you best gift. Then you give him best job." Fisby nobly says this is not the democratic way, and has the villagers themselves choose their men for office. As Chief of Agriculture the ladies pick Mr. Seiko who paints wheat stalks so prettily. Fisby comments: "Drawing pictures of wheat doesn't make him a wheat expert." "Wheat not grow here anyhow," Sakini explains. "Only sweet potatoes." Fisby promises official helmets to Seiko and to Mr. Hokaida, the new Chief of Police. "Now for the ladies," Fisby continues. "We intend to organize a Ladies League for Democratic Action. We'll want to elect a League President." The Okinawan ladies unhesitatingly choose Miss Higa Jiga, who seems a natural for the office. She too demands, and gets, a helmet. Now Fisby announces a question period. "They say," Sakini interprets, "they like to know what time is it?" Fisby looks at his watch and replies, "Quarter of five—why?" "They say," Sakini goes on, "they got to hurry then. They not like to miss sunset. This is time of day they sit around in pine grove, sip tea, and watch sun go down." They're given leave to depart, and Fisby retires to his office for further study of Plan "B," but not for long.

Mr. Sumata now arrives with his gift—a lovely Geisha girl dressed in traditional costume. Mr. Sumata shoos away Mr. Seiko who is hot on her trail, then quickly leaves the Geisha with Sakini and disappears, Sakini brings this "souvenir" in to Fisby, who refuses to believe in—or accept—such a present. He only wants to get rid of her. Sakini would be delighted to house her with his grandpapa and himself, but Fisby won't allow that. Fisby is accordingly stuck with her—Mr. Sumata has rushed off to visit his cousins in the mountains, not at all to the girl's annoyance. She—her name is Lotus Blossom —wants to help Fisby into his sandals and kimono. Sakini tells him, "She trained to please you, boss." "I know what she's trained to do," snaps Fisby. "And I don't need any translation." He sits at his desk, ordering Sakini to clear out the supply shack for Lotus Blossom. "We'll set her up there where I can keep an eye on her." Sakini charges him with: "Not very democratic, boss. You make her lose face if she not make you comfortable, boss. She think she bad Geisha girl." Fisby angrily retorts: "You tell her I've got some face to save, too—so she can just forget this Oriental hanky-panky."

Lotus Blossom then takes charge, ordering Sakini home to his grandpapa. Sakini departs, and as Fisby uncomfortably eyes Lotus Blossom, there is a short blackout.

At this point, the middle bamboo panels are lowered, and the far panel is raised to show Colonel Purdy at his phone. He is having a difficult time getting through to Fisby, while Fisby is shown having an even more difficult time warding off Lotus Blossom's attentions. When he hears Purdy's voice on the phone, he is beside himself with guilt, hiding the Geisha behind his back. Then, what with Purdy's solicitous offers, and Lotus Blossom's oversolicitous movements, things get thoroughly confused on the phone. Purdy asks how Fisby is getting along with the natives, and Fisby—trying to yank his feet away from Lotus Blossom—states the problem: "It seems to be a question of who's going to lose face." Purdy understands: "As Mrs. Purdy says, East is East and West is West and there can be no Twain. But you're making progress?" Lotus Blossom is making the progress, and starts unbuttoning Fisby's jacket. Purdy asks him to send his Progress Report when things get moving. At Fisby's end they're moving at such a clip that he's just about ready to give up. Purdy calls, "Hello? Hello, Fisby—you're getting weak—" and Fisby, looking at the phone, nods in complete agreement. The side panel scenes black out, and Sakini comes forth to announce an intermission.

ACT II

It is a few days later, and the village, Sakini announces, has been turned topsy-turvy by Lotus Blossom. The town chiefs are waiting on her hand and foot, with even old Mr. Oshira competing for her favor. Although the building materials for the school have arrived, nobody is in a mood for work. The town carpenter, Mr. Sumata, has gone away. Fisby thinks his disappearance "fishy." And to all Fisby's troubles, Miss Higa Jiga and her angry followers are about to add another. Sakini tells him they have arrived to protest: "Miss Higa Jiga say do you know what we got in this village, boss? Discrimination."

Miss Higa Jiga rattles away, and Sakini translates: "She say that Ladies League for Democratic Action wait in line for rice rations. Along come Lotus Blossom and ration clerks say, 'Oh, how do you do? Oh, please don't stand in line. You come inside and have a cup of tea.' Then clerks shut up warehouse and leave Ladies League waiting in sun two hours."

FISBY (*pounding his fist*)—It's things like this that undermine the democratic ideal. You tell Miss Higa Jiga I intend to do something about it.

SAKINI—Nantoko shimasuyo. (He'll take measures.) (THE LADIES LEAGUE *wait outside*.)

FISBY—I can see right now we're going to have to get rid of the disrupting factor in our recovery. (*He picks up the field telephone and twists the handle*.) Get me Major McEvoy at Awasi.

SAKINI—What are you going to do, boss?

FISBY—This village isn't big enough for Plan "B" and a Geisha girl.

SAKINI—Oh, boss, Tobiki never have Geisha girl before. We like very much.

FISBY—She has to go. (*Then into telephone*.) Major McEvoy? Captain Fisby at Tobiki. I have a request from one of my people to transfer to your village. Yes—it's a female citizen. Profession? Well— (*He looks at* SAKINI.)

SAKINI—Oh, please not send her away, boss. Not democratic.

FISBY—As a matter of fact her name *is* Lotus Blossom. How did *you* know? What do you mean what am I trying to put over on you? Oh—you did? (*He hangs up angrily and glares at* SAKINI.)

Sakini very innocently asks: "He knows Lotus Blossom, boss?" Fisby angrily tells him: "Very well. She was at Awasi and damn near wrecked his whole plan for recovery. She's been booted out of every village by every commander on the island." "Oh, poor little Lotus Blossom," sympathizes Sakini. Fisby feels no sympathy: "Poor little Lotus Blossom, my eye! She upsets every village she's in."

The carpenter's disappearance into the mountains now makes sense: Major McEvoy has paid him a hundred yen to get rid of Lotus Blossom. Although Sakini is cheered at being stuck with her, Fisby is determined she shall cause no further trouble. But trouble looms in the person of Miss Higa Jiga. She storms in; Sakini tells what's on her mind: "She say she waiting for some democratic action. She say if she don't get it—she thinks she write this Uncle Sam you talk about." Fisby, to head off complaints to headquarters, promises an end to discrimination. Sakini tells him: "Miss Higa Jiga say please not eliminate discrimination. She say—just give *her* some, too." She demands equal footing with Lotus Blossom. Furthermore: "She can't be equal unless she has everything Lotus Blossom has." Fisby retorts: "What Lotus Blossom's got—the government doesn't issue." But Miss Higa Jiga thinks differently, and demands for her Ladies League lipstick and perfume. Fisby finally gives in, promising shaving powder and toilet water from the PX. And possibly bobby pins. But Miss Higa Jiga's demands continue. In her Ladies League's behalf she requests that Lotus Blossom shall teach all the ladies to be Geisha girls. Fisby jumps with horror: "Teach the innocent women of this village to be— No!" This causes Miss Higa Jiga to report back to her girls that Fisby's "No" may mean "Yes."

The cause of all this fuss steps daintily across the square, followed and then overtaken by young Seiko. He passionately presses his suit, but his words only appear to bore Lotus Blossom. She indifferently accepts a flower from him; when he turns tragic, she merely turns haughty and dismisses him. The rejected suitor goes back to his potato fields, while Lotus Blossom continues her untroubled way to Fisby's office. There she is greeted warmly by Sakini, and edgily by Fisby, to whom she presents Seiko's chrysanthemum.

SAKINI—Oh-oh, boss—you know what she give you?
FISBY—The works.
SAKINI—When lady give gentleman chrysanthemum bud—in Okinawa—that mean her heart is ready to unfold.
FISBY—Well—this is one bud that's not going to flower.
LOTUS BLOSSOM (*offering a box she has brought*)—Kore otsuke-mono yo. Dozo.

SAKINI—She say—you like eat some tsukemono?   Tsukemono
nice thing to eat between meals.

FISBY—No.

LOTUS BLOSSOM (*takes sandals and kneels beside him*)—Dozo
ohaki osobase. (Please put these on.)

FISBY—Tell her to *leave my feet* alone.

LOTUS BLOSSOM—Kasa kaburu. Nisshabyo nanoyo. (Ah, maybe
sunstroke, no?)

SAKINI—She worried about you, boss. She say, when you go in
hot sun—should wear "kasa"—that straw hat—on head.

FISBY—Tell her never mind about my feet or my head. I want
her to stop interfering with the recovery program. To stop causing
rebellion and making the men ah—ah—discontented.

Lotus Blossom merely smiles at this, and wishes to make tea and
sing for him. Fisby throws himself on his cot. Lotus Blossom as
a proper Geisha girl offers to listen to his troubles. She tells Sakini
that Fisby is the best boss she has ever had; he doesn't hire her out
and keep her earnings. This bounces Fisby right off the cot, and
he makes plain he has no intention of putting her to work. "Why
not, boss?" Sakini wants to know. "She pay all her dues to Geisha
Guild. She member in good standing." "Obviously," Fisby answers,
"there is a fundamental difference between us that can't be reconciled. I don't say that where I come from—there's no such thing as
prostitution. But, by God—we don't have unions, set rates, and
collect dues!" Sakini insists Fisby is wrong about Geisha girls.
They aren't prostitutes, though he's hard put to explain the "fundamental difference." "Poor man like to feel rich. Rich man like to
feel wise. Sad man like to feel happy. All go to Geisha house and
tell troubles to Geisha girl. She listen politely and say—'Oh, that's
too bad.' She very pretty—she make tea—she sing—she dance,
and pretty soon troubles go away. Is not worth something, boss?"

FISBY—And that's *all* they do?

SAKINI—Very ancient and honorable profession.

FISBY—Look—Sakini—I apologize. I guess I jumped the gun.
And I'm glad you explained. It sort of puts a new light on things.
(*Turns to* LOTUS BLOSSOM *and grins.*)

SAKINI—She say—why are you smiling at her all of a sudden.
You mad or something?

FISBY—Tell her that I'm a dope. That I have a coconut for a
head.

SAKINI—No use, boss—she not believe.

FISBY—Then will you ask her if she'd be kind enough to give Geisha lessons to the Ladies League for Democratic Action?

When this has been agreed to, Fisby has to make an even larger decision. The men of the village assemble outside. They have decided in a democratic fashion—by majority vote—that Tobiki should have a Cha Ya—a real teahouse. Fisby tries to explain that he has no authority for such a thing, that a schoolhouse should satisfy them. Sakini explains: "But majority too old to go to school—they want teahouse." And Lotus Blossom has Sakini add: "Lotus Blossom say—teahouse in Tobiki make recovery program work. Everybody make geta and cricket cages like crazy so they can spend money in a teahouse."

Fisby fights a last-ditch stand against their using the schoolhouse materials for a teahouse, but old Mr. Oshira finishes him off. "There are lovely teahouses in the big cities. But the men of Tobiki have never been inside them. We are too poor and our clothes are too ragged. All of my life I have dreamed of visiting a teahouse where paper lanterns cast a light in the lotus pond and bamboo bells hanging in the pines tinkle as the breezes brush them. But this picture is only in my heart—I may never see it. I am an old man, sir. I shall die soon. It is evil for the soul to depart this world laden with envy or regret. Give us our teahouse, sir. Free my soul for death."

FISBY (*unhappily*)—But—but we haven't got any carpenters.

SAKINI—Oi! daiku-san! daiku-san! (Here carpenters.) (MR. SUMATA *and his* FATHER *come trotting across the stage carrying their tool boxes.*)

FISBY (*knows he is beaten*)—I guess Uncle Sam is going into the teahouse business.

SCENE II

A few weeks later. Colonel Purdy is at his desk, unable to make heads or tails of Fisby's report. He puts through a call to Tobiki.

When the Tobiki panel rises, Fisby is shown taking it easy, feet on desk, while Lotus Blossom fans him. He is dressed in his version of a "kimono"—his old bathrobe. When he answers the irate colonel's ring, it is clear that Tobiki has had its way with him. His speech is studded with Luchuan words, his ideas are pure Okinawan. Purdy explodes as he listens to Fisby's industrial plans. "What

kind of cages did you say?" Fisby explains: "Cricket. Like in
cricket on the hearth. I think we'll find a great market for them.
Of course, we don't supply the crickets." Purdy momentarily hu-
mors him, then hangs up, and asks Gregovich for the name of the
nearest army psychiatrist: "My man at Tobiki has gone completely
off his rocker."

Scene III

A few more days have passed. Now the army psychiatrist, Captain McLean, is making a quick, furtive inspection of Fisby's office,
noting his discoveries in his little black notebook. Fisby's entrance,
in his ersatz kimono, sandals, and straw hat, startles Captain Mc-
Lean. Fisby remains totally unembarassed.

Captain McLean is amazed that the building going up nearby is
Fisby's Cha Ya. Fisby further enlightens him: "Well—it just so
happens, Captain—that I own a Geisha girl—that might sound
strange to you, but you get used to these things after a while. And
if you have a Geisha—you've got to have a Cha Ya." And under
McLean's questioning, Fisby admits to extraordinary happiness and
well-being. He began feeling this way the minute he decided not to
please Colonel Purdy with a pentagon-shaped schoolhouse, but to
please the village with a Cha Ya. Does this sound crazy to McLean?
"Well—yes and no."

Fisby tries to convince McLean of the sensibleness and industry
of these wonderful people. He doesn't get anywhere until suddenly,
talking of his agriculture plans for Tobiki, he says:

Fisby—Next thing I'm going to do for them is find out if this
land here will grow anything besides sweet potatoes. I'm going to
send for fertilizers and DDT—and—
McLean (*leaps to his feet*)—Chemicals!
Fisby—Sure—why not?
McLean—Do you want to poison these people?
Fisby—No, but—
McLean—You've touched on a subject that is very close to me.
For years I've planned to retire and buy a farm—raise specialties
for big restaurants. So let me tell you this—chemicals will kill all
your earthworms, and earthworms aereate your soil.
Fisby—They do?
McLean—Do you know an earthworm leaves castings eight times
its own weight every day?
Fisby—That much!

McLean—Organic gardening is the only thing. Nature's way—compost—manure—but no chemicals.

Once the psychiatrist is allowed to indulge his own mania, he is easily persuaded to stay on at Tobiki to supervise its agricultural program.

McLean at once settles down to compile his extravagantly large list of seeds. Fisby, promising to have the airforce fly them in from the States, leaves McLean happily occupied.

When Colonel Purdy telephones Tobiki, McLean hardly bothers to answer. When he does, he gives Purdy no information, confidential or otherwise. Purdy says: "I was anxious to hear your report on you-know-who." By now McLean is so preoccupied he doesn't know "who." But he does tell Purdy he'll have to stay on in Tobiki for several weeks. A moment later he gives the show away:

McLean—I've lost faith in chemicals. You kill all your worms. I can tell you, when you kill a worm, Colonel—you're killing a friend. (*Pause.*) Hello—hello.

Purdy (*not even listening, he hangs up. To* Gregovich)—Where is Plan "B"!

Gregovich—What did you want, sir?

Purdy—I want to see who I send to analyze an analyst.

Scene IV

A few weeks later, dejected villagers, loaded down with their handmade wares, are gathering in the square outside Fisby's office. Sakini explains to a furious Fisby that after all their work and all their walking to military bases, no one in the village has been able to sell a thing. Fisby in his anger over his countrymen's denseness would like to buy up everything in sight. A sympathetic, bathrobed McLean joins him and asks: "What are you going to do?" The villagers decide to go home: "They say—tell you—not your fault no one wants to buy, boss. They say guess they go home now and get drunk."

Fisby—Tell them I don't blame them. If I had anything to drink —I'd do the same. (*As they start to file out, both* McLean *and* Fisby *have a delayed reaction. They leap to their feet together.*) Wait a minute! (The Villagers *stop.*) What are they going to get drunk *on?*

Sakini (*casually*)—They got nothing but brandy.

McLean—Nothing but *brandy!*

Fisby—How do they manage to get brandy?

Sakini—We make very fine brandy here, from sweet potatoes. Been making for generations.

Fisby—You make brandy *yourselves?*

Sakini orders Hokaida to get some for Fisby, who is suddenly very sure of the future: "Sakini, if this stuff is any good at all, we're in business. This is one thing I *know* our men will buy." Sakini protests that this has been used only for ceremonies in the past. McLean takes a generally dim view of it; it may be so bad that even the troops won't drink it.

Hokaida brings an earthenware jug to Fisby, who gets a wallop from just sniffing it. It turns out the brandy was made only last week, by the village's secret formula. Both Fisby and McLean decline the honor of the first swig. Fisby timidly inquires: "Has anyone ever gone blind or died from this?" McLean answers: "He said they make it for funerals." Sakini protests: "Oh, no—boss. We not blind. We not dead." But McLean feels they simply worked up an immunity. Fisby is loathe to kill off his countrymen, and would like some sort of test made. A goat's bleat suggests the answer, and Sakini is instructed to bring forth Miss Higa Jiga's goat, Lady Astor, to serve as guinea pig.

Lady Astor happily laps up the brandy with no ill effects. Encouraged, Fisby and McLean do likewise, after which Fisby makes a joyous beeline for his office, announcing: "I am about to form the Co-operative Brewing Company of Tobiki." He grabs the phone to call the Officers' Club at Awasi. "Hello—Officers' Club, Awasi? This is Captain Fisby at Tobiki. Oh, hello, Major—how are you? Major—when I was with your unit—you could never keep a supply of liquor in the club, and I stumbled onto something and wondered if you'd be interested. Tobiki, as you know, is in the heart of the brandy industry and—

Fisby (*takes the phone away from his ear*)—Yes—brandy. (*Turns to* McLean.) Doc—look up the word "sweet potato" and see if it has another, fancier name. (*Turns to phone.*) Yes—I'm here— Yes—I could get you some if you could pay their price and would keep the source secret. Oh, yes—it's been made here for generations. Why, you never tasted anything like it!

McLean—The Haitian word for sweet potato is Batata. (*He spells it out.*)

FISBY (*into the phone*)—You've heard of Seven Star Batata, haven't you? Well—Tobiki is where it's made. (*Turns to Mc-Lean.*) The Seven Star did it.

SAKINI—Brandy much better if eight or ten days old, boss.

FISBY—We also have Eight Star and Ten Star. It sells for— (*Looks at* SAKINI *desperately.* SAKINI *holds up ten fingers.*) A hundred occupation yen a gallon.

SAKINI—I mean *ten* yen, boss.

FISBY—Delivered. All right—we'll send up five gallons in about a week. It'll be delivered by our Department of Agriculture. You're welcome. (*Hangs up and turns to* SAKINI.) Sakini—if every family in Tobiki starts making brandy—how much can we turn out in a week?

SAKINI—Oh, maybe—forty—fifty gallons.

Fisby tells him to aim rather at eighty, and then calls the Officers' Club at the Naval Base. After negotiating their excited order, Fisby knows prosperity has come to Tobiki. When the phone begins to ring, Fisby realizes that word gets around fast, and as he tells the villagers, "Get to work, boys!" and they start to go, he calls, "Wait!" They freeze. He reaches into a corner of his office with cupped hands and calls out triumphantly: "I got my cricket!"

ACT III

Sakini comes before the bamboo curtain to announce: "Ability of Americans for mass production equaled only by American capacity for consumption—" Apparently prosperity is indeed smiling on Tobiki. It is now a village of beautiful houses, but the "loveliest of all is Teahouse of August Moon."

Sakini gives the signal for the curtain to rise, and as stringed instruments play soft music the panels rise to reveal an exquisite teahouse. Small bells tinkle from its pagoda roof, soft lights glow through the colored paper panels, dwarf pines edge the walk leading to a small, curved bridge, and over all hangs the full August moon. Lotus Blossom, as she prepares for her guests, is seen silhouetted for a moment against the paper panels, then crosses to light the lanterns. The ladies arrive in their silk kimonos, and the men in their spotless white suits. They remove their shoes and rinse their fingers in a ceremonial bamboo basin before entering the teahouse.

The last guests are Sakini in his new white suit and Fisby and McLean in their bathrobes and sandals. The Americans are delighted and impressed with what has been accomplished.

Lotus Blossom comes forth to greet them and to wish Captain

Fisby her version of "happy birthday," which comes out as "Hoppee." She presents him with a chrysanthemum and points out the mats they are to sit on, while she dances in Fisby's honor.

She performs a traditional dance, full of grace and delicacy. She finishes in front of a much moved Fisby, who rises, bows, and tells her: "What a lovely thing you are!" and returns the chrysanthemum with a flourish. Lotus Blossom accepts this lighthearted gesture seriously, hiding her face in her hands as she seats herself. McLean comments: "She can dance in my Cha Ya any day." Lotus Blossom has next scheduled a wrestling match for their entertainment. It is between Hokaida, Chief of Police, and young Mr. Seiko. This, according to Sakini, is in the nature of a grudge fight. Whoever wins will be allowed to haul Lotus Blossom's sweet potatoes. The wrestling bout, too, is conducted in traditional fashion. Lotus Blossom decorates the ringside posts in symbolic colors, and asks Fisby to start the match by holding a fan over his face, then quickly whipping it away. When, eventually, Hokaida is thrown out of the ring by Seiko, Fisby is startled at Hokaida being declared the winner: "How could he be the winner? He was thrown out of the ring." Sakini concedes: "Maybe so—but judges all cousins of Mr. Hokaida." "But the judges are wrong," Fisby flatly answers. Then Sakini confidentially clears things up for him: "We know who really win—but this way, nobody lose face."

Lotus Blossom now says that the guests wish Fisby and McLean to perform. They are requested to sing. Since their repertory is very limited, they decide to have some fun and they say they will sing "Deep in the Heart of Texas." Fisby, with Sakini's help, instructs the villagers to join in with clapping and singing every time he and McLean get to the chorus. This appeals to everybody, and they all join in lustily.

The sound becomes so great that when Colonel Purdy and Sergeant Gregovich appear, no one pays the slightest attention. Purdy's roar of: "*Captain Fisby!* What in the name of Occupation is going on here?" brings Fisby back to earth with a gasp. He becomes conscious of his bathrobe dress and protruding bare legs, and desperately tries to cover them. As for McLean, he is so panic-stricken he tries to hide behind the villagers, who in turn are so alarmed they try to scatter in all directions. In the midst of this bedlam, the panels are lowered.

Scene II

It looks pretty black for Fisby. Colonel Purdy has taken over his office to conduct a one-man inquiry into the lack of accomplishment at Tobiki these last two months. Hard as he tries to find something that has been done according to army regulations, nothing comes to light. It is clear that Fisby has completely failed the colonel and Plan "B." As for McLean and his worry over his seedlings, he gets his orders from the colonel: "Captain—you will pack your gear and transplant yourself to your unit at once." Purdy wants to be fair, but his temper is barely under control, and when he hears that even the schoolhouse hasn't been built, but a teahouse in place of it, he explodes: "What in the name of Occupation do you mean by saying you built a *teahouse* instead of a *schoolhouse!*"

FISBY—It's a little hard to explain, sir. Everybody in the village wanted one—and Lotus Blossom needed it for her work.

PURDY—And just what is your relationship with this woman?

FISBY—Well—she was a present—so to speak. She's a Geisha girl—after a fashion.

PURDY—You built this teahouse—this place for her to ply her trade—with lumber belonging to the Army of Occupation of the United States Government?

FISBY—Well, it just seemed like lumber at the time.

PURDY—Fisby—are you operating a house of prostitution here on Government rice?

FISBY—No, sir! Geishas aren't what you think.

PURDY—Don't tell me what to think. Army Intelligence warned me I'd find something mighty peculiar going on in Tobiki.

FISBY—What's Army Intelligence got to do with it, sir?

PURDY—You're not very cunning, Fisby. With all the Occupation money on the island finding its way to this village—did you think it wouldn't come to the attention of Intelligence?

And when Purdy finds out that all the women of the village have been taking Geisha lessons, he's not surprised. This war has shown him how degenerate the human race is. He thanks God that his own country is pure; and when Fisby retorts that his teahouse is pure enough for Purdy's mother, Purdy turns apoplectic.

Fisby now has to explain why all the Occupation money comes to Tobiki. He hems and haws at first about cricket cages and the like, but doesn't convince Purdy for a moment. Unhappily, just at this point, the phone rings. Purdy insists on answering and comes up with an order for brandy.

PURDY—Hello? *What* do you want? Who is this? Well, Commander Myers, I think you have the wrong connection. This is not

a brewery. Yes—yes—yes! (*Turns to look at* FISBY.) Oh—I see.
I see. I see.

FISBY—It was the only thing we could make that anyone wanted
to buy, sir.

PURDY—Brandy! (*Sadly.*) I don't know which is worse. Putting your country in the white slave trade or the wholesale liquor
business. Congress will have to decide.

FISBY—We've got the most prosperous village on the island, sir.

PURDY—This ends my Army career. I promised Mrs. Purdy I'd
come out a general. You've broken a fine woman's heart, Fisby.

If the overzealous Purdy hadn't requested a Washington investigation of Tobiki, the two of them might have kept matters to themselves, but now it's too late. Purdy puts Fisby under technical arrest; calls in Sergeant Gregovich to see that every still in town is
smashed to bits. The protesting sergeant must also lead out a wreck-
ing detail and rip up the teahouse. As Gregovich sets forth, Fisby
collapses into his chair.

Scene III

It is a few hours later. Sakini comes before the curtain and
flinches at the sound of destruction going on. He can only manage:
"Oh—no comment."

The panels all rise simultaneously to a view of desolation. Nothing remains of the teahouse except the frame. The panels and roof
are gone.

Fisby finds Lotus Blossom collecting her possessions among the
ruins. She tries to go through the ceremony of pouring him an imaginary cup of tea, but is overcome, and covers her face with her hands
while Fisby sits helplessly watching her.

Sakini, coming upon them, announces that Fisby's jeep is loaded
and waiting, and adds consolingly, "Oh—pretty soon have nice
schoolhouse here." Fisby asks what he can do for Lotus Blossom
before he leaves. Sakini tells him: "Oh, that crazy Lotus Blossom—
she want you to marry her."

FISBY—Why should she want to marry me?

SAKINI—She think you nicest man she ever see, boss.

FISBY—Tell her that I am clumsy—that I seem to have a gift for
destruction. That I'd disillusion her as I have disillusioned her
people.

She still says she would like to go to America—in fact, she has never seen an American she did not like. Fisby unhappily points out: "Some of them wouldn't like her, Sakini. In the small town where I live—there'd be some who would make her unhappy." Neither Sakini nor Lotus Blossom believes him, and as she takes Fisby's hand, Sakini interprets her feelings: "She say not believe that. In America everybody love everybody. Everybody help everybody—that's Democracy."

FISBY—No. That's faith. Explain to her that Democracy is only a method—an ideal system for people to get together. But that unfortunately—the people who get together—are not always ideal.

SAKINI—That's very hard to explain, boss. She girl in love. She just want to hear pretty things.

FISBY—Then tell her that I love what she is—and that it would be wrong to change that. To impose my way of life on her.

SAKINI—Tassha dene!   (Stay in good health.)

FISBY—Tell her that I shall never forget her. Nor this village. Tell her that in the autumn of my life—on the other side of the world—when an August moon rises from the East—I will remember what was beautiful in my youth—and what I was wise enough to leave beautiful.

Lotus Blossom, after remaining silent for a moment, says she too will never forget. "She say," continues Sakini for her, "she guess maybe she be what she is—first-class Geisha girl. She want you to know she make up song-story about you to sing in teahouse. And maybe hundred years from now—you be famous all over Okinawa." And, she would like Fisby to help her select a husband, possibly Mr. Seiko? Fisby leaves that to her, and it's quickly settled by Mr. Seiko entering, grasping—with her permission—the handles of Lotus Blossom's wheelbarrow, and happily trotting off. Lotus Blossom hands Fisby her fan so that he can give the signal for her to follow, but runs off without watching him.

Now it's Sakini's turn to ask to accompany Fisby—but Fisby says Sakini's place is here where he can be of real help. He will miss him though, and he'll miss Tobiki. "I've learned from Tobiki the wisdom of gracious acceptance. I don't want to be a world leader. I'm making peace with myself somewhere between my ambitions and my limitations." Sakini isn't sure: "That's good?" Fisby, waving good-by, assures him: "It's a step backward in the right direction."

But Colonel Purdy prevents Fisby from leaving. He needs Fisby's help to put the village together again. He tells how things stand

Robert Ryan in a scene from "Coriolanus"

DAVID WAYNE
as Sakini in
"The Teahouse
of the August Moon"

SHIRLEY BOOTH
as Lottie Gibson in
"By the Beautiful Se

BEN GAZZARA
as Jocko de Paris in
"End as a Man"

VICTOR BORGE
in his one-man show
"Comedy in Music"

JEANMAIRE
as Lisette in
"The Girl in Pink Tights"

JULIE HARRIS
as Colombe in
"Mademoiselle Colom

LOUIS JOURDAN
as Michel in
"The Immoralist"

PERFORMANCES 1953-1954

INA CLAIRE
as Lady Elizabeth in
"The Confidential Clerk"

ALFRED DRAKE
as Hajj in
"Kismet"

EDNA BEST
as Lulu Ames in
"The Ladies
of the Corridor"

LLOYD NOLAN
as Queeg in
"The Caine Mutiny
Court-Martial"

CAROL HANEY
as Gladys in
"The Pajama Game"

JOSEPHINE HULL
as Mrs. Partridge in
"The Solid Gold
Cadillac"

JOHN KERR
as Tom Lee in
"Tea and Sympathy"

AUDREY HEPBURN
in the title role of
"Ondine"

Hermione Gingold and Billy DeWolfe in "John Murray Anderson's Almanac"

Photo by *LIFE Photographer Gordon Parks*, © *TIME Inc.*

Julie Harris and Eli Wallach in "Mademoiselle Colombe"

David Wayne, Larry Gates, John Forsythe and Mariko Niki in "The Teahouse of the August Moon"

Photo by LIFE Photographer Nina Leen, © TIME Inc.

Loring Smith and Josephine Hull in a scene from "The Solid Gold Cadillac"

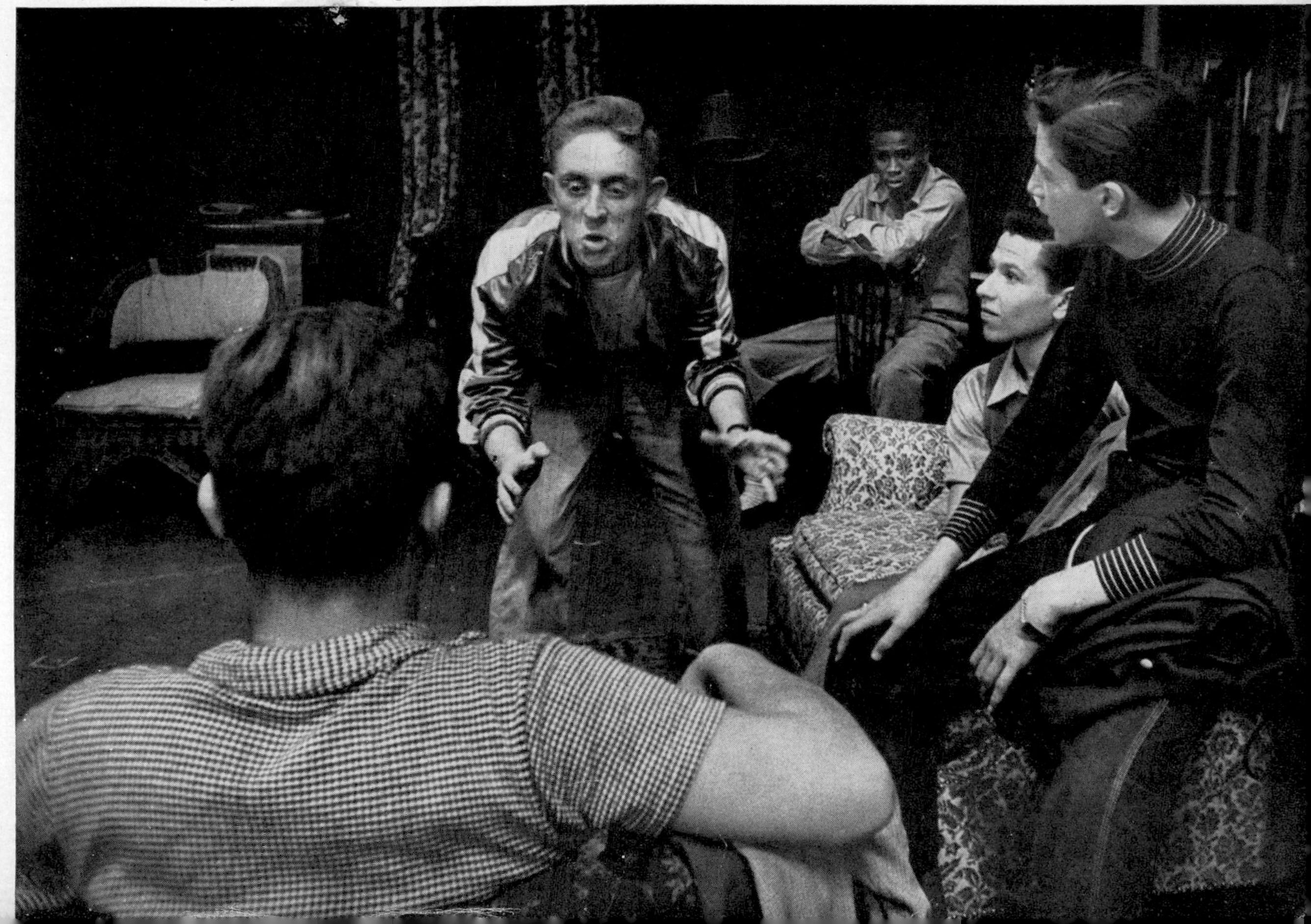

THE BEST SCENE AND COSTUME DESIGNS

Designers of the outstanding sets for plays produced during the 1953-1954 season are the following: Boris Aronson ("Mademoiselle Colombe"), William and Jean Eckart ("The Golden Apple"), Eldon Elder ("The Girl in Pink Tights"), Rolf Gerard ("The Strong Are Lonely"), George Jenkins ("The Immoralist"), Peter Larkin ("The Teahouse of the August Moon"), Jo Mielziner ("Tea and Sympathy"), Donald Oenslager ("Sabrina Fair"), Oliver Smith ("In the Summer House").

The outstanding designers of costumes are: Rolf Gerard ("The Strong Are Lonely"), Motley ("Mademoiselle Colombe"), Irene Sharaff ("By the Beautiful Sea"), Miles White ("The Girl in Pink Tights").

Drawing by William and Jean Eckart for
the stage design for "The Golden Apple"

Costume sketches by Irene Sharaff
for "By the Beautiful Sea"

Sketch for Boris Aronson's set
for "Mademoiselle Colombe"

Sketch by George Jenkins for
the set for "The Immoralist"

Corps de Ballet

Bacchanale

Costume sketch by Miles White for "The Girl in Pink Tights"

now: "I radioed the report to Washington. Some fool Senator misunderstood. He's using the village as an example of American "Get-up-and-go" in the recovery program. The Pentagon is boasting. Congress is crowing. We're all over the papers . . . but it's not wonderful. A Congressional Committee is flying over to study our methods. They are bringing in photographers for a magazine spread. Today—Fisby—today!"

The depressed colonel is even more depressed when Gregovich comes back from destroying all the village stills. Suddenly the sergeant folds. When they get him back on his feet, it turns out he's drunk. Off he's sent to the office to sober up, and Sakini then tells the colonel the stills aren't really destroyed. The natives got Gregovich drunk, then gave him water barrels to chop up; the stills are as good as ever.

Fisby with a rush of hope asks Sakini: "If everybody in the village worked together—how long would it take to rebuild the teahouse?" The chastened colonel carefully adds: "We don't ask the impossible." Sakini answers that it would take three minutes, at the most five, because: "We not destroy. Just take away and hide. You watch now, boss." Sakini calls out and villagers come from all directions. What he tells them makes them very happy, and they dash off. Sakini remarks, "Country that has been invaded many times soon master art of hiding things." Purdy wonders: "You think we can pull it off, Sakini?" He is told to watch, and even as he speaks sections of the teahouse are being carried in and swiftly put in place before his eyes. Music can be heard. The pagoda roof with its tinkling bells is lowered from on high—the dwarf pines and the arched bridge are brought back. Panels slide into place, and once more the lanterns glow. And for a finishing touch, Lotus Blossom comes on with flowers to arrange.

After Fisby ushers a delighted colonel into the teahouse, with a happy McLean and Gregovich bringing up the rear, Sakini comes down front to announce that the story is ended.

THE IMMORALIST *

A Play in Three Acts

By Ruth and Augustus Goetz

(Based on the novel by André Gide)

[Ruth Goetz, *born in Philadelphia and brought up in New York,
was the daughter of the well-known theatrical producer, Philip Goodman. She was taken frequently to Europe, where she met her husband 24 years ago. Their first play was never produced, their second never reached Broadway, their third, "One Man Show," was
produced by Jed Harris, but was not a success. It was "The Heiress"
—adapted from Henry James' "Washington Square"—that brought
them fame. It was after reading "The Heiress" that André Gide
gave them permission to dramatize "The Immoralist."*

Augustus Goetz *was born in Buffalo, and in his early days worked
in Wall Street. He and Mrs. Goetz also collaborated on the screen
version of "The Heiress" and of Dreiser's "Sister Carrie."*]

THE first scene is a country house in France at the turn of the
century. On this particular afternoon the master of the house has
been buried.

The late afternoon light comes through the French door of the
study and adds a cold tone to the room's austere furnishings: the
center table, desk, and chairs.

Marcelline, a slim girl still in her twenties, and her brother, Doctor Robert, have just come back from the funeral to await the arrival
of Michel, the son of the house. Both are somberly dressed, and
Marcelline takes a black scarf from her head, and lays a small bouquet on the table.

Robert thinks it unnecessary to stay on, and would much prefer
leaving a card with a message of sympathy. In fact, he feels his sis-

ter has already been far too attentive to Michel. It would be more suitable for him to call on her occasionally. Robert feels strongly that Michel should make the advances, as other young men do. But Michel, says Marcelline, is not like other young men. Her brother allows that his eminence as an archaeologist does set him apart, and that his books are far more interesting than his father's.

ROBERT (*indicates one on the table*)—Is this a new one?

MARCELLINE (*looks at it*)—Yes—that's three years' work. He and his father gathered most of that material in Greece.

ROBERT—I remember that trip. Michel came home with quite a cough.

MARCELLINE—Are you uneasy about his health, Robert? Is that why you discourage me?

ROBERT—I am not discouraging you. I believe you are sincere in your devotion to him. I don't understand it, but I have to accept it.

MARCELLINE—What is difficult to understand? He is learned, he is considerate, he is gentle—

ROBERT—Those are good qualities, if he was up for Holy Orders, but he isn't. You're talking of a man you want for a husband.

MARCELLINE—Will you let me lead my own life, Robert? Michel and I grew up together and he is the only person I have ever felt safe with.

ROBERT—I don't quite understand that.

MARCELLINE—I don't expect you to. There is a great difference between you and me.

ROBERT—And between you and the other young ladies of the village.

MARCELLINE—I have heard you and your friends discuss the other young ladies of the village—as if you were at a livestock sale. How fat they are or how thin they are or if they have good legs—but never what they think or feel!

ROBERT—Marriage is not all poetry and walks in the garden, Marcie.

And he remarks that his sister had better find out whether Michel expects to share these ideas of hers, for she isn't getting any younger. He is sorry to have been so harsh, and admits that he never really knew Michel. As a boy, Michel was away at boarding school; later he traveled and studied with his father. But Robert was sure that Michel's constant attendance at his father's bedside as he lay dying, was more out of fear than love. As for the old man, he seemed afraid to let Michel out of his sight. "You have never liked him," Marcelline accuses him. "He is an eccentric," Robert replies, "and I don't like eccentrics."

A stout, middle-aged man interrupts them. Bocage has worked for Michel's father for many years, managing both the house and the estate; and for his devotion he has been willed his own stone cottage and fields.

Bocage discusses the funeral services with Robert and Marcelline, and then insists on going for drinks that Robert does not want. Irritated, Robert turns on Marcelline: "How long are you going to sit there?"

MARCELLINE—Until Michel comes.

ROBERT (*with bite*)—Wouldn't it be more proper if *he* came to see *you?*

MARCELLINE—Yes, Robert, it would— Now will you please sit down and be patient? Michel will be here soon.

ROBERT (*stands over her, waiting for her to rise*)—Have a little pride, Marcelline!

MARCELLINE (*quietly*)—I have a great deal of pride, Robert.

ROBERT—Well, nobody in the village thinks you have! Let him come over to see us. Let him act like every other man who's courting a girl!

Michel, a fine-looking young man in a dark suit with a mourning band, comes through the French windows and greets his visitors. Once more the funeral is discussed. Michel finds it difficult to talk about and bursts out: "It amazes me how people gather at funerals. The dead one is gone, so it must be the survivor who interests them. How will he act? What will he do? They stand watching and they weigh the sorrow— Is it small, medium, or great? I wish I could have satisfied them. I wanted to fulfill what they expected of me— but I didn't know how." This produces an embarrassed silence, not much helped by Robert's obvious desire to take his sister home, and her decision to stay. Robert stands around a few minutes more and, to Marcelline's annoyance, fires questions at Michel about his plans for the future. "That's all right, Marcie," Michel placates her, and answers Robert: "I have been invited to lecture at the Royal Society in London. Or I can join an expedition to North Africa. You're right, Robert. I should be making plans." And he knows very well, when Robert suggests he go somewhere to cure his cough, that Robert wants him out of Marcelline's way.

When Robert curtly refuses Bocage's offered refreshments and invitation to supper, Michel tactfully suggests that Marcelline go home with her brother.

Michel is left to Bocage's sympathetic attentions. He is lonely and empty of emotion. Bocage fortifies himself with several drinks and these embolden him to tell Michel of his father's actions, which he considers so unreasonable and wrong. Michel asks him, in a gentle fashion, to explain himself.

"I tried to tell him," Bocage commences, "that I wouldn't be responsible. . . . But he was a stubborn old man and he wouldn't listen. . . . Even the day before he died I tried to explain to him. . . . I tried to make him understand how it would look!" He rises and continues, "I don't know how to tell you this." Michel listens patiently as the old man tells of his father's recent will. Bocage is all for getting rid of it—no one would be the wiser, since Bocage himself wrote it down and was the sole witness. But Michel insists on being shown it.

At first, as Michel reads the will through, it seems usual and perfectly acceptable, with Bocage and two Parisian attorneys to act as trustees of the estate. Bocage would like Michel to stop right there and hand him back the will. But Michel holds onto it and proceeds to read: "The propriety of my son's behavior shall be the sole condition of his enjoying his inheritance. And I appoint the same Bocage as full guardian over him, with power to pay or to withhold all income as it may accrue. Should Bocage fail to exercise his judgment, then I direct my lawyers to assume this guardianship—!" Michel stops reading and, after a pause, he speaks very quietly: "What does it mean? 'The propriety of my behavior' . . . ?"

Bocage is bitter indeed about his father's treatment of him, and says it was because he was such a moral man. But Bocage is sure that any sin Michel committed he has paid for long ago.

MICHEL—I was eleven years old! . . . I had a problem . . . and when you are eleven you are not very good at problems. And I solved mine vilely—I know that!

BOCAGE—If it had been anything else—like stealing or lying—the school would not have expelled you. But this was a sin of the flesh, an offense against yourself and the other boy—it frightened your father! He never forgot it.

MICHEL—*He* never forgot it! Do you think I did? That morning as the teachers packed my boxes, they threw my clothing in as if it were infected. Then they walked me through the courtyard at the recess, so that everybody could watch me leave. I was alone on the earth. At that moment they cut me away from other human beings. I have never been able to make my way back . . . not even to my father. (*In a torment he crumples up the paper.*) What did he want of me that I didn't give him? (*There is a pause, then he continues more calmly.*) The more I tried to appease him, the less he trusted me. In the end he believed that I must always be guilty of the things he suspected. Otherwise why had I tried so hard to please him?

Despite Bocage's wish to burn the will, Michel decides to keep it forever, as a reminder that even his father could not love him.

He vows he is going away where his father cannot touch him. He will leave at once—tonight. Bocage begs him not to go among strangers: "You are liked and trusted here."

MICHEL—Don't lie to me! Even you see in me what he saw.
BOCAGE—Michel! No!
MICHEL—You do! And more terrible than that—they all do!
BOCAGE—You must never believe that!

A bell rings, and Bocage goes to answer it. He returns with Marcelline, who has ostensibly come to apologize for her brother's behavior. Bocage tells her that she's just come in time, because Michel has decided to leave Normandy.

MARCELLINE—Do you mean you might be gone for—a long time?
MICHEL—Yes, Marcie—I think so.
MARCELLINE—Bocage, will you leave us alone? I can ask you to do that, can't I? You're my friend. (*To* MICHEL.) I have a great favor to ask of you.
MICHEL—Can't Bocage hear it? He should. He should hear everything.
MARCELLINE—Very well, I don't care who hears. I was going to wait until Spring— But now there may be no Spring.
MICHEL—What is it, Marcelline?
MARCELLINE—I want to marry you, Michel. I formally ask your hand in marriage. I have half the money our parents left us, and I have been careful with it. It isn't much, but I will be no expense to you. (*The two men listen to her in silence.*) When I would sit with your father, he made me understand how important your work was. I will never interfere with it, Michel.
MICHEL (*to* BOCAGE)—Will you leave us alone, Bocage?

BOCAGE (*picking up will from table, backing to hall*)—He will tell you he is unworthy, Miss Marcelline. But you know better than that.

Michel is deeply touched, and tells the girl what a good friend she is. But he fears all this is due to pity, and perhaps to some promise she had given his father: "Marcie, he told you to love me!"

MARCELLINE—No one can tell another to do that. I have loved you since I was fourteen—every minute of every day. I loved you when you were here, and when you were away. And I will always love you.

MICHEL—Me . . . ?

MARCELLINE—Why is it so hard for you to believe that?

MICHEL—Because no one ever has—

MARCELLINE—Michel, you've never let them— (*Pause.*) Even now you won't let me.

Michel is in despair; he doesn't know what to think, and begs her to wait till he can come to her with true feelings of love. But Marcelline, knowing he won't, pushes her suit. It is only when she starts to go that Michel suddenly comes to a decision: "Wait! You are all I have to cling to! I have no one else! I know that now."

Marcelline smiles a little and is sure that he has only to take her with him, and all will be well. When Michel realizes that she is prepared to leave on a moment's notice, that she will go as she is, he calls Bocage. Then turns to her: "Marcie, I will love you—I know I will!"

MARCELLINE (*smiling at him*)—Of course you will. (BOCAGE *enters.*)

MICHEL—Bocage, we are going away together!

BOCAGE—What?

MICHEL—We are going to be married tonight.

BOCAGE—Yes. Yes. The most respected girl in the village—she does the house great honor.

MICHEL—She does me great honor.

SCENE II

Marcelline and Michel have arrived in Biskra, by way of Genoa, Naples, and Carthage. It is night, a brilliant African night.

Their house on the desert has a small bedroom, only large enough to hold a bed, two night tables, and one chair. A beaded portière covers the doorway to the hall, and a narrow window-door opens on a largish terrace.

Here Marcelline, in dressing gown and night apparel, scans the heavens with a spyglass, and is in raptures over the excitement of the African night. According to Michel, who is stretched out on a deck chair, she delights in everything. But now she wants to be a stay-at-home, and not sight-see for a few days. Michel seems agreeable, though he wishes to see everything—tombs, bazaar, town—immediately.

After Marcelline goes to bed, Michel stays under the stars until, chilled, he goes to the bedroom to borrow her shawl. He is told he needn't sleep on the terrace, but he only says: "Marcelline—dearest —you know it's only because of this cough that I leave you to yourself." Marcelline lovingly places the shawl about her husband's shoulders, telling him: "Yes. Now that we are married, I have the thing I have wanted most in my life." But she dreams that: "One night you will look at me and say—'Heavens, you look pretty tonight—' " Michel repeats: "Heavens, you look pretty tonight." Marcelline hungrily embraces him; it is he who breaks the embrace.

As they sit together on the bed, Marcelline conveys gently that she hasn't everything she hoped for from her marriage. And carefully and sweetly questions Michel: "What did the other women do?" After a brief hesitation, Michel says: "There were no other women."

MARCELLINE—Are we frightened, Michel? Is that what is wrong with us?

MICHEL—Yes.

MARCELLINE—They teach us all the arts, except how to make love.

MICHEL (*rising to stand above the bed*)—It isn't you; it's me! And it has nothing to do with love. (*Kneeling on corner of bed, taking hold of her shoulders.*) I never loved you more than I do right this minute! . . . But I am stopped!

MARCELLINE (*timidly*)—I wonder if you think I will be afraid, or shocked— I won't be, Michel. To be a good animal is sometimes very beautiful. . . . (MICHEL *turns away from her.* MARCELLINE *sees his deep distres*s.) If we had had a courtship like the other young people of the village, we wouldn't be afraid of each other now. We'd be more at ease. I've loved you a long time, and I can wait a little longer—

MICHEL—Wait for what? A magical moment that will turn me into a man?

Marcelline tries to comfort him and reaches the point where, though she finds it hard, she yet can say: "Sometimes people marry, and live together, and *never* feel desire." This reminds Michel of the cold loneliness of his childhood, but Marcelline says they will at least have one another's companionship: "It is a possibility that I have had to accept—" Michel asks: *"What* possibility?" She answers levelly: "That you cannot live with me. That—that you are physically unable. . . ." Michel looks at her and understands: "Do you think I would have married you if that were so? . . . It is not true. . . !"

Marcelline is thoroughly puzzled, and now quite desperately unhappy: "I would rather think that—than that while I have been next to you—" She covers her eyes and manages to finish: "you have wanted someone else." Michel tells her that he does want her, and to prove it takes her in his arms and kisses her. Marcelline clings to him passionately, but almost at once Michel holds her away from him as he starts to cough. Seized with a terrible coughing spell, he is helpless to answer Marcelline's plea of what she can do for him. He can only point to the medicine on the night table, and with a final effort gasp out: "Don't look," as he gives himself up to the hemorrhage. Marcelline holds onto him, and cries out again and again for help: "Help! Oh, won't somebody help. . . . Somebody, please!"

ACT II

A week later, Marcelline is straightening up the house before bringing her husband home from the hospital. She has an Arab boy called Bachir to clean and sweep for her, but he isn't inclined to do much of anything.

As she is about to leave, the Colonial Army doctor, Garrin, arrives at the terrace wall. He has taken it upon himself to get a housewoman for Marcelline, and urges her to go fetch her: "It's important for you to have help here. I will go for your husband, and I will have him here by the time you get back." Marcelline hesitates: "Doctor—I have been wanting to ask you something. . . . Before the hemorrhage last week, my husband must have had fever." Garrin replies: "Undoubtedly," and he agrees that he may have had it for several weeks. "So," concludes Marcelline, "that would account for any weakness—any physical weakness, I mean." Again Garrin concurs. Marcelline, relieved, goes off to meet Sidma, the native woman.

Dr. Garrin catches sight of Bachir squatting on the terrace, and at once recognizes him for a boy caught with some soldiers in the barracks. Bachir denies this, but the doctor isn't so easily fooled. He takes Bachir's cap off, to check the scar he had treated: "Of course, I never forget a face. Stay away from the barracks, or the next time they'll put you in jail."

Michel surprises them by coming home from the hospital under his own steam. The doctor quickly orders Bachir to fix a chair for him in the sun, and to get the food Marcelline had prepared. And before he leaves he gives Michel some friendly advice: "You know, your wife's had a very anxious time of it this past week—so let her see a little light in your face. If she sees you low in your mind, it will be hard for her to help you."

Bachir too is ready to help in his own fashion. After satsifying himself that Michel knows nothing of his reputation, he gobbles up the food intended for Michel and sets out to entertain him.

BACHIR—This [food] is very good for me. I was in the quarter last night and I was the strongest boy of all.

MICHEL (*smiles*)—Why do you have to be the strongest boy of all?

BACHIR (*pauses—then he smiles*)—It is safer that way, in the quarter— (*Finishes a mouthful.*) But soon the warm season will come and I can spend the nights in the orchards.

MICHEL—The orchards?

BACHIR—Yes, sir—the trees are filled with fruit: dates, figs, oranges; everything grows in the orchards. Many boys tend the crops, the earth, the goats. They are very beautiful, those places.

MICHEL—Where are they?

BACHIR—Which one, sir?

MICHEL—I don't know—the one you seem so poetic about.

BACHIR—Ah! That is Moktir's . . . out there beyond the walls. It is always green and cool and they live like a thousand years ago.

MICHEL—And do their families live there, too?

BACHIR—Oh, sir, Moktir has no family. He lives without women —only boys and men are out there. Beautiful men.

MICHEL—Why are you saying these things to me?

BACHIR—You asked me, sir. Besides, many tourists are interested.

MICHEL—I am not interested!

BACHIR—This is Biskra, sir.

Marcelline stops this conversation by her return with the native woman Sidma. Michel and Marcelline embrace. She is so delighted to have him with her again, and determined to take good care of him. He's going to get much better, with her care and Sidma's. Marcelline wants to instruct the housewoman in her duties, and takes her inside so she can begin at once. Sidma notices Bachir on the terrace, and tactfully warns Marcelline: "Many boys like him in Biskra—come from all over—look for rich tourist to charm—make their fortune." Marcelline is puzzled, so Sidma quickly finishes: "You very nice people. This boy bad all through. Be careful," and quietly changes the subject to whether she should launder in the kitchen.

Bachir wastes neither time nor opportunity. He picks up a pair of scissors from Marcelline's sewing box, and snaps them admiringly.

BACHIR—These are good scissors. One could make a jewel of them. They shine. (*Pause.*) Many interesting places in Biskra—I will take you, sir. (*Twirls the scissors.*) Many cafés, bazaars, night places—I know them all. (*Kneeling beside* MICHEL.) The only place I cannot take you is Moktir's.

Michel sharply tells him: "I would not go, even if you could." Forced to shift tactics, Bachir offers Michel in succession a cool drink, a cigarette, a pillow. Turned down three times, he announces: "Then maybe I amuse you, sir. I dance for you." And he dances, first rhythmically snipping with the scissors, then swiftly disposing of them inside his burnoose and snapping his fingers instead. He dances with deliberate sensuousness, his arms extended over his head. He succeeds in fascinating Michel, but the latter suddenly rises from his chair and cries out: "Stop that! Stop that, immediately." Bachir won't, and Marcelline, coming out on the terrace, finds Michel with his back to the dancing boy.

Michel, making an effort to cover the situation, tells her: "Marcelline, as soon as I am able—when I can travel without being a burden to you—we will move on." Marcelline smiles faintly, and picks up her sewing basket, planning to work while keeping him company. She cannot find her scissors. Cagey Bachir denies seeing them. He even suggests that Dr. Garrin might have taken them by mistake. Troubled, Michel starts for the bedroom; he is unable to tell his wife that Bachir has stolen them.

SCENE II

An evening two weeks later; Michel reclines on the terrace, his coffee at his elbow. He has fired Bachir, but to no avail. Marcelline in her softhearted way has given him food and money, and at this moment the boy is accompanying her to the depot to pick up a package of food.

Michel leaves the terrace to get a book from the bedroom. On his return he finds an Arab standing outside the terrace wall. The Arab professes to have sought out the French archaeologist because of something found on his land. Michel inspects the offered stone fragment and the two talk courteously to one another. Michel points out, what the Arab well knew, that the little statue had been out of the earth a long time. The Arab confesses: "I felt I needed to come here with a gift, so I brought what I had." He had heard there was a scholar here, and wished very much to talk with him. He himself had once taught school, at the University of Fez. Michel shows astonishment, and asks why he left such a great university.

ARAB—One must choose, sir. Of the thousand forms of life, each of us can know but one. I came here because I chose to live my life without shame.

MICHEL—Shame of what?

ARAB—I am Moktir, the shepherd.

MICHEL—From the orchards?

ARAB—Yes.

MICHEL—I have heard of you. I want nothing from you. (MICHEL rises.)

ARAB—You didn't begin by insulting me. I am no different now than when I entered here.

MICHEL—You are to me! I didn't know who you were!

ARAB—You don't now. I have given up more freedom than you will ever have in order not to have to lie to you, or to anyone, and above all not to myself.

MICHEL—Everything I have been taught tells me that what you are is wrong.

ARAB—Wrong! How can a man of science use such a word! My instincts are a part of nature.

MICHEL—That is not true!

ARAB—How can you judge what is true for me? I must do that for myself, and I have only a short time on this earth in which to be myself. For me, only the present exists.

MICHEL—My wife will be back here any moment. I would prefer that you leave.

ARAB (rising to him)—I have no fear of your wife—why have you? (Pause.) I came here tonight to borrow a book, to have a few minutes' conversation with a scholar, and suddenly on this terrace I have felt all the aversion, all the ignorance that I came to Biskra to escape.

MICHEL—I am sorry. I come from a different culture . . . and
I am bound by the same standards I was brought up with—

ARAB—Then you must live by them, sir. I respect your feelings.
I accept what you are. I have made a grave mistake. I have forgotten other painful episodes, and I will forget this.

As he turns to go, Michel says he is genuinely sorry. Moktir, with
dignity, tells him: "You should be. If no one else can respect the
human aberration, the scientist should." Michel, now wishing to
make amends, accepts the Arab's hand in friendship, and Moktir
invites him to his orchard: "It is a simple date orchard, but the
shade is dense, the water clear and cool. It might be a peaceful
place in which to read, or work." Michel accepts the invitation and
presents Moktir with a volume of Aristippus. The Arab knows this
well, and quotes as he prepares to go: "The art of life lies in taking
pleasures as they pass, and the keenest pleasures are not intellectual
—nor are they always moral."

SCENE III

Michel and Marcelline, having spent the day at Moktir's orchard,
arrive home in the late afternoon. Tired, hot, and wilted, Marcelline gives the basket she is carrying to Sidma, and retires immediately to the bedroom to change and cool off. Michel puts down the
manuscript and books he has with him and follows Marcelline to
the bedroom door. He knows that she is depressed by more than
the desert heat, and says that if she prefers it he will work at home
instead of in Moktir's orchard. Marcelline picks up the water jug,
answering: "I didn't say I would prefer anything, Michel."

MICHEL—Well, if I stay here in the mornings, will you come with
me for the rest of the day?

MARCELLINE—Why must I do that? Moktir is more helpful than I.

MICHEL—You *are* very helpful.

MARCELLINE (*standing in his path*)—Oh, Michel, you keep saying that. And I don't believe it. When I sit there with you and
Moktir, I feel completely unnecessary.

MICHEL—That's not true.

MARCELLINE—Well, I feel it anyway. (*He goes out on the terrace, sits left of table—she crosses to table, pours water in basin,
puts down jug.*) You keep trying to make a place for me in your
work—as if to reassure me. But I'm not envious of your work, or
your learning! I am proud of it.

Michel worries that if Marcelline is left alone, she will tire of Biskra. She tosses down her towel and picks up a fresh blouse: "I am tired of it now. Look at it. It's sun-baked and dirty. There's no life here!" Michel protests: "There's more living here than any place on earth." Marcelline, coming to him, concedes that he is right "historically speaking." But that isn't enough for her. She yearns for home. Each sip of the French wine Sidma brings her causes her to be more homesick.

MICHEL—You want to go home—

MARCELLINE—I want to do anything you want to do. But we seem to be settling here, and it frightens me. We are not Arabs. We can't be content with the life they lead.

MICHEL (*turns to her*)—Marcie, give me time! For the first time in my life I am at ease among a people. They live without ambition, without judgment, without standards—

MARCELLINE (*interrupting him*)—That's right, Michel! And so they are lying and deceitful and bad!

MICHEL—No, Marcie . . . they are only different.

MARCELLINE (*her hand on his arm*)—You see no faults in anyone.

MICHEL—This is how you help . . . when you reassure me.

MARCELLINE—I need to be assured now— (*Finishes her drink.*) We've been living each day as if the next would never come, but they have come and you have got well. Now I must know whether you will ever *want* me, whether there is a future for us anywhere. Since we have been married you have never wanted us to be separated, not for a day—not for an hour—and yet you have never wanted us to be *one*.

MICHEL (*painfully*)—You say "wanting" as if wanting were deliberate. But it isn't like that.

MARCELLINE (*looks at him and starts to go into the house. Then she stops*)—I could live with you anywhere, without comfort, without children— But I cannot live with your denial of me. It makes me feel half-dead! (*Covers her eyes and blindly goes indoors, to throw herself on the bed.*)

Bachir returns from the cookshop with the supper rice, and his sly remarks about Marcelline draw Michel's wrath. Bachir isn't at all put out. He cagily asks: "You have had a fight, eh?"

MICHEL—Madame and I will eat later. She is resting—get out!

BACHIR—I don't mean her. You have had a fight with Moktir, maybe?

MICHEL (*turns away from the door*)—What—

BACHIR—When Moktir is in good humor, you are—when he is not, you are not. The fight will end. He is very clever—he will not break off. It is too profitable. You are a rich foreigner.

MICHEL (*comes toward him*)—Moktir is an educated man—he has given me the shelter of the orchards in which to work. . . . He is a friend!

BACHIR (*smiles*)—You need not talk like that with me— With Madame, yes. Not with me—

Michel angrily demands he leave at once, and throws money on the table to pay him off. Bachir isn't so easily got rid of; he now takes to taunting Michel with the reason he stays on in Biskra. Michel defends himself: "I was ill. I wanted this climate!" "This climate?" Bachir answers in mock surprise. "You mean the climate of the orchards, sir. The first time I saw you with Madame—the day you took this house—I knew what you were—"

Michel lunges at the boy's throat, then flings Bachir to the ground. When he is ordered away, Bachir stands up and starts to leave, lashing out: "It's no secret— Maybe not even to her—" and his laughter can be heard as he goes, still calling: "It's no secret!"

All this has the effect of driving Michel to his wife's bed. He takes Marcelline in his arms: "Will you be my wife?" he begs. "Yes . . . oh, my dearest . . ." she cries, in his desperate embrace.

SCENE IV

It is still Biskra, several months later. Sidma, returning in the midmorning from market, takes her food and wine supplies to Marcelline in the kitchen. No one is about as Michel arrives home with Moktir. The Arab finds it uncomfortable being at Marcelline's home, and says as much to Michel: "It is not for her sake that I don't want to be here; it is for my own—and yours. One must not be this indifferent, even in Biskra." Furthermore, Moktir thinks it wrong of Michel to allow Sidma to see him here, but Michel reasons: "I cannot hide from a servant. If she doesn't say it, someone else will. I stay away all day, and those nights when I *am* here, Marcelline is asleep. She may know already."

MOKTIR—No—if she knew, she would be gone. That is what you are afraid of, isn't it?

MICHEL—Yes. I cannot face that yet. I cannot live without her.

MOKTIR—You live without her now.

MICHEL—I have been her husband—I love her.

Geraldine Page and Louis Jourdan in "The Immoralist"

MOKTIR—Your love is pity. Can you lead two lives?

MICHEL—Who does not?

MOKTIR—I . . . You should tell her the truth.

MICHEL—I cannot! It would be as if I were glad of the truth, and I am not.

MOKTIR—No one is glad—not even the vicious.

When Sidma answers Michel's call, she is deliberately vague about Marcelline's whereabouts. It is Moktir who advises Michel to look for her in the wine shop, where (local gossip says) much of his money is spent. Michel, followed by Moktir, sets out anxiously to find Marcelline.

After the men have left, Sidma signals to Marcelline, who parts the beaded portières and slowly comes into the bedroom. She is a ravaged, slovenly, desperately unhappy creature. Her lace blouse is unbuttoned and hangs askew, the ends of it untucked. She is quiet and deliberate in her drunken movements, but when she talks there are also tears.

In the begging tones of a child, Marcelline has Sidma join her at cards on the terrace. She tries to recapture the spirit of a card party in France: only here there is no chestnut tree in the garden; here there are no proper prizes; and she is drunk. Sidma pleads with her to eat, and tries to help her into the house, but Marcelline slumps to the terrace floor, and it is thus that the men find her, calling out to Sidma: "I must see if I can win at something!" She sees the cards that her hand has knocked off the table. "You dropped your cards, Sidma!" she announces, then hastily adds, as she picks them up: "I won't look at them—see, I'm covering my eyes." As the men watch her, she continues: "I'll pick them up and put them into your hand, and you play them the way you did before."

MICHEL—What is it, Marcelline?

MARCELLINE (*turns to see him*)—Oh . . . Sidma dropped her cards.

MICHEL—Then let her pick them up.

MARCELLINE—She doesn't want to. She wants to cook . . . And I want to finish our game. (*She is trying to get off the ground, first by holding onto a chair, then by grabbing at a table leg.*) But it was hot out here, and there are no refreshments to offer . . . (*She tries to get up from the uneven balance of one knee and one foot placed flat, but still cannot manage it. MICHEL tries to help her, but she brushes him aside.*) You cannot expect people to sit with you if you have nothing to offer. (MICHEL *goes to her again, but she takes his hands off her shoulders, deliberately. Now she screams hysterically*.) Sidma! Sidma! Sidma! Sidma! (SIDMA *comes to her*.) Help me, Sidma, I'm drunk.

As Sidma puts Marcelline to bed, Moktir points out to Michel: "You have not deceived her. You have deceived yourself."

MICHEL—I have to help her! (MOKTIR *starts out*.) Don't go! Help me, Moktir!

MOKTIR—It is dishonor to live two lives! I return to my own life. I deceive no one. I corrupt no one. Do you think that because I am what I am I have no morality? Do you think that because you have come to our life, you will be able to live without any?

MICHEL—I must help her!

MOKTIR—Your power to help her is not great. You hid behind her. You use her. The only way you could help her is to spare her what is coming—you should bear that alone!

MICHEL—No! No! I will not be alone! I cannot lose her! I cannot live as you do!

MOKTIR (*gravely*)—You harm us all. (*He exits*.)

Once again Michel is forced to do something against his will. He goes to Marcelline stretched out on the bed. At first she weakly turns away with worry in her voice: "Are you going to scold me?" Michel explains: "I have to tell you the truth. I have to tell you everything. You will not understand it, just as I cannot. But if you know about me, you will not destroy yourself any more." This is too much for Marcelline, who tries not to hear what Michel is saying, even to get out of bed and out of his sight. "I am drunk," she cries. "Thank God, I am drunk." As Michel holds her by the arms and lets her know he is everything she fears he is, she almost screams: "How dare you tell me the truth? How dare you?" and struggles to escape.

Michel plans on taking her to Tunis where she can board a boat for France: "If you live with me in Biskra on my terms you will try to die. And if I live with you in Normandy I will do the same thing." Marcelline protests, "It's not true." But Michel is sure: "It is true, Marcie. We both know it." Again she pleads with him, but Michel remains adamant. She must see him as he is, and leave, hating him. She must understand him! Marcelline tries to escape the words, but cannot.

MICHEL—I will say it everywhere!   I will write it!   I will speak it!
MARCELLINE—Don't, Michel . . . don't!
MICHEL (*against her loud protests*)—I will never be silent again!
Whoever knows me will know that about me first.   Whoever hears
of me will hear that before anything!   If there is an ounce of energy
within me, I will say what I am like!   This one thing I can do!   I
can speak out!

ACT III

Marcelline, in a traveling suit, waits stiffly as Sidma and Michel
finish her packing.   She has the sense of being a castoff; and feels
so shaky and ill that she begs Michel for some wine.   When he won't
allow her any, Marcelline draws Sidma aside, and secretly sends her
off for Dr. Garrin.   The bags closed, Michel joins Marcelline on the
terrace.

MICHEL—I will cable Robert that if he cannot meet you in Mar-
seilles he should send Bocage.
MARCELLINE—For God's sake, don't do that!   I want to crawl
back, without anyone seeing me!   I can't answer their questions yet,
Michel!
MICHEL (*gently*)—There will be no questions.   I have written to
Robert and told him everything.
MARCELLINE—Oh, Michel, why did you do that?
MICHEL—So that he can take the proper steps to free you.
MARCELLINE—Free me!   For what?   You are free!   But I am
sent home . . . not wanted!
MICHEL—I will attend to the tickets.   (*He goes through the
house, leaving* MARCELLINE *to lean, sobbing, against the wall for
support.*)

Bachir, with a stay in jail behind him, comes back to his old
haunts and soft touches.   Without much of a preamble, he proceeds
to blackmail Marcelline about Michel's activities.

BACHIR—I could tell Madame such things . . . terrible things!
Madame would be shocked!   And when Michel did not behave,
Madame would know ways to threaten him. . . . Of course, he is a
friend of mine and I would have to have money to tell these things
about him.   Then I could go away and not see him and not feel
ashamed.
MARCELLINE (*revolted*)—You are corrupt into your veins.
BACHIR—I must have money.

MARCELLINE—I won't give you money.
BACHIR—I can sign a complaint against him!

Marcelline indignantly threatens to send Bachir right back to jail.
Whereupon he swiftly changes his tactics, and throws himself on her
mercy. Marcelline sends Bachir for her purse, warning him not to
open it, which of course he does. But the contents appear so skimpy
to him that he decides to leave them untouched and wait for bigger
fish. He decides to blackmail Michel instead: "It will pay better."
Marcelline sighs, "Poor Michel." Bachir is ready with his excuses:
"He will have it everywhere, Madame. It might as well be Bachir
who profits—"

Sidma arrives with Dr. Garrin, and Bachir follows her into the
kitchen. Marcelline tells the doctor of her inability to eat or sleep,
and of her deafening heartbeats. Garrin has her unbutton her blouse
and examines her. He quickly discovers, to his amusement, that she
is several months pregnant. He is very gay about this, and can't
wait to congratulate Michel. Marcelline, miserably upset, bewildered, and frustrated, makes the doctor promise to say nothing to
her husband; her pretext is that she wants to tell him herself.

Michel finds them on the terrace and is disturbed to see the doctor. Garrin assures him his wife will be fine in just a few months;
but after he has gone, Michel asks Marcelline why he should come
after all this time. Marcelline tries to make light of it: "I wanted
something to make me sleep." Yet Michel guiltily worries: "Marcelline, if you are afraid to travel alone, I can take you to Marseilles."

MARCELLINE—And return me to the soil from which I came?
MICHEL—I will take you home. I will take you to the door, if
you want me to.
MARCELLINE—No, Michel . . . I am afraid I would try to hold
you.
MICHEL—You would not want to . . . even if you could. . . .
MARCELLINE (*sits down and folds her arms across her body*)—
I do want to—and I could— But I won't. . . .

SCENE II

At the house in Normandy, six weeks later; supper is over. Dr.
Robert is having his coffee alone when Bocage enters the study with
a message: Marcelline will not join her brother; she wishes him to
leave at once. She cannot bear his righteous attitude, his intolerable
criticism of Michel, the gossip he has spread throughout the village.

ROBERT—Since when have you become so tolerant?

BOCAGE—There are a lot of things going on in the world I don't understand. I don't understand you, either. A fine young doctor in a pressed suit—and half the bordellos in Trouville would close up if it weren't for you.

ROBERT (*enraged*)—You're an old man, Bocage, and you take advantage of it!

BOCAGE (*at the desk*)—Your sister wants to pay you for your visits. Since she's been home you've been here at least three times a week for six weeks. She'd like to pay you and be done with it. What does she owe you?

ROBERT—I'll let her know when I have the stomach to come back into the house.

As soon as he has left, Marcelline comes in to check with Bocage before going to bed, and to make one further request of him: "You have a sister in Lyons, haven't you? . . . I would like you to write to her and ask if she knows of a competent midwife. I don't want one from this village." Bocage says soothingly: "Oh, there's plenty of time for that." But seeing her anxiety, he tries to reassure her: "You don't have to be anxious. You're going to have a fine baby . . . with all your character and quality." "Yes . . ." replies Marcelline, "and his father's."

Bocage is tidying up for the night, closing the desk, turning down the lamp, when Michel emerges from the garden, through the French door. The startled old man greets him, but asks: "Why do you come in like a thief? This is your home." Michel explains: "I went to the front door, but I saw Robert leaving. . . . I only wanted to talk to you! Will you let me?"

Michel felt he had to see Bocage, whom he feels is as sympathetic and kindly as ever. They sit down to talk, but Michel is at a loss how to begin. Bocage, in spite of knowing the contents of his letter to Dr. Robert, hopes he has come back to stay.

MICHEL—No. How can I? I came back because my cruelty to Marcelline haunts me! I should have tempered the truth, but I couldn't.

BOCAGE—Has the truth changed?

MICHEL—No. But if she could understand that I did not invent this problem, that it existed before we did—it might ease her mind. I love her, Bocage, but I married her in desperation—and that was wrong! It was my failure, not hers.

BOCAGE—You could stay, and start again. You have a tie here, now.

MICHEL (*rises*)—I have no tie—! If you knew all the truth about me, even you would put me out.

BOCAGE—No, no!

MICHEL—I have scavenged through the back streets of every town I passed through— There is no loneliness like that! I have been exploited by those who are like me, and shunned by those who are not.

BOCAGE (*not wanting to hear*)—My God, Michel—

MICHEL—And for that freedom I left Marcelline. . . . Tell me about her.

Bocage can only say she is living as best she can, when Robert, having caught a glimpse of Michel, comes bursting into the house. He is all ready to snatch his sister away to safety and forbid her to return until Michel has left the house.

Marcelline enters upon all this commotion, to be told by Robert: "You are leaving this house with me!"

MICHEL—You don't have to . . . I am going.

ROBERT—I don't want her near you for even a minute—and if you value your skin, you'll be gone by morning. (*Takes a step toward him.*) I have your letter here—the one from Biskra—and I'll hold it over your head the rest of your life—and if you ever come back here after my sister's baby is born—I'll post it on the church door! (*A dead silence while* MICHEL *grasps what he has said.*)

MICHEL (*crosses to* MARCELLINE)—Child . . . ?

MARCELLINE—Yes.

MICHEL—Marcelline— (*Then with dignity.*) I would like to talk to my wife—alone. (*Pause.*)

ROBERT (*to* MARCELLINE)—If you need me . . .

MARCELLINE—I need only myself!

When they are alone together, Michel bursts out: "How you must hate me . . . not to have told me!" But Marcelline only remembers her fear: "I thought I might lose my baby. And then I would have nothing. You cannot live with nothing." She is sure that was her reason for not telling Michel in Biskra.

MICHEL—Marcie, you don't think I would have let you go if I had known . . . ?

MARCELLINE—Yes, I do.

MICHEL—Will you listen to me?

MARCELLINE—What is there to say? We stood in this room a year ago and I forced more love on you than you could take, or return . . . I know that! And now when I see you here in front of me, all my pain comes back. There is not a part of me that isn't bruised. How can I forget that?

MICHEL—That will always be between us. All our lives I can only wish me different . . . and you can only wish me dead.

MARCELLINE—We are beyond that, Michel. We both died in Biskra. What is there left?

Michel questions whether they are better apart, but Marcelline finds it difficult to imagine their living together, with all the things they'll never be able to say to each other. Michel answers: "Our life together might destroy us both . . . but it might not. There are many kinds of marriages, Marcie, and people sacrifice many things to hold onto them."

Bocage comes in now and adds his pleas to Michel's: "Oh, Miss, let him stay. Let him stay and face these people down. In time they will listen to him. And if not to him, then to his books." Marcelline is equally sure: "No one will listen! That is a solution for those who come a long time after we are gone. . . . It won't solve our lives." But Bocage persists: "I have watched since you've been home, Miss, and you are as alone as he is— You only have each other, and the baby will only have you. If you send him away now, there is only one life he can go back to . . ." At Marcelline's request, Bocage says his good nights and departs.

MARCELLINE—Is Bocage right? Is that the only life you face?

MICHEL—I wish it were not . . . but there is no place on earth where those who are like me will not seek me out. Only here in this house where I was raised, can I shut them out.

MARCELLINE—Do you think you can?

MICHEL (pause)—Marcelline, I know that what I destroyed in you I cannot ask for, but the child is another chance at life. . . . And the important thing is to live. . . . Will you try?

MARCELLINE—What else can I do? I am like every other woman. . . . I thought my love could hold you . . . and I will probably think that until the day I die. (Pause.) Have you had your supper, Michel?

MICHEL—No.

MARCELLINE—I will get you some. (*She would leave, but he stops her.*)

MICHEL—I promise you one thing: whatever life we may have here, we will live it with dignity.

MARCELLINE (*goes to the door, then turns*)—We must promise each other nothing. My greatest joys I owe to you . . . and also my greatest sorrows. The best, and the most bitter . . . We will have to find a way between. (*She looks at him and leaves.*)

And Michel looks around the familiar room, taking it all in. Then he sits quietly on the couch, waiting for Marcelline.

TEA AND SYMPATHY *

A Play in Three Acts

By Robert Anderson

[Robert Anderson *was graduated from Harvard in 1939 and received his M.A. in 1940. It was while at Harvard that he met his wife, Phyllis, who was head of the Drama Department at the Erskine School for girls. She drafted Harvard boys for Erskine productions and Robert Anderson was one of them. He knew he wanted to be in the theatre but not in what way and it was she who suggested that he write plays. While in the Navy he wrote "Come Marching Home" which won top place in the National Theatre Conference contest of 1944 for plays written by servicemen overseas. It was produced in 1945 at the University of Iowa, and (with two other of his plays) served as the basis for the award of a 1946 Playwriting Fellowship by the National Theatre Conference. He has been everything in the theatre from stagehand to bit actor.*]

THE action takes place in a small, colonial house that serves as the dormitory for a New England boys' school.

We see the housemaster's study downstairs, and to the right of it, at a half-level above, a student's bedroom. Outside the study door a hall leads to the stairs, at the head of which a door opens on the boys' living room, which is out of range. A door from this room opens on the student's cell-like bedroom. Whereas the housemaster's paneled room, with its fireplace and surrounding bookcases, seems warm and friendly, the boy's room is so small there is only room for a bed, a chest of drawers, and a chair. Its present occupant has tried to relieve its bareness with an India print bedspread and drapes; there is also a phonograph.

On this late afternoon in June, before the moment for lighting the lamps, Tom Lee lies on his bed quietly playing his guitar and singing "The Joys of Love." In the downstairs study, the housemaster's wife, Laura Reynolds, works on a costume while she listens to Tom's singing. Her martini-drinking, glass-twiddling guest listens, too, but not for long. Lilly Sears is the pert wife of another master. Her 57th-Street suit is in sharp contrast to Laura's soft sweater and skirt, as is her vivacity to Laura's sensitive, quiet manner. Lilly asks whether Laura knows what the boy is thinking of: "what all the boys in this school are thinking about. Not only now in the Spring, but all the time—sex!" And she wags her head a little wisely and smiles.

LAURA—Lilly, you just like to shock people.

LILLY—Four hundred boys from the ages of thirteen to nineteen. That's the age, Laura. (*Restless, getting up.*) Doesn't it give you the willies sometimes, having all these boys around?

LAURA—Of course not. I never think of it that way.

LILLY—Harry tells me they put saltpeter in their food to quiet them down. But the way they look at you, I can't believe it.

LAURA—At me?

Lilly explains she meant any woman worth looking at. For herself, she is so used to it she even likes to watch them look and suffer. Lilly further explains that Laura is wrong to think these are just boys: according to the best authorities, youths of thirteen to nineteen are far more. "They come here," Lilly goes on, "ignorant as all get out about women, and then spend the next four years exchanging misinformation. They're so cute, and so damned intense." Laura's all wrong in thinking they're being casual. Lilly is convinced this is the right age to play Romeo. Her husband finds their themes all end in death. "Failure; death! Dishonor; death! Lose their girls; death! It's gruesome." Laura, on the contrary, finds this touching.

It occurs to Lilly that she's been chattering too much about the boys and that Laura shouldn't tell her husband, Harry. Then in the next breath Lilly says it's a well-known fact that the boys talk about her too, having her in and out of bed with every master in the school. Bill Reynolds, of course, excepted. Lilly admits that even before Bill met Laura, he was too busy with his mountain climbing and other activities even to glance in her direction. Laura had better be careful he doesn't drag his usual quota of boys up to the Maine lodge this summer! Laura needs no warning; she has planned a Canadian trip for just Bill and herself. "Of course I'd really like to go back to Italy. We had a good time there last summer. It was wonderful then. You should have seen Bill." Lilly has a quick answer: "Look, honey, you married Bill last year on his sabbatical leave, and abroad to boot. Teachers on sabbatical leave abroad are like men in uniform during the war. They never look so good again." Laura loyally sticks up for Bill as Lilly chatters about the farewell party they gave Bill. Laura knew all about it and even has the souvenir from it on a gold chain around her neck.

LILLY—I never thought he'd use that five-and-dime engagement ring we gave him that night. Even though we gave him an awful ribbing, we all expected him to come back a bachelor.

LAURA—You make it sound as though you kidded him into marrying.

LILLY—Oh, no, honey, it wasn't that.

LAURA (*with meaning*)—No, it wasn't.

LILLY—Well, I've got to go. You know, Bill could have married any number of the right kind of girls around here. But I knew it would take more than the right kind of girl to get Bill to marry. It would take something special. And you're something special.

With this backhanded compliment and a thank-you for the drink, plus another admonition not to tell Harry she'd had one, Lilly starts to go. Laura warns her that even though she won't be seeing Harry, Lilly had better stop talking that way, or he'll know without being told. "Now, look, honey," Lilly complains, "don't start going puritan on me. You're the only one in this school I can shoot my mouth off to, so don't change, baby. Don't change." With Laura's assurance that she won't, Lilly gushes: "Someday I'm going to wheedle out of you all the juicy stories you must have, from when you were in the theatre." Laura pleases her immeasurably by saying Lilly would make the most hardened chorus girl blush. Lilly thinks that's the sweetest thing Laura has said to her in days, and cheerfully departs.

Laura sits on, for a moment, listening to Tom's rather plaintive whistling. She then gets up, looks first at the Canadian-trip brochures, next at her watch; and finally goes to the study door to ask Tom down for a cup of tea. Tom needs no urging. He runs the brush over his hair and goes quickly down to the study—that very special place where Laura lives. Tom is full of delayed puppy love for Laura. It shows in his disappointment at having to leave the study door open when Laura says, "Perhaps you'd better leave it ajar, so that if some of the other boys get out of class early, they can come in, too." "Oh, sure." Tom obeys by opening the door the merest crack. When Laura gets all the tea things by the fire, Tom sits on the floor near her chair and answers her queries. Is there

heat enough in their rooms? There's heat enough, but this fire is
nice. When she mentions his singing, he says he hopes it doesn't
bother her. If it does, just bang on the radiator. And what was the
name of the song he was singing?

TOM—It's an old French song—"The Joys of Love." (*He speaks
the lyric.*)
    The joys of love
    Are but a moment long,
    The pain of love
    Endures forever.
LAURA—And is that true? (TOM *shrugs his shoulders.*) You sang
as though you knew all about the pains of love.
TOM—And you don't think I do?
LAURA—Well . . .
TOM—You're right.
LAURA—Only the joys.
TOM—Neither, really. (*Teapot whistles off stage.*)
LAURA—Then you're a fake. Listening to you, one would think
you knew everything there was to know. (*Rises and goes to next
room for tea.*) Anyway, I don't believe it. A boy like you.
TOM—It's true.
LAURA (*off stage*)—Aren't you bringing someone to the dance
after the play Saturday?
TOM—Yes.
LAURA—Well, there.
TOM—You.
LAURA (*reappears in doorway with teapot*)—Me?
TOM—Yes, you're going to be a hostess, aren't you?
LAURA—Yes, of course, but . . .
TOM—As a member of the committee, I'm taking you. All the
committee drew lots . . .
LAURA—And you lost.
TOM—I won.
LAURA (*a little embarrassed by this*)—Oh. My husband could
have taken me. (*Sits down again in her chair.*)
TOM—He's not going to be in town. Don't you remember, the
Mountain Climbing Club has its final outing this week end.

Laura had forgotten, but most tactfully says she'll be honored to
go with him. Tom carefully finds out she will wear yellow that evening: "The boy who's in charge of getting the flowers thinks a cor-

Deborah Kerr in "Tea and Sympathy," Audrey Hepburn in "Ondine" and Margaret Sullavan in "Sabrina Fair"

sage should be something like a funeral decoration. So I'm taking personal charge of getting yours." And he brushes aside her thanks with: "You must have gotten lots of flowers when you were acting in the theatre." Laura, in her turn, brushes this aside by saying that the flowers she was given now and then were quite unspectacular.

To Tom, it seems impossible that she could have given up the theatre to live in a school. Laura answers that if he knew the unromantic statistics of theatre unemployment, he might understand. And besides, she wasn't much good.

It's not only the romance of the theatre, but his love for her, that caused him to read Shaw's *Candida* on his Fall assignment. Laura laughs that it was because it was so short. "No," Tom explains, "because it sounded like the one I'd like the best—one I could understand. Did you ever play Candida?" "Only in stock," Laura answers.

TOM—Do you think she did right to send Marchbanks away?

LAURA—Well, Shaw made it seem right. Don't you think?

TOM (*really talking about himself*)—That Marchbanks sure sounded off a lot. I could never sound off like that, even if I loved a woman the way he did. She could have made him seem awfully small if she'd wanted to.

LAURA—Well, I guess she wasn't that kind of woman. Now stand up. Let's see if this fits. (*She gets up with the dress in her hands.*)

Tom blurts out, as he puts on the top of the dress, that his father will hit the roof when he hears Tom is playing a girl again, even if it's Lady Teazle. Last year he was annoyed when the *Alumni Bulletin* printed Tom's picture in Lady Macbeth costume. Tom's advice to Laura is not to mention this to his father when he comes on alumni business. Laura, buttoning the dress, promises to be careful; but she wonders what his mother's feelings are, and is she coming up for the play? Tom thought Laura knew his parents were divorced and that he didn't see his mother. Laura can only say, "I'm sorry."

Tom—You needn't be. They aren't. I was supposed to hold them together. That was how I happened to come into the world. It didn't work. That's a terrible thing, you know, to make a flop on the first job you've got in life.

Laura—Don't you ever see her?

Tom—Not since I was five. I was with her till five, and then my father took me away. All I remember about my mother is that she was always telling me to go outside and bounce a ball.

Laura (*handing him the skirt of the dress*)—You must have done something before Lady Macbeth. When did you play that character named Grace?

Tom (*stiffens*)—I never played anyone called Grace.

Laura—But I hear the boys sometimes calling you Grace. I thought . . . (*Notices that he's uncomfortable.*) I'm sorry. Have I said something terrible?

Tom—No.

Laura—But I have. I'm sorry.

Tom—It's all right. But it's a long story. Last year, over at the movies, they did a revival of Grace Moore in *One Night of Love*. I'd seen the revival before the picture came. And I guess I oversold it, or something. (But she was wonderful!) Anyway, some of the guys started calling me Grace. It was my own fault, I guess.

Adjusting his costume, Laura recalls how nicknames can be terrible things for most everyone. She adjusts the costume here and there as the boy stands on a footstool in front of her. And under her kindly questioning, Tom relaxes and tells her of his lack of home life these past ten years: his Summers at camp, Winters at boarding school, vacations spent going a round of plays and concerts with his aunt. He knows no girls, and wouldn't dare ask his popular roommate to arrange a blind date. He doesn't even dance. Laura says that she and he can sit out at this dance, but she offers to show him how, anyway, and holds her arms out to him. Tom gets down off the footstool.

Laura—Look, I'll show you how simple it is. (*Assumes the dancing position.*) Hold your left hand out this way, and put your right hand around my— (*She stops, as she sees him looking at her.*) Oh, now you're kidding me. A boy your age and you don't know how to dance.

TOM—I'm not kidding you.

LAURA—Well, then, come on. I had to teach my husband. Put your arm around me. (*Raises her arms.*)

TOM (*looks at her a moment, afraid to touch this woman he loves. Then to pass it off*)—We better put it off. We'd look kind of silly, both of us in skirts.

LAURA—All right. Take it off, then. No, wait a minute. Just let me stand off and take a good look— (*Walks around him.*) You're going to make a very lovely girl.

TOM—Thank you, Ma'am.

As Tom gets out of the dress, Mr. Harris, a young good-looking master, comes down the hall and starts upstairs to Tom's room. Laura wonders who would be coming by at this hour, and Harris explains he must see Tom. When Laura courteously offers him the use of the study, Harris as courteously declines and asks her to send Tom up to his own room, where Harris will wait for him. Tom, thinking it odd of the master to visit him here, takes his costume, thanks Laura, and heads upstairs.

Mr. Harris closes the door behind them. Tom doesn't know what to make of this, and is even more startled when Harris insists on knowing what Tom told the Dean—when Tom hasn't even seen the Dean! But Harris persists: "He didn't call you in and ask you about last Saturday afternoon?" Puzzled, Tom answers: "I'm allowed to leave town for the day in the company of a master." Harris still doesn't believe that Tom hasn't seen the Dean: "About you and me going to the dunes and swimming." Then threateningly: "Why didn't you keep your mouth shut?" "About what? What, for God's sake?" cries Tom.

HARRIS—I never touched you, did I?

TOM—What do you mean, touch me?

HARRIS—Did you say to the Dean that I touched you?

TOM (*turning away from* HARRIS)—I don't know what you're talking about.

HARRIS—Here's what I'm talking about. The Dean's had me on the carpet all afternoon. I probably won't be reappointed next year —and all because I took you swimming down off the dunes on Saturday.

TOM—Why should he have you on the carpet for that?

HARRIS—You can't imagine, I suppose?

Tom—What did you do wrong?

Harris—Nothing! Nothing, unless you made it seem like something wrong. Did you?

Tom—I told you I didn't see the Dean.

Harris—You will. He'll call for you. Bunch of gossiping old busybodies! Well— (*He starts for the door, stops, turns around, and softens. He comes back to the puzzled* Tom.) I'm sorry— It probably wasn't your fault. It was my fault. I should have been more—discreet. Good-by. Good luck with your music.

Three seventeen-year-olds come back from class. They are carrying books and wear the customary sports jackets and odd trousers. They have obviously been gossiping about Tom and Mr. Harris. One of them is Tom's roommate Al. He's both been trying to stop the talk and to stay out of it. Now he tries to shush them in front of Mrs. Reynolds' door, but Ralph, the bully boy, refuses: "Okay, you watch and see. Harris'll get bounced, and I'm gonna lock my room at night as long as Tom is living in this house." And he pretends amazement that Al's not worried over being Tom's roommate.

Since Harris had to pass the boys on his way out, there is now more gossiping and comment. Another youngster, Steve, comes in and diverts the boys' thoughts to other things. "Hey, Al, can I come in and watch Mrs. Morrison nurse her kid?"

Ralph—You're the loudest-mouthed bastard I ever heard. You want to give it away?

Steve—It's time. How about it, Al?

Al (*grudgingly*)—Come on.

Tom (*hears them coming, and moves to bolt his door, but* Steve *and* Ralph *break in before he can reach it. He watches them from the doorway.* Steve *rushes to the bed and throws himself across it and stares through the window.* Ralph *settles down next to him.*)

Al (*to* Tom *as he comes in*)—Hi. These horny bastards.

Steve—Al, bring me the glasses. (Al *goes into sitting room.*)

Ralph—Someday she's going to wean that little bastard and spoil all our fun.

Steve—Imagine sitting in a window . . .

Tom (*has been watching this with growing annoyance*)—Will you guys get out of here?

Ralph (*notices* Tom *for the first time*)—What's the matter with you, Grace?

Tom—This is my damned room.

Ralph—Gracie's getting private all of a sudden.

Tom—I don't want a lot of Peeping Toms lying on my bed watching a—a—
Steve—You want it all for yourself, don't you?
Ralph—Or aren't you interested in women?

Ralph rides Tom unpleasantly. Steve momentarily distracts him with the opera glasses, but when Tom tells them to get out, Ralph gets nasty. Grabbing Tom and holding him down, he says: "Be still, boy, or she'll see, and you'll spoil everything." "Horny bastard," Tom pants. "Get out of here." "Who are you calling a horny bastard?" Ralph cries, and grabs hold of Tom more forcefully and slaps him a couple of times across the face—not to hurt him, only to humiliate him. Steve gets in a few pokes, and in a moment it's not in fun, but verging on the serious. Al comes back from the sitting room and gets the boys off Tom, but Ralph gets in one more crack before he leaves: "I just don't like the son of a bitch calling me a horny bastard. Maybe if it was Dr. Morrison, instead of Mrs. Morrison, he'd be more interested. Hey, wouldn't you, Grace?"

As Ralph and Steve go upstairs, raucously singing "One Night of Love," Bill Reynolds, a large, tweedy man, comes home. He stops Ralph by calling: "Keep it down to a shout, will you?" then continues his conversation with the boy who's with him: "Phil, you come on up to the lodge around—let's see— We'll open the lodge around July first, so you plan to come up, say July third, and stay for two weeks. Okay?" "That'll be swell, sir," the boy answers. Bill goes on: "Frank Hocktor's coming then. You get along with Frank, don't you? He's a regular guy." And goes on to let Phil know what Summer projects he's already thought of for the boys.

Laura hears her husband talking and comes into the study to greet him, but by this time he is too intent on a phone call to the Dean to kiss her. When she asks what is the matter, why this urgency, Bill tells her: "Nothing very pretty," then into the phone: "Oh? How long ago? All right, thanks. I'll give him a couple of minutes, then I'll call him at home." He hangs up and announces: "Well, they finally caught up with Harris." Laura would like to know what he means by "caught up." Bill explains that Harris was seen on the dunes with a student.

Calmly going through his mail, he tells Laura the story because she's bound to hear it sooner or later: "He was lying there naked on the dunes, and one of the students was lying there naked, too. Just to talk about it is disgusting." Laura won't accept this as conclusive evidence. Bill doesn't hesitate for a moment: "With a man like

Harris, it's conclusive enough." And then he reveals that the boy involved was Tom Lee.

Tom at this moment is seen to rise from his bed, grab a towel, and go out of his room to the stairs.

Harris, Bill continues, was called on the carpet this afternoon and will be fired, and Tom may be kicked out, too. Laura, alone among all those who have heard the story, worries over what may happen to Tom. Bill thinks he *should* be kicked out: "I think you've got to let people know the school doesn't stand for even a hint of this sort of thing. He should be booted." According to Bill, this is exactly the punishment for being caught coming out of the rooms of the town whore, Ellie Martin. Laura can't bear to hear it put this way, but Bill isn't thinking of Tom, only of his own relations with Tom's father: "And I'm ashamed and sorry as hell for his father. Herb Lee was always damned good to me—came down from college when I was playing football here—helped me get into college—looked after me when I was in college and he was in law school. And I know he put the boy in my house hoping I could do something with him."

When he goes to the phone again, Laura feels she's never seen her husband so aggressively righteous. She questions him closely. Everyone knew that Tom was Harris's friend, but did anyone know it was because Harris encouraged the boy in his music? Bill won't accept this tack. But Laura continues to press: "What if Tom's roommate, Al, or some other great big athlete had been out with Harris? Would you have jumped to the same conclusion?" It is very simple for Bill: "It would have been different. Tom's always been an off-horse. And now it's quite obvious why. If he's kicked out, maybe it'll bring him to his senses. But he won't change if nothing's done about it." Bill, now that it's in the open, tells her to watch Tom's walk and stance. Laura can only say, "Oh, Bill!" "All right," Bill retorts, "so a woman doesn't notice these things. But a man knows a queer when he sees one."

Laura, at this point, has no desire to talk of Summer plans with Bill, but when he carelessly sweeps her Canadian folders into the wastebasket, her hurt face gives her away. He explains that he wouldn't hurt the boys he had invited to the lodge for anything, but in spite of Laura's patent disappointment, he doesn't return her offered embrace. Instead he gives her a speech on her place in this school: "Look, Laura, when I brought you here a year ago, I told you it was a tough place for a woman with a heart like yours. I told you you'd run across boys, big and little boys, full of problems—problems which for the moment seem gigantic and heartbreaking.

And you promised me then you wouldn't get all taken up with them. Remember?" "Yes," Laura murmurs. He continues, "When I was a kid in school here, I had my problems too. There's a place up by the golf course where I used to go off alone Sunday afternoons and cry my eyes out. I used to lie on my bed just the way Tom does, listening to phonograph records hour after hour." Laura, touched by this, kneels at his side. "But I got over it, Laura. I learned how to take it." Laura looks at him; this touches her. "When the headmaster's wife gave you this teapot she told you what she tells all the new masters' wives. You have to be an interested bystander." Laura says, "I know." And Bill goes on: "Just as she said, all you're supposed to do is, every once in a while, give the boys a little tea and sympathy. Do you remember?" She does, but she also remembers that this was just the age her first husband, John, was when she married him.

Bill breaks off the conversation, wanting to clean up for supper at the Dean's. Laura's preparations for a supper at home mean nothing to him, with the problem of Tom still unsettled. To make things worse for Laura, Bill asks her not to wear the five-and-ten ring to the dining hall. At this point she directly accuses Bill: "I think you're ashamed of the night you gave it to me—that you ever let me see you needed help. That night in Italy, in some vague way, you cried out." Bill's only answer is: "What is the matter with you today? *Me* crying out for help!" And he retires to dress.

Laura then has to greet Herb Lee who comes to their door. This Boston businessman, still collegiate in dress and overhearty in manner, only makes Laura uncomfortable with his greeting to Bill: "I like her, Bill. I like her very much. What I'd like to know is how did you manage to do it?" Cuffing Bill, he adds: "I'll bet you make her life miserable." But it is difficult for the two men to talk to each other with the specter of the son between them. Herb has seen the Dean and found out about Tom. He wants desperately to know what the matter is. "What's happened, Bill? Why isn't my boy a regular fellow? He's had every chance since he was knee-high to a grasshopper—boys' camps every Summer, boarding school—" When he appeals to Laura, she feels Tom is "regular," and brings forth his fine tennis playing as proof. "But, Laura," quickly answers Herb, "he doesn't even play tennis like a regular fellow. No hard drives and cannon-ball serves. He's a cut artist. He can put more damn twists on that ball." He wins, Laura reminds him. But she only brings back uncomfortable memories of locker-room talk about Tom. For Herb and Bill, if Tom isn't considered "regular," he's nothing. Herb even tells of the orphan boy he's befriended who's shaping up much better than his own son.

Herb gives the Dean's personal opinion that Tom was innocently involved. Furthermore, the Dean doesn't go along with some of the faculty who feel it would be easier on Tom if he were to leave the school. Herb and the Dean feel that things have been perhaps too easy for the boy, and he should be made to stick it out as a lesson. Laura suggests that this might prove to be something more. Herb won't listen. He points out that the kidding and the extra effort Tom will have to make are just what he needs to become manly. Laura's protests go unregarded, but they do listen when she says: "Mr. Lee, this may sound terribly naïve of me, and perhaps indelicate, but I don't believe your son knows what this is all about. Why Mr. Harris was fired, why the boys will kid him." And she goes on: "I'm only guessing. But I think when it comes to these boys, we often take too much knowledge for granted. And I think it's going to come as a terrible shock when he finds out what they're talking about. Not just a lesson, a shock." As Herb leaves to see Tom, he answers Laura: "I don't believe he's as naïve as all that. I just don't."

But Herb doesn't know what he's going to tell his son when he sees him; he feels miserably unequipped. He confesses to Bill as they go into the hall that he really talked with Tom only once before. "It was after a Sunday dinner and I made up my mind it was time we sat in a room together and talked about important things. He got sick to his stomach. That's a terrible effect to have on your boy."

Herb girds himself for his visit with Tom, who greets him in a surprised but timidly affectionate fashion. The sight of the Lady Teazle costume in Tom's room makes Herb come to the point of his visit: "Tom, I'd like to be your friend. I guess there's something between fathers and sons that keeps them from being friends, but I'd like to try." Tom is embarrassed, but sits on the bed and listens.

Herb recalls for him advice he had given before: going slow in the choice of friends, since one's known by the company he keeps. "And, instead of making friends with the good guys," says Herb bitterly, "you made friends with people like this Harris guy who got himself fired."

TOM—Why is he getting fired?
HERB—He's being fired because he was seen in the dunes with you.
TOM—Look, I don't—
HERB—Naked.

Tom—You too?

Herb—So you know what I'm talking about?

Tom—No, I don't.

Herb—You do too know. I heard my sister tell you once. She warned you about a janitor in the building down the street.

Tom (*incredulous*)—Mr. Harris—?

Herb—Yes. He's being fired because he's been doing a lot of suspicious things around, apparently, and this finished it. All right, I'll say it plain, Tom. He's a fairy. A homosexual.

Tom—Who says so?

Herb—Now, Tom—

Tom—And seeing us on the beach—?

Herb—Yes.

Tom—And what does that make me?

Herb—Listen, I know you're all right.

Tom—Thanks.

Herb—Now wait a minute.

Tom—Look, we were just swimming.

Herb—All right, all right. So perhaps you didn't know.

Tom—What do you mean, perhaps?

Herb—It's the school's fault for having a guy like that around. But it's your fault for being a damned fool in picking your friends.

Tom—So that's what the guys meant.

Tom's father warns him of the "ribbing" he's going to have to take, but Tom is thinking of the injustice to Mr. Harris, and wants to square him with the Dean. Herb quickly squelches that idea; he is only concerned with patching up his son's reputation. Only two things occur to him: a crew haircut for Tom, and his giving up the part of Lady Teazle.

Tom is upset at giving up the best part in the school play, but is also beginning to grasp what gossip means, what everyone is thinking of him—perhaps even Mrs. Reynolds. Someone on the stairs shouts: "Hey, Grace, who's taking you to the dance Saturday night?" Al shuts the boy up. But Herb now completes his son's sense of humiliation by forcing him, in front of Laura, to call the dramatics coach about giving up his part. Tom is dreadfully unhappy and ashamed to make this call in front of her.

Laura tries to help, but once more is rebuffed by Herb Lee. Seeing how painful it is for Tom to speak his piece, she refuses to go to dinner with Bill and Herb. When, after they leave, the boy is about to break down, she comes to his rescue and speaks into the phone to the dramatics coach: "Hello, Fred . . . Laura. Yes,

Tom's father, well, he wants Tom— He thinks Tom is tired, needs to concentrate on his final exams. You had someone covering the part, didn't you? . . . Yes, of course it's a terrible disappointment to Tom. I'll see you tomorrow."

Through the open door more rough talk is heard as Ralph and his gang go to supper. Tom is beside himself with shame that Laura might hear and believe these things about him. She once more, try-ing to be helpful, tells Tom she's going to have Joan Harrison to tea tomorrow so he can invite her to the dance. This, for Tom, is the most crushing blow of all. "You were to go with me."

LAURA—I know, but—

TOM—Do you think so, too, like the others? Like my father?

LAURA—Tom!

TOM—Is that why you're shoving me off on Joan?

LAURA—Tom, I asked her over so that we could lick this thing.

TOM (*turns to her*)—What thing? What thing? (*He looks at her a moment, filled with indignation, then he bolts up the stairs. But as he goes up,* PHIL *comes down.* TOM *feels like a trapped rat. He starts down the stairs again, but in the state he is in, can't face* LAURA. *He goes on up, cowering to one side.*)

PHIL—What's the matter with you? (TOM *doesn't answer, and* PHIL *shrugs and passes on.* TOM *reaches his room and leans against the door, while* LAURA, *though she wants to comfort him, checks herself. She sits down, and touches her teapot as upstairs* TOM *starts to sob.*)

ACT II

Two days have gone by, and now pressure is being put on Al, Tom's roommate. His father has him on the phone, forbidding him to room with Tom next year. And Ralph, catching Al in the hall, exerts pressure in a cruder fashion when he asks Al whether Tom has made a pass at him yet. Ralph tells Al the boys on the ball team don't like it at all: "The guy they're supposed to elect captain rooming with a queer."

RALPH—So you don't believe me—wait and see. (*Putting on a dirty grin.*) Anyway, my mother said I should save myself for the girl I marry. Hell, how would you like to have to tell your wife: "Honey, I've been saving myself for you, except for one night when a guy— (AL *roughs* RALPH *up with no intention of hurting him.*) Okay, okay. So you don't want to be captain of the baseball team. So who the hell cares? I don't, I'm sure.

AL—Look. Why don't you mind your own business?

RALPH—What the hell fun would there be in that?

AL—Ralph, Tom's a nice kid.

RALPH—Yeah. That's why all the guys leave the shower room
at the gym when he walks in.

Al hadn't heard about that and is outraged, and when Ralph announces that Tom keeps pictures of strong men in his bottom drawer,
Al defends him: "Yes, I've noticed them. His old man wants him
to be a muscle man, and he wrote away for this course in muscle
building, and they send those pictures. Any objections?" Ralph
jeers at him: "Go on, stick up for him. Stick your neck out. You'll
get it chopped off with a baseball bat, you crazy bastard."

After Ralph leaves him, Al, disturbed and unhappy, tries to see
Bill Reynolds. Laura, however, greets him in the study, and does
her utmost to dissuade him from changing rooms.

Laura likes Al, and tells him so. She explains how much it must
mean for Tom to have one of the school's big men for a roommate:
"You wouldn't understand what it means to be befriended. You're
one of the strong people. I'm surprised, Al." He blurts out about
his father's phone call, and then tries to justify himself: "Well, he
does act sort of queer, Mrs. Reynolds." He goes on, giving reasons:
"Well, like the fellows say, he sort of walks lightly, if you know what
I mean. Sometimes the way he moves—the things he talks about—
longhair music all the time." Laura refuses to accept them: "Al,
there are good explanations of all these things you're saying. They're
silly—and prejudiced—and arguments all dug up to suit a point of
view. They're all after the fact." And just to show him how wrong
he is, she flirts with an idea: "Al, what if I were to start the rumor
tomorrow that you were—well, queer, as you put it?"

Al thinks no one would believe it; Laura puts him straight:
"You've got something to learn, Al. I've been around a little and
I've met men, just like you—same setup—who weren't men, some
of them married and with children." But she relents as Al tells her
of his chance to be basebell captain next year. She appreciates how
much this means to him. Then Al shows her where she stands in all
of this: "Excuse me for saying so, but it's easy for you to talk the
way you have. You're not involved. You're just a bystander.
You're not going to be hurt. Nothing's going to happen to you, one
way or the other—" Even after Al is gone, Laura broods over the
criticism.

Al joins Tom in his room. Even though they try to joke about
other things, they quickly get on the subject at issue. Tom has had

a rough day: "I went to a meeting of the dance committee. I'm no longer on the dance committee. Said that since I'd backed out of playing the part in the play, I didn't show the proper spirit. That's what they *said* was the reason." Al is indignant, but he doesn't know what Tom could have done. Tom continues: "I tried to pass it off. Christ, you can't pass it off. You know, when I went into the showers today after my tennis match, everyone who was in there grabbed a towel and—and—walked out." "They're stupid," says Al; "just a bunch of stupid bastards." Tom, wandering nervously about, confesses: "Goddamn it, the awful thing I found myself—Jesus, I don't know—I found myself self-conscious about things I've been doing for years. Dressing, undressing—I keep my eyes on the floor—Geez, if I even look at a guy that doesn't have clothes on, I'm afraid somebody's gonna say something, or— Jesus, I don't know."

And Al, unbuttoning his shirt, suddenly stops, full of this same self-consciousness. Tom edgily advises him to undress in his own room. After this uncomfortable moment Al tries to give Tom some pointers; for one thing recommends his getting a crew haircut. For another, that he do something about his walk. Tom despairingly cries: "No one gave a goddamn about how I walked till last Saturday!" Al makes him walk so he can correct him. Tom just moans: "Now I'm not going to be able to walk any more. Everything I been doing all my life makes me look like a fairy." But he walks, and Al can only say, "Tom, I don't know. You walk sort of light."

Tom—Okay. You walk. Let me watch you. I never noticed how you walked.

Al (*stands there for a moment, never having realized before how difficult it could be to walk if you think about it. Finally he walks*) —If you tell any of the guys about this—

Tom—Do you think I would? (Al *walks again.*) That's a good walk. I'll try to copy it. (*Tries to copy the walk, but never succeeds in taking even a step.*) Do you really think that'll make any difference?

Al—I dunno.

Tom—Not now, it won't. Thanks anyway.

Al (*comes and sits on bed beside* Tom. *Puts arms around* Tom's *shoulder and thinks this thing out*)—Look, Tom— You've been in on a lot of bull sessions. You heard the guys talking about stopping over in Boston on the way home—getting girls—you know.

Al's solution is for Tom to visit the local whore, Ellie Martin, Saturday night. "I know she's a dog," Al continues, "but—" Tom interrupts: "So what good's that going to do? I get caught there, I get thrown out of school." "No one ever gets caught," Al explains. "Sunday morning people'd hear about it—not the Dean—I mean the fellows. Hell, Ellie tells and tells and tells. Boy, you'd be made!" Tom listens with disgusted disbelief to Al, who admits he's never had a woman, but doesn't have to begin with Ellie. Tom understands this: "You mean, you don't have to prove anything?" Al tells him to forget it: "It's probably a lousy idea, anyway."

Al now gets to the real point of his visit: "Hap Hudson's asked me to come to his house. He's got a single there. A lot of the fellows from the team are over there, and well—" Again, Tom understands.

When Tom is left alone, he plays a record to calm himself. Bill Reynolds now returns home with a book of poetry for Laura, only to find that Tom had known she wanted it and had already given it to her. Bill tears the book to pieces and hurls it into the fire, then sullenly sits down to change his shoes. Laura kneels by him, trying to communicate. He won't let her embrace him, and brusquely avoids her caresses. Laura backs away: "Oh, Bill, we so rarely touch any more. I keep feeling I'm losing contact with you. Don't you feel that?"

BILL (*looking at his watch*)—Laura, I—

LAURA—I know, you've got to go. But it's just that, I don't know, we don't touch any more. It's a silly way of putting it, but you seem to hold yourself aloof from me. A tension seems to grow between us —and then when we do—touch—it's a violent thing—almost a compulsive thing. (BILL *is uncomfortable at this accurate description of their relationship. He sits looking troubled. She puts her arms around his neck and embraces him, bending over him.*) You don't feel it? You don't feel yourself holding away from me until it becomes overpowering? There's no growing together any more—no quiet times, just holding hands, the feeling of closeness, like it was in Italy. Now it's long separations and then this almost brutal coming together, and— Oh, Bill, you do see, you do see. (BILL *suddenly straightens up, toughens, and looks at her.* LAURA, *repulsed, slowly draws her arms from around his shoulders.*)

BILL—For God's sake, Laura, what are you talking about? (*Rises and goes to his desk to mark some exams.*) It can't always be a honeymoon.

He remains quite deliberately cold and uncomprehending, and refuses the tea Laura offers. He becomes critical when she tells him

that Joan is coming for tea: "No, she isn't. I just saw her father at
the gym. I don't think that was a very smart thing for you to do,
Laura."

Laura still has ideas of how to help the boy: she now wants Bill
to intercede with the Dean to stop the hazing of Tom. She gets
nowhere. Bill announces with some satisfaction that, although
they're losing Al next year, they at least won't have Tom. This
makes Laura come right out with: "You're not only angry. It's
almost as though you were, well, jealous."

BILL—Oh, come on now.

LAURA—Well, how else can you explain your—your vindictive
attitude towards him?

Bill refuses even to argue, and preparing to leave for class, warns
Laura once more against having Tom down for tea alone: "I think
you should have him down when you have the other boys—for his
own good. I mean that! Well, I'll see you in the dining hall. Try
·to be on time." Laura leans against the back of a chair, and as he
goes out and joins Al, she puts her hands over her face and weeps.

She can't help hearing Tom's call to Ellie Martin on the phone
outside the study door. His reluctance and discomfort at arranging
this Saturday night date only increased her sense of pity for him.
When he knocks on the door, she meets him with tea things in her
hands, and allows him to break the afternoon's date, before she mentions Joan's not coming. He has stopped by to say he won't be
going to the dance, either. She announces: "Look, Tom—now that
neither of us is going, why don't you drop down here after supper
Saturday night. We could listen to some records, or play gin, or
we can just talk." Tom longs to, but pleads another engagement,
one that he is not too anxious to keep. Laura tells him pleasantly:
"Well, I'll be here just in case, just in case you decide to come in."
And she holds out her hand and adds: "Maybe your plans will
change." Tom only wishes they would, as he runs out and down
the hall.

SCENE II

It is about 8:45 Saturday night. In the study, Laura, dressed in
a lovely, soft, informal dress, with a single flower pinned on, sips her
coffee by the fire, and is waiting for Tom.

In his room, Tom is getting all dressed up, too. He has finished
shaving, and is patting on shaving lotion; he is as cheerful as if he
were getting ready for a funeral.

The only person in a gay mood tonight is Lilly. She comes by to pick up Laura. Under her raincoat she wears a very becoming, low-cut dress. As she checks on her appearance in a mirror she tells Laura: "Harry says this neck will drive all the little boys crazy."

LAURA—I don't think so.

LILLY—Well, that's not very flattering.

LAURA—I mean, I think they'll appreciate it, but as for driving them crazy—

LILLY—After all, I want to give them some reward for dancing their duty dances with me.

Laura laughingly tells her she's really lost in a boys' school. But Lilly seems to be happy to settle for her three hundred innocent flirtations a year.

LAURA—Lilly, I've often wondered what you'd do if one of the three hundred attempted to go, well, a little further than innocent flirtation.

LILLY—I'd slap him down—the little beast. (*Laughs and admires herself in the mirror.*) Harry says if I'm not careful I'll get to looking like Ellie Martin. You've seen Ellie?

Laura has, and is sad that the boys settle for something so sordid. She places a chair for Tom before the fire, as Lilly chatters on admiring Laura's flower. She finds it so much better than the monumental corsage the dance committee honored her with. At length she takes up her raincoat to go. Laura says she's not going to the dance, nor will she promise to wait up for Lilly's post-mortems.

When the outside door closes on Lilly, Laura sees to it that the study door is slightly ajar, and then stands, coffee cup in hand, near the fire, waiting for Tom.

Tom, all dressed up in his blue suit, goes back to his room for a reassuring swig from a hidden bottle. He takes down his raincoat and leaves, hoping to slip unnoticed past Laura's door. He doesn't succeed: Laura catches him, and ever so pleasantly maneuvers him into the study.

From then on, she does everything she can to keep Tom from going to Ellie's. Noticing the liquor on his breath, she lets him have some coffee from her cup. She holds his attention with memories of her young, first husband. He was just Tom's age, and: "He was killed being conspicuously brave. He had to be conspicuously brave, you see, because something had happened in training camp—I don't know what—and he was afraid the others thought him a coward. He showed them he wasn't." Tom understands that, and is sorry about his death. Laura tells him: "Yes, so am I. I'm sorry he was killed the way he was killed—trying to prove how brave he was. In trying to prove he was a man, he died a boy." "Still," says Tom, "he must have died happy." Laura asks: "Because he proved his courage?" "That," confesses Tom, "and because he was married to you." With this he is so embarrassed he has an extra reason for leaving quickly. Laura, however, won't let him go. She keeps him talking at the door; and when this fails, she turns on some music and offers to teach him to dance. Tom wants to know: "Why are you so nice to me?" He knows she's not like this to the rest of the fellows. Laura then quite openly tells him: "I guess, Tom—I guess it's because I like you." Tom has been so considerate and nice this first, hard year at school. "We just seem to have hit it off." Tom feels that this is the cause of Bill Reynolds' hate for him.

LAURA—I don't think he hates you.

TOM—Yes, he hates me. Why lie? I think everyone here hates me but you. But they won't.

LAURA—Of course they won't.

TOM—He hates me because he made a flop with me. I know all about it. My father put me in this house when I first came here, and when he left me he said to your husband, "Make a man out of him." He's failed, and he's mad; and then you came along, and were nice to me—out of pity.

LAURA—No, Tom, not pity. I'm too selfish a woman to like you just out of pity.

TOM (*he has worked himself up into a state of confusion, and anger, and desperation*)—There's so much I—there's so much I don't understand.

LAURA (*reaches out and touches his arm*)—Tom, don't go out to-night.

TOM—I've got to. That's one thing that's clear. I've got to!

LAURA (*holds up her arms for dancing*)—Won't you let me teach you how to dance?

TOM (*suddenly and impulsively he throws his arms around her and kisses her passionately, awkwardly, and then in embarrassment he buries his head in her shoulder*)—Oh, God—God.

LAURA—Tom—Tom— (TOM *raises his face and looks at her, and would kiss her again.*) No, Tom— No, I— (*At the first "No,"* TOM *breaks away from her and runs out the door halfway up the stairs.*)

And he finds himself trapped by the returning mountain climbers, Phil and Paul. They had no liking for climbing in the rain.

Bill comes in and calls up to the boys that they have his permission to eat across the street when they've changed their clothes. Then he takes off his equipment and piles it on the floor. Laura doesn't move and doesn't respond when he comes to give her a kiss, and scarcely listens to his complaints about the boys and the weather. She is listening instead for Tom's step, hoping against hope he will go back to his room. But Tom is only waiting for the study door to close before he dashes out. When she hears the street door slam, Laura despairingly turns away to watch her husband settle down in the chair intended for Tom. Bill is now reconciled to his bad luck: "Good to get out, though. Makes you feel alive. Think I'll go out again next Saturday, alone. Won't be bothered by the fellows wanting to turn back." He reaches out his hand for Laura. She stands by the door, staring at his outstretched hand.

ACT III

Late the next afternoon Tom, having locked and bolted his door to everyone, is lying on his back on the bed. Ralph is busy at the pay telephone trying to keep his date happy until teatime, when Steve—with something urgent to tell him—makes him hang up. And as they go upstairs to dress Steve passes on the latest bulletin about Tom's date with Ellie.

A moment after they've disappeared upstairs, Bill comes in and heads for Tom's room. At first the boy refuses to admit him. Bill coldly insists: "You've got to see me. Come on. Open up! I've got to talk to the Dean at four, and I want to speak to you first." When Bill asks if he's afraid to see him, Tom opens the door and says: "You've got the full story. What the hell do you want?" Bill nastily disagrees. Tom tells him: "When the school cops brought me in last night they told you I was with Ellie Martin." Bill once more disagrees: "You weren't with her. You couldn't be with her. Do you understand what I mean?" Tom, trying to brave it out, asks: "Who says so?" Ellie apparently said so. Bill lets him have it: "She says that you couldn't—and that you jumped up and grabbed a knife in her kitchen and tried to kill yourself—and she had to fight with you, and that's what attracted the school cops." Tom mutters: "What difference does it make?" Bill, even though Tom is bound to be expelled, ostensibly wants to set the record straight. The boy knows better, and blurts out that actually Bill is gloating: now he can be happy and spread the news everywhere, even to Laura. Bill virtuously says he won't tell anyone—except, of course, the Dean and possibly Tom's father. As for Laura: "Yes, I think she ought to know." After Bill leaves, Tom locks the door and sits down desolately in the room's one chair.

Laura, as Bill is on his way upstairs, is delayed by Herb Lee, just as she was going to take Tom his raincoat. Herb, although he knows his son is to be expelled, seems almost cheerful. The circumstances this time are so much more normal. Laura remarks that because the police found Tom out of bounds with a whore, Herb for the first time seems actually proud of him. Once again Herb is sure that Bill will understand much better than Laura, and greets him expansively when he comes in.

Bill holds back for a moment, then when Herb imagines his son "telling the boys all about it," Bill straightens him out. Herb pathetically hopes there is some way to shut Ellie up, but he's told it's too late for that: "Ellie talks. She's got no shame—and this apparently is something to talk about." Laura now turns on Herb: "Do you still think it will make a good smoking-car story?" When Laura interrupts, Bill flares up that they won't detain her; she now knows the facts. "Why did you want me to hear?" Laura asks. Bill tells her: "I wanted you to know the facts. That's all. The whole story."

Laura first listens quietly, then begs: "Mr. Lee, please don't go on drawing the wrong conclusion!" Herb says he's not: "This sort of thing can happen to a normal boy. But it's what the others will think—added to the Harris business. And that's all that's important. What will they think?" Neither man seems to care what the boy will be thinking. But Herb tries to prime himself for a talk with his son—and feels his usual inadequate self: "But I've got to go up— Maybe I should have left him with his mother. She might have known what to do, what to say—" And he starts out, asking Bill to come with him. Laura also asks to speak to Bill, but he says he'll be back. The father goes up to his son's room, knocks, and calls out to him. Tom won't open the door or speak. Herb is deeply hurt, but won't let Bill make the boy open the door. The men go back downstairs and this time Laura is so serious in her insistence that Bill stay behind, that he lets Herb go on without him. "Good-by, Laura," Herb tells her, "see you again." "You'll see her," Bill says, "in a couple of days at the reunion." Herb isn't sure: "I may not be coming up for it now— Maybe I will. I don't know. I'll be walking along. Good-by, Laura. Tell Tom I tried to see him."

Left alone with Laura, Bill asks what's the matter. Laura asks at once: "Is there to be no blame, no punishment for the boys and men who taunted him into doing this? What if he had succeeded in killing himself? What then?"

BILL—I wish you'd look at the facts and not be so emotional about this.

LAURA—The facts! What facts? An innocent boy goes swimming with an instructor—an instructor whom he likes because this instructor is one of the few who encourage him, who don't ride him. And because he's an off-horse, you and the rest of them are only too glad to put two and two together and get a false answer—anything which will let you go on and persecute a boy whom you basically don't like. If it had happened with Al or anybody else, you would have done nothing.

BILL—It would have been an entirely different matter. You can't escape from what you are—your character. Why do they spend so much time in the law courts on character witnesses? To prove this was the kind of man who could or couldn't commit such and such a crime.

LAURA—I resent this judgment by prejudice. He's not like me; therefore, he is capable of all possible crimes. He's not one of us—a member of the tribe!

BILL—Now look, Laura, I know this is a shock to you, because you were fond of this boy. But you did all you could for him, more than anyone would expect. After all, your responsibility doesn't go beyond—

LAURA—I know. Doesn't go beyond giving him tea and sympathy on Sunday afternoons. Well, I want to tell you something. It's going to shock you—but I'm going to tell you.

And Laura tells him that she feels responsible for Tom's going to Ellie. She knew of his date and tried to stop him by giving him the affection he needed, but at the last moment she failed because she had to be a "good woman." But good for whom, she asks Bill.

Bill feels this has gone far enough; they can discuss it later. Laura says: "Bill! There'll be no later on. I'm leaving you." He can't believe she's doing this because of Tom.

BILL—You can't leave over a thing like this. You know what it means.

LAURA—I wouldn't worry too much about it. When I'm gone, it will probably be agreed by all that I was an off-horse too, and didn't really belong to the clan, and it's good riddance.

BILL—And you're doing this—all because of this—this fairy?
LAURA—This boy, Bill—this boy is more of a man than you are.
BILL—Sure. Ask Ellie.
LAURA—Because it was distasteful for him. Because for him there has to be love. He's more of a man than you are."

Bill goads her into saying more than she had intended. Everything pours out: his possibly being kidded into marrying her, his really never wanting a wife, and not letting her be a wife to him, and finally: "Did it ever occur to you that you persecute in Tom, that boy up there, you persecute in him the thing you fear in yourself?"

Laura has now hit too close; Bill looks at her with real hate, and says in a controlled voice: "I hope you will be gone when I come back for dinner." She agrees to be gone, but apologizes for having spoken as she did: "This was the weakness you cried out for me to save you from, wasn't it?" Bill leaves her abruptly.

She stands stunned and exhausted. Then after a few minutes, she slowly goes upstairs, with his raincoat, to Tom.

He is lying there, shattered, convinced by the gossip: "I'm no man. Ellie knows it. Everybody knows it. It seems everybody knew it except me. And now I know it."

Laura points out to him that Ellie is no test, because he wasn't in love with her. Tom wishes he were dead. Laura asks him to look at her; she then reminds him of his kissing her. Tom turns away at this reminder: "You sent me away—you— Anyway, when you heard this morning it must have made you sick." But Laura sits beside him and says softly: "Tom, I'm going to tell you something." The boy's head is still turned away. "Tom?" He still doesn't dare look at her. "It was the nicest kiss I've ever had—from anybody." Now Tom looks at her, but with disbelief when she tells him that she's come to say good-by. "I'm leaving Bill— For a lot of reasons —one of them, what he's done to you. But before I left, I wanted you to know, for your own comfort, you're more of a man now than he ever was or will be. And one day you'll meet a girl, and it will be right." She asks Tom to believe her. He's grateful, he smiles at her, but he's sure she's wrong. He shuts his eyes, as she looks at him with compassion and tenderness. She looks at him for a long time, then gets up and leaves the bedroom. A moment later she appears in the hall door, pauses for a moment, then closes it, staying inside. Tom, hearing the door close, collapses on the bed. He is lying there, completely miserable, when he hears the bedroom door close. He watches Laura as, while looking at him, she finds a bolt on the door and slides it to.

LAURA (*stands looking at* TOM, *her hand at her neck. With a slight movement, she unbuttons the top button of her blouse and moves toward* TOM. *When she gets alongside the bed, she reaches out her hand, still keeping one hand at her blouse.* TOM *makes no move, just watches her.* LAURA *makes a little move with the outstretched hand, asking for his hand.* TOM *slowly moves his hand toward hers. She stands there smiling gently at him, then sits, and after a moment murmurs:*)—And now—nothing? (TOM'S *other hand comes up and with both his hands he brings her hand to his lips. After a moment* LAURA *speaks.*) Years from now—when you talk about this—and you will!—be kind. (*Gently she carries the boy's hands toward her opened blouse, as the lights slowly dim out—and—*

CURTAIN

THE GIRL ON THE VIA FLAMINIA *

A Play in Three Acts

BY ALFRED HAYES

[ALFRED HAYES *was born in London but grew up in New York.
He worked there for a time as a newspaperman, magazine writer,
and radio writer. In 1943 he went into the army, serving in Italy,
and while there he met Roberto Rossellini and Luigi Zampa, and
worked with Rossellini on the film "Païsan." Mr. Hayes returned
to the United States in 1945 and after writing "All Thy Conquests,"
went to Hollywood for Warner Brothers. Mr. Hayes' other books
include "Shadow of Heaven"; two books of poems; "The Girl on the
Via Flaminia" which he dramatized in 1954 and which was filmed
under the title of "Act of Love"; and "In Love," a novel. He has
also written two Broadway plays, "Journeyman" (a dramatization
of Erskine Caldwell's novel) and " 'Tis of Thee," a musical. Mr.
Hayes was awarded the Eunice Tietjens poetry award.*]

THIS is the Rome of 1944, liberated, cold, and very hungry. Two
rooms of Signora Pulcini's apartment on the Via Flaminia are to be
seen: the dining room (where she makes money by selling the Allied
soldiers wine and eggs), and the adjoining bedroom (which she rents
out for additional income).

The dining room has a large center table, a radio, the customary
lithograph of the Sacred Heart; and in the rear, French doors leading to a shabby garden. The bedroom consists mostly of a large bed
covered with a red bedspread. It, too, has a garden entrance.

A middle-aged English soldier and a callow American are polishing
off some of Mama's wine while grousing about a soldier's lot. The
Englishman is homesick for his "missus" and the American has girl
trouble—any girl. He wishes he were in France.

ENGLISHMAN—Oh, Rome ain't bad.

AMERICAN—Rome's a city. Cities are different. But you take the
rest of the country. Mountains!

* Copyright 1954 by Alfred Hayes.

234

ENGLISHMAN—Well, it's a pretty country, except for the flies.
AMERICAN—Listen, Sarge. Know what they can do with Europe?
All of it? Fold it three ways and ram it.
ENGLISHMAN—You can get a bellyful of Europe.

Sharp-faced Adele Pulcini, in her late fifties, enters warning them
not to make so much noise or the carabinieri will pay a visit. The
American asks her self-pityingly to feel his ankle: "Busted off a cliff
in Velletri. That's what I got liberating your Goddam city." Adele
retorts drily: "In this house we are all heroes." The Englishman
adds: "Bloody 'eroes."
Little Mimi, the sixteen-year-old servant girl, coming in with another bottle of wine, can't help giggling at the American. Is he
crazy, she asks Adele, and the American cuts in: "Stop talking that
language. Everybody talks foreign languages. Come on, bella mia—
we dance, American tiptop ballata." Adele gives the child permission
in Italian, adding, "He's drunk." No sooner have they started to
dance than the fancy redhead, who has been packing in the bedroom,
emerges. The American immediately stops dancing and heads in
her direction.
Nina efficiently slaps him down: "E proibito," she lightly tells
him. Adele announces that Nina's off for Florence. "To Florence?
What's in Florence?" the American wants to know.

NINA—Love, caro mio. Love, love, love!
AMERICAN—Hell, in Rome there's love, love, love too.
ADELE—She is engaged to an American. A capitano. He takes
her to Florence.
AMERICAN—An officer?

The captain, Nina informs him, is much nicer than he is, besides
being better looking. "He's gentle . . . polite!" . . . and he respects Italian girls.

AMERICAN—Me too. I respect Italian girls.
NINA—Si. In *letto*.
AMERICAN—What's *letto?*
NINA—The bed.

The American can see nothing wrong with that, and asks her to
try him. Nina, gaily brushing him aside and asking them to call her
when Lisa comes, goes into the hall. The American mutters: "Aw,
they save it for the brass," and immediately starts in on Mama Adele

to get him a girl. She is extremely reluctant: "You make trouble. You Americans always make trouble." He shows her all the money he has, with no one to spend it on. Adele gives in, but warns him: "No trouble!" "Honest to God," he promises gratefully, and follows Adele to the phone. She gets him a date. Armed with the address Adele has written down, he can't wait to get going. The Englishman having finished his wine is ready to leave too. Adele tells them both: "Go out through the garden. I do not want you seen leaving the house. Come, I'll open the gate."

Mimi shows Lisa into the dining room: "Accomodatevi, signora. I will call Nina." Lisa, tall, pretty, with fine shoulders, stands examining the room. She is dressed very differently from her red-headed, high-heeled friend Nina—in trench coat, wool skirt, ski stockings, and brogues. Adele, shivering from the garden cold, greets her pleasantly, asking if her husband is with her. "My—?" Adele says again: "The American. Your husband. He is with you?"

LISA—No, signora. He is not with me right now.

ADELE—Eh, you girls! . . . Suddenly all women in Rome love Americans. But it's smart—

LISA—Smart?

ADELE—Escape, my dear. Escape! What's left of Europe? A memory. If I were twenty, I'd do exactly what you've done.

Instead she feeds the "soldati" wine and eggs. "One has only to be a little careful of the carabinieri. . . ." "And your husband?" Lisa asks. "Now and then he works. . . . I have a son, too," she replies, shaking her head. "So one lives."

Nina comes gushing back into the room. Seeing that Adele and Lisa have met, she feels it's all set for Lisa to take her room while she goes off with her American captain. Lisa ventures: "Civilians are forbidden to travel without a permit. But I suppose for a soldier—" "Not a soldier, darling," Nina hastens to explain, "an officer. In the American army there's a great difference." And she tells Adele to make coffee before she starts off. What will they do, Adele wonders, without the coffee from Nina's captain? "Lisa's Roberto will bring American coffee," Nina replies.

When the girls are alone Lisa shyly asks about "Your Roberto." "Mine?" cries Nina. "Yours, dear."

LISA—When will he come?

NINA—I telephoned. Dio! To telephone an American! First one answers: who do I want? I say il sergeanto Roberto. Roberto?

What Roberto? They never heard of a Roberto in their company. Oh, he says—Bob! Si, Bob! Well, he says, this one on the telephone, how about me, babbee, instead of Bob? Finally, he goes. Va bene. Comes another one to the telephone. Again, who do I want? Again the Roberto; again the Bob. Then he says: 'allo, 'allo, who's speaking? I say Nina. Nina! this one shouts, on the telephone. How's the old tomato, Nina? Che pomodoro? Who has a tomato? But that is how one telephones an American.

And Roberto was happy when he learned that Lisa had agreed. "Look how pretty his girl will be . . ." Lisa does not feel pretty: "To wait, like this, in a strange house, for a man I've never seen." Nina considers this no problem at all: "Why do you have to see him? If he's nice, he's nice, sight unseen!" She looks closely at Lisa. "Listen, cara. For three weeks he's bothered me to introduce him to a nice girl. Have you eaten today? . . . And the rent?" When Lisa remains silent, Nina feels it's all settled: "So. At least with Roberto you'll eat, and you'll have somewhere to live. I told Adele you are married to him. I've explained to Roberto how it will be—that you are not a street girl, and that the arrangement will be a permanent one. He's anxious, too. The Army's a cold place. . . ." To Lisa it is not so easily settled. She has never gone with a soldier. She has never talked to an American. She adds bitterly: "The Liberators." Nina gets impatient at this: "We lost the war." Lisa feels more is lost than the war. "Yes, he'll feed me because he's won the war, and that's part of the arrangement, and then after he's fed me, we'll go to bed, because that's part of the arrangement, too. . . ." She turns her head slowly: "But why should I be better or different than the women standing on the bridges? How stupid to think that one is different or better. I'll have my American. Everybody has one now." "No," snaps Nina, "you'll jump in the Tiber." Lisa says: "Why not? It's not important, either way."

NINA—Except I went through all the trouble of getting you a nice one!

LISA—You take him. You like Americans.

NINA—Like them? Some I could spit on. You should see their officers as I've seen them . . . what animals! Screaming in the hotel corridors, and such jokes! To them it's a wonderful joke to hang toilet paper from the chandelier—

LISA—They're gay. For them it's a gay war.

NINA—No, not really; they're not really gay. Really they're a gloomy people, the Americans.

Her American captain is something else, though. But he has an ungrateful, cold wife in Ohio whom he has no intention of divorcing. Lisa sighs: "Che brutta guerra!" Nina agrees but refuses to throw herself in the Tiber: "It's better to eat and go to Florence when one can—" "Or," says Lisa, "wait for some Roberto"—whom she can't even be sure will like her. Nina is willing to bet he will, as Adele comes in with the coffee.

Ugo, Adele's husband, appears the minute he smells the coffee. As soon as he meets Lisa, he is reminded because of her American husband of the American school teacher he once knew. Drinking his coffee, he tells of "this old transgression" that took place in the year 1920. He sighs as he asks Adele: "Do you see how far back I have to go to find a pleasant memory?" "Drink your coffee, Don Giovanni," she tells him. "My husband talks. He talked himself into the Regina Coeli once." They've all been to prison, Ugo adds, as he now gets an American cigarette from Nina: "Even a cigarette has become a luxury in Europe." Nina goes to answer the doorbell, and Ugo asks Lisa: "Your husband, Signora, does he like Italy?" "I don't know," Lisa answers.

Nina comes back with Robert. As she said, he is no animal. A smiling man of about thirty, he too is unsure of the reception he will receive. As Nina introduces him around and chatters away, Robert's eyes hardly leave Lisa. Ugo says courteously: "I was asking your wife, Signor Roberto, just before you came, if you like Italy."

ROBERT (*glancing at the girl*)—Do I? (LISA *doesn't answer.*) Yes, I think it's pretty nice.

UGO—But very much destroyed, no?

ROBERT—No. Surprisingly. I didn't expect it to be as nice as it is. (*Slips the musette bag from his shoulder.*) As a matter of fact, it's much prettier than I thought it would be.

The handsome son of the house, Antonio, arriving home, calls: "Mama," then stops as he sees strangers. "Scusi." Adele introduces him. Nina breaks in to say her farewells, then with mock flirtatiousness offers to kiss Antonio good-by. "Save it for the Alleati," he snaps.

NINA (*to* ADELE)—What a grateful son you have—

ANTONIO—I kissed better girls in Libya.

NINA—But dirtier.

ANTONIO—Only the skin.

Nina—Are you insulting me, darling?
Antonio—Who could insult you, carissima?

Nina shrugs this off, is thanked by Robert, tells him to be good
to Lisa and whisks off, followed by Signora Pulcini.

Robert tries now to break the ice by offering the men cigarettes.
Ugo takes one with a smile, Antonio coldly refuses. He prefers his
own. "Nazionales," says Robert. "Pretty bad, aren't they?" "But
they are ours," Antonio answers.

Ugo recalls the glories of the day the Americans took Rome. "Perhaps we celebrated too soon," Antonio sneers. But Ugo will not be
stopped: he chronicles the hour-by-hour excitement of the German
retreat. Ugo happily remembers when the Americans arrived: "What
a festa it was that day!" "Yes. We are liberated, aren't we,
Signor?" Antonio says to Robert. "Sure," he answers. The boy
makes a convulsive movement, crushes his cigarette in the ash tray.
"You're quite right. Our cigarettes, they stink. Excuse me—" And
Antonio goes out, with his father worriedly following him.

There is a difficult pause. Robert attempts to ease the situation.
"The liberation. It's only six months. We're coming to the first
Christmas we've had since it."

Lisa—Have you been in Italy long?
Robert—Long enough. (*Pause.*) Doesn't it ever snow in Rome?
Lisa—No.
Robert—Never?
Lisa—If you like snow you should go to Switzerland.

Lisa's hostility is quickly apparent. When Robert asks Lisa how
long they're supposed to have been married, and also about her family, she answers that she has a father in Genoa. And ever so politely
adds: "You bombed Genoa and my father thought I would be safer
in Rome." Robert takes this in his stride as he does her talk of
America's wealth. When she asks him if he's rich, he says: "No,
I'm one of the poor ones," and smiles at her. "Are you disappointed?" "I?" said Lisa. "No. Why should I be?" She asks
Robert if he likes Italy. "There's a lot of churches," is his answer.
Lisa says: "St. Paul's is very beautiful. People come from all over
the world to see the cloisters at St. Paul's." St. Paul's leaves Robert
cold. "How old are you?" he asks. Lisa says it doesn't matter.
Robert answers in the same tone: "No, it doesn't matter." As he
starts opening his bag he adds: "Two things surprised me. You're
young and you're pretty." But he loses ground by asking: "Do you

know many soldiers?" Again Lisa bristles with hostility. Robert
grasps that this was not the thing to say. Adele comes back to find
them standing like sticks, and thinking she has neglected them, shows
them the bedroom. Lisa, trapped, has no choice but to follow.

Adele, making conversation, asks when and where they were married. Lisa hesitatingly backs Robert up when he says they were married in Naples.

ADELE—Bella Napoli. Is it as destroyed as they say?
LISA—Terribly.
ADELE—Once upon a time, how they sang!
ROBERT—Well, they don't sing now. (*Looking into garden.*)
What's out there?
ADELE—The Via Flaminia. And the river.
ROBERT—They're both dark.
ADELE—Si. Of darkness we have more than enough. (*A last
survey of the room.*) Well—buonanotte, Signora.

Lisa is wretched. Robert immediately puts his foot into it by telling an unpleasant story. Lisa announces: "It must be wonderful—
to be an American and to be the conqueror of Europe."

ROBERT (*taking a can of peaches from his bag*)—It's all right.
LISA—Wherever you go, flowers, and the people cheering. You
are the liberatori. And drinking wine. And then the girls, every
place.
ROBERT (*as a can of milk comes out*)—I missed a couple of places.

But as she asks him about girls, he casually agrees he knew girls
everywhere, listing the places.

LISA—I think the Americans are liars.
ROBERT (*carefully*)—Why do you say they are liars?
LISA—They make many promises. But they don't keep them.
ROBERT—Depends on the promise. (*Takes some chocolate bars
out of the bag.*)
LISA—I think they are stupid, too.
ROBERT—Oh, we're a little bit of everything. (*Holds up a fruit
cake.*) My mother keeps sending me fruit cake, and I hate it.

Lisa asks him what his fiancée sends him. If he had one, Robert
answers, she'd neglect him. Lisa keeps fighting like a hurt animal;
Robert tries to placate her. Robert offers her chocolate, but she goes

on hurling grievances at his head: American bombing, American boastfulness. Robert can no longer be quiet, and starts talking about Italy. "Baby, it's better than being defeated."

LISA—Italy is not defeated.
ROBERT—No? She's giving a pretty good imitation of it. (*Holds up the cake again.*) Wouldn't you like to try my mother's fruit cake?
LISA—Italy has been invaded by barbarians before.
ROBERT—By what?
LISA—Barbarians!
ROBERT—Now I'm a barbarian.
LISA—You are giving a good imitation of it.
ROBERT (*nettled*)—Look, Baby, you may have Leonardo da Vinci, but we've got U. S. Steel.
LISA—Steel rusts.
ROBERT—Da Vinci peels—(*and he adds*)—it ain't so hot on a tank.

When it reaches the point where Lisa thinks it might be better to have the Germans back, Robert offers to invite them.

LISA—We don't want either of you!
ROBERT—No?
LISA—No!
ROBERT (*slowly*)—Perhaps it was easier sleeping with a kraut—

Lisa cries that's a lie, that they fought them. "Where?" says Robert, "in bed?"

In a cold fury Lisa comes across the room and slaps him. He promptly slaps her back. She heads for the door, which he quickly blocks. "God, you Italians have a temper! Do you always blow your top like that?" Lisa demands he let her go. Instead, the lights begin to flicker out. "I think we are having powerhouse trouble again." Robert doesn't endear himself to Lisa by adding: "Why don't you people get your city fixed up?" They hear Ugo call that he is bringing candles. In the darkness Robert tries again: "Lisa—?" She doesn't answer. "Lisa, can you hear me? I'm sorry. And it's not true. About the girls, I mean." He waits. "It's been a long time. A long time since I've been with a girl. And I'm not your enemy."

Ugo leaves the candles with Robert, who places them by his bag and picks up a package he has taken out of it.

ROBERT—Do you know what this is? Soup. You wouldn't think
they could put soup into a little package like this, and send it all the
way across the ocean. All you have to do is drop it into a pot of
water and boil it five minutes, and there it is—soup. My mother
sent it.

LISA (*slowly*)—In such a small package?

ROBERT—Sure. (*Tentatively.*) Wouldn't you like me to cut you
a piece of fruit cake? (*He does, and extends it to her.*) Please.

LISA (*taking it at last*)—Grazie.

ROBERT—Taste it. It's real good. I don't like cake, but when
my mother sends something it's pretty good. (*Watches her taste the
cake.*) Isn't it good?

LISA—Bonissimo.

ROBERT—It came all the way from America. (*He watches her
begin to eat the cake.*)

ACT II

Early the next evening, Lisa comes in the garden door, puts her
unpacked suitcase in the wardrobe, then after a moment's hesitation
gathers up all the American foodstuffs. She takes them in to Adele
who is pouring the last of the American captain's coffee for her
Antonio. Antonio is drinking the coffee, but while denouncing every
drop of it.

Lisa is a sympathetic listener. He spouts from a poem by Leo-
pardi: "O patria mia, I see the walls and arches and the columns
and the images and the heraldic shields of our ancestors, but the
glory I do not see. . . ." He turns to her: "A captain's coffee I see.
Signor Roberto is a private, isn't he?" His mother cuts in: "Antonio
means that in our Army he was an officer. That is something to
boast about." "I am not boasting. It doesn't matter what I was,"
he says bitterly. "What I was exists only in the Libyan desert. I
only meant a girl like you, Signora, might have married one of their
officers." Visibly uncomfortable, Lisa builds Robert up as a law
student in civilian life. This makes an impression, even though Antonio growls that he doesn't look like one. Antonio lives in the past:
he was in the catastrophic retreat at Bardia, where he played an
inglorious role. He envies an American like Lisa's husband: "I envy
the fact that he has an army he is not ashamed of. I envy him the
fact that he has not had to endure a defeat or remember a desertion."
Abruptly, he asks Lisa: "Are you happy, Signora?" He means with
a foreigner. Again she comes to Robert's defense: "They are generous, and not all of them are alike." Antonio says he was merely

asking a question: he has forgotten what it means to be happy. Suddenly he gets up and leaves the house.

Another unhappy Italian enters. This short fat neighbor tells a sad and angry story of being gypped in the Black Market. The man who fooled him was an American soldier, a Negro. The neighbor was stung because he felt sorry about Italy's role in Ethiopia. So he paid two thousand lire for what he thought were cigarettes and turned out to be straw or dung.

Robert overhears this from the bedroom door and bursts into laughter. Lisa joins him in the room, saying she doesn't think it's at all funny.

She throws herself on the bed, taking her raincoat as cover, and lies silent as Robert puts an alarm clock on the bed table, saying: "That looks almost matrimonial, doesn't it? The clock next to the bed." He asks why Lisa doesn't unpack her suitcase, but gets no answer. He confesses, as he pours himself a glass of vermouth, that when he came home tonight he was afraid she wouldn't be there. "What would you have done?" she is curious enough to ask. He doesn't know. "Last night, when we were together," he says, "you looked cute." He sits by her on the bed, glass in hand: "I was pretty happy being with you—last night." "Grazie. I'm glad you were," is all she will answer. Last night, Robert continues, was the first time he had slept in a house, except for being billeted in a shelled house in Piombino. "Last night I thought: here it is, a real pillow in a real bed, and both of them clean." He drinks his vermouth as Lisa tells him how, when Antonio inquired about him, she said he was studying law. "Who, me?" Robert exclaims. "I'm no lawyer. I'm not even an engineer. I used to work for a newspaper." Lisa is momentarily hopeful until Robert tells her: "No. Not even a journalist. I used to sell ads. Advertisements. Like these." He shows her ads in a newspaper. "That isn't much to boast of to Antonio, is it?" "Non importa," says Lisa, ". . . but nothing is—you are not a lawyer; I am not a prima ballerina."

Robert asks if she will go to church Sunday. "I have nothing to go to church for." "Well, people go to pray." "I don't go to church right now," she tells him. "I'm in anger." "All right." Robert is amused. "We'll go to Bracciano. You're not in anger with Lake Bracciano, are you?"

Robert puts down his glass carefully: "Last night I knew you didn't like me. I thought you would learn to . . . later. But that wasn't important. It was just the fact that you were here. And I couldn't tell you that. I thought you wouldn't understand—how tremendous it was, just your being here . . ." He pauses. "And

besides, you didn't run away, and I was afraid you might. And
that was important to me—your being with me."

But she did run away, she tells him. This morning, after looking
at herself in the mirror. She went to an elegant hotel where the
French military stay. She saw a French major who admires Pinturic-
chios in Siena, independence in women, and women's usual talents.
Robert tells her: "You're not that independent."

LISA—No. I am not that independent. So you see? I ran in a
circle. Back to the mirror. (*Leans back again, looking at him.*)
And you are not even a lawyer.

ROBERT—No, I'm not even a lawyer.

LISA—You are nothing.

ROBERT—Practically nothing.

Lisa asks Robert to leave the room; he joins Ugo in the dining
room, while she lies quiet for a moment, then switches off the bedroom light. Ugo talks to Robert while they smoke. Antonio, his
father says, likes Lisa so much—she's the first girl who's come to the
house he's liked. Ugo talks of Antonio's disappointments, of all of
theirs: "Nothing has turned out like we expected. . . . We thought
that if the Fascisti were gone—well, the Fascisti are gone, and now?
We thought that prison was one of the worst indignities one could suffer—now how simple the going to prison looks!" "What are you,
Ugo? A socialist?" Robert asks him. "A kind of socialist, who is more
of an old man than he is a socialist. You see, in Italy, we're always a
kind of something. Not the exact thing—like the Germans or the
English. But only a kind of, with many shades." It's only because
of the war, Robert tells him: "Afterwards, you'll be all right." Ugo
says: "We live in hope." And Robert says: "Good night."

The bedroom is in darkness. Robert gropes his way to the closet,
where he discovers Lisa has unpacked her suitcase. "Si," she says
from the bed. Robert goes over to her and sits on the edge of the
bed, saying that Sunday they'll go to Lake Bracciano.

LISA—Va Bene.

ROBERT (*pauses;* ROBERT *lights a match, looks at her lying there,
her shoulders naked*)—Christ, you are beautiful.

LISA (*blows out the match*)—I'm not an animal in a stable.

ROBERT—I didn't mean it like that. (*Pause.*) What are you
thinking about?

LISA—Nothing.

ROBERT—You're so quiet, you must be thinking about something.

LISA—About God.

ROBERT—God?

LISA—Yes. That he has a lot to forgive me. And I have a lot to forgive Him.

SCENE II

New Year's Eve is pretty grim at the Pulcinis'. The English soldier finds nothing better than a kiss from the maid. Ugo refuses a glass of his wine.

ENGLISHMAN—Oh, vino's vino. Pop it into you, puke it out—

UGO—Before the war you should have gone to Frascati. There was a wonderful wine—famous!

ENGLISHMAN—You know, you're not such bad chaps, considerin', you Eyeties. Bunch of excitable Johns, though. Always full of bellyaches. Always cheering a bloke or shootin' him.

UGO (*smiling*)—There are many we would like to shoot we will not have the pleasure of shooting.

Robert arrives with his New Year's bottle of bad cognac. Ugo won't touch it, and implies that Robert had been grossly overcharged for such swill. Robert minds this far less than that Lisa's not there; it's almost midnight. When she finally arrives, she brushes aside his questions of where she's been and refuses a drink of the brandy. Antonio's arrival is even more depressing. He's in one of his violently angry moods, this time over the actions of a drunken American couple who took over his billiard room.

The Englishman tries to shut him up: "Shove off, Antonio. It's a bloody party." Antonio answers: "It's an army of parties."

ENGLISHMAN—Look here, mate. There's a lot of our chaps lying out there dead, from El Alamein to Tripoli. And it ain't Jerry's bullets in them—

ANTONIO—No, they are ours.

ENGLISHMAN—Bloody well right yours!

ANTONIO—And our dead? With whose bullets do they lie in the desert? Whose wound did I carry from Bardia to Mersa Matrûh?

His mother upbraids him in Italian; this time he apologizes, for her sake. Then he drops the English and takes on the Americans. Robert pays as little attention as possible to his remarks. This time Adele makes Antonio go to his room, while Ugo apologizes for his behavior.

When the midnight noises start, everyone except Lisa and Robert troops into the garden to hear the excitement. Lisa goes instead to the bedroom, with Robert trailing behind her with his bottle. When he fails to get even a New Year's kiss from her, he tries to find out where she's been all evening. She won't tell, only gives her usual answer that it doesn't matter. Robert tells her that if she says that again he'll break her neck. She very deliberately says: "It does not matter," and gets the expected reaction: "Goddamit!" Lisa says of course he can't be angry: "I thought you were angry. But I forgot. The Americans are above anger. Only Antonio is stupid enough to get angry." Robert grabs her arms: "Are you trying to get me to blow my cork?" Lisa says that would be impossible, since she's: ". . . just an Italian girl you met in a war. An adventure." This adventure will be very amusing to tell his fiancée. It will make a very funny story. So, "Why should it matter what I do or where I go?" It just happens, he says, that he likes her. "Should I be flattered?" says Lisa. "Yes, I'm flattered." "I think I will break your neck," he decides. Lisa can't stop: "You know, perhaps this Winter it will snow, too. Just for the Americans. I think it may snow just for them." Robert begs her to say what it is she wants. "I? Nothing. I have everything, haven't I? You heard Antonio— how lucky I am! I'm going to America. They won't escape, but I will. Che buona fortuna!"

Robert asks for the truth: does she like him at all? Lisa says slowly: "I think I hate you." The whole thing was impossible from the very beginning. From Lake Bracciano, where the people on the road shouted ugly things at her for being at Robert's side, and the waiter refused to wait on them. "Then why did you start?" Robert asks. "Why did you tell Nina, yes? Why did you have me come here?" "Because," Lisa answers, "I thought nothing was important any more. Because I thought everybody had a soldier. The Americans were rich, they had so much, I thought: why not? Take one, too. It's so simple!" Robert stubbornly insists he thought it was simple. Then, says Lisa, he should have found someone who thought so, too. ". . . You were kind enough, even generous—you brought the food, and I had real coffee, just as we had arranged. And you asked so little—"

ROBERT—I wanted a girl.

LISA—And it was not important how. Or what she felt. So little —that she should be warm, that she should be here when you wanted her—

ROBERT—Is that wrong?

LISA—No. Why should it be wrong if you don't think it's wrong?

ROBERT—You needed food.

LISA—The food! Yes. Didn't I? I did not need anything but the food!

ROBERT (*slowly*)—I don't think I care any more about the other things. (*Pauses.*) I wanted a girl. I don't think I wanted love. I wanted a girl because I didn't want to have to stand under the trees on the Via Veneto or to go under the bridges. I wanted to get away from the army. I wanted to have a house I could come to, and a girl there, mine. I wanted it as simple as that, as simple as it could possibly be. And I thought I would just be exchanging something somebody needed for something I needed. Something somebody wanted for something I wanted.

LISA—The Black Market.

ROBERT—Yes. The black market, if you want to call it that. Everything's on the black market now. But you don't want it simple like that, do you? That's wrong. That's ugly. You have to complicate it with something else. Oh, you'll climb up in the hayloft, all right, but you have to be in love before you use the ladder, don't you?

LISA—You are so delicate! You understand a woman so well!

ROBERT—I'm a dumb American. You said that before.

LISA—From such a great country! With such sympathy for human happiness!

She taunts him further, until he says he's not interested in Europe; what he's interested in is himself. And that's that. "Well, it was a lovely New Year's. I guess this finishes it. You figure out some excuse to tell the Pulcinis tomorrow. Tell them my outfit left town. We moved up north—" He would like that New Year's kiss, though. Lisa turns her face away. He bends her over and places a kiss on her reluctant mouth, then goes into the garden.

Lisa, who would like to nurse her wounds in private, now has to let Antonio into the bedroom. He has chosen an inconvenient moment to be gallant—to apologize about her American husband. Lisa sits down at the dressing table, listening numbly and combing her hair. She tells Antonio Robert wasn't insulted.

ANTONIO—They are not all bad—but it's hard for me to distinguish. I am always angry. Besides, our women—they're worse than the soldiers. The soldiers have some excuse.

LISA—I imagine our women have, too.

ANTONIO—Some excuse? No. (*Pauses.*) If they were all like you, Signora—

LISA (*her comb pausing*)—Like me?
ANTONIO—One should respect one's countrywomen. Not to feel
they are degrading you—isn't that true, Signora?
LISA (*briefly*)—Yes.

He has to tell her this, and give her the bullet that was his souvenir of the war, because he respects her. As for himself, he may
turn thief and steal tires, like other ex-soldiers, or die a frost-bitten,
patriot's death in the hills. His advice to Lisa is to: "Go to America.
In the end one is happiest away from the scene of one's mistakes—
or one's suffering." And he goes away, closing the bedroom door
behind him.

The New Year's excitement being over, they all come back in
from the garden. The Englishman orders another bottle of wine, but
before he can settle down to it, the doorbell rings and there is loud
talk in the hall. "A bit of a row, sounds like," says the Englishman
indifferently.

The American with the bad ankle has come back with a carabinière, making unpleasant accusations against Adele. "The old bitch,"
he yells. The carabinière, consulting his little black books, asks:
"Did you solicit for this American a woman named—Maria Galluzo
who lives at the Via Angelico, 38?" "I solicit for no one," Adele
says frigidly. She admits she telephoned: "The drunkard whined to
me how lonesome he was." The Englishman backs her up: "He
asked her all right. I heard him ask the old lady." In any case,
Maria was sick, and the police are going to find the source of the
infection. What kind of a house does Adele have here? "A house
like any house," she snaps. "I serve wine and eggs. Is that a
crime?" The carabinière starts checking on the people in the house.
Mimi is cleared—she lives with her family. Next he knocks on Lisa's
door. Adele hastens to tell the police: "The Signora is the wife of
this American." "So? Congratulations." He asks Lisa for her
identification card. She gets it for him; then he asks to see the marriage documents. Robert says quickly he has them at his billet.
"So? How unfortunate." The carabinière starts writing out a sum-
mons. "Tomorrow you can exhibit them to the magistrate—"
"What magistrate?" Robert demands. "At the Questura. The Signora is aware of the address, no?" "Si, I know it," answers Adele.
The carabinière was sure she did, and tells Lisa to be there at eight
the next morning. Robert breaks in: "Why should she have to go
to the Questura at all? I told you we're married," and adds, "We
have a room." "Of course; a room," the carabinière repeats. "Rome

is full today of just such rooms." He presents a slip to Lisa: "To-morrow, Signora—at eight o'clock. May I suggest you search well for the documents? He is difficult, the magistrate. Buona sera." And he departs.

Antonio sees the police leaving and finds out what's going on, which hastens the Englishman's feeling that he has had enough of this "Bloody party." Lisa just stands looking at the slip of paper, crying she won't go. Robert asks what would happen if she didn't. Adele tells him: "To you? Nothing. You are a soldier—the soldier is always innocent. But the girl—if she does not report, they will come here and arrest her anyway, and take away her identity card." "Let them take it away," Robert says. Adele explains patiently: "You are an American—you don't understand. In Europe, without an identity card, one doesn't exist."

When Ugo says there is nothing to worry about; after all they are married, Robert asks Adele: "What if we aren't married? I mean, what if I can't find the certificate? If I can't prove our marriage?" He is told that would be bad—bad for Lisa. "Tomorrow she would go to the Questura. There she would be questioned. If she could not prove she is married, or that she works, then she is taken away from the Questura in a police truck—to the hospital for the doctors to examine—to see if she is sick. And if she is sick, then one goes to San Gallicano,"—which is a terrible place. "If it is the first time, she is given a small sentence. And cured. And then, later, when she is released, she is given a card. The small yellow card." At this Lisa whimpers. Adele continues: "One gets a card of the profes-sional. It is stamped officially. One reports every week. One has to carry it, always. Wherever one goes." "But what if she's not sick?" Robert wants to know. "If she's innocent?" "Do you know the European police system?" Adele asks wearily. "Once the doc-tors examine them, there are no innocent girls. Sick or healthy, innocent or guilty—the yellow card is given to them all. You see? It would be very bad, Roberto, if you and Lisa were not married."

Before them all, Robert confesses how bad it is: there are no mar-riage documents. With that Antonio begins to carry on. Robert tries to shut him up, and finally grabs at him: "Get him out of here, Adele, or I'll knock his teeth out!" Antonio wrenches himself free, shouts: "Whores and thieves!", spits, and leaves the room.

They all try to comfort the shaking girl. Robert kneels at her side and promises to go with her to the Questura—they can't do anything to his girl: "They can't hold her if she's my girl. They can't send her to San Callicano or whatever the name of it is, if she's my girl—

Can they?" Adele can only say: "They are afraid of disease in the city." And Ugo has to add: "In the Piazza Colonna last week they arrested a hundred girls on the street." Lisa, in tears, tries to have Robert take his hands off her; she thinks he is holding her for San Gallicano. Adele says there is no place to go. Lisa thinks differently: "There is always a place to go. Please, Adele. Tell him not to hold me." Robert won't let go. Ugo hopelessly watches, then goes out to warm the coffee: "Che mondo."

Robert strokes the weeping girl and Adele bursts out: "Madonna mia, what is the disgrace? You crawled into bed together. That should be the least of your sins." Robert tries, in his clumsy way, to be consoling. Adele bursts out again: "What fools. What fools I'm lost among! To throw oneself into the river because of the police. If I had gone to the river each time they knocked, I'd be dead and drowned a hundred times!" She tells Robert that Lisa is frightened: "She wants to be Tosca! Take her in your arms!" But he can't calm her, and Adele takes over, pushing him aside. "Is she still crying? Well, let her cry. Tomorrow we'll have a festa. When she comes home, free, and it's all nothing, we'll have a festa. Madonna, they bomb each other, they destroy cities—but a girl in bed is a crime. Here, go away. Let me sit with her. She had to take an American! With one of her own, this would not have happened."

ACT III

Late in the afternoon of New Year's Day, Robert is still worriedly awaiting Lisa's return. Watching him looking for her out the window, Ugo asks Robert if he loves Lisa. For Robert, it is not a question of love: he doesn't enjoy feeling like a heel. But what will happen to Lisa, Ugo persists. "That's not my responsibility," says Robert. "Whose is it?" Ugo asks. "Hers! God's! The World's! How do I know?" "You see," Ugo shows him, "it is a question of love."

When Robert wants to help with money, or whatever she needs, Ugo says: "What a hard people you are!" Robert is consciously getting tough; he is not Lisa's husband; he is: "Il conquistadore!"

Nina, to all appearances as indomitable as ever, though dustier than usual, arrives unexpectedly. She irritably tells of her captain's sudden leaving of her bed, and how she found a magnificent British major with a magnificent staff car to bring her back to Rome. She takes Ugo into the kitchen, to eat and to get the latest news. Antonio, disapproving as always, follows.

When there is no one in the dining room, Lisa, completely spent, slips in from the garden and sinks into a chair. When little Mimi sees her, she goes to her side, trying to bring some comfort and sympathy. But Antonio comes in, gets rid of the maid, and brutally takes over. What Lisa has gone through already is not enough; she now must listen to Antonio denouncing her for dishonoring her country: ". . . and now the dream comes to its ugly finish. The police! What is one American? There will be dozens. They'll come to you —drunk, stupid, ugly. In some room somewhere. At night. They'll drop their big boots on the floor, sprawl in your arms—the conqueroros! And you? Every week to San Gallicano! Every night on the Via Veneto!

LISA—Antonio!

ANTONIO—Yes, cara mia—that's what you can look forward to. And what shall I say? What shall I feel? I'll see you drinking with them in the cafés. I'll see you walking with them on the boulevards. No. (*He puts his hand into her hair.*) Don't look down. Don't look away. Look at me!

LISA—You're hurting me.

ANTONIO—Am I? Not much. Not enough. But one must pay a little; one must suffer a little. Is it just that the decent should have all the suffering, and you nothing? Yesterday, in the bedroom, I believed you. You were one of the good ones! I was stupid, no? I was easily deceived. Because I could not tell. One should be able to tell, isn't that true, Signorina? You shouldn't be allowed to deceive people. When you walk in the streets people should know. They are also hungry, they are also poor, but they haven't sold themselves. People with wounds—they ought to be able to say: "There's a girl who has dishonored herself and her country." Else, how is one to tell? (*Takes a knife from the fruit bowl.*) Isn't what I have said true?

LISA (*in terror*)—Antonio!

Mimi comes in on this miserable business and rushes to Lisa's defense while crying for help. Everyone crowds back into the room; Robert hits Antonio. Ugo, as always, suffers for his son: "He's ashamed." This causes Nina to burst out: "Ashamed! Some day he'll kill somebody with that shame of his! Go bring a glass of wine, Mimi." Nina makes Lisa drink the wine and chafes her hands: "There, darling, is it better?" Lisa says numbly: "They wouldn't believe me at the Questura." They were put into trucks and driven through the streets in full view of everyone: ". . . then in the hospital they put us into a big room and they said undress, and we undressed, and they examined us." She looks straight ahead as she continues: "Have you ever seen, Nina, many girls naked together in a big, cold room?"

NINA—I don't want to see it.
LISA—I was afraid of touching anything. I was so afraid of the disease.
UGO—Eh—but they released you—
NINA—Of course!
LISA—Yes.
NINA—Why should they hold her? She's innocent—
LISA—They released me.

They released her, but to herself, she is now like all the others. She turns to Robert: "It will be so much easier now that I am what the others are." Robert, getting rid of Ugo and Nina, tries to make her understand that he wants to help her, to do anything he can. Lisa takes her yellow police card from her pocket: "And this? Can you do anything about this?" Humiliated and desolated, Lisa can only think of this "souvenir" of the war.

Robert begs her to tell him what she wants. Lisa cries: "Go home! Take your tanks, take your money, take your coffee and your sugar and all your generous gifts, and go home!" Robert replies: "It's seven thousand miles away." "The dancing in the streets is over! The celebration is finished. Go home!" cries the trembling girl.

Robert talks quietly to Lisa, reminding her of what he had said when they first met—that the Americans were a little bit of everything. She remembers, but it doesn't matter any more. "Except," Robert says, "it might have been different. Who knows? Perhaps, if I'd met you when there was no war—" Lisa protests it wouldn't have been different. Trying to convince her, holding her by the arms, Robert asks did she go to the opera before the war? Lisa says: "Yes." Which opera does she like best? "Traviata." "We'd have gone to Traviata. Then we'd travel," Robert tells her. What town does she like best? "Portofino—in the north—by the sea," she gasps. "All right," says Robert, "we'd go to Portofino, in the north by the sea. Why did you like Portofino?" Like a drowning person, Lisa says she remembers being happy there when she was seventeen. "Would I be happy in Portofino?" he asks.

LISA—I don't know.

ROBERT—I'd be in love. You're supposed to be happy when you're in love. Would I be happy?

LISA (*desperately*)—Yes! Yes!

ROBERT—Then, after Portofino, and after being in love, we'd go to the States, wouldn't we? To America. Just to show them how pretty an Italian girl can be— Besides, I'd have to show my mother who ate her fruit cake. Tell me what kind of a wife would you have made—would you have made a good wife?

LISA—Yes.

ROBERT—How good?

LISA—Very good.

ROBERT—All Italians make good ones, they tell me. But you'd have been one of the best, wouldn't you?

LISA—Yes—

Robert takes the card from her hand in spite of her protests. He tears it up, saying: "What card? I don't know of any card."

LISA—Roberto, you mustn't! You mustn't do this to me!

His answer is why not, they love each other, don't they? Doesn't she? "Yes, yes!" Lisa cries desperately. Then he has her kiss him as any wife does a husband. Adele comes in, finds them together, takes Robert's word that everything went well at the Questura, and goes off to prepare a fine festa. Lisa begs Robert to let her go now, to wash. "Okay—but one kiss, first," he says as he releases her. She runs out.

Ugo comes in and asks where Lisa is. "Making herself pretty," Robert says cockily. And how does "the conquistadore" feel? "Me? Great," answers Robert, thinking of Portofino and how he's "going to be seventeen years old in Portofino one of these days."

The Englishman arrives—just in time, they joke, for an invitation to the festa. He accepts, then casually wonders: "I say, Yank— wasn't that your gel I saw outside?"

ROBERT—Outside?

ENGLISHMAN—She was in an awful hurry. Didn't even have her coat on. Where's the fire, I said, but she was rushin' so, she didn't seem to hear me.

ROBERT (*tense*)—Where did she go?

ENGLISHMAN—Down the Via Flaminia, last time I saw her. (ROBERT *rushes out. The door slams behind him.*)

ADELE (*offstage*)—Roberto! Where are you running? The macaroni is almost ready!

ENGLISHMAN—Now what's wrong with him? What'd he lose?

UGO (*slowly gets up*)—What we've all lost, my friend. (*Sadly.*) Viva la Chicago!

THE GOLDEN APPLE *

A Musical In Two Acts

Written by John Latouche
Music Composed by Jerome Moross

[Jerome Moross *had his first show, "Parade," produced by the Theatre Guild when he was 21. Born in Brooklyn, he attended De Witt Clinton High School and New York University; he received a Juilliard Fellowship and two Guggenheim Fellowships. He has done incidental music for Broadway plays and for radio, and won critical acclaim for his ballets such as "Frankie and Johnny." His very successful "Ballet Ballads" which he did with John Latouche was the incentive for their collaboration on "The Golden Apple." His most recent ballet, "The Last Judgement," was commissioned by Ruth Page for a European production. Among his numerous works for concert are "A Tall Story for Orchestra" commissioned by C.B.S. and his "First Symphony," premiered by Sir Thomas Beecham and the Seattle Symphony. He has had a long though intermittent association with Hollywood as composer, orchestrator, and musical adviser.*]

[John Latouche *came to New York at 15 from Richmond, Va., and entered the Riverdale Preparatory School on a scholarship. He then went to Columbia and was the first freshman to win the Columbia Award for both poetry and prose. In his sophomore year he wrote the lyrics and some of the music for the varsity show. He adapted into English Erika Mann's "The Pepper Mill" and had two numbers in the revue "Pins and Needles." He wrote the very popular "Ballad for Americans." His lyrics for "Cabin in the Sky" estab-*

---

*lished him on Broadway. In 1942 he served as American Observer
on an expedition in the Belgian Congo.*]

THIS turn of the century mock-Homeric starts on the slope of
Mt. Olympus, in the outskirts of Angel's Roost, state of Washington, U.S.A.

With all the men away at the Spanish-American war, sultry Helen
is plain bored. She sits high on a stepladder near an apple tree
laden with fruit, the peaks of Mt. Olympus creating a background
that she ignores. Helen is longing for the excitement of the big city.
"Nothing," she sighs, "ever happens in Angel's Roost."

Three important ladies of the town: Lovey Mars, Mrs. Juniper—
the mayor's wife—and a schoolmarm, Miss Minerva, come to load
their baskets with apples. They are markedly sniffy about Helen,
and Helen's attitude. Lovey Mars suggests that Helen show some
civic zeal for the "Greatest Little Town on Earth," but Helen remains unmoved as she listens to the three ladies sing a chamber of
commerce aria to Angel's Roost. After the trio rises to such heights
as:

> "Blessed be thou O Angel's Roost.
> Blessed be the products that thou hast produced,
> Blessed be thy population,
> Thy annual rain precipitation.
> Blessed be thou O Angel's Roost!"

Helen, as bored as ever, adds:

> "Nothing ever happens
> In Angel's Roost."

Mother Hare, the local crystal-gazer, rushes on. At the sight of
her batik scarves and jangling beads, Helen perks up. Mrs. Juniper
admits to having enjoyed her last seance. Helen can't wait for her
to go to work, and urges Mother Hare:

> "So gaze into your crystal ball,
> And keep it cheerful, dear!
> This jerkwater town,
> Is wearing me down.
> How can I get out of here?"

Mother Hare can sense a situation, and looks into the ball:

"I predict that Mrs. Juniper
And Miss Minerva Oliver
Will split the town asunder,
Through a blunder
Of Lovey Mars.

"And Helen, you'll kick the traces, dear.
A man will take you places, dear.
You'll leave your old man wailing,
And go sailing
Through the stars."

The Ladies want to know when the war will end. Mother Hare assures them it will last for years—her spirits never lie to her. But at this moment, Penelope, a lissome bouncy beauty, comes on with highly contradictory news and has Menelaus, the sheriff that she drags with her, read a telegram:

"Our war with Spain at last is through.
They've demobilized our boys in blue.
And President McKinley wired to say,
They'll all be coming home today."

The Ladies enjoy themselves vastly, sniping at Mother Hare for being a false prophet. Helen, however, can't be bothered; she can think of nothing except all those boys coming home.

Penelope dismisses Mother Hare:

"At last we have no need of you
To paint out futures black.
At last the town is freed of you."

Helen's one-track mind adds:

"The men are coming back!"

Mother Hare, still banking on her spirits, stalks angrily off. Menelaus, sensing Helen's present mood, hustles her off to get her safely under lock and key.

Penelope, her mind on Ulysses, sings joyously: "My love is on his way," and waltzes off.

The Townspeople quickly prepare for their heroes' home-coming; they wheel in a bandstand topped with an enormous eagle, and a curtained stage. A huge banner reads: "Welcome Home, Boys." With the village green looking like a lithograph poster of the early

1900's, the twelve brave boys in blue march proudly on. At their head is Captain Mars, while Ulysses brings up the rear.

When the cheering is over, Mrs. Juniper self-importantly announces the pageant that the town has prepared; Miss Minerva wrote the words, Lovey Mars set the tunes, and Mrs. Juniper whipped the whole thing into shape. While the Townspeople intone Miss Minerva's verses a child hands out flowers, and the Spirit of Columbia stands bearing a scroll of honor for Captain Mars, Ajax Finucane, Agamemnon Nimmin, Nester Neider, Bluey Weinerwitz, Thirsty Miller, Silas Protes, Homer Pickins, Diomede Kunkel, Achilles Akins, Patroclus Whiting, Doc Macahan, and "Last but not least," Ulysses Spelvin.

The young girls are dying to hear of the boys' wild adventures. The boys decide that Ulysses should tell them:

> "He's crazy like a fox he
> Just overflows with moxie.
> When we get in a tangle
> He figgers out an angle.
> He's smarter
> Than Nick Carter,
> He's the one to tell you all."

Ulysses, in all modesty, can only sing:

> "It was a glad adventure.
> The Philippine scenes were so sweet,
> Them wee Igoroots,
> In their birthday suits,
> Made life just a Sunday-school treat.
>
> "Wherever we went they loved us,
> So dazzled were they with our charms.
> The folks in them lands
> Ate right out of our hands,
> But why did they chew off the arms?"

All sing in conclusion: "Oh, we're lucky to get home alive," and everyone dances happily. Lovey Mars interrupts the dance to announce a fancy, church supper that night in the boys' honor. The boys and girls dance gaily, figuring: "We're going to raise a ruckus tonight . . ." and the crowd dances off.

Penelope and Ulysses, finally alone together, embrace tenderly and sing of their longing for each other when they were apart. Ulysses sings:

"It's the being home together
When the shadows rise.
Someone looks into your eyes
And takes you by the hand.

"It's a dear familiar face
That can light up a place,
And little private jokes
Only you two understand."

Penelope sings with him:

"It's the being home together
Through the changing years.
It's the talk about the weather,
And the laughter and the tears."

Ulysses adds:

"It's to love the you that's me
And the me that's you. . . ."

Both conclude:

"It's the going home together
All life through!"

Mother Hare—a darkening sky and a bit of forked lightning be-
token her approach—sees things differently. She is all for having
Ulysses go forth to meet the wonders of the twentieth century. She
bids Ulysses see things through her eyes and, where before he saw a
valley rich in forest, streams, and farms, now with Mother Hare's
help he sees a wasteland created to make room for the scientific
changes to come.

At once Ulysses gets excited, but Penelope realizes that Mother
Hare is up to her old tricks again and is weaving another spell.
Mother Hare brushes this neatly aside:

"Good is a word that fools believe,
And evil's a word that the wise achieve.
Fools who are good fools try to deny
That evil exists—they pass it by.

"But life without evil is empty and strange.
Without evil, how can the good ever change?
Without change, how can any man ever grow?
Ask Ulysses. He's clever. He'll tell you it's so."

And off she goes, leaving Ulysses, that great lover of change, raring to follow. Poor Penelope despairs of his ever settling down, but this time he promises:

> "I promise I'll not travel
> Farther than our pasture track.
> When my eyes
> Can't see the smoke rise
> From our chimney stack,
> I shall turn back."

Penelope begs him:

> "Oh, don't ever promise
> A thing you cannot do."

He means to, though. Clinging to each other, they go home together.

Gay, colored Japanese lanterns descend from on high to light the twelve young veterans ambling with only one thought, to track down Helen. To find her they're prepared to bust up Angel's Roost. Each veteran dances, imagining Helen is in his arms. Doc Macahan sums up the general feeling about her:

> "Our Helen ain't neat, her hair is a mess.
> She can't cook a meal that is fillin',
> So what is the secret of her success?
> Well, Dear Helen,
>   Fair Helen,
>   My Helen,
>   His Helen,
>   Their Helen's
> Always willin'!"

And on she comes with news to break their hearts: she's "kind of quieted down." Then, when old Menelaus comes on, she gives him a kiss, causing general consternation:

> "Oh, Helen, Helen, you can't betray us,
> You ain't gonna marry ol' Menelaus."

Says Helen:

> "I married him over a year ago.
> I couldn't keep flitting to and fro.

"He's bent with age, his feet are flat,
But his bank account will straighten that!
I love him."

The boys are out to murder Menelaus, when Ulysses enters in time
to prevent any serious damage. He persuades them to admit that
what's done is done—they all couldn't have married her, anyway.
Ulysses makes them swear:

". . . a sacred vow
To steer clear of Helen
And protect her from the rest of all

"The men in the mountains,
The men from the valley.
For Helen has a tendency
To dilly-dally."

Smug Menelaus leads a reluctant Helen away, while the boys follow Ulysses in the other direction.

Scene II

The Townspeople whisk a gaily decorated picnic table on stage, a
fair stall drops from the flies, and all is ready for the simple pleasures of a country fair. The dancers give imitations of potato races,
square dances, and a carrousel. Suddenly, in the midst of a tug of
war, the contestants collapse in amazement as a gorgeous balloon
settles in their midst. The balloon, gaily striped and spelling out
Paris Notions, Inc. in electric lights, is the vehicle for Mr. Paris, a
traveling salesman.

Dapper, cocksure Paris blithely tosses out his throwaway leaflets,
leaps from the balloon's basket, opens suitcase, and sets up shop.
Ulysses, noting his wares, calls for Penelope to see:

". . . this traveling man from the city
With brand-new things,
Fur muffs and rings,
And dresses to fix you up pretty!"

In the mad scramble for Paris' merchandise, Penelope comes up
with a new bonnet and Ulysses with the new idea of flying to the
city in the balloon. This time Penelope manages to keep him home.
Ulysses, agreeing to tend to the crops now, and to put off the trip
to another day, tells his anxious wife as they go home:

"You know I'd rather
Stay here with you."

Lovey Mars, bearing a freshly-baked angel cake, meets Mrs.
Juniper carrying her prize mince pie. The ladies watch Miss Minerva approach, her seven-layer cake only matched in size by the
bird on her hat. All three march ceremoniously to the contest table
where they place their specialities. At once Mother Hare, preceded
by her usual clap of thunder and smidgen of lightning, arrives to
make trouble.

Mother Hare is miffed at these ladies, who have given her "the
go-by since the men came back." The three apologize, but that does
little good. Mother Hare sings:

"I'm so mad I could spit!
Mother has pride after all.
But I came to do my bit
For the general festival."

And she brings forth a gleaming, golden apple from under her cape.
Amidst gasps of wonder:

"It's a pretty, golden apple
That glitters in the sun,
A symbol of our proud state
Of Washington."

She releases the apple; it hangs glittering in mid-air:

" 'Twill be sure to bring your ship in
Through storm and stress,
If you own this lucky pippin
You'll be certain of success."

And she starts making trouble by singing:

"I offer this . . .
As the general prize
For the one who makes
The very best cakes and pies."

She then stalks happily off. The ladies are too refined to pull one
another's hair, but they are becoming increasingly grim as Mr. Paris
dances on. They at once choose him as judge of their baked goods,
and coyly go away while he makes his decision. As Paris looks at
the cakes with loathing, each contestant briefly slips on-stage with a

bribe. Mrs. Juniper, the mayor's wife, guarantees Paris popularity and business success. Miss Minerva promises she will make him so learned he can become anything, even *President*. Lovey Mars offers what is closest to a traveling salesman's heart: a charm that will let him make any girl he wants. Lovey wins hands down. Off dances Lovey with the apple and Mr. Paris, leaving the two losers to exit in a rage.

Meanwhile the scene has changed to Helen's veranda, where she sits fanning herself. Helen hasn't a thought in her head, until Lovey dances by with Paris. From then on, there is just a single thought; and Lovey leaves the young people to their own devices.

As Paris and Helen reach out to each other, Ulysses and the Boys pass by on their way to a ball game. Ulysses mockingly calls back over his shoulder:

> "My, it's *awful* hot,
> Isn't it?"

Taking no chances, Helen grabs at Paris from over the porch rail. His coat comes off as she yanks, revealing Paris in a dickey, suspenders, and shirt cuffs. Helen pulls him down beside her, and ever so languidly serenades him:

> "It's a lazy afternoon
> And the beetle bugs are zoomin'
> And the tulip trees are bloomin'
> And there's not another human
> In view
> But us two."

She continues to sing the bucolic charms of the countryside, and asks Paris to spend the lazy afternoon with her. Seizing Paris by the hair, she—between stanzas—whirls him around, and leaves no doubt what she'd like to do this lazy afternoon.

Paris, in an elegant dance, entices Helen, then with a flick of his wrist brings down his balloon. Whereupon Helen throws herself into his arms: "All right, my dear," she modestly yields, "you talked me into it." She kisses him, rushes into the house, begins throwing packages and clothes out to the bewildered Paris, then reappears dressed in a linen duster and motoring hat, with a jewel box and *cash* box tucked under her arm.

Menelaus, sauntering along, sees Helen floating happily off with a stranger. Mrs. Juniper and Minerva come on and size up the situation at once; Lovey is in for it. Everyone except the Boys begs

Scene from "The Golden Apple"

Helen to come back. The Boys look up from their ball game, note her disappearing act, and couldn't care less.

But Menelaus and the Old Men of Angel's Roost call for vengeance. They remind the Boys of their oath. Ulysses, trying to quiet them down, asks if they aren't distorting the principle of the thing. The Old Men leap at the phrase:

> "That's it! That's it!
> It's the principle of the thing.
> Get sore! Make war
> On wicked Rhododendron."

Ulysses dismisses this—and Menelaus'—warmongering with:

> "Pay no mind to all that pouting.
> Pay no mind to their disputing.
> Old men always do the shouting;
> Young man have to do the shooting."

But the Old Men, though, with their martial pacing and carryings on, begin to sway the Boys, and the Boys finally decide:

> "Of course, of course,
>   We can't stand by
>   And let the guy
> Take our good Helen off by force!

> "It's vengeance! Vengeance! Vengeance!"

Penelope and the Three Ladies entreat:

> "Will you never learn?"

But even Penelope's clinging to Ulysses no longer helps, as Mother Hare does her worst:

> "Do not go, Ulysses,
>   Stay home and die in bed."

That decides Ulysses; he gives Penelope a fond embrace and joins up. The Boys and Ulysses go off to war in a bunting-draped float with a highly-alive and vocal girl as its figurehead. At the last minute Menelaus hops on too; the Old Men wave, the women weep, and Mother Hare stands gloating.

ACT II

Helen, dressed to the teeth and toting a lacy parasol, is having a fine old time in the city of Rhododendron. Paris is at her side as she strolls along the streets, but so is most of the male population of Rhododendron. All are singing: ". . . it's grand to see her picture in the papers." Helen loves it and doesn't give a hoot:

> ". . . my reputation's battered,
>   But it really hasn't mattered,
>   Every lad about is mad about this bird of paradise."

The men break in:

> ". . . her future may be stormy dear"

Helen begs:

"But, Heavens, don't reform me, dear.
I'm nicer as a nice girl who is really not too nice."

The future begins to be stormy right then and there. Ulysses and
his contingent—including mournful Menelaus—arrives in Rhododendron. When Ulysses sees Helen he promises her forgiveness if
she will go home. Menelaus pleads with her too, but instead of
going back, she brazenly walks off with her new friends.

The Boys, feeling like hicks, want to go home, but Ulysses is excited by the look and feel of the city:

> "Don't give up so easy.
> Come back, you guys,
> Let's get in a huddle
> And organize . . ."

Boys—
But they are so many
And we are so few.
We will never break
This town in two.

Ulysses—
I figured out a simple trick,
It's elementary arithmetic.

They're bored and aimless,
Their brains are blotto.
Divide and conquer
Will be our motto.

Watch me take the city!
Watch me take the city!

The Boys are won over and do as Ulysses orders. First Ulysses
stops busy citizens scurrying past and bids them form a committee
with him. When they want to know what for, Ulysses answers:

> "Don't ask questions!
> Are you joining or not?
> All you have to do is sign,
> Right here on the dotted line."

As soon as they have signed, Ulysses has another group sign for a
"countercommittee." After he primes the Rhododendrons that an
invisible "They" are out to ruin them, he prompts his Boys to join
both groups and get them going:

FIRST GROUP—
  Give up Helen.
  She's a public scandal,
  She's too hot to handle.

SECOND GROUP—
  Don't ditch Helen!
  You're a rat unless you're
  Loyal to Helen.
  Don't give in to pressure.

  Send back Helen!
  Give that baby doll up.
  Get rid of Helen,
  Helen is a trollop.

  Save our Helen!
  Listen here to this, you,
  Raise hell for Helen,
  She's a civic issue.

As Ulysses planned, all is pandemonium, with wild street fighting until the mayor appears. This natty, smiling, top-hatted fellow presents himself to Ulysses. His tactics are blandly lethal, as he urges compromise.

MAYOR HECTOR—
  Why break the town up? Nothing is solved.
  I have a practical plan.
  Let's have the two galoots involved
  Fight it out man to man!

Ulysses is mollified, and agrees. A fight arena is quickly set up and Paris dances on in a silk robe. Ulysses unexpectedly takes over for Menelaus, and at the end of a prize fight with much of the atmosphere of a George Bellows picture, Ulysses knocks Paris out. The Boys collect their winnings, and Paris is borne off in a funeral procession by the Townspeople.

Hector gives Helen back to Menelaus, who immediately forgives her. The Boys feel put out by this:

  "Is there no justice?
  Does virtue never triumph?
  The wicked like a bay tree
  Keep right on flourishing."

They're now to see this for themselves, as darkness falls upon Rhododendron, for Ulysses gets the idea of spending Saturday night in the city, before heading back to the hills. With their fight winnings in their pockets, the Boys are easily tempted. Mayor Hector starts them on their way, urging them to spruce up:

  "In store bought suits
  You raw recruits
  Will look as chic
  As the sleekest city dude."

As the Boys head for the stores, Mayor Hector silkily and sunnily confides in the audience:

> "Now we will have our revenge on them.
> The bait is ready, the trap is set.
> The city itself will be our stratagem.
> There'll be a bitter reckoning, yet.

> "They speak of seven sins in the Scripture,
> But our age has invented many more,
> So subtle and sweet that once you've slipped you're
> Never, never able to go home any more."

Mayor Hector happily lists the pitfalls of money, fame, empty knowledge, liquor, and sex, and concludes:

> "Some go for empty knowledge,
> And some think sex will set their body free.
> The man of the hour
> Will settle for power,
> Yes, every soul alive has his fee,

> Except for noble people,
>   Lovely people,
>   Wonderful people,
>   Marvelous people,
>   Exceptional people
>   Like you
> And
>   Like me!

And he struts off vaudeville-fashion.

Meanwhile, back in Angel's Roost, Penelope has managed to keep her suitors at arms' length, and herself busy, by working on a patch-work quilt. She calmly receives the suddenly virtuous Helen, who has just returned, cashbox and all, with Menelaus. Helen has no qualms about relaying news of Ulysses: "He is off on a spree. . . ."

And Menelaus adds his tactless bit:

> "He and the fellers,
> Those fellers
> Are rowdydowdy hellers."

Helen doesn't mind saying she was shocked, but Penelope serenely sings:

"The shape of the world is round,
Is round,
And no matter how far he'll stray,
When the thread of his dream's unwound
He's bound
To turn up at his own back door one day. . . ."

Helen tells her:

"Penelope, you're a good girl,
But your good man likes to roam.
Oh, why can't a good woman
Ever keep a good man home. . . ."

Penelope is no more affected by Helen's gloating than by Mene-laus' misplaced pity. She goes on with her patchwork and holds on to her love.

Scene II

The Big Spree

In revue style, Ulysses' adventures begin. He and the Boys, dressed in dark suits trimmed with gay piping, are quickly tempted by Hector's barker spiel:

"Hurry, hurry!
Right this way
For Rho
      do
          dendron
On display.
The wonder of the twentieth century.
Here's
      Money,
            Power,
                  Booze,
And wenchery."

Led on by a smirking Paris, Madame Calypso, the lion tamer, is on their trail. She is Mrs. Juniper, a stately creature in an extrava-gant ball gown, diamonds, and osprey plumes, bent on displaying the Boys and Ulysses, since she's the "hostess who only handles—Big Names." She flutily sings:

> "Ulysses and Doc,
> Achilles and *all*,
> You mustn't be late to the Victory Ball"

that she's giving in their honor.

Calypso waves her wand, the curtains open, and a ballroom, complete with chandelier, columns, and gorgeously clothed guests flies into view. The guests gush and fawn over the Boys, and compliment Calypso for daring to have them here. Calypso explains her social success:

> "The Old Guard is dying to stop me
> Because I am up to the minute.
> The Social Register surely would drop me,
> Except,
> I've never been in it!"

Ulysses and Calypso become coy with one another and, as she leads the toast "to you darlings from the hills," Ulysses and the Boys eat it up, while protesting that they're just simple farmers. Calypso, the hostess, sings:

> "Dear Milton was a farmer, too,
> My late lamented husband Milton,
> A simple farmer just like you,
> With big broad shoulders I could wilt on.

> "But Milton struck it rich!
> He peeled a hazel switch—
> *He* called it a divining rod,
> A simply *too* divining rod,
> That showed him soil
> Just *soaked* in oil.
> It rushed,
>   And gushed,
>   And made a wad.

> "And now he's dead
> And under the sod.
> But Milton struck it rich, thank God.
> Milton struck it rich. . . ."

The Boys and Ulysses now feel like cocks of the walk, and start preening and strutting about. Calypso and her guests begin to yawn, a pall of boredom settling over them. The twentieth century has so

accelerated things that Ulysses' seven-year visit to Calypso is whit-
tled down to a few minutes. Quickly the guests and Calypso, the
ballroom, and Patroclus, who couldn't bear being left out, fade away.
Ulysses and the rest of the Boys are left in utter darkness. They
shrug off the loss of their companion, and immediately are ready for
a try at "Paradise Alley."

Mayor Hector has other ideas, as a "runner" on one roller skate
rolls on with a whispered message, and then rolls off. Hector passes
around his flask to loosen up his suckers, and in a jiffy has them on
the floor of the stock exchange. He advises:

> "Step into these stately portals
> Where the Golden Calf is fed.
> Shun the humbler working materials,
> Let them work for you instead."

Hector—now broker Charybdis—is joined by Menelaus—now
broker Scylla. Their Gallagher-and-Sheen routine quickly induces
the Boys to throw their money around.

SCYLLA—
I say there, Charybdis.
HECTOR—
Oh, yes, good friend Scylla.
SCYLLA—
Did you corner the hemp market in Manila?
HECTOR—
I did corner it, old sport
But I had to sell it short.
SCYLLA—
Positively, Mister Charybdis?
HECTOR—
Absolutely, Mister Scylla.

Scylla confides in the Boys:

> "He pretends he sold hemp short
> So as not to let the rest in.
> If you are the clever sort
> Hemp's the thing you will invest in."

Ajax is all for buying shares:

> "If we pool our railroad fares
> And those bets we won, we'll cash in."

Ulysses and the Boys know:

> "If we lose our railroad shares,
> Gettin' home will be a nuisance."

But Ajax insists:

> "If we win we're millionaires,
> By investing just a few cents!"

After Ajax snatches their money from them and hands it over the counter, hemp quickly toboggans and the Boys are busted. Ajax, in elaborate despair, takes a running jump out the nearest window. Hector discreetly pulls the window shade down, while Ulysses and the Boys briefly eulogize: "Poor Ajax," and that's that.

Hector consoles the survivors with a turn in a waterfront dive, complete with a background volcano and tropical moon. Lovey Mars, as a black-wigged Siren swathed in leis, adorns a platform dragged on-stage by four sirenettes.

In Aloha style, Lovey sings:

> "By a goona, goona, goona,
> By a goona, goona, goona lagoon
> We will croona, croona, croona,
> We will croona, croona real jungle tune. . . ."

The Boys, in spite of Ulysses' warning, quickly succumb to the dancing hula girls, while Ulysses soon forgets his own advice and yields to the Siren's attentions. The Siren tells them:

> "The passion fruit is in blossom now,
> So come along cuties and shake the bough."

Suddenly Ulysses realizes that all his men—except Doc, Achilles, and Bluey—have been shanghaied:

> *"Shanghaied!*
> This is one hell of a bender.
> These town folks are mean as can be.
> Of glory they've stripped us.
> They've clipped us
>   And gypped us.
> This is one *hell* of a spree!"

Bluey takes fright when a blandly smiling Hector comes on. He disappears into someone's waiting arms, and Achilles, Doc, and Ulysses alone remain of the crew.

Ulysses is beginning to distrust Hector and his slick ideas:

> "Don't trust me, put your reliance
> In the cold hard facts of science.
> It will free you from vain superstitions,
> From demons, taboos, and angels with wings.
> It will shatter your antiquated traditions.
> Just hark to the hymn that the scientist sings!"

To a burst of ragtime, Miss Minerva, now dressed in bloomers and high-laced boots, is seen monkeying around in a place filled with rheostats, dynamos, retorts, and a rocket straight out of Rube Goldberg.

LADY SCIENTIST—
> I've prodded the atom to its foundation,
> Cross-indexed the human mind,
> Reduced the universe to an equation.

ULYSSES, DOC & ACHILLES—
> What, oh, what did you find?

LADY SCIENTIST (*cheerfully*)—
> Oooo, the Polar Cap is slowly expanding,
> In a million years we'll freeze to death, I guess.
> If the Ice Age hasn't floored us,
> There's a planet heading toward us.
> When it hits, we'll be an interstellar mess!
>
> Oh, our continent is crumbling and dissolving
> As our rivers wash the topsoil out to sea,
> And what land we can retrieve'll
> Be devoured by pest and weevil,
> And there won't be nothing left for you and me.

ALL—
> Oh, we're doomed,
> Doomed, doomed.
> Oh, we're doomed,
> Doomed, doomed.
> Oh, we're doomed to disappear without a trace!

Miss Minerva feels certain this is so:

> "Because all of us are just
> Little specks of cosmic dust"

and "man is just a biological mistake." Gaily the Lady Scientist dances back to her laboratory, fiddles with the levers of the huge, glistening rocket, and gets an admiring Doc to volunteer to ride in it. Doc is stuffed into the rocket, the Scientist pulls a switch, and off goes Doc in a flash of light. The Scientist is in raptures that the rocket works. Ulysses asks: "But how is he gonna get back?"

SCIENTIST—
Oh, dear! Oh, dear!
I never thought of that.

Well, back to work!

And with a shrug, she and her assistants march back into the laboratory, which blacks out.

ULYSSES—
Enough is enough.
The game is played out,
And all of our pals
Have pulled a fade-out!

When Hector blithely comes on, Ulysses grabs him by the lapels:

"I'm wise to this joint now,
It's fight or get beaten.
I get the point now,
It's eat or be eaten."

As Hector brushes him off, the city, looking squalid and sinister, appears behind him. In a flash, slinky Circe—Penelope veiled and clad in black—undulates over the roof tops. Paris dances a dance of longing for this creature, whose attentions are already fixed on Ulysses.

HECTOR—
She's the city when it's evil,
In her veins flows rock and rye.
You had better hide in a doorway
When you see her passing by.

A crowd of the People of the Night, cold and evil in appearance, say of her:

"Circe, Circe,
The woman without mercy.
Circe turns men into swine."

Hector now suggests to Ulysses:

"Ulysses, we've mystified you,
Oh, we've tried to drag you down.
But boy with this gal beside you
You can rule this doggone town."

Achilles tries his best to prevent it, but Ulysses goes after Circe,
who sings to him:

"There are just two kinds of people,
Those who follow and those who lead.
I will make you so cold and clever,
You'll be certain to succeed."

As Ulysses and Circe weave slowly among the dancing Night
People, Hector gets a knife from one of them and offers it to Paris,
saying:

"Paris!
This is all your doin',
Cause you went wooin'.

"You dragged that fool in,
And now he's rulin'.

"But we all hate him,
So liquidate him
And Circe will love you."

Paris at first refuses. But when Circe suddenly holds out the
golden apple to Ulysses, and starts to lead him over the rooftops,
Paris enviously grabs the knife, intending to do Ulysses in. But it is
Achilles who, intercepting the blow, falls dead in Ulysses' place.

The bender is almost over. Ulysses, now completely alone, receives Hector's almost affectionate farewell:

"It was grand,
Really grand,
To have known you,
And all of your wonderful crew.
But you've lost the friends you've known,
And at last you're on your own,
And it's certain to be curtains for you too."

And Hector disappears after the others over the rooftops.

Ulysses tosses the golden apple away, and the illusion of the city
begins to fade. A starry sky descends to cover the rooftops, while

Ulysses puzzles over the meaning of his existence. He asks questions out loud about life and death, love and faith. Mother Hare, seemingly suspended in space, echoes his words. As Ulysses finds his answers, the city fades completely away and the skies brighten:

> "Yes, life is life's answer,
> And death is the same.
> Love, faith, hope, and dreams,
> All the things I can name,
> All answer themselves.
> Together, not apart,
> In the unspoken wisdom
> Of the living heart.
>
> "I know that I am myself,
> And I am also other men.
> And knowing this truly,
> I can go home again.
>
> "I can go home again."

His decision made, Penelope's house in Angel's Roost appears. There are morning-glories on the picket fence, and the ladies are at their usual occupation of meddling in Penelope's life, of urging her to forget Ulysses, and marry one of her suitors. Still, after ten years at work on the patchwork quilt, Penelope says firmly:

> "I vowed I would not choose before
> I finished up my sewing chore."

But the end seems near; the suitors crowd impatiently around as the girls take the quilt from Penelope and toss it in the air. Penelope gaily counts out:

> "Eeny, meeny, miney, mo,
> Whichaway shall my heart go?
> The Parson, Banker Carson,
> The Smith, or Farmer Joe?"

She is interrupted by the battered barge's return. Ulysses stands alone in it. The figurehead is all knocked out, her crown askew, her gown in tatters. When Ulysses leaps out, the boat can barely stagger off.

Penelope greets Ulysses, not with an embrace, but with a violent push and caustic words:

"Oh, it's you back, is it?
Are you home for a visit?"

What did he expect?   That she would be as good as gold, refusing
to cut up, just waiting for him with that lamp in the window?

"Well, you're wrong, Ulysses.
Ulysses, you're wrong!
I got along without you,
So you had better get along, too!"

But her toughness doesn't last.   She bursts into tears.   Seeing the
quilt, Ulysses recognizes the scraps it's made of, and all it represents.   He holds it out to her beseechingly.   He argues that if he'd
never gone away, he could never have been so sure that all he wishes
in life was at Angel's Roost.   And he reminds her:

"It's the coming home together
When your work is through . . ."

And it's knowing someone's there.
Penelope yields and joins him in singing:

"It's the being home together
When the shadows rise.
Someone looks into your eyes,
And takes you by the hand.

"It's a dear familiar face
That can light up a place,
And little private jokes
Only you two understand."

The whole town joins in the chorus; and the sky is bathed in
bright, clear light as Penelope and Ulysses go home.

THE MAGIC AND THE LOSS *

A Play in Three Acts

By Julian Funt

[Julian Funt *attended New York University and later entered the newspaper field doing publicity and editorial work. Then he began writing radio and television scripts, becoming one of the top writers in the business. He was coauthor (1946) of "The Dancer," a play which served Anton Dolin for his first, and only, appearance on Broadway in a legitimate play. Actually, however, Mr. Funt considers "The Magic and the Loss" his first play.*]

GRACE WILSON and her son Nicki live in a slightly crowded but pleasant three-room village apartment on one of the numbered side streets off Washington Square. We can see the living room (off which is a bedroom we can't see) and the small hall to the kitchenette and bathroom. When the door to the hall is open we can get a glimpse of the kitchenette.

The living room is attractively furnished. On the wall hang a Chagall reproduction and Picasso line drawings; the shelves are crowded with records and books, and near the couch, which also serves as Nicki's bed, there is a fine record-player.

It is late afternoon when two fourteen-year-olds enter the dark apartment. Nicki was in the park trying to beat up a boy who had made cracks about his mother when Al Maccio came along. Nicki isn't the fighter type; he's a slender and precocious boy. Al, on the other hand, though small looks pretty tough.

While Nicki goes to wash off the stains of battle, Al takes a look around the flat, and the Picasso nudes immediately catch his eye: "Hey, what kind of a house is this? Dirty pictures." Nicki comes out to see what Al is het up about, and explains that Picasso is a very famous painter. Al is sure his cousin could do better, and she's not even twelve.

There are other things Al can't understand: for instance, Nicki's habit of calling his mother "Grace." "Geez, if I called my old man Salvatore, he'd mobilize me. Well, I better get goin'." When Nicki offers him a coke, Al feels the least he can do is give Nicki some friendly advice: "Hey, look—these guys around the fountain start pickin' on you again, why don'tcha smack 'em in the mouth?" Nicki says: "Maybe if I could fight like you, I would." Al has an easy solution: "Maybe if you went to a real school instead of the fancy-pants dump you go to, you'd learn how." Nicki stands up for his progressive school, and asks Al: "Anyway, what's so great about being an athlete?" "Are you kidding? Do you know how much Phil Rizzuto makes?" Nicki certainly does, and isn't in the least impressed because he also knows how short a time an athlete has to cash in. To Al, this kind of heresy sounds just like his old man, who thinks "if you play ball, you're a dope." Nicki tactfully assures him this isn't true: ". . . Lots of them get started on college teams."

AL—Try and tell him that. I flunk algebra in the mid-terms—so he has to holler like I blew up the BMT or something.

NICKI—Your mother's dead?

AL—Yeah. . . . My old man! Work in the store after school—he tells me. Sure, I tell him—I'll work. Pay me. He heard that. I thought he was gonna blow his gasket. Boy, oh, boy, would I like to see his ugly puss the day I take off for Palm Beach, Florida. Only I won't be aroun' to see it.

NICKI—You're going to run away from home?

AL—You're damn right! Palm Beach—that's the place. I got a cousin down there—Vinnie Ignante. You oughta get a load of the doll he's got. And she drives a 1952 Buick convertible. And is she nuts about him. Any time he wants to.

NICKI—Any time he wants to what?

AL—What the hell do you think?

When Nicki goes on asking questions about this trip, Al thinks he sounds like the truant officer. But Nicki would really like this new friend to have dinner with his mother and himself. When Grace Wilson arrives, loaded down with flowers, a brief case, and a bag of groceries, she is rather startled at Al's appearance. She greets him in friendly fashion, and hearing that Nicki has asked him to dinner, she repeats the invitation. This time Al is really uncomfort-

able and wants to leave. Which he does, first making a date with
Nicki for the following afternoon at the fountain. Grace, crossing
to the phone, admits she's curious: "He isn't exactly the kind of boy
who—" Nicki bristles, so she is quick to admit her error. While she
waits for her office number, she tells Nicki: "Darling—would you
mind putting that bag in the refrigerator—and bringing me something to put these in? And Nicki—one more thing—comb your hair,
put on a clean shirt. In fact, why not shoot the works and wash
your face, too?" The company he is to get ready for is Larry Graves.
Nicki protests—does she have to see him all the time? Tonight,
Grace says, Larry is coming especially to meet Nicki.

GRACE (*gets her call*)—Hello, Bill . . . Grace . . . Did you get
that memo from the Moose? . . . He never neglects us in the copy
department. . . . Bill, would I be a pig if I asked you to dig up
the 1951-52 figures as well? I really would like to rock 'em. . . .
I know, I know, that's advertising. . . . You will? . . . Wonderful.
. . . I don't know what I'd do without you, Bill. . . . I really don't.
. . . Good night, Bill. (*Abruptly.*) Oh, Bill—did you hear anything? . . . About me, of course. . . . Oh . . . Well, keep your
pretty little ears wide, wide open, will you, pal? . . . Right. (*Re-
places receiver.*)
NICKI—How does it look? What did he say?
GRACE—Patience, darling, patience. Your old lady's going to be
a vice-president, yet. You wait and see.

With a husband's interest, Nicki asks Grace whether she saw the
Moose today. She admits she didn't, so Nicki gives her a bit of
advice: "You know something? You let him push you around too
much." Nicki thinks she should threaten to quit. Grace smiles at
this. Things are looking up so much, she may hear something very
special tonight. She playfully crosses her fingers and knocks on wood
in front of her disapproving and superior son.
Things aren't looking up for the lady who now drops in on Grace.
Anita Harmon, Grace's boss, who is just out of the hospital after a
major operation, had to stop off to see Grace—nor is this her first
stop: she's been to the office, too.

ANITA—I—I dropped in on my way home from the hospital. How
neurotic can you get about your job—huh?
GRACE—I'm sorry I missed you.
ANITA—I was only there about ten minutes. And the Moose
wasn't exactly ecstatic when he saw me.

GRACE—Maybe his ulcer was acting up again—or his daughter—or both.

The Moose had shown Anita the presentation Grace prepared for the Winchester account. Anita thinks it's a slick job, bound to be bought. "Anyway the Moose was very much impressed." Anita uneasily gets to the point of her visit: "Grace, I did a funny thing this afternoon. You may not like it. I told him we worked up this presentation together."

GRACE (*startled, dismayed*)—How could we?

ANITA—You came up to my room at the hospital. We were in constant touch by telephone.

GRACE—I see.

ANITA—Do you mind very much?

GRACE—Very much.

ANITA (*pulling a bank book out of her pocket and thrusting it into* GRACE's *hand*)—Grace, take a look at this. I have $6,485 between me and whatever happens to women of 52 who have the ground pulled from under them. And I'm not 52. I'm 54. And I don't have someone like Larry Graves—

GRACE—What's he got to do with it?

ANITA—I'm sorry.

GRACE—Anita, this was a test for me—a trial run—my big chance. I have—problems, too. I'm getting too old to be an assistant, and there's the boy.

ANITA—I know. (*Begins to sob.*)

GRACE—Don't do that— For God's sake, Anita, cut it out! That's what they're always sneering at—the way we crack up—when things get rough— Anita, will you cut it out, please?

Anita subsides, then bursts out with what is she doing so wrong these days? Why doesn't she get along fine with the Moose as she used to? Grace tells her: "You make him uncomfortable, I guess." "*I* make *him* uncomfortable . . . ?" Grace adds: "He wants to be superior, protective. Why don't you give him a chance?" This is the very advice Anita gave Grace years ago, but today is unable to follow. To Anita, men (particularly the Moose) are arrogant bastards. She asks for a drink, which she shouldn't have, and holding up her glass, toasts:

ANITA—Here's to nothing. (*Takes a sip, shudders.*) After thirty years I still have trouble getting the first one down. I really should

be drinking this to you. Because if they tie the can to me, you're
the one that's going to get the job. Well, maybe you should at that.
You're certainly better able to cope with the bastards than I am.

GRACE—Cope?

ANITA—Or something. Anyway you haven't got my problem.
That's still fifteen years off. I'd better blow.

Anita is about to leave, when Grace hesitantly tells her: "If he asks
me, we worked on this presentation together." "You are out of
your head, you know," Anita tells her. "But then, you can afford
to make sentimental gestures, and it's been so long since I could."

After she leaves, Nicki reappears. Naturally he's heard everything, and he's full of advice. He thinks Mrs. Harmon should quit,
just like that, so Grace can have her job. "Now wait a minute.
Anita's been with the firm for over twenty years," she tells her son.
But Nicki feels sure that Grace does all the work: "You mean you
don't want her job?" "I mean," corrects Grace, "I'm not rooting
for her collapse—and I don't want you to be, either. Things are
tough enough at her age." Nicki seems to understand this, and is
pleased his mother doesn't look her age. Grace sighs for, ". . . all
those poor women who don't have sons like you." "No, I mean it,"
insists Nicki. Grace hugs him: "I know you do. That's the nicest
part." Nicki, the male, wants to know what's for dinner, but beautiful lamb chops are no attraction: he's decided to become a vegetarian.

NICKI—Eating the corpses of living things—it's cannibalism. Besides, people don't really need meat. Scientists have found out that
—two-thirds—

GRACE—Nicki, not so loud. The Meat Packers Institute is one of
our best accounts.

NICKI—So what? The Agency can't control my life.

Nicki is plainly disappointed that Grace is going out for dinner.
Grace asks him if he really minds, and he gives a muttered: " 'course
not." Grace says gently she wouldn't mind if he went out oftener,
for instance to Sally Wheelock's party. Nicki dismisses Sally as a
big horse, and various other young ladies as creeps, baby-talkers,
and show-offs. Grace sums up: "One girl's a tomboy—another's too
feminine—still another's too smart. Darling, wait a year or two
before you join the Great Conspiracy." Before Grace can wash up,
the doorbell rings. Nicki accuses her of being nervous over a vice-
president of R. H. R. and C. Grace, before opening the door, says

pleadingly: "I want you two to like each other. I want it very much."

Larry Graves, a good-looking, self-assured vice-president in his early forties, has arrived determined that Nicki shall like him. It's something of an uphill job. The gramophone record he's brought, Nicki announces he already has and scarcely says thank you for. When Larry says something about Nicki's joining them for dinner, Nicki pleads too much homework. Larry offers him a rain check: "Maybe some Friday, when there's no school the next day— Well, shall we get started, Grace." Grace suggests a drink first, and Nicki offers to get the ice.

LARRY—I'm afraid I'm not doing too well.
GRACE—Well. Don't forget he's as nervous as you are.
LARRY—Yeah—I guess he is. (*Kisses her.*) Hello.
GRACE—Hello.
LARRY—Hey, remember me?
GRACE (*nodding warningly toward the kitchen*)—I never forget an account executive.
LARRY—I talked to Mason White today.
GRACE—What did he say?
LARRY—You're beautiful. Do you know that?
GRACE—Mason White said that?

Larry tells her the gentleman is for her. This is pleasant news, but at once the thought of Anita spoils it. Larry says they don't like her: ". . . they're going to get somebody to take her place. And you certainly rate a crack at the job." Grace with a grateful smile asks: "Do you want to repeat that for the Front Office?" "Be glad to," says Larry as he starts toward her again.

Nicki comes back with the ice. Suddenly, as Grace talks shop with Larry, Nicki calls attention to himself by ordering whiskey— neat. First Grace protests, but then she gives it to him, and asks what they should drink to.

NICKI—What do you mean?
GRACE—A toast. This is something of an occasion. Isn't it?
NICKI—Why?
GRACE (*groping*)—Your first drink—among other things. What'll we drink *to?*
NICKI—To George Bernard Shaw.
LARRY—Good man.

NICKI—He was a vegetarian, too. (NICKI *takes a gulp and his eyes and mouth spring wide open. He swallows air in large doses. Gasping.*) That's terrible!

GRACE (*soothingly*)—If it's any comfort, Nicki, George Bernard Shaw felt exactly the same way.

LARRY—Here you are.

GRACE—Take a sip of water, darling.

NICKI (*recovering*)—How can you drink this stuff?

After hitting Nicki on the back, Larry apologizes for his choice of record. Nicki begins to relax and the two talk folk-singers. When Larry seems to know what he's talking about, Nicki starts to warm up and even accepts the dinner invitation, provided he needn't dress. Grace feels things are going so well that she can go off to dress, herself.

The phone rings. Nicki answers and when he hears the voice at the other end of the wire, becomes excited. It's his father, George, calling from the 8th St. Whelan's. He hasn't seen him in two years, and now he's going out to dinner with him. This time, Nicki can't wait to get all spruced up; but, despite his excitement, he remembers to ask Larry: "Are you sure you don't mind? It's my father." And he apologizes to Grace, who rises to the occasion: "If he had given us a little warning you could have had your hair cut. Put on a tie. We want to make a good impression on your father."

And Grace wants Larry to wait for George so she can make a good impression by showing *him* off. ". . . Besides, having a third party around at this point isn't a bad idea at all." Larry regards her affectionately: "You're wonderful and slightly crazy." Larry is curious, too, as to what her former husband is like. Grace finds it hard to pigeonhole him—he's a teacher at Reed College, a small college somewhere in Oregon. And his going way out there was no accident: ". . . For George it's in complete character. Wait till you meet him. He's the thoughtful observer, the man with the appraising eye—the not-quite-so-innocent bystander."

When the bell rings, Grace asks the startled Larry how she looks, and then confesses: "Boy—I'm in great shape— Pay no attention." Larry gives her the reassurance she needs: "Grace, just for the record—you look great."

George, a pleasant-looking, reticent man, also in his early forties, comes in. He too carries a package. Grace takes his coat and introduces him to Larry. Apparently George's sudden arrival in New York is all due to editing a book for Doubleday. He apologizes for not warning her.

Grace asks politely about his wife; then says that Nicki is putting on a tie. "Could any father get a more touching tribute?" Grace asks. George turns to Larry: "You in the advertising business, too, Mr. Graves?" "Does it show?" Larry asks. "Not everybody in New York," says Grace, "is in the advertising business—although some days it looks like it." George apologizes. Larry wonders why. "You don't insult a man by asking if he's in the advertising business —I hope."

Nicki comes in and after a formal handshake with his father, and visible emotion on his father's part, has to go out of the room: "I've got something in my eye." George tells him to take his time, and apologizes after the boy goes: "I'm sorry. I guess I kind of swarmed all over him." And he accepts a drink from Larry.

The grownups start to make polite conversation while waiting for Nicki's return, but it takes on warmth and color as Grace and George begin to reminisce. They talk of people they used to know—Grace had met an artist friend coming out of the Waldorf: ". . . looking for all the world like he belonged there."

LARRY—Is that Phil West the illustrator?
GRACE—Uh huh.
GEORGE—He was once a very talented painter.
GRACE—Talented and hungry.
LARRY—Well—what Art has lost, Commerce has gained.
GEORGE—Yeah.
LARRY—And as the fella says—Them's the conditions that prevail.
GEORGE—So I hear.

Grace gossips that Phil is married again—to an athletic blonde whom George remembers very well indeed.

GEORGE—Not the one he had in Provincetown that Summer?
GRACE—He had until she latched onto you. I never could figure out what you two were doing on that ladder.
GEORGE—I never could figure out what you suspected—on a ladder.
GRACE (smiles)—I guess I was a little violent.
GEORGE—Well, it was a pretty violent Summer all around, wasn't it?
GRACE—I guess it was. They don't make Summers like that any more. . . .

To cover up in front of Larry, Grace asks about the book George is doing. Nicki finally arrives, and doesn't soothe Larry's vanity by begging to stay out late, after dinner with his father. As they leave, George assures Grace they'll be back by eleven.

Grace now has no thoughts for Larry or for what Larry is thinking. She doesn't respond to his passionate kiss; she thinks they'd better go out to dinner, too. Larry tries again. "Don't you see that it wouldn't be any good?" Grace asks him. Larry becomes angry. "What made you suddenly decide to cut the evening so short?"—She made a date, didn't she? "You mean I— Do you think I'm planning to go to bed with him?" Grace is horrified. Larry insists she's still in love with George. "I'm in love with you," Grace assures him. "Are you?" Larry says bitterly. " 'They don't make Summers like that any more.' End of quote."

Grace asks why must there be comparisons? "I'm a different person now—and this is a different country." Larry refuses to understand her talk of old scars, just tells her to get her coat. Grace begs him not to look like that: he simply goes for his own coat and tells her to come along.

GRACE—Larry, please! So our moods didn't coincide for a moment. But believe me, darling—I never felt closer to you than I do right now—

LARRY—Let's not talk about it any more, Grace.

GRACE (*wearily*)—All right, Larry. (*Slips out of her coat.*) We won't talk about it any more. (*They embrace.*)

SCENE II

At 11:30 Grace is looking thoughtfully out of the window, waiting for George to bring Nicki home. When they arrive, she shoos Nicki to bed, and offers George coffee. He has wanted a chance to talk to her, and this is a fine one.

First he tells a little about his life at Reed, and Grace is delighted to tell of her own work: "I love it. I really do—the challenge and the excitement and the money. And I still like the look of respect on the faces of the boys when I come up with a good idea. And, though modesty should forbid, I come up with quite a few of them." George is sure she does. "Of course," Grace adds, "it's not all a breeze. It's like the Army, this business I'm in. When you reach a certain age, you have to move up or out. They don't want middle-aged lieutenants."

GEORGE (*laughs*)—Middle-aged?

GRACE—Don't laugh. I was stopped by a policeman the other day for crossing against the light—and he was a kid. It comes as quite a jolt when you suddenly discover that you're older than the cops. Tell me about your wife.

GEORGE—What do you want to know?

GRACE—Everything— No, I don't. Tell me what you think of your son.

As she asks this, George finds her on the defensive. "Because," she answers, "I won't accept platitudes from you?" "What do you want me to say?" George asks. "I think he's a fine kid. And I think you've done a wonderful job under the circumstances." Says Grace: " 'A boy needs a father,' I know."

George now asks her why she never answered his letter two months back. She won't say; asks instead, why, after all these years, he wants the boy?

GEORGE—Well, for one thing, I didn't feel I could handle it then. And when he was younger, he needed you much more than he needed me.

GRACE—That makes sense—as far as it goes.

GEORGE—Where doesn't it make sense?

GRACE—I'm not sure that he'd do well in a climate of resignation and withdrawal.

GEORGE—Is that what a college campus means to you?

GRACE—No, what I think it means to you.

GEORGE—Why? Just because our values are different from Madison Avenue? Because we want different things?

GRACE—Because you don't want them hard enough.

GEORGE—Hard enough? Or loud enough?

Grace tells him to wait a minute. She knows the advertising business is lunatic, but she also feels Nicki's too young to be exposed, "to the idea that everything ends on a note of betrayal, so why bother?" She believes life should be competitive. George wonders if after fourteeen years of the competitive life, it mightn't be a good thing to give the boy a change. "A change to what? What's wrong with him that a change will help?" George thinks he is terribly insecure. Grace agrees. "Did you ever meet a boy without a father who wasn't? Nicki needed you, he needed you badly. And you weren't there. You didn't walk out on me. You walked out on a family." "Walked out?" he asks. "What would you call it?" Grace would like to know.

George refuses to be attacked for the way of life *she* chose, or to apologize because he, "couldn't be a streamline operator in the right income bracket like Larry Graves." "Operator?" repeats Grace. "Is that how he strikes you?" George waves the red flag at her: "Well, evidently he's better able to cope than I was . . ." Grace flings back that she was a pretty good homemaker, as well as business woman. George doesn't agree: ". . . for you, work was in competition with the home." "Or," says Grace, "in competition with you?"

Nicki, who should have been in bed, can't stay away from his father and invents pretexts for staying up. When he goes to the kitchen for the glass of milk he is sure he needs, he discovers the sink full of dishes: "I thought you were going out to dinner," he says to his mother. They changed their minds. Grace answers his "Why?" with: "People sometimes do," and offers to take his empty glass. Nicki has something on his mind that must be settled at once: Can he go with George to Washington for a few days? Grace is perfectly willing. So now, Nicki thinks, he'll start in on his packing. Grace stops this by offering to help him in the morning, and Nicki finally goes to bed.

George reminds her that she still hasn't answered whether Nicki can go to Reed with him. Grace says he knows her answer. She doesn't make snap decisions about Nicki. Perhaps, she adds, he feels Nicki's insecure from a twinge of conscience? George concedes that's possible, but not the whole story. After watching Nicki for a whole evening, he feels the boy just doesn't know where he belongs. "And why doesn't he?" Grace asks. "Because you don't," George answers. "You don't know where you fit in. You talked about a complete life, but you don't have one. You're not as happy as you say you are."

Grace doesn't contend she's always ecstatically happy, but she'd rather take life as it comes than lead the usual woman's existence. "But that's my problem." George insists that it's Nicki's too.

Grace answers that she's not ashamed of the job she's done on the boy. She tells George to observe him while they're away together, and then say whether he's been hurt by Grace's kind of life. George agrees that's fair.

ACT II

It is 8:30 several mornings later. Nicki has arrived home ahead of schedule and is asleep on his couch as Grace brings in his breakfast tray. He sleeps straight through a disconcerting phone call from Larry, who has left his suitcase in Grace's apartment, and for obvious reasons she won't bring it to the office. She decides Larry should pick it up after Nicki goes off to school: she'll leave the key in the mail box.

Her next problem is to waken Nicki, who murmurs there's plenty of time. "No, there isn't," he's told as he rolls over again. "No, you don't," Grace continues. "Now that you're back, I don't want you to miss another day of school." She glances at her watch. "Look, darling, it's late and I've got to run. Today's the day your old lady may come home a vice-president. Wake up and wish me luck." Off she goes, with Nicki promising he'll get to school on time. Nicki climbs out of bed and eats breakfast while dressing with spectacular adolescent technique and speed. He's finished within three minutes, just as the doorbell rings and Al asks to come in.

Al, having flunked three subjects, has been thrown out by his father. He's been on the town all night and needs breakfast and some "shut-eye." He scorns Rice Krispies, settles for a meat sandwich, and taunts Nicki for wanting to get to school on time. He himself is heading for Palm Beach, Florida. Could he phone the girl who gave him the brush-off, and make her feel sorry he's leaving town? "She'll beg me not to go. Nothin' doin', I'll tell her," he fantasies. "Not even if she comes crawlin'. I bet she'll even come up here—if I ask her." He has a sudden thought: "Hey—would it be okay? We'll have a ball!" Nicki refuses him the apartment, certain that his mother would disapprove. Al lets it pass, and Nicki is asking him for a letter from Florida, when a key turns in the lock.

Larry lets himself in, then with enormous embarrassment sees and greets the two boys. Nothing he can say eases the situation. At the best, conversation about Washington and folk-singers would be difficult at this hour of the morning, but with Larry toting a suitcase, it becomes grim. The suitcase, he explains, is one that Grace borrowed to bring home some lay-outs. He exits as fast as he decently can.

Al now takes it upon himself to wise Nicki up: "Lay-outs in a suitcase? What a cock-eyed liar he is." Nicki tells him to shut up. Al doesn't care to: "What are you getting so high-horse about? Get a load of him. And when I wanted to bring Maria up here you wouldn't let me. Your mother wouldn't like it. Well, she likes it fine when he comes around, huh?" Nicki tells him to shut up. As Al peers nastily into the bedroom, Nicki tries to force him out. Things get ugly, Nicki hits Al, and Al, cursing, knocks Nicki to the floor. As he falls, he brings a lamp crashing down with him.

Larry, hearing the noise at the elevator, rushes in just in time. He drags the tough-mouthed Al to the door, and shoves him out. With that Nicki scrambles to his feet and orders Larry out, refusing to listen to Larry's plea: "Nicki, please. It's important for you to understand."

NICKI—Get out! . . . Get out!
LARRY—All right, Nicki. (*Picks up the suitcase and crosses to the door. He looks back at* NICKI *for a moment, then exits.* NICKI *looks at the door, then collapses in tears on the hassock.*)

SCENE II

Grace is tense and nervous when she arrives home that evening. Nicki is lying on the couch and won't look up or speak to her. When Grace notices the broken lamp, Nicki mutters he broke it. "Is that why you're upset? Because you broke the lamp?" "I'm not upset," he says. "What's the matter, Nicki?" Grace asks. "Something wrong at school?" In a surly voice, he says he didn't go to school. Grace gives up.

George, finding he's tied up with business matters that evening, arrives to break his date with Nicki. The boy becomes sharp and rebellious, and insists he has to talk to George. When Grace tries to smooth things over, "Darling, if George has a business appointment . . . ," Nicki tells her to keep out of it. "It's none of her business," he cries to George. "When you go at your mother, go with a whip," murmurs Grace. "Excuse me, George, I have to change. Remember the good old days," she adds, "when children used to be scared of their parents?"

Left alone with Nicki, George finds out pretty quickly what is bothering the boy. Nicki is violent about his mother: "I could kill her!" George tells him to stop. "How could she do a thing like that?" the boy goes on, and tells about Larry's spending the night. Nicki, in belligerent tones, wants to know what George is going to do about it. "Nothing," says his father. "It's none of my business—and it's not yours either."

George has the amazed Nicki sit beside him, and then—after an apprehensive look at Grace's door—tries to straighten him out. George first tells him how pleased he was with Nicki in Washington, and, "depressed because I had so little to do with it."

NICKI—What's all this got to do with—
GEORGE—Let me finish, Nicki. Not every kid of your age would have reacted the way you did. In fact, darn few I know of. You know, a boy growing up these days is exposed to all kinds of things—

some good—a lot not so good. It's pretty easy to get side-tracked unless someone has given you a sense of direction. And you're lucky —because someone has. Your respect for ideas and for people—your warmth towards people—you don't find these things in bargain basements—they're pretty special, take my word. And so's your mother . . . *very* special.

NICKI—Not any more.

GEORGE—Grace hasn't changed.

NICKI—Yes, she has.

GEORGE—She's still the same warm human being that she always was. And I don't think it's been easy. To keep her job she had to be hard and tough. And raising a boy, that called for tenderness and love. And she had that, too. It was there whenever you needed it, wasn't it?

NICKI—Sure, I know, but—

GEORGE—But she needs, too, Nick— To be able to give love— you have to get it. In the case of a woman like Grace—a lot of it— even more than you can give her. And there is something else she has to get from you, Nicki—understanding. If Larry Graves is the man she needs, if she wants to marry him—

Nicki is horrified—she can't marry him. "That's not for you to say," George answers. "I know, but—" "Look, Nicki," George breaks in, "it's a wonderful thing to have a mother like Grace. But it imposes obligations, too." Grace's entrance cuts this short. She is ready for dinner. George now decides to cancel his business date and have dinner with Nicki. Grace considers this senseless—he's just had four days in Nicki's company. George is sharp with her as Nicki goes to the bedroom and slams the door behind him.

When Grace learns what is disturbing Nicki, she is utterly miserable. When she learns, too, that George told Nicki she and Larry would be married, she feels sunk: "The truth is—he hasn't asked me."

Grace wonders whether George is outraged or if he understands. George says: "I understand a single woman has needs, too. I'm not outraged. I'm not scandalized, Grace. But there is such a thing as discretion—if not for yourself—at least for the boy." She dejectedly agrees.

When Nicki opens the bedroom door with the announcement that he's going out, Grace is ready to turn him over to his father: "Nicki, how would you like to live with George for a year?" Nicki is overjoyed and can't wait to get going. "Take it easy, Nicki," George cautions.

At this very inconvenient moment, Anita has to make a very, very drunken appearance. Nor is her errand one of mercy. Grace gives her a drink because there's no way not to, and offers her sympathy: "I'm terribly sorry about the way things turned out for you." Anita is calm about it; she has news to spill.

ANITA—Want to know why I'm here? Tell you precisely and without flourishes. Tit for tat. Noblesse oblige. And quid pro quo.

GRACE—Fair enough. I'll make you some coffee.

ANITA—You consoled me. Now I console you. You've been mousetrapped, Grace girl. You've been harpooned, hung out to dry.

GRACE—What's this—

ANITA—They're not giving you my job. Oh, they deliberated. Had a good meeting. Everybody in there thinking every bleeding minute of the time. Almost gave it to you. Almost but not quite.

GRACE—Where did you get this?

ANITA—I have my sources. You're not moving up, Grace. You're staying put. Didn't want a woman, they decided. No sirree bob. Not enough hemoglobin. Pretty poor specific gravity, let me tell you.

GRACE (*sick with dismay*)—Do you know what you're talking about?

ANITA—Could take offense at a question like that. Could get sensitive and wounded. No, no, ma'am. I'm not going to. In spite of your vascular system, I was rooting for you. If I couldn't keep the job—wanted to see you get it. But—"women are too damned emotional." The Moose said it—and now it's the law of the land.

Grace wants to call the office; George offers to do it for her, but she does it herself, and finds that Anita was right.

Larry arrives to pick up Grace for dinner, and seeing Anita in a stupor offers to find her a cab. Nicki is sent with her instead: "He can do it," says Grace. Anita answers: "What's more I want him to. And a little child shall lead them. A man child. They're not really offensive until they grow up, are they? Do you suppose the Moose was ever a child? Hard to believe. Come on, Nicki." George thinks that, as he must go anyway, he can drop Anita off; so he's going with her and Nicki.

Grace and Larry are left alone with all the signs of a mess on their hands. Larry speaks of this morning and Nicki: "It must have been awfully rough on him." Then he wonders: "What was Anita doing here?" "She brought the glad tidings," Grace tells him. Larry is not only sorry about Nicki, and themselves, but about the job, too. Only somehow Grace doesn't feel he's sorry enough. At first she doesn't accuse him of anything: she simply fires question after question at him. For instance, what did the Moose say when Larry made his pitch for her? When Larry hesitatingly says he didn't get in to the Moose, Grace wants to know why not. The Moose was in his office all afternoon—she had kept tabs on all his visitors. Larry takes a different tack: he had felt it would be rather raw, pushing beyond a certain point.

GRACE—What point? How much did you actually do and say?
LARRY—I did everything I felt I could.
GRACE—Up to a certain point. But if it had been one of the boys you play gin with—instead of the girl you sleep with—would you have felt you could do more?
LARRY—That's a helluva thing to say.
GRACE—If I couldn't handle the job—if there had been any doubt —but even the Moose had conceded—
LARRY—But if they wanted a man— You know damn well how I feel.
GRACE—Then why did you keep your feelings to yourself? Where did this sudden reticence come from? You promised to help. We talked it over, planned it. My God, how careful and circumspect can you get?

Larry at this point tells her angrily to stop pressing. "That's the trouble with you! Always pressing! At home and at the office, keeping tabs on everyone, covering all the bases. And there's another thing he doesn't like: her contempt for the boys, and for him. At this point Grace begins to pull back: she pleads that she is acting this way because she's so upset over Nicki. Larry is upset, too. So upset, that he wouldn't go through with it again for the world. "It's no good, Grace. It won't work." Grace fights back again, point for point, but Larry shows he's through. For a moment, with feminine despair, Grace begs forgiveness and promises never to embarrass him at the office again. She is even willing to forget the job. When Larry tells her not to be an idiot, Grace in a dazed way starts pulling herself together and says quietly: "You said you were going. I think that's a good idea. This has been an exhausting evening—and we have to be bright and clear-eyed in the morning." Larry meets Nicki at the door, and says with a note of finality: "Good-by."
Nicki has instructions for Grace about picking up his and George's tickets, along with a check to pay for them: "There's an office in your building. I told him you'd pick them up, tomorrow." Grace

is oddly abstracted as she asks about the check: Nicki accuses her of not listening—what's the matter?

GRACE—I don't know. Maybe I'm getting awfully tired of listening—I'd like the feeling of—being listened to—for a change. (*Tears up the check.*)
NICKI—What are you doing?
GRACE—Asking to be heard.
NICKI—Are you crazy?
GRACE—Not asking for it—demanding it. No, not demanding it. Pleading for it. Look, darling, you'll have to leave eventually, I know. But this is the wrong time for it, Nicki—the wrongest possible time! (*Runs crying into the bedroom.* NICKI *stands looking after her.*)

ACT III

At four the next afternoon, Grace is in a state. She pours herself another drink while re-reading a note on her desk.

She is scared, and is terribly grateful when George arrives. Nicki has run away, leaving this note behind him. Neither parent has any idea where he could have gone, and George can't understand why he left. Grace is so tense that when the phone rings, she says: "Oh, God!" then picks up the receiver: "Oh, hello, Jane, I'm sorry I ran out like that but— Whose script? . . . Look, baby, I can't talk about it right now. . . . No, nothing's wrong. . . . I'll call you later. All right?" Then she says abruptly, "Jane, at the moment nothing could interest me less," and hangs up. "They're picking Anita's successor today," she continues to George. "The place was impossible. Everybody so damned discreet and sympathetic—hot tips from the office boys— They were even making book. I couldn't take it. I came home. Then I found that."

She wants to call the police but George won't let her. What could she tell them? George asks did Nicki have any money, does Grace have even an idea where he may have gone? Then, getting nowhere, George probes deeper. Had anything happened, can she explain why Nicki did it? Grace is hesitant but finally confesses: "Last night I told him he couldn't go with you." George is furious.

GEORGE—What did you think would happen? Didn't it occur to you the kid might need to hit back?
GRACE—Nicki hits back. He's never had to be docile or obedient with me.

GEORGE—You don't give a kid something like this and take it away from him.

GRACE—George, please!

The phone rings again. This time Grace says an exasperated Hello. It's not the office; it's no one. Only after she hangs up does she realize it must have been Nicki—it's just like him to ". . . call up and then freeze." Now she is determined to call the police. George puts his foot down: "In the first place if that *was* Nicki, then he's all right. After all he's not a six-year-old who's lost. He's a fourteen-year-old who ran away. There's a big difference. We can't have him dragged back here."

Grace understands this, then tries to think of the name of a detective who went to school with Larry. Larry could tell her his name— Abruptly she remembers: "The next voice you hear will be that of the Village Idiot."

GEORGE—What do you mean?

GRACE—Larry doesn't live here any more. That is, he never did. But the next time you and Nicki go to Washington or wherever— you can go with completely untroubled minds. It'll be very uneventful here on the home front.

GEORGE—When did this happen?

GRACE—Yesterday. Oh, it was probably building up for a long time. Nothing happens in one day.

GEORGE—Oh. I see. Then that was why you told Nicki—

GRACE—No, it wasn't. All right! Maybe it was. Everything suddenly seemed to be slipping away. So I lost my head and cried "Help . . ." (*Pause—sighs.*) I was over it by this morning.

Grace doesn't want too much sympathy: "Maybe I do try to hold on too hard. I was trying to hold on to Nicki and look what happened. Maybe a woman has to ease up—to be—what are those words they use for the female of the species? Passive, receptive."

The phone rings: this time George insists on answering. It *is* Nicki. George talks to him reasonably and finds he's already on his way home from New Jersey. George says they're both waiting for him—his mother hadn't meant it about the trip.

George reports that Nicki's first thought was whether Grace was upset. Grace lets go and sobs with relief; George puts his hands on her shoulders and says: "I've got news for you. You weren't the only one who was scared." She tries to compose herself, complaining: "What's the matter with me? What's ever happened to my stiff upper lip?" George tells her tenderly that nothing is wrong with her and gives her a kiss, which seems to help. She's so grateful he was around: without him, it would have been impossible. Having pulled herself together, her next thought is the office; but before she can call, George insists on straightening out the business of the trip. He insists there be no reservations to her approval: "When he walks in here, he's got to feel it's something you want him to do." Grace begins to balk. She's willing to play along while Nicki's here, ". . . but don't ask me to play charades with you."

GEORGE—I'm not asking that. I'm only trying to tell you what you already know—what you have to do.

GRACE—No. You're telling me what I have to *feel*. I said I'd do what you want. But that's not good enough! You want me to say I like it. Well, I don't like it. I don't like it at the office where I *have* to take it, and I don't like it here.

GEORGE—All right. Then don't. But you've got to be logical. Now remember, the boy did run away. Something here made him do it.

GRACE—What? The same thing that drove you away—that drove Larry— Is that what you're trying to say?

GEORGE—I don't even know the man. Larry? Why drag him into this?

GRACE—The difference between you isn't as wide as you think. There's a great area of agreement. With minor variations. For Larry I'm not passive enough. For the Moose I'm not stable enough. For you I'm not compliant enough. You all want something different, but it adds up to the same thing. I'm not submissive enough. But don't let that worry you. The woods are full of women who are. . . ."

Nicki, having formally rung the doorbell, walks in. Grace tries to keep calm, as she asks how he is. Is he hungry? Would he like to put his bag down? She's all ready to go through with what George wants when Nicki says to his father: "I hope you won't be too disappointed but I don't think I want to go out to Oregon after all." George gently asks him to explain. Nicki says: "Not that it wouldn't be fun out there but—well, you've got to think of other things, too." It wouldn't be fair, he adds, to everybody. Grace asks: "To me?"

NICKI (*looking away*)—When people have had a tough time on account of you—you owe them something. In fact, you owe them a lot.

GEORGE—Your first obligation is to yourself.   Your mother agrees
with me.

NICKI (*doggedly*)—I know.   But there's a right time and a wrong
time.   And—well, this is the wrong time.

Grace, fumbling for her handkerchief, chokes: "Oh, Nicki."   Nicki
is embarrassed and decides to go out for a walk—assuring them that
he'll be back.   Grace now makes a gesture, too: "Nicki, I think
you should go with George."   This amazes Nicki after what she
said last night.   "That was last night," says Grace.   "And maybe
that's all it takes for the wrong time to become the right time."
Nicki says he doesn't mind staying: in fact he wants to.   But Grace
has made up her mind: "It will be a wonderful trip for you.   Boys
should travel.   Girls, too, for that matter.   But that's another story.
Go on, Nicki.   You'll want to say good-by to Al."   Nicki doesn't
stir; then deeply moved, kisses Grace before going out.

George doesn't think it necessary to cross their fingers about the
boy; he'll be all right.   He'll find the answers—even if he has to
hunt for them in New Brunswick, New Jersey. . . . You have to
take them where you find them."   "If," corrects Grace, "you find
them."

George tells her he'd forgotten how wonderful she was.   He's sorry
about everything.   "It's okay," Grace says.   "For a gal who wants
what I want, there are always calculated risks."   The two of them
are pleased with each other; Grace says: "I kind of like you."   When
the phone rings once more, the call is from the office, and this time
is *the call*.   Grace is being offered the job after all, for the interesting
reason that the man they picked wanted too much money: "And
now I'm supposed to call the Moose back—choke up with gratitude—
and say 'thank you, coach.'   Well, to hell with him!"

GEORGE—I know just what you mean.

GRACE—Of all the degrading, scabrous ways to be offered a job.
The gall of that guy.   I'll bet he's not even uncomfortable.   I've got
a good mind to call him up and really tell him off.

GEORGE—If that's what you really want to do.

GRACE—I'm sorely tempted.

GEORGE—Well, the best way to overcome a temptation is to yield
to it.

GRACE (*starts to the phone, then stops*)—You're pretty smart,
aren't you?

GEORGE—I've known you for quite a while.

GRACE—Yeah. I can't step out of character at this late date, can I? I can't start pouting and getting coy now—

GEORGE—You always knew what you wanted.

GRACE—And you always understood it.

GEORGE—You know it's too bad you can't call up the Moose and tell him off the way you wanted.

GRACE—Uh huh. But them's the condition that prevail. I'm going to take that job, I'm afraid. And what's more, I'm going to kick the daylights out of it. (*Crosses to the phone. Pauses. Turns to* GEORGE.) I wonder how much that guy was actually asking for?

PLAYS PRODUCED IN NEW YORK

June 1, 1953—May 31, 1954

(Plays marked "continued" were still running on June 1, 1954)

OKLAHOMA!

(40 performances)

Musical comedy in two acts, based on the play *Green Grow the Lilacs* by Lynn Riggs; book and lyrics by Oscar Hammerstein II; music by Richard Rodgers. Revived by Rodgers and Hammerstein at the New York City Center of Music and Drama, August 31, 1953.

Cast of characters—

Aunt Eller	Mary Marlo
Curly	Ridge Bond
Laurey	Florence Henderson
Cord Elam	Charles Hart
Fred	Charles Scott
Slim	Charles Rule
Will Parker	Harris Hawkins
Jud Fry	Alfred Cibelli, Jr.
Ado Annie Carnes	Barbara Cook
Ali Hakim	David Le Grant
Gertie Cummings	Judy Rawlings
Ellen	Maggie Nelson
Kate	Barbara Reisman
Silvie	Patti Parsons
Armina	Lynne Broadbent
Aggie	Cathy Conklin
Andrew Carnes	Owen Martin
Chalmers	George Lawrence
Mike	Bob Lord

Dancers: Lynne Broadbent, Bette Burton, Cathy Conklin, Betty Koerber, Gayle Parmelee, Patti Parsons, Cynthia Price, Georganne Shaw, Louellen Sibley, Marguerite Stewart, Payne Converse, Nick Dana, Jack Ketcham, Ronnie Landry, John Pero, Jr., Tom Pickler, Joe Ribeau.

Singers: Lenore Arnold, Lois Barrodin, Marylin Hardy, Frances Irby, Heidi Palmer, Barbara Reisman, Jeanne Shea, William Ambler, Dino Dante, James Fox, Christopher Golden, Bob Lord, Charles Rule, Charles Scott.

Staged by Rouben Mamoulian; dances by Agnes de Mille; setting by Lemuel Ayers; costumes by Miles White; dances reproduced by Betty Gour; production stage manager, Jerome Whyte.

Oklahoma! was first produced March 31, 1943, by The Theatre Guild. It set the long-run record for American musicals with 2,248 performances.

(Closed October 3, 1953)

ANNA RUSSELL'S LITTLE SHOW

(16 performances)

Revue in two acts; music and lyrics by Miss Russell. Produced by Eastman Boomer and Arthur Klein at the Vanderbilt Theatre, September 7, 1953.

The principals—

Anna Russell
Arthur Barnett
Jane Ashlock
Jean Leon Destine and Company

Paul Duke
Joseph Scandur
Arthur Harris

Staged by Arthur Klein; lighting by Ralph Alswang; musical arrangements by Arthur Harris; stage manager, Milton Stern.

Sketches and musical numbers—

ACT I

Overture

Jane Ashlock and Arthur Harris
Duo Pianists

Arthur Barnett

Jean Leon Destine and Company
with Yolanda Gaffne
Drummers: Alphonse Cimber, Ti-Marcel
in "The Spider and the Lady"

Paul Duke
"A Symphony in Smoke"
(Assisted by Doris Haley)

Arthur Barnett

Miss Anna Russell
"Habanera"
"O Night! O Day!"
"Da Nyet, Da Nyet!"
"Anameia's Death Scene"
"I Gave My Love a Cherry"
"The Prince of Philadelphia" or "How to Write Your Own
Schubert Operetta" (Assisted by Joseph Scandur)
"Les Cigarettes"
"Trink"

ACT II

Arthur Barnett

Miss Anna Russell
Music Appreciation—"The Bagpipes"

Jean Leon Destine and Company
"The Witch Doctor"

Paul Duke
"Magic in Rhythm"
(Assisted by Doris Haley)

Arthur Barnett

Miss Anna Russell
"Hello! Hello! Oh, a Jolly Good Show" (Assisted by Joseph
Scandur)
"Guarda la Bella Tomato"
"Night and Day"

THE DECLINE AND FALL OF THE POPULAR SONG
(As witnessed by Miss Russell)
"Feeling Grand"
"I'd Be a Red Hot Momma"
"Chlorophyll Solly"
"Miserable"
"Mad"

Pianists

Finale

(Closed September 19, 1953)

CARNIVAL IN FLANDERS

(6 performances)

Musical comedy in two acts, based on *La Kermesse Heroique* by
C. Spaak, J. Feyder, and B. Zimmer; book by Preston Sturges;
music by James Van Heusen; lyrics by Johnny Burke. Produced by
Paula Stone and Mike Sloane and Burke & Van Heusen at the New
Century Theatre, September 8, 1953.

Cast of characters—

Siska ....Pat Stanley
Jan Breughel ....Kevin Scott
Tailor ....Paul Reed
Butcher ....Paul Lipson
Barber ....Bobby Vail
Innkeeper ....Lee Goodman
Mayor ....Roy Roberts
Cornelia ....Dolores Gray
Martha ....Dolores Kempner
Courier ....Matt Mattox
The Three Mourning Women ......Sandra Devlin, Julie Marlowe,
Lorna Del Maestro
1st Officer ....Ray Mason
2nd Officer ....George Martin
3rd Officer ....Jimmy Alex
The Duke ....John Raitt
1st Citizen ....Wesley Swails
2nd Citizen ....Norman Weise
Lisa ....Jean Bradley
Katherine ....Undine Forrest
Orderly ....William Noble
Dancers: Lorna Del Maestro, Sandra Devlin, Pat Ferrier, Patti
Karkalits, Mary Alice Kubes, Julie Marlowe, Billie Shane, Emy
St. Just, Elfrieda Zieger, Jimmy Alex, John Aristides, Harry Day,
Ronnie Field, Skeet Guenther, George Martin, Greg O'Brien, Paul
Olson, Richard Reed, Michael Spaeth.
Singers: Jean Bradley, Jean Cowles, Undine Forrest, Dolores Kemp-
ner, Mara Landi, Mary Stanton, Gloria Van Dorpe, Lee Barry, Fred
Bryan, Bill Conlon, Stokley Gray, William Noble, Dick Stewart,
Wesley Swails, Norman Weise.

The action takes place in and around the town of Flacksenburg in Flanders in 1616.

Staged by Preston Sturges; carnival ballet and musical numbers staged by Helen Tamiris; scenery by Oliver Smith; costumes by Lucinda Ballard; musical director, Harold Hastings; vocal arrangements by Elie Siegmeister; orchestrations by Don Walker; production stage manager, Fred Hebert; stage manager, Dennis Murray.

Musical numbers—

ACT I

"Ring the Bell" ....Mayor, Butcher, Barber, Tailor, Innkeeper, Jan, Siska, Ensemble
"The Very Necessary You" ....Jan and Siska
"It's a Fine Old Institution" ....Cornelia
"I'm One of Your Admirers" ....Cornelia
"The Plundering of the Town"......Cornelia, Courier, 2nd Officer, Emy St. Just, John Aristides, Julie Marlowe, Ensemble
"The Stronger Sex" ....Cornelia
"The Sudden Thrill" ....Duke
"It's an Old Spanish Custom" ....Cornelia and Duke
"A Seventeen Gun Salute" .....Cornelia, Duke, Courier, 1st Officer, 2nd Officer, Ensemble

ACT II

"You're Dead!" ....Mayor, Butcher, Barber, Innkeeper, Tailor
"Rainy Day" ....Cornelia
"Take the Word of a Gentleman" ....Duke

THE CARNIVAL BALLET

The Virgin ....Emy St. Just
The Bats ....Greg O'Brien, Paul Olson
The Monk ....John Aristides
The Goat ....Harry Day
The Youngest One ....Pat Stanley
The Plumed Swains .....Jimmy Alex, Ronnie Field, Skeet Guenther, Michael Spaeth, George Martin, Richard Reed
The Seven Virgins ....Sandra Devlin, Lorna Del Maestro, Pat Ferrier, Julie Marlowe, Patti Karkalits, Mary Alice Kubes, Elfrieda Zeiger
The Spanish Trio ....Matt Mattox, George Martin, Jimmy Alex, Singers of the Town

"A Moment of Your Love" ....Cornelia and Duke
"How Far Can a Lady Go?" ....Cornelia

(Closed September 12, 1953)

A RED RAINBOW

(16 performances)

Play in three acts by Myron C. Fagan. Produced by Bruce Fagan at the Royale Theatre, September 14, 1953.

Cast of characters—

Inspector Scanlon (Chief of Homicide) ....Howard Smith
Boris Sarno ....Hans Josef Schumm
District Attorney Britt ....Winston Ross
Gorman, a Detective ....William Martel

Roxy Gainsborough ....Effie Afton
Major Robert (Bob) Brainard ....William Kemp
Arline Mason ....Mary Alice Moore
Jensen ....William Remick
Senator Derlin ....Fred Irving Lewis
Mrs. Russell Meadow ....Ruthelma Stevens
J. Kerrigan Kane ....Robert Middleton
Congressman Felz ....Spencer James
Rourke ....William Adler

The action takes place in J. Kerrigan Kane's penthouse on Park Avenue, New York City, in the spring of 1946. Act I.—Ten o'clock in the morning. Act II.—Six o'clock the previous evening. Act. III.—The same as Act I.

Staged by Myron C. Fagan; setting by Louis Kennel; stage manager, Al Jones.

Wooden anti-Communist melodrama that starts off as a whodunit (a well-known columnist is murdered) and develops into a who-done-America-dirt (the murderer turns out to be a fanatical Communist).

(Closed September 26, 1953)

END AS A MAN

(137 performances *)

Play in three acts by Calder Willingham. Produced by Claire Heller at the Theatre de Lys, September 15, 1953. After thirty-two performances at the Theatre de Lys, it moved to the Vanderbilt Theatre on October 14.

Cast of characters—

Robert Marquales ....William Smithers
Maurice Maynall Simmons ....Arthur Storch
Harold Koble ....Pat Hingle
Jocko de Parls ....Ben Gazzara
Perrin McKee ....Paul Richards
First Orderly ....Eli Rill
Second Orderly ....Warren Slocum
Starkson ....Anthony Franciosa
Larrence Corger ....Mark Richman
General Draughton ....Frank M. Thomas
Roger Gatt ....Albert Salmi

Cadet Officers ....⎧ Richard Vogel
⎪ Steven Ross
⎪ Richard Heimann
⎨ Robert Dirk
⎪ Harry Gardino
⎩ Martin Greenlee

The action takes place at a military college in the South. Act I.—Scene 1—Robert Marquales' room; morning of the second day of the Academy year. Scene 2—The same; Friday afternoon one month later. Act II.—Scene 1—The same; an afternoon one week later. Scene 2—The same; just before midnight the same day. Act III.—Headquarters of the Regimental Cadet Committee; the next morning.

Staged by Jack Garfein; production designed by Mel Bourne; stage manager, Irving Buchman.

* Includes off-Broadway performances.

Laid in a Southern military academy, the play introduces a variety of cadets—a blabbing prig, a maliciously conniving homosexual, a dull-witted football husk—most of them under the heel of suavely evil and ingratiating Jocko de Paris. Some vicious midnight hell-raising, with Jocko as ring leader, is followed by expulsion.

(Closed January 16, 1954)

A PIN TO SEE THE PEEPSHOW

(1 performance)

Play in two acts by F. Tennyson Jesse and H. M. Harwood, adapted from Miss Jesse's novel of the same name. Produced by Nancy Davids at The Playhouse, September 17, 1953.

Cast of characters—

Julia Almond	Joan Miller
Anne Ackroyd	Martha Farrar
Herbert Starling	Claude Horton
George Almond	Bill Griffis
Mrs. Almond	Eva Leonard Boyne
Dr. Ackroyd	Basil Howes
Elsa	Joy Saunders
Lily Kitt	Valerie Cardew
Bertha Starling	Margaretta Warwick
Marian Lestrange	Marie Paxton
Gipsy Danvers	Winnifred Cushing
Captain Embury	Frederic Warriner
Leo Carr	Roger Moore
Police Constable	James Morley
Police Inspector	Ronald Long
Another Constable	Pat Malone
Matron	Nell Clarke
Mr. Ringwood	Jerome Kilty
Dr. Ogilvie	Frederic Warriner
A Wardress	Shirley Gale

Prison Officials and Others: Winnifred Cushing, Pat Malone, Richard Towers, Len Bedsow, Charles Shelvey, Crandall Diehl, Richard Lederer.

Act I.—Scene 1—St. Clement's Square, London; Spring, 1916. Scene 2—The parlor at Mrs. Almond's; later that evening. Scene 3—A dress shop on Bond Street; the next day. Scene 4—The same; six months later. Scene 5—Sitting-room of the Starlings' flat; Winter, 1920. Scene 6—The same; Spring, 1922. Act II.—Scene 1—The dress shop; late Summer, 1923. Scene 2—St. Clement's Square; near midnight the following night. Scene 3—A police station; after midnight. Scene 4—A waiting-room in a women's prison; September, 1923. Scene 5—The doctor's room in the jail; late November, 1923. Scene 6—The condemned cell; later. Scene 7—The same; the next morning.

Staged by Peter Cotes; setting by Ariell Ballif; lighting by Feder; costumes by Ruth Morley; stage manager, Len Bedsow.

An English drama based on a real-life, love-triangle murder. Unfolded in thirteen scenes—at a pace that resembled slow-motion—the play was less concerned with raising goose pimples than with providing a biography of the hanged, but conceivably innocent, wife.

(Closed September 17, 1953)

Joan Miller, Roger Moore and Ronald Long in "A Pin to See the Peepshow"

AT HOME WITH ETHEL WATERS

(23 performances)

Songs by Ethel Waters with Reginald Beane at the piano. Produced by Charles Bowden and Richard Barr at the Forty-Eighth Street Theatre, September 22, 1953.

Staged by Richard Barr; setting by Oliver Smith; costumes by Robert Mackintosh; production stage manager, Elliot Martin.

Musical numbers—

MISS WATERS

"I Ain't Gonna Sin No More" ....Lennerts
"Sleepy Time Down South" ....Muse-René
"Throw Dirt" ....Brooks
"Am I Blue" ....Clarke-Akst
"Half of Me" ....Thomas
"Washtub Rubsudy" ....Written for Miss Waters by Mann Holiner
and Alberta Nichols

(from "Rhapsody in Black," 1931)

Miss Waters and Mr. Beane

"Bread and Gravy" .... Hoagy Carmichael

Mr. Beane

Moods (from Jazzantasy Suite) .... Beane
   Blues
   Syncopation
   Boogie
"Love for Sale" .... Porter-Beane

Miss Waters

"Dinah" .... Lewis-Young-Akst
   (introduced by Miss Waters in "Plantation Revue," 1924)
"Go Back Where You Stayed Last Night" ...... Ethel Waters and
                             Sidney Easton
"My Man" .... Willemetz-Charles-Pollock-Yvain
"St. Louis Blues" .... W. C. Handy
"Suppertime" .... Irving Berlin
   (from "As Thousands Cheer," 1933)

Miss Waters

"Dance Hall Hostess" .... Mann Holiner and Alberta Nichols
   (from "Rhapsody in Black," 1931)

Mr. Beane

"Odd Moments" .... Beane
"Jerome Kern Medley" .... Kern-Beane

Miss Waters

"Takin' a Chance on Love" .... Latouche-Fetter-Duke
"Somethin' Told Me Not to Trust That Man" ... Mann Holiner and
                            Alberta Nichols
"Happiness Is Jes' a Thing Called Joe" .... Harburg-Arlen
"Lady Be Good" .... Ira and George Gershwin
"Stormy Weather" .... Koehler-Arlen
"Mammy" .... Original version by the late Will Marion Cook
"Motherless Chile" .... Spiritual
"Crucifixion" .... Spiritual
"Cabin in the Sky" .... Latouche-Duke

(Closed October 10, 1953)

TAKE A GIANT STEP

(76 performances)

Play in six scenes by Louis Peterson. Produced by Lyn Austin and Thomas Noyes at the Lyceum Theatre, September 24, 1953.

Cast of characters—

Spencer Scott .... Louis Gossett
Grandmother .... Estelle Hemsley
Tony .... Fred Vogel
Iggie .... Bernard Rich
Frank .... Frank Wilson
Man .... Maxwell Glanville
Violet .... Pauline Myers
Poppy .... Helen Martin
Rose .... Margaret Williams
Carol .... Jane White
Lem Scott .... Frederick O'Neal

May Scott ....Estelle Evans
Christine ....Dorothy Carter
Gussie ....Robert Brivic
Johnny Reynolds ....Warren Berlinger
Bobby Reynolds ....Tarry Green
      The action takes place in a town in Connecticut in early Spring of
the present year. Scene 1—The Scott home; late afternoon. Scene
2—A bar in the Negro section; a few hours later. Scene 3—Violet's
room; immediately following. Scene 4—The Scott home; later that
evening. Scene 5—Spencer's bedroom; two weeks later. Scene 6—
The Scott home; the following day.
      Staged by John Stix; setting and lighting by Eldon Elder; cos-
tumes by Ruth Morley; production stage manager, David Kanter;
stage manager, Charles Pratt, Jr.

See page 135.

(Closed November 28, 1953)

THE STRONG ARE LONELY

(7 performances)

Play in two acts by Fritz Hochwalder, adapted by Eva Le Gallienne. Produced by Walter P. Chrysler, Jr., at the Broadhurst Theatre, September 29, 1953.

Cast of characters—

Alfonso Fernandez, S.J. (Father Provincial of the
      Society of Jesus in Paraguay) ....Victor Francen
Ladislaus Oros, S.J. ....Wesley Addy
Rochus Lieberman, S.J. (Father Superior) ......Earl Montgomery
Candia   ⎱ (Indian Chiefs) .... ⎰ Edward Groag
Naguacu ⎰   ⎱ Junaluska
Andre Cornelis ....Nils Asther
William Clark, S.J. (Father Procurator) ....Paul Ballantyne
Don Pedro de Miura ....Dennis King
Sergeant of the Guard ....Stuart Vaughan
Captain Villano ⎱ (Officers of the Spanish Army) ⎰ Martin Rudy
Captain Arago ⎰   ⎱ Frederick Rolf
Lorenzo Querini ....Philip Bourneuf
Carlos Gervazoni, Bishop of Buenos Aires ....Kermit Murdock
Jose Bustillos ....John Marley
Gracia Queseda ....Dion Allen
Alvaro Catalde ....John Straub
Father Reinegg, S.J. ....Joseph Dooley
Father Torres, S.J. ....Ray Rizzo
Father Claussner, S.J. ....Dion Allen
Acatu   ⎱ (Indian Chiefs) .... ⎰ Kuruks Pahitu
Barrigua ⎰   ⎱ Dehl Berti
Young Indians .... ⎰ Ernesto Gonzalez
                                             ⎱ Tuktu
Soldiers of the Spanish Army .... ⎰ Robert Ludlum
                                             ⎱ Wyatt Cooper
      The action takes place at the College of the Jesuit Fathers at
Buenos Aires in the study of the Father Provincial during a single
day, July 16, 1767. Act I.—Scene 1—Morning. Scene 2—Two
hours later. Act II.—Scene 1—Afternoon. Scene 2—Evening.
Scene 3—Night.
      Staged by Margaret Webster; scenery and costumes by Rolf Gerard;
incidental music by Lehman Engel; stage manager, Thelma Chandler.

The scene is eighteenth-century Buenos Aires, where some Spanish Jesuits have created a kind of self-contained Utopia. This gets them into difficulties with the Spanish government whose sovereignty they endanger, and at length provokes them to defiance. But when their own religious superiors—fearful of consequences for the Order as a whole—command them to submit, they face a bitter ordeal.

(Closed October 3, 1953)

TEA AND SYMPATHY

(280 performances)
(Continued)

Play in three acts by Robert Anderson. Produced by The Playwrights' Company, in association with Mary K. Frank, at the Ethel Barrymore Theatre, September 30, 1953.

Cast of characters—

Laura Reynolds	Deborah Kerr
Lilly Sears	Florida Friebus
Tom Lee	John Kerr
David Harris	Richard Midgley
Ralph	Alan Sues
Al	Dick York
Steve	Arthur Steuer
Bill Reynolds	Leif Erickson
Phil	Richard Franchot
Herbert Lee	John McGovern
Paul	Yale Wexler

Act I.—A dormitory in a boys' school in New England; late afternoon of a day early in June. Act II.—Scene 1—Two days later. Scene 2—Eight-thirty Saturday night. Act III.—The next afternoon.

Staged by Elia Kazan; setting and lighting by Jo Mielziner; clothes designed by Anna Hill Johnstone; production stage manager, Seymour Milbert.

See page 208.

COMEDY IN MUSIC

(VICTOR BORGE'S ONE-MAN SHOW)

(275 performances)
(Continued)

Produced by Harry D. Squires at the John Golden Theatre, October 2, 1953.

Stage manager, Lester Hamilton.

See "The Season in New York."

THE LITTLE HUT

(29 performances)

Comedy in three acts by André Roussin, adapted by Nancy Mitford. Produced by John C. Wilson and H. M. Tennent, Ltd., at the Coronet Theatre, October 7, 1953.

Cast of characters—

Henry	Colin Gordon
Susan	Anne Vernon
Philip	Roland Culver
A Stranger	John Granger
Second Stranger	Ray Gil

The action takes place on a desert island. Act I.—Morning. Act II.—Evening—two weeks later. Act III.—The following morning.

Staged by Peter Brook; décor by Oliver Messel; stage manager, Samuel Liff.

A husband, a wife and a lover are shipwrecked on a tropical island. The husband is studiously enlightened as to the lover's status, and the obliging wife is thereafter openly shared. As time goes on, the lover grows jealous and glum, the husband ever more carefree. Later, a "native"—who is actually the shipwrecked cook in disguise—enters the lists (and the hut) with the lady. And finally the marooned party catch a boat—though the play distinctly misses it.

(Closed October 31, 1953)

LATE LOVE /

(95 performances)

Comedy in three acts by Rosemary Casey. Produced by Michael Abbott at the National Theatre, October 13, 1953.

Cast of characters—

Billy Gordon	Frank Albertson
Matthew Anderson	Cliff Robertson
Sarah	Ann Dere
Graham Colby	Neil Hamilton
Janet Colby	Elizabeth Montgomery
Mrs. Colby	Lucile Watson
Constance Warburton	Arlene Francis

The action takes place in the living room of the Colby home in Connecticut early in September of the present year. Act I.—Sunday afternoon. Act II.—The following Saturday morning. Act III.—Ten seconds later.

Staged by John C. Wilson; setting and lighting by Stewart Chaney; costumes supervised by Frank Thompson; associate producers, Howard Erskine and Bonnie Alden; stage manager, Ward Bishop.

Tale of a household presumably tyrannized over by a puritanical dowager, but actually, it turns out, kept in chains by her priggish novelist of a son. A lady painter arrives to do the novelist's portrait, quickly sizes him up, and remains to set his people free.

(Closed January 2, 1954)

THE TEAHOUSE OF THE AUGUST MOON

(265 performances)
(Continued)

Comedy in three acts by John Patrick, based on the novel by Vern Sneider. Produced by Maurice Evans, in association with George Schaefer, at the Martin Beck Theatre, October 15, 1953.

Cast of characters—

Sakini	David Wayne
Sgt. Gregovich	Harry Jackson
Col. Wainright Purdy III	Paul Ford
Capt. Fisby	John Forsythe
Old Woman	Naoe Kondo
Old Woman's Daughter	Mara Kim
The Daughter's Children	Moy Moy Thom / Joyce Chen / Kenneth Wong
Lady Astor	Saki
Ancient Man	Kame Ishikawa
Mr. Sumata	Kaie Deei
Mr. Sumata's Father	Kikuo Hiromura
Mr. Hokaida	Chuck Morgan
Mr. Seiko	Haim Winant
Mr. Oshira	William Hansen
Mr. Omura	Kuraji Scida
Mr. Keora	Yuki Shimoda
Villagers	Jerry Fujikawa / Frank Ogawa / Richard Akagi / Laurence Kim / Norman Chi
Miss Higa Jiga	Shizu Moriya
Ladies League for Democratic Action	Vivian Thom / Naoe Kondo / Mary Anne Reeve / Mara Kim
Lotus Blossom	Mariko Niki
Capt. McLean	Larry Gates

Act I.—Scene 1—Okinawa, Col. Purdy's Office, G.H.Q. Scene 2—Outside Capt. Fisby's Quarters, G.H.Q. Scene 3—Tobiki Village. Act II.—Scene 1—Tobiki Village. Scene 2—Capt. Fisby's Office, Tobiki. Scene 3—The same. Scene 4—Tobiki Village. Act III.—Scene 1—The Teahouse of the August Moon. Scene 2—Capt. Fisby's Office, Tobiki. Scene 3—The Teahouse of the August Moon.

Staged by Robert Lewis; settings and lighting by Peter Larkin; costumes by Noel Taylor; music composed by Dai-Keong Lee; production stage manager, Billy Matthews; stage manager, Tom Hughes Sand.

See page 161.

THE FROGS OF SPRING

(15 performances)

Comedy in three acts by Nathaniel Benchley. Produced by Lyn Austin and Thomas Noyes, in association with Robert Radnitz and Robert Sagalyn, at the Broadhurst Theatre, October 20, 1953.

Cast of characters—

Kay Allen	Haila Stoddard
Virginia Belden	Barbara Baxley
Danny Shaw	Kevin Coughlin
James Allen	Anthony Ross
Alice Kemp	Mary Grace Canfield
Charles Belden	Hiram Sherman
Bobby Belden	Billy Quinn
Chris Allen	Kenneth Kakos
John Allen	Malcolm Brodrick
Dr. Lindquist	Roland Wood
Asa McK. Gelwicks	Jerome Kilty
Luther Raubel	Fred Gwynne

The action takes place during six days in the garden behind the Allens' and Beldens' apartments in New York in the present year.

Act I.—Scene 1—Wednesday afternoon. Scene 2—Friday afternoon. Act II.—Scene 1—Saturday morning. Scene 2—That afternoon. Act III.—Scene 1—Sunday morning. Scene 2—Monday afternoon.

Staged by Burgess Meredith; setting and lighting by Boris Aronson; costumes by Alvin Colt; production stage manager, Robert Sagalyn; stage manager, Robert Radnitz.

A comedy concerned with two New York families who live in adjoining houses—or, for stage purposes, backyards. Both husbands are boyishly irresponsible, and after removing the fence between the yards, install such gear as helium tanks, portable swimming pools, and stilt houses. Their bourbon leads to excessive bonhomie, the bonhomie to loss of jobs and decline in brotherliness. A play with bright lines and bubbly moments, but with nothing to keep it in motion or even to hold it together.

(Closed October 31, 1953)

THE LADIES OF THE CORRIDOR

(45 performances)

Play in two acts by Dorothy Parker and Arnaud d'Usseau. Produced by Walter Fried at the Longacre Theatre, October 21, 1953.

Cast of characters—

Mr. Humphries	Robert Van Hooton
Mrs. Gordon	June Walker
Mrs. Lauterbach	Vera Allen
Mrs. Nichols	Frances Starr
Charles Nichols	Shepperd Strudwick
Harry	Lonny Chapman
Casey	Louis Criss

June Walker, Edna Best, Vera Allen, Betty Field, Frances Starr and Margaret Barker in "The Ladies of the Corridor"

Lulu Ames .... Edna Best
Sassy .... Tassle
Mildred Tynan .... Betty Field
Robert Ames .... Clement Brace
Betsy Ames .... Carol Wheeler
Constance Mercer .... Margaret Barker
Irma .... Kate Harkin
Paul Osgood .... Walter Matthau
Tom Linscott .... Donald McKee
Mary Linscott .... Harriet MacGibbon
        The action takes place during the course of a year in the Hotel
Marlowe in the East Sixties in New York City.
        Staged by Harold Clurman; settings and lighting by Ralph Alswang;
costumes by Noel Taylor; stage manager, James Gelb.

A play about the lonely, empty-lived women—most of them
widows—in a quiet, "refined" New York apartment hotel. Besides
a number of minor characters, there are three major ones. Middle-
aged Lulu Ames, having moved East after her husband's death to
be with her family, gets caught up in an affair with a younger man

and loses him through proving too possessive. Elderly Mrs. Nichols rules her middle-aging son from a wheelchair, and quashes his rebellion by threatening to expose a homosexual scandal in his past. Mildred Tynan is driven by an ill-made and short-lived marriage first to drink and ultimately to suicide.

(Closed November 28, 1953)

GENTLY DOES IT

(37 performances)

Play in three acts by Janet Green. Produced by Edward Choate and George Ross (by arrangement with Wauna Paul) at The Playhouse, October 28, 1953.

Cast of characters—

Monica Bare	Phyllis Povah
Emmie	Mabel Taylor
Philip Mortimer	Andrew Duggan
Edward Bare	Anthony Oliver
Freda Jefferies	Brenda Bruce
Charlotte Young	Joyce Heron

The action takes place in the sitting room of Monica Bare's house at the top of Sunrise Hill, just outside a small market town in Kent. Act I.—Scene 1—An afternoon in November. Scene 2—Afternoon—a few days later. Act II.—Scene 1—Afternoon—eight weeks later. Scene 2—Noon—two months later. Scene 3—Noon—ten days later. Act III.—After tea, the same day.

Staged by Bretaigne Windust; setting and lighting by George Jenkins; costumes by Virginia Volland; stage manager, Daniel S. Broun.

Edward Bare neatly does in his wife for her money, only to find that financially he has done himself in as well. To recoup, he courts and marries a well-to-do ex-barmaid, but she proves more than a match for him. A third lady now crosses his path—a path that leads, eventually, but to the grave.

An English thriller of sorts whose excitement is severely rationed and whose merits are largely incidental.

(Closed November 28, 1953)

A GIRL CAN TELL

(60 performances)

Comedy in three acts by F. Hugh Herbert. Produced by Richard Aldrich and Richard Myers, in association with Julius Fleischmann, at the Royale Theatre, October 29, 1953.

Cast of characters—

Hannah ....Eulabelle Moore
Nancy, Jennifer's Daughter ....Natalie Trundy
Vernon ....Barry McGuire
Jennifer Goodall ....Janet Blair
Artie ....Marshall Thompson
Mr. Benton, Jennifer's Father ....Paul McGrath
Mrs. Benton, Jennifer's Mother ....Lulu Mae Hubbard
Bill ....Tod Andrews
Freddie ....Donald Symington
George ....Dean Harens
J. G. ....Jack Whiting
Natasha ....Joan Wetmore
Emmett ....William Kester

PHONE VOICES

David ....Bill Windom
D. F. ....Henry Hart

Act I.—Scene 1 (Prologue)—The Bentons' living room, Washington Square; the present—a sunny afternoon in Spring. Scene 2—the same; 1936—or seventeen years ago—an evening in December. Act II.—Scene 1—An executive office in midtown Manhattan; a week later, about 5 P.M. Scene 2—Living room of Bill's bachelor apartment, ten days later, evening. Act III.—Scene 1—The Bentons' living room; a month later—January, 1937—late afternoon. Scene 2 (Epilogue)—The Bentons' living room; the present, two hours or so later than Act I, Scene 1.

Staged by F. Hugh Herbert; settings by Stewart Chaney; costumes by Edith Lutyens; production stage manager, Nick Mayo; stage manager, Charles Vocalis.

A teen-ager's mother leafs back through her memories to the time of her own teens—to the 'thirties when she was besieged by a variety of suitors, necked in the family parlor, came home unscathed from a bachelor's apartment, unscathed as well from a business trip with the boss. Another exercise—by the author of *Kiss and Tell* and *The Moon Is Blue*—in discreetly amorous girlhood, one written under the sign of Virgo but in the spirit of Capricorn. But on this occasion the tone is coarse and the writing hand seems tired.

(Closed December 19, 1953)

SHERLOCK HOLMES/

(3 performances)

Play in three acts by Ouida Rathbone, based on the original stories of Sir Arthur Conan Doyle. Produced by Bill Doll at the New Century Theatre, October 30, 1953.

Cast of characters—

Dr. John Watson ....Jack Raine
Sherlock Holmes ....Basil Rathbone
Mrs. Hudson ....Elwyn Harvey
Rt. Hon. Trelawney Hope ....John Dodsworth
Arthur Cadogan West ....Richard Wendley
Lady Hope ....Eileen Peel
Eduardo Lucas ....Gregory Morton

Anna ....Margit Forssgren
Count Louis De Rothiere ....Chester Stratton
Irene Adler ....Jarmila Novotna
Walker ....Terence Kilburn
Lestrade ....Bryan Herbert
Miss Alice Dunbar ....Mary Orr
Andrew ....Evan Thomas
Professor Moriarty ....Thomas Gomez
Hugo Oberstein ....Martin Brandt
Captain Von Herling ....Ludwig Roth
Prince Bulganin ....St. John Phillipe
Gregson ....Arthur N. Stenning
Villard ....Alfred A. Hesse

Act I.—Scene 1—221B Baker Street, London; an evening, March, 1895.   Scene 2—16 Godolphin Square; the same night.   Scene 3—A dressing room at Queen's Hall; the same night.   Act II.—Scene 1—221B Baker Street; the same night.   Scene 2—13 Caulfield Gardens; early the following morning.   Scene 3—A chalet overlooking the Reichenbach Falls; three days later.   Act III.—The chalet overlooking Reichenbach Falls; two months later.

Staged by Reginald Denham; settings, costumes, and lighting by Stewart Chaney; incidental music by Alexander Steinert; production stage manager, George Greenberg.

Not William Gillette's famous old warhorse, but a new pastiche of Holmes material concerned chiefly with the theft of the Bruce-Partington submarine plans. After bouncing all over London, the play shifts to the Swiss chalet of Professor Moriarity, with Holmes and the professor vanishing in that locked-together death plunge from which Holmes had later, by popular demand, to be restored to life. In the present case, the plunge hardly mattered, since Holmes was scarcely alive to begin with.

(Closed October 31, 1953)

THE TRIP TO BOUNTIFUL /

(39 performances)

Play in three acts by Horton Foote. Produced by The Theatre Guild and Fred Coe at Henry Miller's Theatre, November 3, 1953.

Cast of characters—

Mrs. Carrie Watts ....Lillian Gish
Ludie Watts ....Gene Lyons
Jessie Mae Watts ....Jo Van Fleet
Thelma ....Eva Marie Saint
Houston Ticket Man ....Will Hare
A Traveler ....Salem Ludwig
Second Houston Ticket Man ....David Clive
Harrison Ticket Man ....Frederic Downs
Sheriff ....Frank Overton
Travelers ....⎰ Patricia MacDonald
                                         ⎱ Neil Laurence
                                           Helen Cordes

Act I.—A Houston apartment.   Act II.—The trip.   Act III.—A country place.

Staged by Vincent J. Donehue; settings by Otis Riggs; costumes by Rose Bogdanoff; lighting by Peggy Clark; production stage manager, Henry Weinstein; stage manager, David Clive.

Story of a meek, unhappy widow who lives in Houston, Texas, with her struggling, half-henpecked son and his wife, and who is bullyingly exploited by her giddy, discontented daughter-in-law. Liking Houston hardly better than home life, in time she runs away to the small town of Bountiful where she had lived years before. She is briefly happy among the ghosts of Bountiful before her son and his wife force her back to the city.

(Closed December 5, 1953)

KIND SIR

(166 performances)

Comedy in two acts by Norman Krasna. Produced by Joshua Logan at the Alvin Theatre, November 4, 1953.

Cast of characters—

Anna Miller .... Margalo Gillmore
Margaret Munson .... Dorothy Stickney
Jane Kimball .... Mary Martin
Alfred Munson .... Frank Conroy
Philip Clair .... Charles Boyer
Carl Miller .... Robert Ross
    The action takes place in the New York apartment of Miss Jane Kimball. Act I.—Scene 1—Early Fall, six P.M. Scene 2—One A.M. Scene 3—Two weeks later. Act II.—Scene 1—Six months later. Scene 2—Five hours later. Scene 3—The following evening before midnight.
    Staged by Joshua Logan; settings and lighting by Jo Mielziner; costumes by Main Bocher; associate producer and director, Marshall Jamison; production stage manager, Robert Linden; stage manager, Douglas McLean.

An unmarried stage star meets an unmarried State Department charmer—who pretends to be married. By doing this, he can woo ladies without the faintest suggestion of wedding them. When, in time, his actress conquest finds out the truth, she sets out to be avenged, and winds up at the altar.

(Closed March 27, 1954)

THE SOLID GOLD CADILLAC

(238 performances)
(Continued)

Comedy in two acts by Howard Teichmann and George S. Kaufman. Produced by Max Gordon at the Belasco Theatre, November 5, 1953.

Lillian Gish in "The Trip to Bountiful"

Cast of characters—

T. John Blessington	Geoffrey Lumb
Alfred Metcalfe	Wendell K. Phillips
Warren Gillie	Reynolds Evans
Clifford Snell	Henry Jones
Mrs. Laura Partridge	Josephine Hull
Miss Amelia Shotgraven	Mary Welch
Mark Jenkins	Jack Ruth
Miss L'Arriere	Charlotte Van Lein
Edward L. McKeever	Loring Smith
Miss Logan	Vera Fuller Mellish
The A. P.	Carl Judd
The U. P.	Al McGranary
I. N. S.	Howard Adelman
A Woman	Gloria Maitland

NEWS BROADCASTERS

Bill Parker	Henry Norell
Dwight Brookfield	Mark Allen
Estelle Evans	Lorraine MacMartin

The action takes place in New York and Washington.

Staged by George S. Kaufman; settings by Edward Gilbert; production stage manager, Joseph Olney; stage manager, Carl Judd.

A "fairy tale" about an elderly ex-actress who is also a tiny stockholder in a huge corporation. Turning up at a stockholders' meeting, she starts to ask a lot of embarrassing questions, and as a way of shushing her the executives offer her a job with the company. Once installed, she engineers all sorts of ticklish incidents and by the final curtain has become head of the corporation.

CYRANO DE BERGERAC

(15 performances)

Play in five acts by Edmond Rostand, adapted by Brian Hooker. Produced by the New York City Theatre Company at the New York City Center of Music and Drama, November 11, 1953.

Cast of characters—

Porter	Benedict MacQuarrie
A Cavalier	Peter Brandon
A Musketeer	Carl Albertson
A Lackey	Richard Cowdery
Another Lackey	Tom Tryon
A Guardsman	Charles Summers
Flower Girl	Carmen Alvarez
A Citizen	Wallace Widdecombe
His Son	Sandy Campbell
A Cut Purse	Peter Buchan
Orange Girl	Lori March
A Marquis	Jack Fletcher
Brissaille	Albert Whitley
Ligniere	Gordon Nelson
Christian de Neuvillette	Douglas Watson
Rageneau	Jacques Aubuchon
Le Bret	Philip Huston

```
Roxane, nee Madeleine Robin .........................Arlene Dahl
Her Duenna .......................................Paula Laurence
Comte de Guiche ..................................Ralph Clanton
Vicomte de Valvert ..............................Dean Cetrulo
Montfleury .......................................Leopold Badia
Cyrano de Bergerac .............................José Ferrer
Bellerose ........................................Stanley Carlson
Jodelet .........................................Robinson Stone
A Meddler .......................................Bill Butler
A Soubrette .....................................Tamar Cooper
A Comedienne ....................................Jill Kraft
                                                { Sandy Campbell
Pastry Cooks ...................................{ Philip Prindle
                                                { Peter Buchan
Lise ............................................Betty Bartley
Carbon de Castel-Jaloux .........................G. Wood
A Poet ..........................................Vincent Donahue
Another Poet ....................................John Glennon
Third Poet ......................................Benedict MacQuarrie
A Capuchin ......................................Robinson Stone
Sister Marthe ...................................Jarmila Daubek
Mother Marguerite ...............................Viola Roache
Sister Claire ...................................Linda Berlin
A Nun ...........................................Ann Chisholm
Another Nun .....................................Marijane Maricle
```

Cadets of Gascoyne: Peter Harris, Arthur Walsh, Lee Danna, Garry Cowen, Toby Allen, Robert Lansing.

Court Ladies, Nuns, etc.: Louise de la Parra, Honey Waldman, Muriel Dooley, Lily Lodge, Jill McAnney, Eva Rubinstein, Roberta MacDonald.

The first four acts take place in 1640; the fifth in 1655. Act I.—A performance at the Hotel de Bourgogne. Act II.—The bakery of the poets. Act III.—Roxane's kiss. Act IV.—The Cadets of Gascoyne. Act V.—Cyrano's Gazette.

Staged by José Ferrer; in charge of production, Jean Dalrymple; assistant director, Jess Kimmel; settings by Richard Whorf; costumes by Emeline Roche; technical scenic director, Paul Morrison; incidental music composed by Paul Bowles; production stage manager, Buford Armitage; stage manager, Jess Kimmel.

(Closed November 22, 1953)

SABRINA FAIR

(223 performances)
(Continued)

Comedy in four scenes by Samuel Taylor. Produced by The Playwrights' Company at the National Theatre, November 11, 1953.

Cast of characters—

```
Maude Larrabee ..................................Cathleen Nesbitt
Julia Ward McKinlock ............................Luella Gear
Linus Larrabee, Jr. .............................Joseph Cotten
Linus Larrabee ..................................John Cromwell
Margaret ........................................Katharine Raht
David Larrabee ..................................Scott McKay
Gretchen ........................................Ruth Woods
Sabrina Fairchild ...............................Margaret Sullavan
Fairchild .......................................Russell Collins
A Young Woman ...................................Harriette Selby
```

Joseph Cotten and Margaret Sullavan in "Sabrina Fair"

A Young Man ....Gordon Mills
Another Young Woman ....Loraine Grover
Another Young Man ....Michael Steele
Paul D'Argenson ....Robert Duke
   The action takes place on the north shore of Long Island about an
hour from New York.   Scene 1—A Saturday afternoon in September.
Scene 2—Friday evening, two weeks later.   Scene 3—The following
morning.   Scene 4—Immediately afterwards.
   Staged by H. C. Potter; setting and lighting by Donald Oenslager;
costume supervision by Bianca Stroock; production stage manager,
David Gray, Jr.

Set among Long Island's rich, the play tells of a chauffeur's daughter who returns, chic and hep, after five years in Paris, to the estate
where her father works.   She acquires three suitors: two rich young
men she had grown up with and a third she met in Paris.   There are
difficulties with the old playmate she wants and finally gets: his
family dislike his marrying beneath him, and he has no desire to
marry at all.

ESCAPADE

(13 performances)

Comedy in three acts by Roger MacDougall. Produced by Alfred de Liagre, Jr., and Roger L. Stevens, with Henry Sherek, at the Forty-Eighth Street Theatre, November 18, 1953.

Cast of characters—

Stella Hampden	Ursula Jeans
Mrs. Hampden	Margery Maude
Peter Henderson	Murray Matheson
William Saxon	Peter Pagan
Sir Harold Cookham	Arthur Marlowe
John Hampden	Brian Aherne
Walters	John Moore
Dr. Skillingworth	Melville Cooper
Miss Betts	Marie Paxton
Paxton	Rex Thompson
Daventry	Roddy McDowall
Andrew Deeson	Felix Deebank
Molly	Carroll Baker
George	Nicholas Howard

The action takes place in and nearby London at the present time. Act I.—Scene 1—The Hampdens' living room; late afternoon. Scene 2—The same; three hours later. Act II.—Dr. Skillingworth's study at Ferndale; the next morning. Act III.—Scene 1—The same as Act I; early that evening. Scene 2—The same; the next morning.

Staged by Alfred de Liagre, Jr.; production designed by Donald Oenslager; stage manager, Arthur Marlowe.

An English play that tells of a self-important British pacifist who spends his time fecklessly bumbling and bellowing about peace manifestoes. In contrast to his empty noise are his three hell-raising schoolboy sons (all off-stage characters) who, in order to get to Geneva to make a militant peace appeal, first shoot a teacher and then steal an airplane.

(Closed November 28, 1953)

SPANISH THEATRE REPERTORY COMPANY

(31 performances)

Repertory of seven plays. Produced by Domingo Blanco and J. G. Del Pozo at the Broadhurst Theatre, starting November 19, 1953.

Repertoire—

Don Juan Tenorio (Don Juan the Lover) by José Zorrilla
El Alcalde de Zalamea (The Mayor of Zalamea) by Calderón, adapted by Tomas Borras

La Vida es Sueño (Life Is a Dream) by Calderón
Reinar Después de Morir (Rule After Death) by Guevara
El Cardenal (The Cardinal) by Luis N. Parker, Spanish adaptation by Linares Rivas and Reparaz
Cyrano de Bergerac by Edmond Rostand, Spanish adaptation by the Sres. Vila y Tintore
La Otra Honra (The Other Honor) by Jacinto Benavente

Repertory Company—

Alejandro Ulloa	Francisca Ferrandiz
Manuel Calzada	Miguel Garcia
Rafael Calvo	Emilio Menendez
Enrique Cerro	José Poveda
Pedro Gil	Francisco Camacho
Luis Garcia	A. Mendez
Rosario de la Torre	Pilar Olivar
Carmen Pradillo	Laura Bove
Luis Torner	Leonor Hernandez
Pedro Calis	Maria Rollan
Luis Calvo	Antonio Mora
Luis Vinas	Manuel Alvarez
Manuel Sanchez	Luis Rosson

Staged by Alejandro Ulloa; décor by Ramon Batlle; stage manager, Pedro Cadiz.

(Closed December 12, 1953)

THE SHRIKE

(15 performances)

Play in three acts by Joseph Kramm. Revived by the New York City Theatre Company at the New York City Center of Music and Drama, November 25, 1953.

Cast of characters—

Miss Cardell	Rica Martens
Fleming	Tom F. Reynolds
Miss Hansen	Jane Buchanan
Dr. Kramer	Leonard Patrick
Perkins	Ellsworth Wright
Grossberg	William Bush
Dr. Barrow	Isabel Bonner
Patient	Vincent Donahue
Ann Downs	Judith Evelyn
Jim Downs	José Ferrer
Dr. Schlesinger	Somer Alberg
Don Gregory	Philip Huston
Sam Tager	Arny Freeman
George O'Brien	Martin Newman
Joe Major	Van Prince
John Ankoritis	Jacques Aubuchon
Frank Carlisle	Leigh Whipper
William Schloss	Billy M. Greene
Dr. Bellman	Kendall Clark
Miss Wingate	Mary Bell

Harry Downs ....Carl Frank
Tom Blair ....Donald Foster
Attendants ....T. J. King, Addison Powell
Visitors ....Margaret Ropp, Antoinette Griffith,
                                    James Clark, Kenneth Sleeper
   Staged by Joseph Kramm and José Ferrer; in charge of produc-
tion, Jean Dalrymple; setting and lighting by Howard Bay; cos-
tumes by Emeline Roche; production stage manager, Buford Armitage;
stage manager, Herman Shapiro.

The Shrike was first produced January 15, 1952, at the Cort
Theatre for 161 performances.

(Closed December 6, 1953)

MADAM, WILL YOU WALK

(42 performances)

Comedy in three acts by Sidney Howard. Produced by the Phoenix Theatre at the Phoenix Theatre, December 1, 1953.

Cast of characters—

Mrs. Broderick ....Madeleine King
Broderick ....Arthur Jarrett
Officer Mallon ....John Randolph
Mrs. Fanaghy ....Susan Steell
Father Christy ....William Roerick
Judge Moskowitz ....Edwin Jerome
Miss Auchincloss ....Dorrit Kelton
Mr. Dockwiler ....Norman Lloyd
Mary Doyle ....Jessica Tandy
Dr. Brightlee ....Hume Cronyn
Scupper ....Robert Emmett
Alderman Doyle ....David Clarke
Magistrate ....Leon Janney
Court Clerk ....David Hooks
Marshal ....Buff Shurr
   Assorted Citizens of New York City: Nora Dunfee, Jill Andre,
Donald Draper, Dan Hogan, Elizabeth Johnstone, Mavis Mitchell,
Fred Smith.
   The time is the present. Act I.—The Doyle residence on Fifth
Avenue, New York City. Act II.—Scene 1—Behind the bandstand
on the Mall in Central Park; the same evening. Scene 2—The 72nd
Street lake in Central Park; later. Scene 3—A night court; an hour
later. Act III.—Same as Act I; the following morning.
   Staged by Hume Cronyn and Norman Lloyd; settings and lighting
by Donald Oenslager; costumes supervised by Alvin Colt; dances by
Anna Sokolow; incidental music by Max Marlin; production stage
manager, Paul A. Foley; company stage manager, Robert Woods.

The heiress-daughter of "a Tammany grafter who died in Sing
Sing" has turned into a guilt-ridden recluse. Into her parlor steps
a persuasive Dr. Brightlee, who is clearly the devil, but a devil on
the side of the angels—on the side, at least, of all who show courage
and resist conformity. With the doctor for an escort, the heiress

takes a night out, meets a hackie who wants to be a hoofer, wanders in Central Park, ends up in night court. Though the doctor becomes smitten, it is the hackie who gets the girl.

(Closed January 10, 1954)

KISMET

(209 performances)
(Continued)

Musical in two acts, based on the play by Edward Knoblock; an Edwin Lester production; book by Charles Lederer and Luther Davis; music from Aleksandr Borodin; musical adaptation and lyrics by Robert Wright and George Forrest. Produced by Charles Lederer at the Ziegfeld Theatre, December 3, 1953.

Cast of characters—

Imam of the Mosque	Richard Oneto
Muezzins	Gerald Cardoni, Kirby Smith, Ralph Strane, Louis Polacek
Doorman	Jack Mei Ling
First Beggar	Earle MacVeigh
Second Beggar	Robert Lamont
Third Beggar	Rodolfo Silva
Dervishes	Jack Dodds, Marc Wilder
Omar	Philip Coolidge
A Public Poet, later called Hajj	Alfred Drake
Marsinah, His Daughter	Doretta Morrow
A Merchant	Kirby Smith
Hassan-Ben	Hal Hackett
Jawan	Truman Gaige
Street Dancer	Florence Lessing
Akbar	Jack Dodds
Assiz	Marc Wilder
The Bangle Man	Richard Oneto
Chief Policeman	Tom Charlesworth
Second Policeman	Hal Hackett
The Wazir of Police	Henry Calvin
Wazir's Guards	Stephen Ferry, Steve Reeves
Lalume	Joan Diener
Attendants	Mario Lamm, John Weidemann
The Princesses of Ababu	Patricia Dunn, Bonnie Evans, Reiko Sato
The Caliph	Richard Kiley
Slave Girls	Carol Ohmart, Joyce Palmer, Sandra Stahl, Lila Jackson
A Peddler	Earle MacVeigh
A Servant	Richard Vine
Princess Zubbediya of Damascus	Florence Lessing
Ayah to Zubbediya	Lucy Andonian
Princess Samaris of Bangalore	Beatrice Kraft
Ayah to Samaris	Thelma Dare
Street Women	Jo Ann O'Connell, Lynne Stuart
Prosecutor	Earle MacVeigh
The Widow Yussef	Barbara Slate
Diwan Dancers	Neile Adams, Jack Dodds, Marc Wilder

Singers: Gerald Cardoni, Robert Lamont, Richard Oneto, Louis Polacek, Kirby Smith, Ralph Strane, Richard Vine, George Yarick,

Anita Coulter, Thelma Dare, Lila Jackson, Jo Ann O'Connell, Barbara Slate, Sandra Stahl, Lynne Stuart, Erica Twiford.

Dancers: Neile Adams, Patricia Dale, Devra Kline, Ania Romaine, Vida Ann Solomon, Roberta Stevenson.

The action takes place in Baghdad.

Staged by Albert Marre; dances and musical numbers staged by Jack Cole; settings and costumes by Lemuel Ayers; lighting by Peggy Clark; orchestral and choral arrangements by Arthur Kay; musical direction by Louis Adrian; production manager, Peter Bronte; stage manager, Phil Friedman.

Musical numbers—

ACT I

"Sands of Time" .... Imam of the Mosque
"Rhymes Have I" .... Hajj and Marsinah
"Fate" .... Hajj
"Bazaar of the Caravans" .... Street Dancer, Akbar, Assiz, Merchants, Shoppers
"Not Since Nineveh" .... Lalume, Wazir, Three Princesses of Ababu, Akbar, Assiz, Merchants, Shoppers
"Baubles, Bangles and Beads" .... Marsinah
"Stranger in Paradise" .... Caliph and Marsinah
"He's in Love!" .... Chief Policeman, Second Policeman, Prosecutor, Three Princesses of Ababu, Akbar, Assiz, Caliph, Omar
"Gesticulate" .... Hajj and Wazir's Council
"Fate" .... Hajj and Ladies of the Wazir's Harem

ACT II

"Night of My Nights" .... Caliph and Entourage
"Was I Wazir?" .... Wazir, Policemen, Guards
"Rahadlakum" .... Hajj, Lalume, Princess Zubbediya, Princess Samaris, Three Princesses of Ababu, Ladies of the Wazir's Harem
"And This Is My Beloved" .... Marsinah, Caliph, Hajj, Wazir
"The Olive Tree" .... Hajj
"Ceremonial of the Caliph's Diwan" .... Diwan Dancers
"Presentation of Princesses" .... Princess Zubbediya, Ayah, Princess Samaris, Princesses of Ababu
Finale .... Ensemble and Hajj

RICHARD III

(15 performances)

Play in two acts by William Shakespeare. Produced by the New York City Theatre Company at the New York City Center of Music and Drama, December 9, 1953.

Cast of characters—

Richard, Duke of Gloucester (later Richard III) ......José Ferrer
George, Duke of Clarence (his brother)........... Staats Cotsworth
Brackenbury (Lieutenant of the Tower) .... Paul Ballantyne
Lord Hastings (Lord Chamberlain) .... William Post, Jr.
Anne (widow of the son of Henry VI) .... Maureen Stapleton
Tressel .... Tom Tryon
Berkeley .... Benedict MacQuarrie
A Priest .... G. Wood
Queen Elizabeth (wife of Edward IV) .... Jessie Royce Landis
Earl Rivers (her brother) .... Philip Huston
Lord Grey (her son) .... John Glennon

Duke of Buckingham ....Vincent Price
Lord Stanley, Earl of Derby ....John Straub
Marquis of Dorset (Elizabeth's son) ....Robert Lansing
Queen Margaret (widow of Henry VI) ....Florence Reed
Catesby (Richard's follower) ....Eugene Stuckmann
1st Murderer ....Martin Kingsley
2nd Murderer ....Jack Bittner
Edward IV (Richard's elder brother) ....Norman Roland
Young Clarence ....John Glennon
Dowager Duchess of York (mother of Edward, Richard,
  and Clarence) ....Viola Roche
1st Citizen ....Stanley Carlson
2nd Citizen ....Jack Fletcher
3rd Citizen ....Will Davis
Richard, Duke of York (Edward's younger son) ......Charles Taylor
Edward, Prince of Wales (Edward's elder son) ...John Connoughton
The Lord Mayor of London ....Leopold Badia
Bishop of Ely ....James Arenton
Another Bishop ....Wallace Widdecombe
A Messenger (servant to the Earl of Derby)..........Dehl Berti
Duke of Norfolk ....Charles Summers
Sir Richard Ratcliff } (followers of Richard) .... { Jay Barney
Lord Lovel   }   { Robinson Stone
A Scrivener ....Bill Butler
A Page ....Sandy Campbell
Sir James Tyrell ....Kendall Clark
1st Messenger }   { Peter Harris
2nd Messenger } (soldiers in Richard's army) ... { Richard Cowdery
3rd Messenger }   { Robert Ludlum
Henry, Earl of Richmond (afterwards Henry VII)...Douglas Watson
Sir James Blunt ....Bill Butler
Sir William Brandon } (followers of Richmond) { Vincent Donahue
The Earl of Oxford }   { John Glennon
  Citizens, Soldiers, Monks, Priests, Nobles, etc.: Jack Betts, Dehl
Berti, Jack Bittner, Marc Breaux, Peter Buchan, Bill Butler, David
Post, Sandy Campbell, Stanley Carlson, Wyatt Cooper, Garry Cowen,
Will Davis, John Devoe, Vincent Donahue, Jack Fletcher, John Glen-
non, Martin Kingsley, Walter Lawrence, Benedict MacQuarrie, Ray
MacDonnel, Phil Prindle, Ray Rizzo, Kenneth Sleeper, Stanley Tan-
nen, Tom Tryon, Bruce Webster, Bert Whitley, G. Wood, David
Wright, Stefan Olsen.
  Staged by Margaret Webster; in charge of production, Jean Dal-
rymple; production designed by Richard Whorf; music composed and
conducted by Alex North; costume director, Emeline Roche; production stage manager, Buford Armitage; stage manager, Jess Kimmel.

(Closed December 20, 1953)

JOHN MURRAY ANDERSON'S ALMANAC

(198 performances)
(Continued)

Revue in two parts: music and lyrics by Richard Adler, Jerry Ross,
Cy Coleman, Michael Grace, Joseph McCarthy, Jr., Henry Sullivan,
John Rox, and Bart Howard; sketches by Jean Kerr, Sumner Locke-
Elliot, Arthur Macrae, Herbert Farjeon, Lauri Wylie, and Billy K.
Wells. Produced by Michael Grace, Stanley Gilkey, and Harry
Rigby at the Imperial Theatre, December 10, 1953.

The principals—

Hermione Gingold	Billy DeWolfe
Harry Belafonte	Polly Bergen
Orson Bean	Nanci Crompton
Carleton Carpenter	Harry Mimmo
Elaine Dunn	Celia Lipton

James Jewell

Devised and staged by John Murray Anderson; sketches directed by Cyril Ritchard; dances and musical numbers staged by Donald Saddler; scenery by Raoul Pène du Bois; costumes by Thomas Becher; musical director, Buster Davis; orchestrations by Ted Royal; vocal arrangements by Buster Davis; dance music arranged by Gerald Alters; production stage manager, Arthur Barkow; stage managers, Perry Bruskin, Dennis Murray.

Sketches and musical numbers—

PART I

PROLOGUE

HARLEQUINADE
By Richard Adler and Jerry Ross

Harlequin ....Carleton Carpenter
Puncinello ....Harry Mimmo
Pierrot ....James Jewell
Pierrette ....Celia Lipton
Columbine ....Nanci Crompton
Pierrettes: Lee Becker, Imelda DeMartin, Dorothy Dushock, Greb Lober, Illona Murai, Margot Myers, Gwen Neilson, Gloria Smith.
Pierrots: Jimmy Albright, Hank Brunjes, Ronald Cecill, Dean Crane, Ralph McWilliams, Gerard Leavitt.

THE ALMANAC

Page 1

THE CORONATION
"Queen for a Day"
By Richard Adler and Jerry Ross

The Four Queens: Jacqueline Mickles, Colleen Hutchins, Monique Van Vooren, Tina Louise.
The Bridegrooms: Larry Kert, Bob Kole, George Reeder, Jay Harnick, Ronald Cecill, Ralph McWilliams, Hank Brunjes, Gerard Leavitt.
Miss Reingold ....Hermione Gingold

Page 2

"MY COUSIN WHO?"
By Jean Kerr

David ....Billy DeWolfe
Butlers ....Jimmy Albright, Kenneth Urmston, Ronald Cecill, Ralph McWilliams
Witch Doctor ....Dean Crane
Maids ....Toni Wheelis, Gwen Neilson
Rebecca ....Celia Lipton
Louise ....Illona Murai

Page 3

"YOU'RE SO MUCH A PART OF ME"
By Richard Adler and Jerry Ross

The Pierrot of 1953 ....Sung by Carleton Carpenter
The Pierrette of 1953 ....Sung by Elaine Dunn

Page 4

"I DARE TO DREAM"
Music by Michael Grace and Carl Tucker; lyrics by Sammy Gallup
Sung by Polly Bergen

Page 5
"THE CELLO"
By Leslie Julian Jones
The Cellist .... Hermione Gingold

Page 6
DON BROWN'S BODY
By Jean Kerr
Mike Hammer .... Orson Bean
Sally Duprey .... Kay Medford
Man .... Carleton Carpenter
  Chorus: Jay Harnick, Colleen Hutchins, Jacqueline Mickles, Tina
Louise, Bob Kole, Monique Van Vooren, Siri, George Reeder, Larry
Kert.

Page 7
"MARK TWAIN"
Written by Harry Belafonte
Sung by Harry Belafonte
Guitarist .... Millard Thomas

Page 8
"THE NIGHTINGALE AND THE ROSE"
(Adapted from the story of Oscar Wilde by John Murray Anderson)
"Nightingale, Bring Me a Rose"
Music by Henry Sullivan; lyric by John Murray Anderson
Sung by James Jewell
The Story Teller .... Celia Lipton
The Student .... Dean Crane
The Prince .... Gerard Leavitt
The Coquette .... Margot Myers
The Nightingale .... Nanci Crompton
  Guests at the Ball: Siri, Monique Van Vooren, Tina Louise, Colleen
Hutchins, Greb Lober, Dorothy Dushock, Gloria Smith, Gwen Neil-
son, Hank Brunjes, Ralph McWilliams, Ronald Cecill, George Reeder,
Jimmy Albright.

Page 9
EUROPEAN EXPRESS
Mrs. A .... Hermione Gingold
Mrs. B .... Billy DeWolfe

Page 10
"MY LOVE IS A WANDERER"
Music and lyrics by Bart Howard
Sung by Polly Bergen

Page 11
"TIN PAN ALLEY"
Music by Cy Coleman; lyric by Joseph McCarthy, Jr.
The Song Plugger .... Carleton Carpenter
and
Ronald Cecill, Jay Harnick, Larry Kert, Bob Kole
"Mammy Songs"
Ralph McWilliams and Kenneth Urmston
"Rhythm Songs"
George Reeder, Imelda DeMartin, Lee Becker, Greb Lober, Dorothy
Dushock
"Torch Songs"
Gloria Smith, Illona Murai, Margot Myers, Hank Brunjes, Gerard
Leavitt, Dean Crane
"Patriotic Songs"
Elaine Dunn

Page 12
ORSON BEAN
(The song "Merry Little Minuet" is by Sheldon Harnick)

Page 13
"HOPE YOU COME BACK"
By Sumner Locke-Elliot
Music and lyrics by Richard Adler and Jerry Ross

Meg ....Polly Bergen
Beth ....Nanci Crompton
Jo ....Elaine Dunn
Amy ....Hermione Gingold
Marmee ....Kay Medford
Laurie ....Billy DeWolfe
Friends ....James Jewell and Entire Company

PART II

Page 1

ZIEGFELDIANA

"If Every Month Were June"
Music by Henry Sullivan; lyrics by John Murray Anderson
Sung by Celia Lipton

The Spring Bride ....Colleen Hutchins
The Summer Bride ....Siri
The Autumn Bride ....Jacqueline Mickles
The Winter Bride ....Monique Van Vooren
The Bouquet ....Nanci Crompton
    The Train Bearers: Imelda DeMartin, Lee Becker, Dorothy Du-
shock, Gwen Neilson.

Page 2

"WHICH WITCH?"
Lyric by Allan Melville; music by Charles Zwar
Sung by Hermione Gingold

Page 3

"LA LOGE"
(Renoir)
By Herbert Farjeon
"FINI"
By Richard Adler and Jerry Ross
Sung by Polly Bergen

The Man in the Box ....Jay Harnick

Page 4

CARTOON
By Arthur Macrae

First Secretary ....Kay Medford
Second Secretary ....Colleen Hutchins
The New Manager ....Orson Bean

Page 5

"ACORN IN THE MEADOW"
By Richard Adler and Jerry Ross
Sung by Harry Belafonte

Page 6

HARRY MIMMO
The Ladies
Tina Louise, Jacqueline Mickles, Monique Van Vooren
Sedan Chair Bearers
Jay Harnick and Larry Kert

Page 7

"WHEN AM I GOING TO MEET YOUR MOTHER?"
By Richard Adler and Jerry Ross
Sung and Danced by
Elaine Dunn and Carleton Carpenter

Page 8

"DINNER FOR ONE"
By Lauri Wylie

The Lady ....Hermione Gingold
The Butler ....Billy DeWolfe

Page 9

ORSON BEAN
(The Chinese monologue was written by Orson Bean and Phil Green)

Page 10

"Hold 'em Joe"
By Harry Belafonte
Sung by Harry Belafonte
Danced by Illona Murai, George Reeder, Gloria Smith, Monique Van
Vooren, Colleen Hutchins, and the "Almanac" Dancers

Page 11

"La Pistachio"
By Billy K. Wells
(Adapted for the "Almanac" by Sumner Locke-Elliot)
Bobo ....Hermione Gingold
Cornelius ....Billy DeWolfe
Fifi ....Kay Medford

Page 12

"The Earth and the Sky"
Music and lyrics by John Rox
Sung by Polly Bergen

Finale

The Entire Company

THE PRESCOTT PROPOSALS

(125 performances)

Play in three acts by Howard Lindsay and Russel Crouse. Produced by Leland Hayward at the Broadhurst Theatre, December 16, 1953.

Cast of characters—

Mary Prescott, U.N. Delegate from the United
   States ....Katharine Cornell
Kathleen Murray, Secretary to Mrs. Prescott ......Emily Lawrence
Emma ....Helen Ray
Elliott Clark ....,...Lorne Greene
Jan Capek, U.N. Delegate from Czechoslovakia ...Bartlett Robinson
Sir Audley Marriott, U.N. Ambassador from the
   United Kingdom ....Felix Aylmer
Paul-Emile D'Arceau, U.N. Delegate from France .....Roger Dann
Dr. Ali Masoud, U.N. Delegate from Pakistan ....Minoo Daver
Alexis Petrovsky, U.N. Delegate from the Soviet Union ..Ben Astar
Miguel Fernandez, Conference Officer ....Edward Groag
Alan Draper, Press Attaché ....Robert M. Culp
Miroslav Babicka, U.N. Alternate Delegate from
   Czechoslovakia ....Boris Tumarin
Russian Aide ....Jan de Ruth
British Aide ....,.....J. P. Wilson
Precis-Writer ....John Drew Devereaux
   Experts and Aides to the United Nations Delegates: Bijou Fernandez, Joe Masteroff, John Leslie, Sheppard Kerman, Richard Bengali, Ward Costello, Bernard Reines, Hubert Beck.
   The action takes place in late Autumn. Act I.—Mary Prescott's apartment. Act II.—Scene 1—A committee room at the United Nations; the next afternoon. Scene 2—Mary Prescott's apartment; that night. Act III.—A committee room at the United Nations; the next afternoon.
   Staged by Howard Lindsay; settings by Donald Oenslager; costumes by Main Bocher; production stage manager, Edmund Baylies; stage manager, Ross Hertz.

A Czech delegate to the U.N. calls on an American lady delegate, years before his mistress in Prague, now the sponsor of important U.N. proposals. He dies during his visit of a heart attack. Were the fact to leak out, it might wreck the proposals, so that there is the old problem of how to get rid of a corpse. Thereafter, there is also the problem of how to combine a moderately serious theme with a largely popular plot; politics with thrills. Despite a good beginning, the play is by no means up to Lindsay and Crouse's blend of politics and humor in *State of the Union*.

(Closed April 3, 1954)

OH, MEN! OH, WOMEN!

(200 performances)
(Continued)

Comedy in three acts by Edward Chodorov. Produced by Cheryl Crawford, in association with Anderson Lawler, at Henry Miller's Theatre, December 17, 1953.

Cast of characters—

Miss Tacher	Joan Gray
Alan Coles	Franchot Tone
Grant Cobbler	Larry Blyden
Myra Hagerman	Betsy von Furstenberg
Dr. Krauss	Henry Sharp
Mildred Turner	Anne Jackson
Arthur Turner	Gig Young
Steward	Paul Andor

Act I.—Dr. Coles's office on a morning in Spring. Act II.—Myra's apartment; that evening. Act III.—Suite on the S. S. *Miramar;* the following morning.

Staged by Edward Chodorov; settings by William and Jean Eckart; costumes supervised by Paul du Pont; stage manager, Al West.

A middle-aged psychoanalyst, on the eve of taking a bride half his age, learns from a patient that his fiancée has a considerable past. Then he learns from another patient that her movie-star husband plans to seduce the fiancée to see whether the analyst "can take it as well as dish it out." Complications thereafter abound.

CHARLEY'S AUNT

(15 performances)

Comedy in three acts by Brandon Thomas. Revived by the New York City Theatre Company at the New York City Center of Music and Drama, December 22, 1953.

Cast of characters—

```
Brassett .......................................Rex O'Malley
Jack Chesney ..................................Robert Lansing
Charles Wykeham ..............................Terence Kilburn
Lord Fancourt Babberley .........................José Ferrer
Kitty Verdun ....................................Lori March
Amy Spettigue ................................Sarah Marshall
Colonel Sir Francis Chesney .......................Kent Smith
Stephen Spettigue ............................Jacques Aubuchon
Farmer .......................................Richard Cowdery
Donna Lucia D'Alvadorez .........................Peggy Wood
Ela Delahay ....................................Patricia Wheel
Maud ........................................Beverly Dennis
```

Staged by José Ferrer; in charge of production, Jean Dalrymple; assistant director, Jess Kimmel; production designed by Raoul Pène du Bois; costume director, Emeline Roche; production stage manager, Buford Armitage stage manager, Herman Shapiro.

Charley's Aunt was first produced in New York October 2, 1893.

(Closed January 3, 1954)

DEAD PIGEON

(21 performances)

Play in three acts by Lenard Kantor. Produced by Harald Bromley and Haila Stoddard at the Vanderbilt Theatre, December 23, 1953.

Cast of characters—

```
Lieutenant Monahan ............................James Gregory
Sherry Parker ....................................Joan Lorring
Detective Ernest Brady .........................Lloyd Bridges
```

The action takes place in a room in a resort hotel near the ocean in a suburb of a large American city at the present time. Act I.— Early in May, Sunday, 11 A.M. Act II.—Scene 1—Two o'clock the same afternoon. Scene 2—Three o'clock. Scene 3—At dusk. Act III.—Early the next morning.

Staged by Harald Bromley; setting by William and Jean Eckart; production stage manager, James Hagerman.

A young girl is released from the penitentiary for twenty-four hours to give the D. A. information about her recently murdered gangster lover. Set to guard her in a resort hotel are two detectives (both on the gangster's payroll), one of whom falls in love with her, the other of whom is determined to do her in. In the end the captivated detective disarms the intended killer.

(Closed January 9, 1954)

SING TILL TOMORROW

(8 performances)

Play by Jean Lowenthal. Produced by Dorothy Natter at the Royale Theatre, December 28, 1953.

Cast of characters—

Evie	Eileen Ryan
Hank	John Marley
A. J. Alexander	Raymond Bailey
Dan	Michael Sheehan
Fred Lyon	Edward Cary
Nick Di Giorgio	Ted Campbell
George Faulkner	Maurice Brenner
John Lowery	Arthur Oshlag
Sue Alexander	Virginia Bradley
Jake Levin	Wolfe Barzell

The action takes place within 24 hours. The time is the present.
Staged by Basil Langton; scenery and lighting by Ralph Alswang; stage manager, Morgan James.

Pretentiously bad drama, rife with tortured lives and reeling with tortured language, about a druggist, his second wife, and his son, who sins with the wife and writes a play attacking the father.

(Closed January 2, 1954)

IN THE SUMMER HOUSE

(55 performances)

Play in two acts by Jane Bowles. Produced by Oliver Smith and The Playwrights' Company at The Playhouse, December 29, 1953.

Cast of characters—

Gertrude Eastman-Cuevas	Judith Anderson
Molly, Her Daughter	Elizabeth Ross
Mr. Solares	Don Mayo
Mrs. Lopez	Marita Reid
Frederica	Miriam Colon
Esperanza	Isabel Morel
Alta Gracia	Marjorie Eaton
Quintina	Phoebe Mackay
Lionel	Logan Ramsey
A Figure-Bearer	Paul Bertelsen
Another Figure-Bearer	George Spelvin
Vivian Constable	Muriel Berkson
Chauffeur	Daniel Morales
Mrs. Constable	Mildred Dunnock
Inez	Jean Stapleton

The time is the present. Act I.—Scene 1—Gertrude Eastman-Cuevas's garden, on the coast, Southern California. Scene 2—The beach; one month later. Scene 3—The garden; one month later. Act II.—Scene 1—The Lobster Bowl; ten months later, before dawn. Scene 2—The same; two months later, late afternoon.
Staged by José Quintero; music by Paul Bowles; scenery by Oliver Smith; costumes by Noel Taylor; lighting by Peggy Clark; associate producer, Lyn Austin; stage manager, Elliot Martin.

See page 84.

(Closed February 13, 1954)

THE REMARKABLE MR. PENNYPACKER

(178 performances)
(Continued)

Comedy in three acts by Liam O'Brien. Produced by Robert Whitehead and Roger L. Stevens at the Coronet Theatre, December 30, 1953.

Cast of characters—

Laurie Pennypacker .... Nancy Devlin
1st Pupil .... Betty Lou Keim
2nd Pupil .... Kathleen Gately
Ben Pennypacker .... Billy Quinn
David Pennypacker .... Lewis Scholle
Edward Pennypacker .... Jackie Scholle
Elizabeth Pennypacker .... Roni Dengel
Aunt Jane Pennypacker .... Una Merkel
Wilbur Fifield .... Michael Wager
Kate Pennypacker .... Phyllis Love
Ma Pennypacker .... Martha Scott
Henry Pennypacker .... John Reese
Teddie Pennypacker .... Joel Crothers
Grampa Pennypacker .... Thomas Chalmers
Quinlan .... William Lanteau
A Young Man .... Roger Stevens
Dr. Fifield .... Glenn Anders
Sheriff .... Howard Fischer
Pa Pennypacker .... Burgess Meredith
Policeman .... James Holden

The action takes place in the Pennypacker home in Wilmington, Delaware, in late Spring, 1890. Act I.—Scene 1—A Friday afternoon. Scene 2—The next day. Act II.—Immediately following. Act III.—Two hours later.

Staged by Alan Schneider; setting and costumes by Ben Edwards; stage manager, Frederic de Wilde.

Comedy, laid in Wilmington, Delaware, in 1890, concerning a middle-class paterfamilias with a large brood and advanced social views. It is soon revealed that he has sired an even larger brood in Philadelphia. Unlike his Wilmington wife, he sees nothing untoward in bigamy, and is no less devoted a family man for having one family too many. Bourgeois complications necessarily ensue; nor, despite revealing at the end that the Philadelphia wife is dead, can Mr. Pennypacker ever really wriggle out of his predicament.

MADEMOISELLE COLOMBE

(61 performances)

Play in two acts by Jean Anouilh, adapted by Louis Kronenberger. Produced by Robert L. Joseph and Jay Julien at the Longacre Theatre, January 6, 1954.

Cast of characters—

Colombe ....Julie Harris
Julien ....Eli Wallach
Mme. Georges.......................................Edna Preston
Mme. Alexandra ....Edna Best
Chiropodist ....Edward Julien
Manicurist ....Joanne Taylor
Hairdresser ....Nehemiah Persoff
Gourette ....Sam Jaffe
Edouard ....William Windom
Deschamps ....Frank Silvera
Poet-Mine-Own ....Mikhail Rasumny
Gaulois ....Harry Bannister
Dancers ....{ Lee Philips
                                               { Jeanne Jerrems
Stagehand ....Gregory Robins

The action takes place in a Paris theatre around 1900. Act I.—
Scene 1—A backstage corridor and Mme. Alexandra's dressing-room.
Scene 2—The stage; a few days later. Act II.—Scene 1—A corridor
and Colombe's dressing room; three months later.   Scene 2—The
stage; three hours later. Epilogue—The stage; two years earlier.

Staged by Harold Clurman; production designed by Boris Aronson;
costumes by Motley; production associate, Shirley Bernstein; production stage manager, James Gelb.

Called up for military service, the neglected, embittered son of a
famous turn-of-the-century Parisian actress leaves his attractive
young wife in his mother's hands. Given a small part in a play,
Colombe comes to life in the gay, unmoral world of the theater, and
proves unfaithful with her husband's brother. When her husband
suspects, Colombe tries in vain to conceal the truth: afterwards there
are bitter scenes and a doomed marriage. An epilogue, taking place
two years before the rest of the action, depicts the rapturous, idyllic
first meeting of the pair.

(Closed February 27, 1954)

HIS AND HERS

(76 performances)

Comedy in three acts by Fay and Michael Kanin. Produced by
Albert Selden and Morton Gottlieb at the Forty-Eighth Street Theatre, January 7, 1954.

Cast of characters—

Jean ....Helen Harrelson
Avis.......................................Elizabeth Patterson
Maggie Palmer ....Celeste Holm
The Super ....Lou Gilbert
Lydia ....Perry Wilson
George ....Herbert Nelson
Dr. Carl Halek ....George Voskovec
Mike Foster ....Howard St. John
Clem Scott ....Robert Preston
The Judge ....Donald McKee
Her Lawyer ....Heywood Hale Broun

His Lawyer ....Harry Mehaffey
Bunty ....Roy Monsell
    Act I.—Scene 1—Maggie Palmer's apartment in New York City;
early afternoon, last Summer. Scene 2—The Supreme Court of the
State of New York, in New York City. Act II.—Scene 1—Maggie's
apartment; a Monday morning, a week later. Scene 2—The same;
a Saturday evening, early Fall. Scene 3—The same; the following
noon. Act III.—Maggie's apartment; opening night, about two
months later.
    Staged by Michael Gordon; settings by Charles Elson; costumes by
Frank Thompson; Miss Holm's clothes by Oleg Cassini; stage manager, James Awe.

The play tells of a playwriting couple who got divorced after two
Broadway flops. Now they go to court because each has thought
up a play with the same plot; and the court decrees that they write
the play together. While collaborating they feel the stirrings of an
old passion, and decide that if the play clicks they will remarry.
Then they decide that love outweighs success, and that they'll remarry whatever happens.

With so cut and dried a plot, the play needed real gaiety in the
writing; but all it had was an awful glibness.

(Closed March 13, 1954)

THE STARCROSS STORY

(1 performance)

Play in three acts by Diana Morgan. Produced by John C. Wilson, the Messrs. Shubert and S. S. Krellberg at the Royale Theatre,
January 13, 1954.

Cast of characters—

James Trenchard ....Anthony Ross
Chloe Gwynn ....Marta Linden
George Phillips ....Christopher Plummer
Christine Starcross ....Lynn Bailey
Ellen ....Una O'Connor
Lady Starcross ....Eva Le Gallienne
Alice Venning ....Margaret Bannerman
Laura Shipman ....Philippa Bevans
Jean Benson (Halliday) ....Doris Patston
Anne Meredith ....Mary Astor
    The action takes place in the drawing room of Lady Starcross's
home in Chiswick Mall, London, at the present time. Act I.—An
April afternoon. Act II.—Scene 1—Evening, a few weeks later.
Scene 2—Later that evening. Act III.—The next morning.
    Staged by John C. Wilson; setting by Watson Barratt; stage man-
ager, Ward Bishop.

The play concerns a movie to be made about a heroic expedition
that cost Explorer Christian Starcross and his men their lives.
Wrangling over the movie project are Starcross's widow and his former mistress; and their feuding reveals that Starcross himself was a
scheming egomaniac who knowingly went off on a phony quest. The

widow still insists, however, that the movie be made—in an era of despair, she argues, heroic legends (even though false) count for more than the truth does.

Loaded down with exposition and limp from reminiscence, the play had only a fitful—and even then, stagy—force.

(Closed January 13, 1954)

CORIOLANUS

(48 performances)

Tragedy by William Shakespeare. Produced by the Phoenix Theatre at the Phoenix Theatre, January 19, 1954.

Cast of characters—

1st Citizen	Frederick Rolf
2nd Citizen	David Clarke
3rd Citizen	Jack Bittner
4th Citizen	Carl Jacobs
5th Citizen	Jerry Stiller
6th Citizen	Jack Klugman
7th Citizen	Gene Saks
Menenius Agrippa, a Patrician	Alan Napier
Caius Martius Coriolanus	Robert Ryan
Senatorial Messenger	Michael Tolan
Titus Lartius, a Roman General	Lou Polan
1st Senator	Joseph Macaulay
2nd Senator	George Fells
Cominius, Commander-in-Chief of the Roman Army	Joseph Holland
1st Aedile } Officers of the Tribune	{ Jamie Smith
2nd Aedile }	{ Carl Jacobs
Junius Brutus } Tribunes of the People	{ John Randolph
Sicinius }	{ Will Geer
Volumnia, Mother to Coriolanus	Mildred Natwick
Virgilia, Wife to Coriolanus	Lori March
Gentlewoman Attending on Volumnia	Nora Dunfee
Valeria, Friend to Virgilia	Paula Laurence
Tullus Aufidius, General of the Volscians	John Emery
Lieutenant to Aufidius	Jamie Smith
1st Volscian Servant	Gene Saks
2nd Volscian Servant	Jack Klugman
3rd Volscian Servant	Jerry Stiller
1st Sentinel	Michael Tolan
2nd Sentinel	Carl Jacobs
Son to Coriolanus	Terry Nardin
1st Conspirator	Carl Jacobs
1st Lord	Lou Polan

Roman and Volscian Senators, Aediles, Lictors, Soldiers, Citizens, Messengers, Servants to Aufidius and Other Attendants: Norman Beim, Peter Benzoni, Peter Buchan, Nat Burns, Donald Draper, Mel Fillini, Jack Friend, Joseph Elic, Erle Hall, Richard Lederer, Frank Lucas, Paul Lukather, Richard Marr, Hugh Mosher, Joseph Nathan, Jim Oyster, Richard Shull, Tim Squires, Laurence Vide.

The action takes place in Rome and in Antium and Corioles, two cities of the Volsces.

Staged by John Houseman; settings by Donald Oenslager; costumes by Alvin Colt; music by Alex North; production stage manager, Robert Woods; company stage manager, George Quick.

(Closed February 28, 1954)

THE CAINE MUTINY COURT-MARTIAL

(152 performances)
(Continued)

Play in two acts by Herman Wouk, adapted by Mr. Wouk from his novel *The Caine Mutiny*. Produced by Paul Gregory at the Plymouth Theatre, January 20, 1954.

Cast of characters—

Stenographer	John Huffman
Orderly	Greg Roman
Lt. Barney Greenwald	Henry Fonda
Lt. Stephen Maryk	John Hodiak
Lt. Cdr. John Challee	Ainslie Pryor
Captain Blakely, President of the Court	Russell Hicks
Lt. Cdr. Philip Francis Queeg	Lloyd Nolan
Lt. Thomas Keefer	Robert Gist
Signalman 3rd Class Junius Urban	Eddie Firestone
Lt. (Jr. Grade) Willis Seward Keith	Charles Nolte
Capt. Randolph Southard	Paul Birch
Dr. Forrest Lundeen	Stephen Chase
Dr. Bird	Herbert Anderson
Members of the Court	Larry Barton Jim Bumgarner T. H. Jourdan Richard Farmer Richard Norris Pat Waltz

The action takes place in the General Court-Martial Room of the 12th Naval District, San Francisco, in February, 1945. At the end of Act II the scene shifts to a private dining room of the Hotel Fairmount, San Francisco. Act I.—The Prosecution. Act II.—The Defense.

Staged by Charles Laughton; stage manager, Len Smith, Jr.

See page 54.

RUTH DRAPER

(58 performances)

Monologues by Ruth Draper. Produced by Charles Bowden and Richard Barr at the Vanderbilt Theatre, January 25, 1954.

Monologues—

PROGRAM I

The Italian Lesson
A Dalmatian Peasant in the Hall of a New York Hospital
Doctors and Diets
On the Porch in a Maine Coast Village
In a Church in Italy

PROGRAM II

Opening a Bazaar
In County Kerry—1919
At an Art Exhibition in Boston
Three Women and Mr. Clifford
A Scottish Immigrant at Ellis Island

PROGRAM III

A Children's Party in Philadelphia
Three Generations in the Court of Domestic Relations
Showing the Garden
A Class in Greek Poise
A Debutante at a Dance
"Vive La France"

Stage manager, Gerry O'Brien.

(Closed March 13, 1954)

LULLABY

(45 performances)

Comedy in two acts by Don Appell. Produced by Jerome Mayer and Irl Mowery, in association with Toby Ruby, at the Lyceum Theatre, February 3, 1954.

Cast of characters—

A Bellhop ....Al Ramsen
Johnny ....Jack Warden
Eadie ....Kay Medford
The Mother ....Mary Boland
    Act I.—Scene 1—The wedding night. Scene 2—The honeymoon morning. Act II.—Scene 1—The first week. Scene 2—The first month.
    Staged by Jerome Mayer; settings and lighting by Ben Edwards; stage manager, Robert Downing.

A comedy about a thirty-eight-year-old truck driver who wriggles out from under his mother's thumb to marry a nice nightclub cigarette girl. First chronicling a honeymoon in Scranton complicated by Mother's rampagious arrival from New York; then recounting household arrangements in New York disturbed by Mother's inching her way inside the household, *Lullaby* has its bright moments and its sassy scenes, but is half ready-made realism and half routine farce.

(Closed March 13, 1954)

THE IMMORALIST

(96 performances)

Play in three acts by Ruth and Augustus Goetz, based on André Gide's novel of the same name. Produced by Billy Rose at the Royale Theatre, February 8, 1954.

Cast of characters—

Marcelline ....Geraldine Page
Dr. Robert ....John Heldabrand
Bocage ....Charles Dingle

Michel .... Louis Jourdan
Bachir .... James Dean
Dr. Garrin .... Paul Huber
Sidma .... Adelaide Klein
Moktir .... David J. Stewart
Dolit .... Bill Gunn
    Act I.—Scene 1—Normandy, France; November, 1900. Scene 2—
Biskra, North Africa; two months later.   Act II.—Scene 1—Biskra;
the following week.   Scene 2—Biskra; February.   Scene 3—Biskra;
late Spring.   Scene 4—Biskra; Summer.   Act III.—Scene 1—Biskra;
the next day.   Scene 2—Normandy; that Autumn.
    Staged by Daniel Mann; settings by George Jenkins; lighting by Abe
Feder; costumes by Motley; stage manager, Lucia Victor.

See page 184.

(Closed May 1, 1954)

THE GIRL ON THE VIA FLAMINIA

(111 performances *)

Play in three acts by Alfred Hayes. Produced by Circle in the
Square at Circle in the Square, February 9, 1954. After forty-three
performances at Circle in the Square (through March 21) it moved
to the Forty-Eighth Street Theatre on April 1.

Cast of characters—

The English Sergeant .... James Greene
The American G.I. .... Andy Milligan
Adele Pulcini .... Lola D'Annunzio
Mimi .... Emilie Stevens
Nina .... Sylvia Daneel
Lisa .... Betty Miller
Ugo Pulcini .... Carl Harms
Robert .... Leo Penn
Antonio .... Felice Orlandi
Bologinini .... Louis Guss
Police Inspector .... Jason Wingreen
    The action takes place in newly liberated Rome in the dining room
and one bedroom in the apartment of the Pulcini family.   Act I.—
Evening, just before Christmas, 1944.   Act II.—Scene 1—Evening,
the following day.   Scene 2—New Year's Eve.   Act III.—Afternoon, New Year's Day, 1945.
    Staged by José Quintero; setting and lighting by Klaus Holm;
music by Arnold Black; stage manager, Elliot Martin.

See page 234.

(Closed May 29, 1954)

THE CONFIDENTIAL CLERK

(117 performances)

Comedy in three acts by T. S. Eliot. Produced by Henry Sherek
and The Producers' Theatre at the Morosco Theatre, February 11,
1954.

* Includes off-Broadway performances.

Cast of characters—

```
Sir Claude Mulhammer ...............................Claude Rains
Eggerson .........................................Newton Blick
Colby Simpkins ...................................Douglas Watson
B. Kaghan .......................................Richard Newton
Lucasta Angel ....................................Joan Greenwood
Lady Elizabeth Mulhammer ...........................Ina Claire
Mrs. Guzzard ....................................Aline MacMahon
```

Act I.—The study in Sir Claude Mulhammer's West End house; early afternoon. Act II.—The flat in the mews; two months later. Act III.—The study at Sir Claude's house; several mornings later.

Staged by E. Martin Browne; settings, costumes, and lighting by Paul Morrison; production stage manager, Del Hughes.

See page 109.

(Closed May 22, 1954)

THE WINNER

(30 performances)

Play in four scenes by Elmer Rice. Produced by The Playwrights' Company at The Playhouse, February 17, 1954.

Cast of characters—

```
Eva Harold .......................................Joan Tetzel
Martin Carew .....................................Tom Helmore
David Browning ................................Whitfield Connor
Newscaster ......................................P. Jay Sidney
Arnold Mahler ...................................Lothar Rewalt
Irma Mahler .....................................Jane Buchanan
Haggerty ........................................Phillip Pruneau
Dr. Clinton Ward ...............................Charles Cooper
Miss Dodd .......................................Lily Brentano
A Stenographer ..................................David Balfour
Judge Samuel Addison ..........................Frederick O'Neal
Hilde Kranzbeck .................................Vilma Kurer
```

Scene 1—New York, Eva's apartment; a night in midsummer. Scene 2—Eva's apartment; several days later. Scene 3—Bridgeport, Judge Addison's chambers; several months later. Scene 4—Eva's apartment; a few weeks later.

Staged by Elmer Rice; settings by Lester Polakov; stage manager, David Clive.

Tale of an attractive cigar-counter girl who is engaged to a married lawyer. Another married suitor brings scandal without sin upon the heroine by dying of a heart attack in her room. He also leaves her his fortune, compelling her to fight his widow for the money in court. She wins the suit, only to learn that the money belongs in back taxes to the Government, and to discover that she prefers marrying the rich opposition lawyer to her own lawyer-fiancé.

An unconvincing rigmarole full of curious plot "twists," that shift at will from romance to realism or from melodrama to comedy.

(Closed March 13, 1954)

ONDINE

(117 performances)
(Continued)

Play in three acts by Jean Giraudoux, adapted by Maurice Valency. Produced by The Playwrights' Company at the Forty-Sixth Street Theatre, February 18, 1954.

Cast of characters—

Auguste	John Alexander
Eugenie	Edith King
Ritter Hans	Mel Ferrer
Ondine	Audrey Hepburn
The Ondines	{ Dran Seitz Tani Seitz Sonia Torgeson
The Old One	Robert Middleton
The Lord Chamberlain	Alan Hewitt
The Superintendent of the Theatre	Lloyd Gough
The Trainer of Seals	James Lanphier
Bertha	Marian Seldes
Bertram	Peter Brandon
Violante	Anne Meacham
Angelique	Gaye Jordan
Venus	Jan Sherwood
Matho	Barry O'Hara
Salammbo	Lily Paget
A Lord	William Le Massena
A Lady	Stacy Graham
The Illusionist (The Old One)	Robert Middleton
The King	William Podmore
A Servant	James Lanphier
The First Fisherman	Lloyd Gough
The Second Fisherman (The Old One)	Robert Middleton
The First Judge	Alan Hewitt
The Second Judge	William Le Massena
The Executioner	Robert Crawley
The Kitchen Maid	Stacy Graham

The action takes place during the Middle Ages. Act I.—A fisherman's cottage. Act II.—A hall in the king's palace. Act III.—The courtyard in the Castle of the Wittenstein.

Staged by Alfred Lunt; settings by Peter Larkin; lighting by Jean Rosenthal; costumes by Richard Whorf; Miss Hepburn's gowns by Valentina; music by Virgil Thomson; stage manager, William Chambers.

See "The Season in New York."

THE BURNING GLASS

(28 performances)

Play in three acts by Charles Morgan. Produced by The Theatre Guild and John C. Wilson at the Longacre Theatre, March 4, 1954.

Cast of characters—

Christopher Terriford	Scott Forbes
Lady Terriford	Isobel Elsom
Mary Terriford	Maria Riva
Tony Lack	Walter Matthau

Gerry Hardlip ....William Roerick
Lord Henry Strait ....Ralph Clanton
Montagu Winthrop ....Cedric Hardwicke
Inspector Wigg ....Basil Howes
    The action takes place in the South Room at Terriford House, sixty miles from London, in the near future. Act I.—An evening before dinner, early September. Act II.—The same night, 1:30 A.M. Act III.—Scene 1—The following Sunday, near nightfall. Scene 2—Eight days later.
    Staged by Luther Kennett; setting by Oliver Smith; lighting by John Davis; costumes by Noel Taylor; stage manager, Karl Nielsen.

An intellectual thriller about a young English scientist who discovers a new source of power in harnessing solar heat. Feeling that spiritual values, today, lag far behind scientific ones, he refuses to give Britain his formula except in time of war or dire necessity. Kidnaped by "the Enemy" after his chief assistant blabs too much, the scientist is returned unharmed; and the assistant, for fear he may blab again, nobly takes poison.

(Closed March 27, 1954)

THE GIRL IN PINK TIGHTS

(101 performances)
(Continued)

Musical comedy in two acts; book by Jerome Chodorov and Joseph Fields; music by Sigmund Romberg; lyrics by Leo Robin. Produced by Shepard Traube, in association with Anthony B. Farrell, at the Mark Hellinger Theatre, March 5, 1954.

Cast of characters—

Boris ....Joshua Shelley
Volodya Kuzentsov ....Alexandre Kalioujny
Lisette Gervais ....Jeanmaire
Maestro Gallo ....Charles Goldner
Lotta Leslie ....Brenda Lewis
Clyde Hallam ....David Atkinson
Eddington ....David Aiken
Hattie Hopkins ....Dania Krupska
Van Beuren ....Robert Smith
British Tars ....Tom Rieder, John Taliaferro
Policeman ....John Stamford
Newspaper Boy ....Maurice Hines
Shoe Shine Boy ....Gregory Hines
Mike ....Kalem Kermoyan
Bruce ....John Stamford
Nellie ....Lydia Fredericks
Hollister ....Ray Mason
Simone ....Katia Geleznova
Mimi ....Eva Rubinstein
Lucette ....Lynne Marcus
Odette ....Nancy King
Gisele ....Lila Popper
Paulette ....Mickey Gunnersen
Fire Chiefs ....Ted Thurston, John Taliaferro
Jenny ....Jenny Workman
Blanchette ....Beryl Towbin

Emile .... Ted Thurston
Sommelier .... John Taliaferro
Gypsy Violinist .... Douglas Rideout

Singers: Lydia Fredericks, Jane House, Deedy Irwin, Peggy Kinard, Marni Nixon, Michelle Reiner, Joanne Spiller, Beverly Weston, David Aiken, Herbert Banke, Robert Driscoll, Kalem Kermoyan, Ray Mason, Stas Pajenski, Douglas Rideout, Tom Rieder, James Schlader, John Stamford, John Taliaferro, Ted Thurston.

Dancers: Meredith Baylis, Joan Bowman, Katia Geleznova, Mickey Gunnersen, Mary Haywood, Rhoda Kerns, Nancy King, Lynne Marcus, Julie Marlowe, Ellen Matthews, Lila Popper, Eva Rubinstein, Dorothy Scott, Beverly Simms, Beryl Towbin, Diana Turner, Jenny Workman, Harry Asmus, Louis Kosman, Paul Olson, Edward Stinnett, William Weslow.

The action takes place immediately following the Civil War in the theatrical district of New York.

Staged by Shepard Traube; dances and musical numbers staged by Agnes de Mille; music developed and orchestrated by Don Walker; scenery and lighting by Eldon Elder; costumes by Miles White; musical direction by Sylvan Levin; ballet music arranged by Trude Rittman; production stage manager, Bill Ross; stage managers, Bruce Savan, Perry Bruskin.

Jeanmaire, Alexandre Kalioujny, David Atkinson, Brenda Lewis and Charles Goldner in "The Girl in Pink Tights"

Musical numbers—

ACT I

Ballet Class ....Danced by the French Ballet Company
Lisette ....Jeanmaire
Volodya ....Alexandre Kalioujny
Soloists ....Diana Turner, William Weslow, Lynne Marcus,
    Harry Asmus, Beverly Simms, Paul Olson,
    Dorothy Scott, Edward Stinnett
"That Naughty Show from Gay Paree" ...Sung by Singing Ensemble
"Lost in Loveliness" ....Sung by Clyde Hallam
Lisette ....Jeanmaire
1st Lover ....Paul Olson
2nd Lover ....Harry Asmus
Lovers ....Edward Stinnett, Louis Kosman
"I Promised Their Mothers" ....Sung by Maestro Gallo
"Up in the Elevated Railway" ...Sung and danced by Lisette, Clyde,
    Volodya, Hattie, Shoe Shine Boy,
    Newspaper Boy, the Singing Ensemble
"In Paris and in Love" ....Sung by Clyde and Lisette
"You've Got to Be a Little Crazy" ....Sung by Lotta Leslie,
    Nellie, Mike, Bruce

"When I Am Free to Love" ....Sung by Lisette
Pas de Deux ....Danced by Lisette and Volodya
"Out of the Way" and "Roll Out the Hose,
 Boys" ....Sung by Members of the Singing Ensemble
Finale ....Entire Company

ACT II

"My Heart Won't Say Goodbye" ......Sung by Clyde, Lisette, the
 Singing Ensemble
"We're All in the Same Boat" ....Sung and danced by the
 Entire Company
Bacchanale ....Danced by the French Ballet Company
 Dionysius ....Alexandre Kalioujny
 The Wayward Nymph ....Jenny Workman
 Nymphs...........Meredith Baylis, Joan Bowman, Dorothy Scott,
 Beverly Simms, Diana Turner
 Satyrs ....Harry Asmus, Paul Olson, Edward
 Stinnett, William Weslow
 Messenger ....Beryl Towbin
 Attendants ....Maurice Hines and Gregory Hines
"Love Is the Funniest Thing" ......Sung by Lotta and the Maestro
"The Cardinal's Guard Are We" ....Sung by Lotta and Members
 of the Singing Ensemble
Grand Imperial Ballet ....Danced by the Ballet Company
 Lucifer ....Alexandre Kalioujny
 Hecate ....Jeanmaire
 Devils ....Harry Asmus, Paul Olson, Edward
 Stinnett, William Weslow
 Evil Spirits ....Katia Geleznova, Lynne Marcus,
 Dorothy Scott, Beverly Simms
 Bats ....Mary Hayward, Meredith Baylis, Joan Bowman,
 Julie Marlowe, Lila Popper, Diana Turner
 Dancing Batlets ....Nancy King, Ellen Matthews, Eva
 Rubinstein, Jenny Workman
 Batlets ....Mickey Gunnersen, Rhoda Kerns, Beryl Towbin
 Attendants ....Maurice and Gregory Hines
Finale ....Entire Company

THE GOLDEN APPLE

(95 performances *)
(Continued)

Musical in two acts written by John Latouche; music composed by
Jerome Moross. Produced by the Phoenix Theatre at the Phoenix
Theatre, March 11, 1954. After forty-eight performances at the Phoe-
nix Theatre (through April 18) it moved to the Alvin Theatre on
April 20.

Cast of characters—

Helen ....Kaye Ballard
Lovey Mars ....Bibi Osterwald
Mrs. Juniper ....Geraldine Viti
Miss Minerva Oliver ....Portia Nelson
Mother Hare ....Nola Day
Penelope ....Priscilla Gillette
Menelaus ....Dean Michener

* Includes off-Broadway performances.

The Heroes:
Captain Mars ....Frank Seabolt
Ajax ....Marten Sameth
Agamemnon ....Crandall Diehl
Nestor ....Maurice Edwards
Bluey ....Murray Gitlin
Thirsty ....Don Redlich
Silas ....Peter De Maio
Homer ....Barton Maumaw
Diomede ....Robert Flavelle
Achilles ....Julian Patrick
Patroclus ....Larry Chelsi
Doe MacCahan ....Gary Gordon
Ulysses ....Stephen Douglass
Theron ....David Hooks
Mayor Juniper ....Jerry Stiller
Paris ....Jonathan Lucas
Hector Charybdis ....Jack Whiting
     The Local Girls: Sara Bettis, Dorothy Etheridge, Nelle Fisher,
Dee Harless, Janet Hayes, Lois McCauley, Ann Needham, Joli Roberts, Jere Stevens, Tao Strong, Helen Ahola.
     The Local Boys: Santo Anselmo, Bob Gay, Charles Post, Arthur
Schoep.
     The action takes place in the State of Washington between 1900
and 1910.
     Staged by Norman Lloyd; choreography by Hanya Holm; musical
director, Hugh Ross; orchestral arrangements by Jerome Moross and
Hershey Key; settings by William and Jean Eckart; costumes by
Alvin Colt; lighting by Klaus Holm; production stage manager, Robert Woods; company stage manager, Thelma Chandler.

Musical sequences—

ACT I

"Nothing Ever Happens in Angel's Roost" ......Helen, Lovey Mars, Mrs. Juniper, Miss Minerva
Mother Hare's Séance
"My Love Is on the Way" ....Penelope
The Heroes Come Home ....Entire Company
"It Was a Glad Adventure" ....Ulysses and the Heroes
"Come Along, Boys" ....The Heroes and the Ensemble
"It's the Going Home Together" ....Ulysses and Penelope
Mother Hare's Prophecy
"Helen Is Always Willing" ....The Heroes
The Church Social ....The Heroes and the Ensemble
"Introducin' Mr. Paris" ....Paris and the Ensemble
The Judgment of Paris ....Lovey Mars, Mrs. Juniper, Miss Minerva, Mother Hare, Paris
"Lazy Afternoon" ....Helen and Paris
The Departure for Rhododendron ....Entire Company

ACT II

"My Picture in the Papers" ....Helen, Paris, Male Ensemble
The Taking of Rhododendron ....Ulysses, Hector, Paris
Hector's Song
"When We Were Young" ....Penelope
"Store-bought Suit" ....Ulysses
Calypso ....Mrs. Juniper
Scylla and Charybdis ....Menelaus and Hector
"By Goona-Goona Lagoon" ....Lovey Mars
"Doomed, Doomed, Doomed" ....Miss Minerva
"Circe, Circe" ....Circe, Mother Hare, the Ensemble
Ulysses' Soliloquy
The Sewing Bee ....Penelope, Helen, Miss Minerva, Mrs. Juniper, Lovey Mars, the Suitors, Ulysses
"We've Just Begun" ....Ulysses and Penelope

See page 255.

KING OF HEARTS

(69 performances)
(Continued)

Comedy in three acts by Jean Kerr and Eleanor Brooke. Produced by Elaine Perry at the Lyceum Theatre, April 1, 1954.

Cast of characters—

Dunreath Henry	Cloris Leachman
Larry Larkin	Donald Cook
Jeniella	Hilda Haynes
Mike	John Drew Devereaux
Francis X. Dignan	Jackie Cooper
Joe Wickes	David Lewis
Norman Taylor	Rex Thompson
Mr. Hobart	Carl Low
Billy	Darryl Richard
Happy	Patchwork Peggy
Policeman	William Sharon

The action takes place in Larry Larkin's studio in New York City at the present time. Act I.—January, late afternoon. Act II.—Several weeks later, midafternoon. Act III.—Eight o'clock that evening.

Staged by Walter F. Kerr; setting and lighting by Frederick Fox; production stage manager, Ben Kranz.

A satiric farce treating of an egomaniac cartoonist who regards his comic strips as cosmic profundities and himself as an omniscient Adonis. The play makes mincemeat of him through a series of scenes involving interviewers, assistants, syndicate chiefs, the small boy he adopts, and his secretary, who is also—but not at the final curtain—his fiancée.

ANNIVERSARY WALTZ

(62 performances)
(Continued)

Comedy in three acts by Jerome Chodorov and Joseph Fields. Produced by Joseph M. Hyman and Bernard Hart at the Broadhurst Theatre, April 7, 1954.

Cast of characters—

Millie	Pauline Myers
Okkie Walters	Warren Berlinger
Alice Walters	Kitty Carlisle
Debbie Walters	Mary Lee Dearring
Bud Walters	Macdonald Carey
Chris Steelman	Andrew Duggan
Janice Revere	Jean Carson
Harry	Don Grusso
Sam	Donald Hylan
Mr. Gans	Howard Smith
Mrs. Gans	Phyllis Povah
Handyman	Terry Little

The action takes place in the living room of the Walters' apartment in New York City at the present time. Act I.—Scene 1—About seven o'clock on a Spring evening. Scene 2—Four hours later. Act II.—Scene 1—The following morning. Scene 2—That evening. Act III.—Scene 1—A few minutes later. Scene 2—A week later. Staged by Moss Hart; setting and lighting by Frederick Fox; costumes by Robert Mackintosh; production stage manager, Donald Hershey; stage manager, Terry Little.

Hack domestic comedy: at a party celebrating his fifteenth wedding anniversary, the husband, after too many highballs, lets slip that he and his wife had lived together before marriage. Just when he has his horrified in-laws pacified, his teen-age children start acting up, one of them Telling All on TV. The irate husband walks out on his wife, then comes home to a wife irate enough to walk out on him, only she discovers she is going to have a baby.

BY THE BEAUTIFUL SEA

(61 performances)
(Continued)

Musical comedy in two acts; book by Herbert and Dorothy Fields; music by Arthur Schwartz; lyrics by Dorothy Fields. Produced by Robert Fryer and Lawrence Carr at the Majestic Theatre, April 8, 1954.

Cast of characters—

Quartet ....John Dennis, Reid Shelton, Ray Hyson, Larry Laurence
Acrobats ....Ray Kirchner, Rex Cooper
Cora Belmont ....Mary Harmon
Molly Belmont ....Cindy Robbins
Lillian Belmont ....Gloria Smith
Ruby Monk .... Mae Barnes
Mrs. Koch ....Edith True Case
Carl Gibson ....Cameron Prud'Homme
Lottie Gibson ....Shirley Booth
Half-Note ....Robert Jennings
Diabolo ....Thomas Gleason
Baby Betsy Busch ....Carol Leigh
Mickey Powers ....Richard France
Dennis Emery ....Wilbur Evans
Flora Busch ....Anne Francine
Willie Slater ....Warde Donovan
Lenny ....Larry Howard
Sidney ....Eddie Roll
Mr. Curtis ....Paul Reed
Burt Mayer ....Larry Laurence
Viola ....Gaby Monet
Dancers: Cathryn Damon, Dorothy Donau, Lillian Donau, Pat Ferrier, Sigyn, Mona Tritsch, Rex Cooper, Bob Haddad, Larry Howard, Ray Kirchner, Victor Reilly, Eddie Roll, Arthur Partington.
Singers: Suzanne Easter, Lola Fisher, Colleen O'Connor, Pat Roe, Jean Sincere, Libi Staiger, John Dennis, Warde Donovan, Thomas Gleason, Ray Hyson, Franklin Kennedy, Larry Laurence, George Lenz, Reid Shelton.
The action takes place in Coney Island during the early 1900's.
Staged by Marshall Jamison; choreography by Helen Tamiris; setting and lighting by Jo Mielziner; costumes by Irene Sharaff; musical

Mae Barnes, Robert
Jennings, Shirley Booth
and Wilbur Evans in
"By the Beautiful Sea"

direction by Jay Blackton; orchestrations by Robert Russell Bennett; production associate, Simon P. Herman; production stage manager, Samuel Liff; stage manager, Len Bedsow.

Musical numbers—

ACT I

"Mona from Arizona" ......John Dennis, Reid Shelton, Ray Hyson,
Larry Laurence
"The Sea Song" ....Shirley Booth, Boarders, Neighbors
"Old Enough to Love" ....Richard France
"Coney Island Boat" ......Shirley Booth, Robert Jennings, Visitors
"Alone Too Long" ....Wilbur Evans
"Happy Habit" ....Mae Barnes
"Good Time Charlie" ......Richard France, Larry Howard, Eddie
Roll, Mary Harmon, Cindy Robbins, Gloria Smith
"I'd Rather Wake Up by Myself" ....Shirley Booth
"Hooray for George the Third" .....Thomas Gleason, Libi Staiger,
Visitors

ACT II

"Hang Up" ....Mae Barnes, Boarders, Neighbors
"More Love Than Your Love" ....Wilbur Evans
"Lottie Gibson Specialty" ....Shirley Booth
"Throw the Anchor Away" .....Larry Laurence, Arthur Partington,
Mary Harmon
Finale ....Entire Company

THE MAGIC AND THE LOSS

(27 performances)

Play in three acts by Julian Funt. Produced by Alexander H. Cohen and Ralph Alswang at the Booth Theatre, April 9, 1954.

Cast of characters—

Nicki Wilson	Charles Taylor
Al Massio	Danny Dennis
Grace Wilson	Uta Hagen
Anita Harmon	Edith Meiser
Larry Graves	Lee Bowman
George Wilson	Robert Preston

The action takes place in the living room of Grace Wilson's apartment near Washington Square, New York City. Act I.—Scene 1—Late afternoon. Scene 2—The same evening. Act II.—Scene 1—

Early morning, several days later.   Scene 2—That afternoon.   Act III.—Afternoon, the next day.
Staged by Michael Gordon; setting by Ralph Alswang; clothes by Jocelyn; stage manager, John Barry Ryan.

See page 278.

(Closed May 1, 1954)

SHOW BOAT

(15 performances)

Musical comedy in two acts, based on the novel by Edna Ferber; music by Jerome Kern; book and lyrics by Oscar Hammerstein II. Revived by the New York City Light Opera Company at the New York City Center of Music and Drama, May 5, 1954.

Cast of characters—

Windy McLain	Arthur Newman
Steve	Robert Gallagher
Pete	Boris Aplon
Queenie	Helen Phillips
Parthy Ann Hawks	Marjorie Gateson
Captain Andy	Burl Ives
Ellie	Diana Drake
Frank	Donn Driver
Rubberface	Thomas R. Powell
Julie	Helena Bliss
Gaylord Ravenal	Robert Rounseville
Vallon	Lawrence Haynes
Magnolia	Laurel Hurley
Joe	Lawrence Winters
Backwoodsman	Arthur Newman
Jeb	Lawrence Haynes
Barker	Thomas R. Powell
Fatima	Ann Barry
Second Barker	Charles Kuestner
Sport	Roland Miles
Strong Woman	Meri Miller
Landlady	Sara Floyd
Ethel	Gloria Wynder
Jake	Milton Lyon
Jim	Boris Aplon
Man with Guitar	Charles Kuestner
Doorman at Trocadero	Bill Smith
Mother Superior	Ellen Gleason
Nun	Barbara Ford
Kim (as a child)	Adele Newton
Drunk	Charles Kuestner
Lottie	Marilyn Bladd
Dolly	Dorothy Mirr
Sally	Gloria Sacks
Old Lady on Levee	Sara Floyd
Kim (in her twenties)	Greta Thormsen

Singing Ensemble: Benjamin Bajorek, Marilyn Bladd, Adelaide Boatner, Eugene S. Brice, Doryce Brown, Walter P. Brown, Joseph E. Crawford, Dawin Emanuel, Rina Falcone, John Fleming, Barbara Ford, Mareda Gaither, Ellen Gleason, Russell Goodwin, Louise Hawthorne, Ida Frances Johnson, Charles Kuestner, Sheila Mathews, James Martindale, William McDaniel, Roland Miles, Dorothy Mirr, John Neilsen, Benjamin Plotkin, Madeline Porter, William W. Reynolds, Gloria Sacks, Christine Spencer, William Starling, Joseph Tanner, Frederick L. Thomas, Greta Thormsen, DeLoyd Tibbs, Rodester Timmons, Clyde S. Turner, Rose Virga, Gloria Wynder.

Congress of Beauties: Joanne Budill, DeAnn Mears, Peg Shirley, Barbara Sohmers.

Children: Ginger Brooks, Georgianna Catal, Claudia Crawford, Dale Dennard, Leonard Grinnage, Joan Nickel, Bonnie Sawyer.

Staged by William Hammerstein; conductor, Julius Rudel; settings by Howard Bay; costumes by John Boyt; lighting by Jean Rosenthal; assistant to director, Michael Shurtleff; production stage manager, Lucia Victor; stage manager, Hans Sondheimer.

Show Boat was first produced December 27, 1927, by Florenz Ziegfeld at the Ziegfeld Theatre for 572 performances.

(Closed May 16, 1954)

THE SEA GULL

(24 performances)
(Continued)

Play in two acts by Anton Chekhov, adapted by Mira Rostova, Kevin McCarthy, and Montgomery Clift. Produced by the Phoenix Theatre at the Phoenix Theatre, May 11, 1954.

Cast of characters—

Madame Irina Arkadina ....Judith Evelyn
Constantin Treplev, Her Son ....Montgomery Clift
Peter Sorin, Her Brother ....Sam Jaffe
Nina Zarechnaya ....Mira Rostova
Shamrayev, Manager of Sorin's Estate ....Will Geer
Paulina, His Wife ....June Walker
Masha, Their Daughter ....Maureen Stapleton
Boris Trigorin, a Writer ....Kevin McCarthy
Dr. Dorn, a Physician ....George Voskovec
Medvedenko, a School Teacher ....John Fiedler
Yakov, a Laborer ....Karl Light
Cook ....Lou Polan
Housemaid ....Sarah Marshall

The action takes place on the country estate of Peter Sorin in Southern Russia. Act I.—Scene 1—A part of the park; evening, 1895. Scene 2—The same; noon, a week later. Act II.—Scene 1—The dining room in Sorin's house; noon, several days later. Scene 2—The same; evening, two years later.

Staged by Norris Houghton; settings by Duane McKinney; costumes by Alvin Colt; lighting by Klaus Holm; music arranged by Max Marlin; production stage manager, Robert Woods; company stage manager, John Cornell.

THE PAJAMA GAME

(21 performances)
(Continued)

Musical comedy in two acts, based on the novel *7½ Cents* by Richard Bissell; book by George Abbott and Richard Bissell; music and lyrics by Richard Adler and Jerry Ross. Produced by Frederick Brisson, Robert E. Griffith, and Harold S. Prince at the St. James Theatre, May 13, 1954.

Cast of characters—

Hines	Eddie Foy, Jr.
Prez	Stanley Prager
Joe	Ralph Farnworth
Hasler	Ralph Dunn
Gladys	Carol Haney
Sid Sorokin	John Raitt
Mabel	Reta Shaw
1st Helper	Jack Drummond
2nd Helper	Buzz Miller
Charlie	Ralph Chambers
Babe Williams	Janis Paige
Mae	Thelma Pelish
Brenda	Marion Colby
Poopsie	Rae Allen
Salesman	Jack Waldron
Eddie	Jim Hutchison
Pop	William David
Worker	Peter Gennaro

Dancers: Carmen Alvarez, Marilyn Gennaro, Lida Koehring, Shirley MacLaine, Marsha Reynolds, Ann Wallace, Robert Evans, Eric Kristen, Jim Hutchison, Dale Moreda, Augustin Rodriguez, Ben Vargas.

Singers: Rae Allen, Sara Dillon, Mara Landi, Virginia Martin, Mary Roche, Mary Stanton, Rudy Adamo, Bob Dixon, Jack Drummond, Ralph Farnworth, John Ford, Gordon Woodburn.

The action takes place in a small town in the Middle West at the present time.

Staged by George Abbott and Jerome Robbins; scenery and costumes by Lemuel Ayers; choreography by Bob Fosse; musical director, Hal Hastings; orchestrations by Don Walker; dance music arrangements by Roger Adams; stage manager, Jean Barrere.

Musical numbers—

ACT I

"The Pajama Game"	Eddie Foy, Jr.
"Racing with the Clock"	Girls and Boys
"A New Town Is a Blue Town"	John Raitt
"I'm Not at All in Love"	Janis Paige and Girls
"I'll Never Be Jealous Again"	Eddie Foy, Jr., and Reta Shaw
"Hey There"	John Raitt
"Her Is"	Stanley Prager and Carol Haney
"Sleep-Tite"	Janis Paige and Boys and Girls
"Once a Year Day"	Sung by John Raitt, Janis Paige, and Company
	Danced by Carol Haney, Buzz Miller, Peter Gennaro
"Small Talk"	John Raitt and Janis Paige
"There Once Was a Man"	John Raitt and Janis Paige

ACT II

"Steam Heat"	Carol Haney, Buzz Miller, Peter Gennaro
"The World Around Us"	John Raitt and Janis Paige
"Think of the Time I Save"	Eddie Foy, Jr., and Girls
"Hernando's Hideaway"	Carol Haney, John Raitt, and Company
"Jealousy Ballet"	Eddie Foy, Jr, Carol Haney, Reta Shaw, and Boys
"7½ Cents"	Janis Paige, Stanley Prager, and Girls and Boys

FLEDERMAUS

(15 performances)

Operetta in three acts; music by Johann Strauss; libretto by C. Haffner and Richard Genee; English book and lyrics by Ruth and Thomas Martin. Produced by the New York City Light Opera Company at the New York City Center of Music and Drama, May 19, 1954.

Cast of characters—

Alfredo, an operatic tenor ....Lloyd Thomas Leech
          Alternate: Harold R. Brown
Adele, chambermaid ....Adelaide Bishop
Rosalinda, Eisenstein's wife ....Gloria Lind
          Alternate: Guen Omeron
Gabriel von Eisenstein, a banker ....Jack Russell
          Alternate: Lloyd Thomas Leach
Blind, Eisenstein's lawyer ....Carl Nicholas
Dr. Falke, a friend of the Eisensteins' ....John Tyers
Frank, prison warden ....Stanley Carlson
Sally, Adele's sister, a ballet dancer ....Lidija Franklin
Prince Orlofsky, a very wealthy Russian Prince .....Donald Gramm
Ivan, servant to Orlofsky ....Thomas R. Powell
Boris, a dancer ....Robert Pagent
Frosch, a jailer ....Colee Worth
     Servants: Stanley Bakis, Hill Eller, Alan James, Don Ratka, James Spicer, George Tucker.
     Guests: Marilyn Bladd, Rina Falcone, Barbara Ford, Ellen Gleason, Sheila Mathews, Dorothy Mirr, Gloria Sacks, Greta Thormsen, Rose Virga, Benjamin Bajorek, Dawin Emanuel, Russell Goodwin, Charles Kuestner, James Martindale, Roland Miles, Benjamin Plotkin, William W. Reynolds, Joseph Tanner.
     Staged by Glenn Jordan; conductor, Thomas Martin; choreography by Robert Pagent; costumes by John Boyt; lighting by Jean Rosenthal; production assistant, Michael Shurtleff; production stage manager, Lucia Victor; stage manager, Hans Sondheimer.

(Closed May 30, 1954)

OFF BROADWAY

By Garrison P. Sherwood

It can certainly be said that the Off Broadway theatre has gone this year from the "little theatre" class to big business. There were more of them than you could shake a critic at. Indeed, some Off Broadway went ON Broadway. The added importance of the Off Broadway stage derives from two impulses. Theatregoers want to see plays that don't make such a hole in their budgets that they have to wait a month or so between shows. Another factor is that every actor likes to act. For many, indeed for most of them, the opportunity comes pretty seldom. There are all kinds of actors in Off Broadway productions—amateur, semiprofessional, and professional, Equity card-holders. Some of the acting—let's face it—is pretty awful. Some of it is so good that a Broadway engagement follows immediately. This is also true of the productions; and this is the real incentive.

This has been Off Broadway's best year. The new Phoenix Theatre (see "The Season in New York") at 12th Street and Second Avenue is at least geographically one of the group. That harsh, brutal play "End as a Man" with its vivid acting started as an Off Broadway production at the Theatre de Lys.

This same Theatre de Lys was host to a number of productions during the year. It began, early in June, with a revival of Simon Gantillon's "Maya," first done in New York in 1928. Although the cast was headed by Helen Craig, I am afraid that "Maya" will have to wait for at least another revival before coming into its own. Percy MacKaye's "The Scarecrow" was next, with Patricia Neal, Eli Wallach, and Douglas Watson giving buoyant and shining performances in this romantic, imaginative play. Patricia Neal remained to play Lady Teazle in what turned out to be a less than adequate revival of "The School for Scandal." "The Little Clay Cart" was the last of this series of four revivals presented by Terese Hayden. It was an excellent production of the kind of fanciful play that uptown theatres seldom offer. In October "The Knight of the Burning Pestle" took over the stage of the Theatre de Lys but briefly and not successfully, followed late in the month by "Moon in Capricorn" which also fell considerably short of success. A new play by Leslie

356

Josephine Hull in "The Solid Gold Cadillac"

Stevens entitled "Bullfight" with Hurd Hatfield heading the cast came along in January. It got a rather mixed reaction but most audiences felt that it was an intelligent and stimulating, though not a perfectly finished bit of playwriting. The acting received high praise. The theatre's biggest hit was Brecht's "The Threepenny Opera" with a new book and lyrics by Marc Blitzstein, and the famous score by Kurt Weill. It was remarkably successful and proved to be just what the doctor ordered for an intimate theatre such as the de Lys. The performance had verve and charm.

The Circle-in-the-Square presented, in November, a new play by Victor Wolfson, "American Gothic" (based on the author's book "The Lonely Steeple"). It was a sensitive and well-thought-out work especially well played by Clarice Blackburn and Jason Robards, Jr. This held the boards until the Circle's production of Alfred Hayes' "The Girl on the Via Flaminia" opened in February. This, also, had first been a novel, and "Act of Love," a motion picture made from the novel, opened the same week as the dramatization. The situation portrayed in the play is not new but it is tenderly written with genuine insight, and the acting leaves little to be desired. As usual under José Quintero's direction, the play comes beautifully alive. In fact this may be said to be one of Mr. Quintero's best directorial jobs. It moves with spontaneity and sharpness. The play was a genuine hit, but late in March the Fire Commissioner condemned the Circle Theatre and the play had to close. Not for long, for on April 5th it reopened uptown at the 48th Street Theatre to attract further critical acclaim. One critic called it "one of the most thoughtful and disarming plays of the season."

The Equity Library did their usual fifteen productions which this year included "The Madwoman of Chaillot," "Scrapbook" (a selection of scenes from Wilde, Shakespeare, and Schnitzler), "Shadow and Substance," "Heavenly Express," "Goat Song," "Detective Story," "The Corn Is Green," "The Hasty Heart," "Kiss Me, Kate," "The Master Builder," "White Wings," "Montserrat," "Thunder on the Left," "Naked," and "Jacobowsky and the Colonel." Surely an impressive and varied list. "Kiss Me, Kate" was especially successful. And it must be said again that considering the budget and the physical handicaps of the Lenox Hill Playhouse the plays are remarkably well done.

At the Jan Hus Auditorium on East 74th Street Summer patrons could have seen "Ten Nights in a Barroom" and later Ken Parker's "There's Always a Murder." Early in October there was a production of "Everyman." Later in the same month there was an exciting revival of "Othello" with Earle Hyman giving an outstanding performance in the title role and William Thornton distinguishing himself as Iago. The run was extended well into the Spring as indeed it should have been. Later in the Spring the Jan Hus gave a very interesting and creditable production of "Hamlet" with Mr. Thornton as the Dane.

Then there was an organization known as the Green Room Studio that did a pedestrian production of Strindberg's "Miss Julia"; Current Stages gave an attractive performance of "Penguin," a new play by Norm Vein and in the fall put on an extremely good version of Moss Hart's "The Climate of Eden" which ran all year. During the Summer the American Lyric Theatre had its second season at the Provincetown; Paul Vincent Carroll's "The Wise Have Not Spoken" attracted attention in February at the Cherry Lane. "The World of Sholom Aleichem" reopened at the Barbizon-Plaza in September and received enough praise to carry it through the Winter. The Blackfriars Guild did two very effective productions, a comedy "Late Arrival," and a play about the martyrdom of Sir Thomas More called "Praise of Folly." At the Davenport Theatre there was a barely passable revival of Shaw's "The Simpleton of the Unexpected Isles" and an unsuccessful effort, "Cyanamide," by Burt Marnick. At the Greenwich Mews Theatre they revived "The Emperor's Clothes" and in February produced Sheldon Stark's "The Time of Storm," an unusually interesting drama which dealt with the Massachusetts witch hunt of 1693. It was said to have been written before "The Crucible." It had a splendid set designed by Robert Soule who also did the sets for Equity Library's "Heavenly Express" and "Kiss Me, Kate." For several years Mr. Soule has been doing such fine work that it is time someone gave him a chance ON Broadway.

There were other productions—many others—such as the Club Theatre's very poor one of Jean Cocteau's "The Infernal Machine"; "Haven in the Dark" and a group of one-act thrillers at Originals Only; and several attempts by the Artists' Theatre that never fulfilled their noble ambitions.

All in all it was a very busy season, and a decidedly effective one. Off Broadway really assumed importance on the theatrical map.

HIT TUNES OF THE SEASON

MORE LOVE THAN YOUR LOVE from *By the Beautiful Sea*

Music by Arthur Schwartz

Lyrics by Dorothy Fields

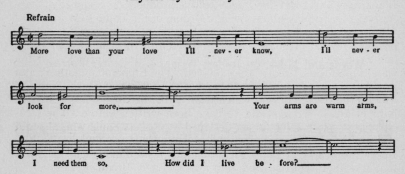

HEY THERE from *The Pajama Game*

Words and Music by Richard Adler and Jerry Ross

STRANGER IN PARADISE from *Kismet*

Words and Music by Robert Wright and George Forrest
Based on themes of A. Borodin

VARIETY'S TABULATION
OF FINANCIAL HITS AND FLOPS

HITS

Caine Mutiny Court-Martial
Confidential Clerk
Kind Sir
Oh, Men! Oh, Women!

Sabrina Fair
Solid Gold Cadillac
Tea and Sympathy
Teahouse of the August Moon

STATUS NOT YET DEFINITE

Anniversary Waltz
By the Beautiful Sea
Girl in Pink Tights
Golden Apple
John Murray Anderson's Alma-
nac

King of Hearts
Kismet
Ondine
Pajama Game
Remarkable Mr. Pennypacker

FAILURES

Anna Russell's Little Show
Burning Glass
Carnival in Flanders
Dead Pigeon
End as a Man
Escapade
Frogs of Spring
Gently Does It
Girl Can Tell
Girl on the Via Flaminia
His and Hers
Immoralist
In the Summer House
Ladies of the Corridor
Late Love

Little Hut
Lullaby
Mademoiselle Colombe
Magic and the Loss
Pin to See the Peepshow
Prescott Proposals
Red Rainbow
Sherlock Holmes
Sing Till Tomorrow
Starcross Story
Strong Are Lonely
Take a Giant Step
Trip to Bountiful
Winner

NON-COMMERCIAL

Charley's Aunt
Coriolanus
Cyrano de Bergerac
Fledermaus
Golden Apple
Madam, Will You Walk
Oklahoma!

Richard III
Ruth Draper
Sea Gull
Show Boat
Shrike
Spanish Theatre

CLOSED OUT OF TOWN

Daphne
Dear Charles
Flame-Out
Little Jesse James

Make Momma Happy
Mardi Gras
Paradise Question

Holdovers from 1952-53 Season, Since Clarified

HITS

Can-Can
Me and Juliet

Picnic
Wonderful Town

FAILURES

Crucible
Hazel Flagg

Misalliance
My 3 Angels

Note: *The Golden Apple* was produced by the Phoenix Theatre, but was subsequently transferred to Broadway for a regular run.

STATISTICAL SUMMARY

(LAST SEASON PLAYS WHICH ENDED RUNS AFTER JUNE 1, 1953)

Plays	Number Performances	
The Crucible	197	(Closed July 11, 1953)
Dial "M" for Murder	552	(Closed February 27, 1954)
Guys and Dolls	1,200	(Closed November 28, 1953)
Hazel Flagg	190	(Closed September 19, 1953)
The King and I	1,246	(Closed March 20, 1954)
Me and Juliet	358	(Closed April 3, 1954)
Misalliance	146	(Closed June 27, 1953)
My 3 Angels	344	(Closed January 2, 1954)
Picnic	477	(Closed April 10, 1954)
Porgy and Bess	305	(Closed November 28, 1953)
South Pacific	1,925	(Closed January 16, 1954)
Time Out for Ginger	248	(Closed June 27, 1953)
Wish You Were Here	598	(Closed November 28, 1953)

LONG RUNS ON BROADWAY

To June 1, 1954

(Plays marked with asterisk were still playing June 1, 1954)

Plays	Number Performances	Plays	Number Performances
Life with Father	3,224	Three Men on a Horse	835
Tobacco Road	3,182	Where's Charlie?	792
Abie's Irish Rose	2,327	The Ladder	789
Oklahoma!	2,248	State of the Union	765
South Pacific	1,925	The First Year	760
Harvey	1,775	Death of a Salesman	742
Born Yesterday	1,642	Sons o' Fun	742
The Voice of the Turtle	1,557	The Man Who Came to Dinner	739
Arsenic and Old Lace	1,444		
Hellzapoppin	1,404	Call Me Mister	734
Angel Street	1,295	High Button Shoes	727
Lightnin'	1,291	Finian's Rainbow	725
The King and I	1,246	Claudia	722
Guys and Dolls	1,200	The Gold Diggers	720
Mister Roberts	1,157	I Remember Mama	714
Annie Get Your Gun	1,147	Junior Miss	710
Pins and Needles	1,108	Seventh Heaven	704
Kiss Me, Kate	1,070	Peg o' My Heart	692
Anna Lucasta	957	The Children's Hour	691
Kiss and Tell	957	Dead End	687
The Moon Is Blue	924	The Lion and the Mouse	686
Carousel	890	Dear Ruth	683
Hats Off to Ice	889	East Is West	680
Follow the Girls	882	The Doughgirls	671
The Bat	867	Irene	670
My Sister Eileen	865	Boy Meets Girl	669
White Cargo	864	Blithe Spirit	657
Song of Norway	860	The Women	657
A Streetcar Named Desire	855	A Trip to Chinatown	657
You Can't Take It with You	837	Bloomer Girl	654
		Rain	648

Plays	*Number Performances*	*Plays*	*Number Performances*
Call Me Madam	644	Ziegfeld Follies	553
Janie	642	Floradora	553
The Green Pastures	640	Dial "M" for Murder	552
* The Seven Year Itch	637	Good News	551
The Fourposter	632	Let's Face It	547
Is Zat So?	618	Within the Law	541
The Happy Time	614	The Music Master	540
Separate Rooms	613	Pal Joey	540
Affairs of State	610	What a Life	538
Star and Garter	609	The Red Mill	531
The Student Prince	608	The Boomerang	522
Broadway	603	Rosalinda	521
Adonis	603	Chauve Souris	520
Street Scene	601	Blackbirds	518
Kiki	600	Sunny	517
Wish You Were Here	598	Victoria Regina	517
A Society Circus	596	* Wonderful Town	516
Blossom Time	592	The Vagabond King	511
The Two Mrs. Carrolls	585	The New Moon	509
Detective Story	581	Shuffle Along	504
Brigadoon	581	Up in Central Park	504
Brother Rat	577	Carmen Jones	503
Show Boat	572	The Member of the Wedding	501
The Show-Off	571	Personal Appearance	501
Sally	570	Panama Hattie	501
One Touch of Venus	567	Bird in Hand	500
Happy Birthday	564	Sailor, Beware!	500
* The Fifth Season	563	Room Service	500
The Glass Menagerie	561	Tomorrow the World	500
Rose Marie	557		
Strictly Dishonorable	557		

NEW YORK DRAMA CRITICS CIRCLE AWARDS

At their annual Spring meeting, the New York Drama Critics Circle chose John Patrick's *The Teahouse of the August Moon* as the best new American play of the season, with Herman Wouk's *The Caine Mutiny Court-Martial* as runner-up. As the best foreign play the Circle chose Jean Giraudoux's *Ondine* (adapted by Maurice Valency), and as the best musical, *The Golden Apple*.

Circle awards have been—

1935-36—Winterset, by Maxwell Anderson
1936-37—High Tor, by Maxwell Anderson
1937-38—Of Mice and Men, by John Steinbeck
1938-39—No award.
1939-40—The Time of Your Life, by William Saroyan
1940-41—Watch on the Rhine, by Lillian Hellman
1941-42—No award.
1942-43—The Patriots, by Sidney Kingsley
1943-44—No award.
1944-45—The Glass Menagerie, by Tennessee Williams
1945-46—No award.
1946-47—All My Sons, by Arthur Miller
1947-48—A Streetcar Named Desire, by Tennessee Williams
1948-49—Death of a Salesman, by Arthur Miller
1949-50—The Member of the Wedding, by Carson McCullers
1950-51—Darkness at Noon, by Sidney Kingsley
1951-52—I Am a Camera, by John van Druten
1952-53—Picnic, by William Inge
1953-54—The Teahouse of the August Moon, by John Patrick

PULITZER PRIZE WINNERS

For the fifth time, in the nineteen years that both awards have been made, the Pulitzer Prize went to the same play as the Critics Circle Award. Besides *The Teahouse of the August Moon*, the double award has gone to *The Time of Your Life, A Streetcar Named Desire, Death of a Salesman* and *Picnic*.

Pulitzer awards have been—

1917-18—Why Marry?, by Jesse Lynch Williams
1918-19—No award.
1919-20—Beyond the Horizon, by Eugene O'Neill
1920-21—Miss Lulu Bett, by Zona Gale
1921-22—Anna Christie, by Eugene O'Neill
1922-23—Icebound, by Owen Davis
1923-24—Hell-bent fer Heaven, by Hatcher Hughes
1924-25—They Knew What They Wanted, by Sidney Howard
1925-26—Craig's Wife, by George Kelly
1926-27—In Abraham's Bosom, by Paul Green
1927-28—Strange Interlude, by Eugene O'Neill
1928-29—Street Scene, by Elmer Rice
1929-30—The Green Pastures, by Marc Connelly
1930-31—Alison's House, by Susan Glaspell
1931-32—Of Thee I Sing, by George S. Kaufman, Morrie Ryskind, Ira and George Gershwin
1932-33—Both Your Houses, by Maxwell Anderson
1933-34—Men in White, by Sidney Kingsley
1934-35—The Old Maid, by Zoë Akins
1935-36—Idiot's Delight, by Robert E. Sherwood
1936-37—You Can't Take It with You, by Moss Hart and George S. Kaufman
1937-38—Our Town, by Thornton Wilder
1938-39—Abe Lincoln in Illinois, by Robert E. Sherwood
1939-40—The Time of Your Life, by William Saroyan
1940-41—There Shall Be No Night, by Robert E. Sherwood
1941-42—No award.
1942-43—The Skin of Our Teeth, by Thornton Wilder
1943-44—No award.
1944-45—Harvey, by Mary Coyle Chase

1945-46—State of the Union, by Howard Lindsay and Russel
          Crouse
1946-47—No award.
1947-48—A Streetcar Named Desire, by Tennessee Williams
1948-49—Death of a Salesman, by Arthur Miller
1949-50—South Pacific, by Richard Rodgers, Oscar Hammer-
          stein II and Joshua Logan
1950-51—No award.
1951-52—The Shrike, by Joseph Kramm
1952-53—Picnic, by William Inge
1953-54—The Teahouse of the August Moon, by John Patrick

BOOKS ON THE THEATRE

1953-1954

Altman, George, et al. *Theater Pictorial*. University of California Press. $10.00.
A history of world theatre as recorded in drawings, paintings, engravings, and photographs.

Anouilh, Jean. *Mademoiselle Colombe*. Adapted by Louis Kronenberger. Coward-McCann. $3.00.

Aristophanes. *Lysistrata*. Translated by Dudley Fitts. Harcourt, Brace. $3.50.

Beaton, Cecil, and Tynan, Kenneth. *Persona Grata*. Putnam. $5.00.

Beerbohm, Sir Max. *Around Theatres*. Simon & Schuster. $6.00.
Long out of print, this contains the cream of Max's drama criticism.

Boughner, Daniel C. *The Braggart in Renaissance Comedy*. University of Minnesota Press. $5.00.

Bowers, Faubion. *The Dance in India*. Columbia University Press. $4.00.
With numerous illustrations.

Bowles, Jane. *In the Summer House*. Random House. $2.75.

Cassidy, Claudia. *Europe—on the Aisle*. Random House. $3.50.
A European vacation journey with much reference to theatre and music.

Chapman, John (Editor). *Theatre '53*. Random House. $5.00.

Chute, Marchette. *Ben Jonson of Westminster*. Dutton. $5.00.
A biography in the manner of the author's biographies of Chaucer and Shakespeare.

Dekker, Thomas. (Edited by Fredson Bowers.) *The Dramatic Works of Thomas Dekker*, Vol. I. Cambridge University Press. $7.00.
A much-needed definitive text.

Burl Ives in "Show Boat"

Eliot, T. S. *The Complete Poems and Plays of T. S. Eliot.* Harcourt, Brace. $6.00.

—— *The Confidential Clerk.* Harcourt, Brace. $3.00.

Engel, Edwin A. *The Haunted Heroes of Eugene O'Neill.* Harvard University Press. $4.75.
A comprehensive study of O'Neill.

Gassner, John. *The Theatre in Our Times.* Crown. $5.00.
A many-sided survey of men and movements from Ibsen to the present.

Giraudoux, Jean. *Ondine.* Adapted by Maurice Valency. Random House. $2.75.

Greene, Graham. *The Living Room.* Viking. $2.75.
Greene's London stage hit.

Hatcher, Harlan (Editor). *A Modern Repertory.* Harcourt, Brace. $2.75.
A small but varied anthology of modern plays.

Hodges, C. Walter. *The Globe Restored.* Coward-McCann. $7.50.
The physical facts about the Elizabethan stage.

Kronenberger, Louis (Editor). *Best Plays of 1952-1953.* Dodd, Mead. $5.00.

—— *Cavalcade of Comedy.* Simon & Schuster. $7.50.
21 Plays from Ben Jonson to John van Druten.

—— *G.B.S.: A Critical Survey.* World. $6.00.

Laurie, Joe, Jr. *Vaudeville: From the Honky Tonks to the Palace.* Holt. $5.00.

Lucas, F. L. *Greek Drama for Everyman.* Macmillan. $4.00.

Mayorga, Margaret (Editor). *Best Short Plays of 1953-1954.* Dodd, Mead. $3.00.

Morris, Lloyd. *Curtain Time.* Random House. $5.00.
A history of the New York theatre.

Nathan, George Jean. *The Theatre in the Fifties.* Knopf. $4.50.

Nicoll, Allardyce (Editor). *Shakespeare Survey 7.* Cambridge University Press. $3.75.
The latest issue in an annual series.

O'Brien, Liam. *The Remarkable Mr. Pennypacker.* Random House. $2.75.

Pedicord, Harry William. *The Theatrical Public in the Time of Garrick.* Columbia University Press. $4.00.

Pirandello, Luigi. *Right You Are.* Columbia University Press. $4.00.
A stage version, with introduction and notes by Eric Bentley.

Prideaux, Tom (Editor). *World Theatre in Pictures.* Greenberg. $7.50.
A comprehensive pictorial stage history.

Reese, M. M. *Shakespeare: his World and his Work.* St. Martin's Press. $6.75.

Restoration Plays. Modern Library. $1.45.

Richman, Robert. *The Arts at Mid-Century*. Horizon Press. $5.00.
Contains articles on the theatre in the United States, England, France and Italy.

Shaw, Bernard. *Four Plays (Candida, Caesar and Cleopatra, Pygmalion, Heartbreak House)*. Modern Library. $1.45.

Sobel, Bernard. *Broadway Heartbeat*. Hermitage House. $3.50.
The memoirs of one of Broadway's best-known press agents.

Sophocles. *Oedipus the King*. Translated by David Grene. *Oedipus at Colonus*. Translated by Robert Fitzgerald. *Antigone*. Translated by Elizabeth Wyckoff. University of Chicago Press. $3.00.

Sothern, E. H. (Edited by Fairfax Downey.) *Julia Marlowe's Story*. Rinehart. $3.50.
Miss Marlowe's autobiography, as told to her husband: edited and published twenty years after Sothern's death and three years after Julia Marlowe's.

Stephens, Frances (Editor). *Theatre World Annual*. Macmillan. $3.75.
An illustrated record of London's 1952-1953 season.

Taylor, Deems. *Some Enchanted Evenings: the Story of Rodgers and Hammerstein*. Harper. $3.95.

Taylor, Samuel. *Sabrina Fair: or a Woman of the World*. Random House. $2.75.

Thomas, Dylan. *Under Milk Wood*. New Directions. $3.00.

Whiting, Frank M. *An Introduction to the Theatre*. Harper. $6.00.
All aspects, from playwriting to make-up.

Williams, Raymond. *Drama from Ibsen to Eliot*. Oxford University Press. $2.90.

Williams, Tennessee. *27 Wagons Full of Cotton, and Other One-Act Plays*. New Directions. $3.50.

Wilson, Edmund. *Five Plays*. Farrar, Straus & Young. $6.50.
Cyprian's Prayer; The Crime in the Whistler Room; This Room and This Gin and These Sandwiches; Beppo and Beth; The Little Blue Light.

Wilson, F. P.   *Marlowe and the Early Shakespeare*.   Oxford University Press. $2.00.

Wodehouse, P. G., and Bolton, Guy.   *Bring on the Girls*.   Simon & Schuster. $3.95.
The story of their "life in musical comedy."

Wouk, Herman.   *The Caine Mutiny Court-Martial*.   Doubleday. $2.75.

PREVIOUS VOLUMES OF BEST PLAYS

Plays chosen to represent the theatre seasons from 1899 to 1953 are as follows:

1899-1909

BARBARA FRIETCHIE, by Clyde Fitch. Life Publishing Co.
THE CLIMBERS, by Clyde Fitch. Macmillan.
If I WERE KING, by Justin Huntly McCarthy. Samuel French.
THE DARLING OF THE GODS, by David Belasco. Little, Brown.
THE COUNTY CHAIRMAN, by George Ade. Samuel French.
LEAH KLESCHNA, by C. M. S. McLellan. Samuel French.
THE SQUAW MAN, by Edwin Milton Royle.
THE GREAT DIVIDE, by William Vaughn Moody. Samuel French.
THE WITCHING HOUR, by Augustus Thomas. Samuel French.
THE MAN FROM HOME, by Booth Tarkington and Harry Leon Wilson. Samuel French.

1909-1919

THE EASIEST WAY, by Eugene Walter. G. W. Dillingham and Houghton Mifflin.
MRS. BUMPSTEAD-LEIGH, by Harry James Smith. Samuel French.
DISRAELI, by Louis N. Parker. Dodd, Mead.
ROMANCE, by Edward Sheldon. Macmillan.
SEVEN KEYS TO BALDPATE, by George M. Cohan. Published by Bobbs-Merrill as a novel by Earl Derr Biggers; as a play by Samuel French.
ON TRIAL, by Elmer Reizenstein. Samuel French.
THE UNCHASTENED WOMAN, by Louis Kaufman Anspacher. Harcourt, Brace and Howe.
GOOD GRACIOUS ANNABELLE, by Clare Kummer. Samuel French.
WHY MARRY?, by Jesse Lynch Williams. Scribner.
JOHN FERGUSON, by St. John Ervine. Macmillan.

1919-1920

ABRAHAM LINCOLN, by John Drinkwater. Houghton Mifflin.
CLARENCE, by Booth Tarkington. Samuel French.
BEYOND THE HORIZON, by Eugene G. O'Neill. Boni & Liveright.

DÉCLASSÉE, by Zoë Akins. Liveright, Inc.
THE FAMOUS MRS. FAIR, by James Forbes. Samuel French.
THE JEST, by Sem Benelli. (American adaptation by Edward Sheldon.)
JANE CLEGG, by St. John Ervine. Henry Holt.
MAMMA'S AFFAIR, by Rachel Barton Butler. Samuel French.
WEDDING BELLS, by Salisbury Field. Samuel French.
ADAM AND EVA, by George Middleton and Guy Bolton. Samuel French.

1920-1921

DEBURAU, adapted from the French of Sacha Guitry by H. Granville Barker. Putnam.
THE FIRST YEAR, by Frank Craven. Samuel French.
ENTER MADAME, by Gilda Varesi and Dolly Byrne. Putnam.
THE GREEN GODDESS, by William Archer. Knopf.
LILIOM, by Ferenc Molnar. Boni & Liveright.
MARY ROSE, by James M. Barrie. Scribner.
NICE PEOPLE, by Rachel Crothers. Scribner.
THE BAD MAN, by Porter Emerson Browne. Putnam.
THE EMPEROR JONES, by Eugene G. O'Neill. Boni & Liveright.
THE SKIN GAME, by John Galsworthy. Scribner.

1921-1922

ANNA CHRISTIE, by Eugene G. O'Neill. Boni & Liveright.
A BILL OF DIVORCEMENT, by Clemence Dane. Macmillan.
DULCY, by George S. Kaufman and Marc Connelly. Putnam.
HE WHO GETS SLAPPED, adapted from the Russian of Leonid Andreyev by Gregory Zilboorg. Brentano's.
SIX CYLINDER LOVE, by William Anthony McGuire.
THE HERO, by Gilbert Emery.
THE DOVER ROAD, by Alan Alexander Milne. Samuel French.
AMBUSH, by Arthur Richman.
THE CIRCLE, by William Somerset Maugham.
THE NEST, by Paul Geraldy and Grace George.

1922-1923

RAIN, by John Colton and Clemence Randolph. Liveright, Inc.
LOYALTIES, by John Galsworthy. Scribner.
ICEBOUND, by Owen Davis. Little, Brown.
YOU AND I, by Philip Barry. Brentano's.
THE FOOL, by Channing Pollock. Brentano's.

MERTON OF THE MOVIES, by George Kaufman and Marc Connelly, based on the novel of the same name by Harry Leon Wilson.

WHY NOT? by Jesse Lynch Williams. Walter H. Baker Co.

THE OLD SOAK, by Don Marquis. Doubleday, Page.

R.U.R., by Karel Capek. Translated by Paul Selver. Doubleday, Page.

MARY THE 3D, by Rachel Crothers. Brentano's.

1923-1924

THE SWAN, translated from the Hungarian of Ferenc Molnar by Melville Baker. Boni & Liveright.

OUTWARD BOUND, by Sutton Vane. Boni & Liveright.

THE SHOW-OFF, by George Kelly. Little, Brown.

THE CHANGELINGS, by Lee Wilson Dodd. Dutton.

CHICKEN FEED, by Guy Bolton. Samuel French.

SUN-UP, by Lula Vollmer. Brentano's.

BEGGAR ON HORSEBACK, by George Kaufman and Marc Connelly. Boni & Liveright.

TARNISH, by Gilbert Emery. Brentano's.

THE GOOSE HANGS HIGH, by Lewis Beach. Little, Brown.

HELL-BENT FER HEAVEN, by Hatcher Hughes. Harper.

1924-1925

WHAT PRICE GLORY? by Laurence Stallings and Maxwell Anderson. Harcourt, Brace.

THEY KNEW WHAT THEY WANTED, by Sidney Howard. Doubleday, Page.

DESIRE UNDER THE ELMS, by Eugene G. O'Neill. Boni & Liveright.

THE FIREBRAND, by Edwin Justus Mayer. Boni & Liveright.

DANCING MOTHERS, by Edgar Selwyn and Edmund Goulding.

MRS. PARTRIDGE PRESENTS, by Mary Kennedy and Ruth Warren. Samuel French.

THE FALL GUY, by James Gleason and George Abbott. Samuel French.

THE YOUNGEST, by Philip Barry. Samuel French.

MINICK, by Edna Ferber and George S. Kaufman. Doubleday, Page.

WILD BIRDS, by Dan Totheroh. Doubleday, Page.

1925-1926

CRAIG'S WIFE, by George Kelly. Little, Brown.
THE GREAT GOD BROWN, by Eugene G. O'Neill. Boni & Liveright.
THE GREEN HAT, by Michael Arlen.
THE DYBBUK, by S. Ansky, Henry G. Alsberg-Winifred Katzin translation. Boni & Liveright.
THE ENEMY, by Channing Pollock. Brentano's.
THE LAST OF MRS. CHEYNEY, by Frederick Lonsdale. Samuel French.
BRIDE OF THE LAMB, by William Hurlbut. Boni & Liveright.
THE WISDOM TOOTH, by Marc Connelly. George H. Doran.
THE BUTTER AND EGG MAN, by George Kaufman. Boni & Liveright.
YOUNG WOODLEY, by John van Druten. Simon & Schuster.

1926-1927

BROADWAY, by Philip Dunning and George Abbott. George H. Doran.
SATURDAY'S CHILDREN, by Maxwell Anderson. Longmans, Green.
CHICAGO, by Maurine Watkins. Knopf.
THE CONSTANT WIFE, by William Somerset Maugham. George H. Doran.
THE PLAY'S THE THING, by Ferenc Molnar and P. G. Wodehouse. Brentano's.
THE ROAD TO ROME, by Robert Emmet Sherwood. Scribner.
THE SILVER CORD, by Sidney Howard. Scribner.
THE CRADLE SONG, translated from the Spanish of G. Martinez Sierra by John Garrett Underhill. Dutton.
DAISY MAYME, by George Kelly. Little, Brown.
IN ABRAHAM'S BOSOM, by Paul Green. McBride.

1927-1928

STRANGE INTERLUDE, by Eugene G. O'Neill. Boni & Liveright.
THE ROYAL FAMILY, by Edna Ferber and George Kaufman. Doubleday, Doran.
BURLESQUE, by George Manker Watters and Arthur Hopkins. Doubleday, Doran.
COQUETTE, by George Abbott and Ann Bridgers. Longmans, Green.
BEHOLD THE BRIDEGROOM, by George Kelly. Little, Brown.
PORGY, by DuBose Heyward. Doubleday, Doran.
PARIS BOUND, by Philip Barry. Samuel French.
ESCAPE, by John Galsworthy. Scribner.

THE RACKET, by Bartlett Cormack. Samuel French.
THE PLOUGH AND THE STARS, by Sean O'Casey. Macmillan.

1928-1929

STREET SCENE, by Elmer Rice. Samuel French.
JOURNEY'S END, by R. C. Sherriff. Brentano's.
WINGS OVER EUROPE, by Robert Nichols and Maurice Browne. Covici-Friede.
HOLIDAY, by Philip Barry. Samuel French.
THE FRONT PAGE, by Ben Hecht and Charles MacArthur. Covici-Friede.
LET US BE GAY, by Rachel Crothers. Samuel French.
MACHINAL, by Sophie Treadwell.
LITTLE ACCIDENT, by Floyd Dell and Thomas Mitchell.
GYPSY, by Maxwell Anderson.
THE KINGDOM OF GOD, by G. Martinez Sierra; English version by Helen and Harley Granville-Barker. Dutton.

1929-1930

THE GREEN PASTURES, by Marc Connelly (adapted from "Ol' Man Adam and His Chillun," by Roark Bradford). Farrar & Rinehart.
THE CRIMINAL CODE, by Martin Flavin. Horace Liveright.
BERKELEY SQUARE, by John Balderston.
STRICTLY DISHONORABLE, by Preston Sturges. Horace Liveright.
THE FIRST MRS. FRASER, by St. John Ervine. Macmillan.
THE LAST MILE, by John Wexley. Samuel French.
JUNE MOON, by Ring W. Lardner and George S. Kaufman. Scribner.
MICHAEL AND MARY, by A. A. Milne. Chatto & Windus.
DEATH TAKES A HOLIDAY, by Walter Ferris (adapted from the Italian of Alberto Casella). Samuel French.
REBOUND, by Donald Ogden Stewart. Samuel French.

1930-1931

ELIZABETH THE QUEEN, by Maxwell Anderson. Longmans, Green.
TOMORROW AND TOMORROW, by Philip Barry. Samuel French.
ONCE IN A LIFETIME, by George S. Kaufman and Moss Hart. Farrar & Rinehart.
GREEN GROW THE LILACS, by Lynn Riggs. Samuel French.
AS HUSBANDS GO, by Rachel Crothers. Samuel French.

ALISON'S HOUSE, by Susan Glaspell. Samuel French.

FIVE-STAR FINAL, by Louis Weitzenkorn. Samuel French.

OVERTURE, by William Bolitho. Simon & Schuster.

THE BARRETTS OF WIMPOLE STREET, by Rudolf Besier. Little, Brown.

GRAND HOTEL, adapted from the German of Vicki Baum by W. A. Drake.

1931-1932

OF THEE I SING, by George S. Kaufman and Morrie Ryskind; music and lyrics by George and Ira Gershwin. Knopf.

MOURNING BECOMES ELECTRA, by Eugene G. O'Neill. Horace Liveright.

REUNION IN VIENNA, by Robert Emmet Sherwood. Scribner.

THE HOUSE OF CONNELLY, by Paul Green. Samuel French.

THE ANIMAL KINGDOM, by Philip Barry. Samuel French.

THE LEFT BANK, by Elmer Rice. Samuel French.

ANOTHER LANGUAGE, by Rose Franken. Samuel French.

BRIEF MOMENT, by S. N. Behrman. Farrar & Rinehart.

THE DEVIL PASSES, by Benn W. Levy. Martin Secker.

CYNARA, by H. M. Harwood and R. F. Gore-Browne. Samuel French.

1932-1933

BOTH YOUR HOUSES, by Maxwell Anderson. Samuel French.

DINNER AT EIGHT, by George S. Kaufman and Edna Ferber. Doubleday, Doran.

WHEN LADIES MEET, by Rachel Crothers. Samuel French.

DESIGN FOR LIVING, by Noel Coward. Doubleday, Doran.

BIOGRAPHY, by S. N. Behrman. Farrar & Rinehart.

ALIEN CORN, by Sidney Howard. Scribner.

THE LATE CHRISTOPHER BEAN, adapted from the French of René Fauchois by Sidney Howard. Samuel French.

WE, THE PEOPLE, by Elmer Rice. Coward-McCann.

PIGEONS AND PEOPLE, by George M. Cohan.

ONE SUNDAY AFTERNOON, by James Hagan. Samuel French.

1933-1934

MARY OF SCOTLAND, by Maxwell Anderson. Doubleday, Doran.

MEN IN WHITE, by Sidney Kingsley. Covici-Friede.

DODSWORTH, by Sinclair Lewis and Sidney Howard. Harcourt, Brace.

AH, WILDERNESS, by Eugene O'Neill. Random House.
THEY SHALL NOT DIE, by John Wexley. Knopf.
HER MASTER'S VOICE, by Clare Kummer. Samuel French.
NO MORE LADIES, by A. E. Thomas.
WEDNESDAY'S CHILD, by Leopold Atlas. Samuel French.
THE SHINING HOUR, by Keith Winter. Doubleday, Doran.
THE GREEN BAY TREE, by Mordaunt Shairp. Baker International
    Play Bureau.

1934-1935

THE CHILDREN'S HOUR, by Lillian Hellman. Knopf.
VALLEY FORGE, by Maxwell Anderson. Anderson House.
THE PETRIFIED FOREST, by Robert Sherwood. Scribner.
THE OLD MAID, by Zoë Akins. Appleton-Century.
ACCENT ON YOUTH, by Samson Raphaelson. Samuel French.
MERRILY WE ROLL ALONG, by George S. Kaufman and Moss Hart.
    Random House.
AWAKE AND SING, by Clifford Odets. Random House.
THE FARMER TAKES A WIFE, by Frank B. Elser and Marc Connelly.
LOST HORIZONS, by John Hayden.
THE DISTAFF SIDE, by John van Druten. Knopf.

1935-1936

WINTERSET, by Maxwell Anderson. Anderson House.
IDIOT'S DELIGHT, by Robert Emmet Sherwood. Scribner.
END OF SUMMER, by S. N. Behrman. Random House.
FIRST LADY, by Katharine Dayton and George S. Kaufman. Ran-
    dom House.
VICTORIA REGINA, by Laurence Housman. Samuel French.
BOY MEETS GIRL, by Bella and Samuel Spewack. Random House.
DEAD END, by Sidney Kingsley. Random House.
CALL IT A DAY, by Dodie Smith. Samuel French.
ETHAN FROME, by Owen Davis and Donald Davis. Scribner.
PRIDE AND PREJUDICE, by Helen Jerome. Doubleday, Doran.

1936-1937

HIGH TOR, by Maxwell Anderson. Anderson House.
YOU CAN'T TAKE IT WITH YOU, by Moss Hart and George S. Kauf-
    man. Farrar & Rinehart.
JOHNNY JOHNSON, by Paul Green. Samuel French.
DAUGHTERS OF ATREUS, by Robert Turney. Knopf.

STAGE DOOR, by Edna Ferber and George S. Kaufman.   Doubleday,
Doran.
THE WOMEN, by Clare Boothe.   Random House.
ST. HELENA, by R. C. Sherriff and Jeanne de Casalis.   Samuel
French.
YES, MY DARLING DAUGHTER, by Mark Reed.   Samuel French.
EXCURSION, by Victor Wolfson.   Random House.
TOVARICH, by Jacques Deval and Robert E. Sherwood.   Random
House.

1937-1938

OF MICE AND MEN, by John Steinbeck.   Covici-Friede.
OUR TOWN, by Thornton Wilder.   Coward-McCann.
SHADOW AND SUBSTANCE, by Paul Vincent Carroll.   Random House.
ON BORROWED TIME, by Paul Osborn.   Knopf.
THE STAR-WAGON, by Maxwell Anderson.   Anderson House.
SUSAN AND GOD, by Rachel Crothers.   Random House.
PROLOGUE TO GLORY, by E. P. Conkle.   Random House.
AMPHITRYON 38, by S. N. Behrman.   Random House.
GOLDEN BOY, by Clifford Odets.   Random House.
WHAT A LIFE, by Clifford Goldsmith.   Dramatists' Play Service.

1938-1939

ABE LINCOLN IN ILLINOIS, by Robert E. Sherwood.   Scribner.
THE LITTLE FOXES, by Lillian Hellman.   Random House.
ROCKET TO THE MOON, by Clifford Odets.   Random House.
THE AMERICAN WAY, by George S. Kaufman and Moss Hart.
Random House.
NO TIME FOR COMEDY, by S. N. Behrman.   Random House.
THE PHILADELPHIA STORY, by Philip Barry.   Coward-McCann.
THE WHITE STEED, by Paul Vincent Carroll.   Random House.
HERE COME THE CLOWNS, by Philip Barry.   Coward-McCann.
FAMILY PORTRAIT, by Lenore Coffee and William Joyce Cowen.
Random House.
KISS THE BOYS GOOD-BYE, by Clare Boothe.   Random House.

1939-1940

THERE SHALL BE NO NIGHT, by Robert E. Sherwood.   Scribner.
KEY LARGO, by Maxwell Anderson.   Anderson House.
THE WORLD WE MAKE, by Sidney Kingsley.
LIFE WITH FATHER, by Howard Lindsay and Russel Crouse.   Knopf.

THE MAN WHO CAME TO DINNER, by George S. Kaufman and Moss Hart. Random House.

THE MALE ANIMAL, by James Thurber and Elliott Nugent. Random House, New York, and MacMillan Co., Canada.

THE TIME OF YOUR LIFE, by William Saroyan. Harcourt, Brace.

SKYLARK, by Samson Raphaelson. Random House.

MARGIN FOR ERROR, by Clare Boothe. Random House.

MORNING'S AT SEVEN, by Paul Osborn. Samuel French.

1940-1941

NATIVE SON, by Paul Green and Richard Wright. Harper.

WATCH ON THE RHINE, by Lillian Hellman. Random House.

THE CORN IS GREEN, by Emlyn Williams. Random House.

LADY IN THE DARK, by Moss Hart. Random House.

ARSENIC AND OLD LACE, by Joseph Kesselring. Random House.

MY SISTER EILEEN, by Joseph Fields and Jerome Chodorov. Random House.

FLIGHT TO THE WEST, by Elmer Rice. Coward-McCann.

CLAUDIA, by Rose Franken Meloney. Farrar & Rinehart.

MR. AND MRS. NORTH, by Owen Davis. Samuel French.

GEORGE WASHINGTON SLEPT HERE, by George S. Kaufman and Moss Hart. Random House.

1941-1942

IN TIME TO COME, by Howard Koch. Dramatists' Play Service.

THE MOON IS DOWN, by John Steinbeck. Viking.

BLITHE SPIRIT, by Noel Coward. Doubleday, Doran.

JUNIOR MISS, by Jerome Chodorov and Joseph Fields. Random House.

CANDLE IN THE WIND, by Maxwell Anderson. Anderson House.

LETTERS TO LUCERNE, by Fritz Rotter and Allen Vincent. Samuel French.

JASON, by Samson Raphaelson. Random House.

ANGEL STREET, by Patrick Hamilton. Constable & Co., under the title "Gaslight."

UNCLE HARRY, by Thomas Job. Samuel French.

HOPE FOR A HARVEST, by Sophie Treadwell. Samuel French.

1942-1943

THE PATRIOTS, by Sidney Kingsley. Random House.

THE EVE OF ST. MARK, by Maxwell Anderson. Anderson House.

THE SKIN OF OUR TEETH, by Thornton Wilder. Harper.
WINTER SOLDIERS, by Dan James.
TOMORROW THE WORLD, by James Gow and Arnaud d'Usseau.
    Scribner.
HARRIET, by Florence Ryerson and Colin Clements. Scribner.
THE DOUGHGIRLS, by Joseph Fields. Random House.
THE DAMASK CHEEK, by John van Druten and Lloyd Morris. Ran-
    dom House.
KISS AND TELL, by F. Hugh Herbert. Coward-McCann.
OKLAHOMA!, by Oscar Hammerstein 2nd and Richard Rodgers.
    Random House.

1943-1944

WINGED VICTORY, by Moss Hart. Random House.
THE SEARCHING WIND, by Lillian Hellman. Viking.
THE VOICE OF THE TURTLE, by John van Druten. Random House.
DECISION, by Edward Chodorov.
OVER 21, by Ruth Gordon. Random House.
OUTRAGEOUS FORTUNE, by Rose Franken. Samuel French.
JACOBOWSKY AND THE COLONEL, by S. N. Behrman. Random
    House.
STORM OPERATION, by Maxwell Anderson. Anderson House.
PICK-UP GIRL, by Elsa Shelley.
THE INNOCENT VOYAGE, by Paul Osborn.

1944-1945

A BELL FOR ADANO, by Paul Osborn. Knopf.
I REMEMBER MAMA, by John van Druten. Harcourt, Brace.
THE HASTY HEART, by John Patrick. Random House.
THE GLASS MENAGERIE, by Tennessee Williams. Random House.
HARVEY, by Mary Chase.
THE LATE GEORGE APLEY, by John P. Marquand and George S.
    Kaufman.
SOLDIER'S WIFE, by Rose Franken. Samuel French.
ANNA LUCASTA, by Philip Yordan. Random House.
FOOLISH NOTION, by Philip Barry.
DEAR RUTH, by Norman Krasna. Random House.

1945-1946

STATE OF THE UNION, by Howard Lindsay and Russel Crouse.
    Random House.
HOME OF THE BRAVE, by Arthur Laurents. Random House.

DEEP ARE THE ROOTS, by Arnaud d'Usseau and James Gow. Scribner.

THE MAGNIFICENT YANKEE, by Emmet Lavery. Samuel French.

ANTIGONE, by Lewis Galantière (from the French of Jean Anouilh). Random House.

O MISTRESS MINE, by Terence Rattigan. Published and revised by the author.

BORN YESTERDAY, by Garson Kanin. Viking.

DREAM GIRL, by Elmer Rice. Coward-McCann.

THE RUGGED PATH, by Robert E. Sherwood. Scribner.

LUTE SONG, by Will Irwin and Sidney Howard. Published version by Will Irwin and Leopoldine Howard.

1946-1947

ALL MY SONS, by Arthur Miller. Reynal & Hitchcock.

THE ICEMAN COMETH, by Eugene G. O'Neill. Random House.

JOAN OF LORRAINE, by Maxwell Anderson. Published by Maxwell Anderson.

ANOTHER PART OF THE FOREST, by Lillian Hellman. Viking.

YEARS AGO, by Ruth Gordon. Viking.

JOHN LOVES MARY, by Norman Krasna. Copyright by Norman Krasna.

THE FATAL WEAKNESS, by George Kelly. Samuel French.

THE STORY OF MARY SURRATT, by John Patrick. Dramatists' Play Service.

CHRISTOPHER BLAKE, by Moss Hart. Random House.

BRIGADOON, by Alan Jay Lerner and Frederick Loewe. Coward-McCann.

1947-1948

A STREETCAR NAMED DESIRE, by Tennessee Williams. New Directions.

MISTER ROBERTS, by Thomas Heggen and Joshua Logan. Houghton Mifflin.

COMMAND DECISION, by William Wister Haines. Random House.

THE WINSLOW BOY, by Terence Rattigan.

THE HEIRESS, by Ruth and Augustus Goetz.

ALLEGRO, by Richard Rodgers and Oscar Hammerstein 2d. Knopf. Music published by Williamson Music, Inc.

EASTWARD IN EDEN, by Dorothy Gardner. Longmans, Green.

SKIPPER NEXT TO GOD, by Jan de Hartog.

AN INSPECTOR CALLS, by J. B. Priestley.
ME AND MOLLY, by Gertrude Berg.

1948-1949

DEATH OF A SALESMAN, by Arthur Miller. Viking.
ANNE OF THE THOUSAND DAYS, by Maxwell Anderson. Sloane.
THE MADWOMAN OF CHAILLOT, by Maurice Valency, adapted from
the French of Jean Giraudoux. Random House.
DETECTIVE STORY, by Sidney Kingsley. Random House.
EDWARD, MY SON, by Robert Morley and Noel Langley. Random
House, New York, and Samuel French, London.
LIFE WITH MOTHER, by Howard Lindsay and Russel Crouse.
Knopf.
LIGHT UP THE SKY, by Moss Hart. Random House.
THE SILVER WHISTLE, by Robert Edward McEnroe. Dramatists'
Play Service.
TWO BLIND MICE, by Samuel Spewack. Dramatists' Play Service.
GOODBYE, MY FANCY, by Fay Kanin. Samuel French.

1949-1950

THE COCKTAIL PARTY, by T. S. Eliot. Harcourt, Brace.
THE MEMBER OF THE WEDDING, by Carson McCullers. Houghton
Mifflin.
THE INNOCENTS, by William Archibald. Coward-McCann.
LOST IN THE STARS, by Maxwell Anderson and Kurt Weill. Sloane.
COME BACK, LITTLE SHEBA, by William Inge. Random House.
THE HAPPY TIME, by Samuel Taylor. Random House.
THE WISTERIA TREES, by Joshua Logan. Random House.
I KNOW MY LOVE, by S. N. Behrman. Random House.
THE ENCHANTED, by Maurice Valency, adapted from a play by Jean
Giraudoux. Random House.
CLUTTERBUCK, by Benn W. Levy. Dramatists' Play Service.

1950-1951

GUYS AND DOLLS, by Jo Swerling, Abe Burrows and Frank Loesser.
DARKNESS AT NOON, by Sidney Kingsley and Arthur Koestler. Ran-
dom House.
BILLY BUDD, by Louis O. Coxe and Robert Chapman. Princeton
University Press.
THE AUTUMN GARDEN, by Lillian Hellman. Little, Brown & Co.

BELL, BOOK AND CANDLE, by John van Druten. Random House.
THE COUNTRY GIRL, by Clifford Odets. Viking Press.
THE ROSE TATTOO, by Tennessee Williams. New Directions.
SEASON IN THE SUN, by Wolcott Gibbs. Random House.
AFFAIRS OF STATE, by Louis Verneuil.
SECOND THRESHOLD, by Philip Barry. Harper & Bros.

1951-1952

MRS. MCTHING, by Mary Coyle Chase.
THE SHRIKE, by Joseph Kramm. Random House.
I AM A CAMERA, by John van Druten. Random House.
THE FOURPOSTER, by Jan de Hartog.
POINT OF NO RETURN, by Paul Osborn. Random House.
BAREFOOT IN ATHENS, by Maxwell Anderson. Sloane.
VENUS OBSERVED, by Christopher Fry. Oxford.
JANE, by S. N. Behrman and Somerset Maugham. Random House.
GIGI, by Anita Loos and Colette. Random House.
REMAINS TO BE SEEN, by Howard Lindsay and Russel Crouse.
     Random House.

1952-1953

THE TIME OF THE CUCKOO, by Arthur Laurents. Random House.
BERNARDINE, by Mary Coyle Chase.
DIAL "M" FOR MURDER, by Frederick Knott. Random House.
THE CLIMATE OF EDEN, by Moss Hart. Random House.
THE LOVE OF FOUR COLONELS, by Peter Ustinov.
THE CRUCIBLE, by Arthur Miller. Viking.
THE EMPEROR'S CLOTHES, by George Tabori. Samuel French.
PICNIC, by William Inge. Random House.
WONDERFUL TOWN, by Joseph Fields, Jerome Chodorov, Betty
     Comden and Adolph Green. Random House.
MY 3 ANGELS, by Sam and Bella Spewack.

WHERE AND WHEN THEY WERE BORN

(Compiled from the most authentic records available)

Abbott, George .... Forestville, N. Y. 1889
Abel, Walter .... St. Paul, Minn. 1898
Addy, Wesley .... Omaha, Neb. 1912
Aherne, Brian .... King's Norton, England 1902
Aldrich, Richard .... Boston, Mass. 1902
Anders, Glenn .... Los Angeles, Cal. 1890
Anderson, Judith .... Australia 1898
Anderson, Maxwell .... Atlantic City, Pa. 1888
Arthur, Jean .... New York City 1905
Ashcroft, Peggy .... Croydon, England 1907

Bainter, Fay .... Los Angeles, Cal. 1892
Bankhead, Tallulah .... Huntsville, Ala. 1902
Barrymore, Ethel .... Philadelphia, Pa. 1879
Barrymore, Lionel .... Philadelphia, Pa. 1878
Barton, James .... Gloucester, N. J. 1890
Behrman, S. N. .... Worcester, Mass. 1893
Bellamy, Ralph .... Chicago, Ill. 1904
Bergman, Ingrid .... Stockholm 1917
Bergner, Elisabeth .... Vienna 1900
Berlin, Irving .... Russia 1888
Best, Edna .... Hove, England 1900
Blackmer, Sidney .... Salisbury, N. C. 1898
Bolger, Ray .... Dorchester, Mass. 1904
Bondi, Beulah .... Chicago, Ill. 1892
Bourneuf, Philip .... Boston, Mass. 1912
Boyer, Charles .... Figeac, France 1899
Brando, Marlon .... Omaha, Neb. 1924
Brent, Romney .... Saltillo, Mex. 1902
Brown, Joe E. .... Holgate, Ohio 1892
Burke, Billie .... Washington, D. C. 1885
Byington, Spring .... Colorado Springs, Colo. 1898

Cagney, James .... New York City 1904
Cagney, Jeanne .... New York City 1920

388

Ethel Waters in "At Home with Ethel Waters"

Chase, Ilka ....New York City 1905
Chatterton, Ruth ....New York City 1893
Claire, Ina ....Washington, D. C. 1895
Clark, Bobby ....Springfield, Ohio 1888
Clift, Montgomery ....Omaha, Neb. 1921
Clive, Colin ....St. Malo, France 1900
Clurman, Harold ....New York City 1901
Cobb, Lee ....New York City 1911
Coburn, Charles ....Macon, Ga. 1877
Collinge, Patricia ....Dublin 1894
Collins, Russell ....New Orleans, La. 1897
Colt, Ethel Barrymore .. .. Mamaroneck, N. Y. 1911
Colt, John Drew ....New York City 1914
Conroy, Frank ....London, England 1885
Cook, Donald ....Portland, Ore. 1902
Cook, Joe ....Evansville, Ind. 1890
Cooper, Melville ....Birmingham, England 1896
Corbett, Leonora ....London, England 1908
Cornell, Katharine ....Berlin, Germany 1898
Coulouris, George ....Manchester, England 1906
Coward, Noel ....Teddington, England 1899
Cromwell, John ....Toledo, Ohio 1888
Cronyn, Hume ....London, Ontario 1912
Crothers, Rachel ....Bloomington, Ill. 1878
Crouse, Russel ....Findlay, Ohio 1893
Cummings, Constance ......Seattle, Wash. 1911

Dale, Margaret ....Philadelphia, Pa. 1880
Dana, Leora ....New York City 1923
Daniell, Henry ....London 1894
Davis, Owen ....Portland, Me. 1874
Derwent, Clarence ....London 1884
Dixon, Jean ....Waterbury, Conn. 1905
Douglas, Melvyn ....Macon, Ga. 1901
Dowling, Eddie ....Woonsocket, R. I. 1894
Drake, Alfred ....New York City 1914
Duncan, Todd ....Danville, Ky. 1900
Dunning, Philip ....Meriden, Conn. 1890
Durante, Jimmy ....New York City 1893

Eldridge, Florence ....Brooklyn, N. Y. 1901
Elsom, Isobel ....Cambridge, England 1893
Evans, Edith ....London, England 1888

Evans, Maurice .... Dorchester, England 1901
Evans, Wilbur .... Philadelphia, Pa. 1908
Evelyn, Judith .... Seneca, S. Dak. 1913
Ewell, Tom .... Owensboro, Ky. 1912

Fabray, Nanette .... New Orleans, La. 1921
Fay, Frank .... San Francisco, Cal. 1897
Ferber, Edna .... Kalamazoo, Mich. 1887
Ferrer, José .... Puerto Rico 1912
Field, Betty .... Boston, Mass. 1918
Field, Virginia .... London 1917
Fields, Gracie .... Rochdale, England 1898
Fitzgerald, Barry .... Dublin, Ireland 1888
Fitzgerald, Geraldine .... Dublin, Ireland 1914
Flemyng, Robert .... Liverpool 1912
Fletcher, Bramwell .... Bradford, Yorkshire, Eng. 1904
Fonda, Henry .... Grand Island, Neb. 1905
Fontanne, Lynn .... London, England 1887
Forbes, Brenda .... London, England 1909
Foy, Eddie, Jr. .... New Rochelle, N. Y. 1907
Francis, Arlene .... Boston, Mass. 1908
Fry, Christopher .... England 1907

Gahagan, Helen .... Boonton, N. J. 1900
Gaxton, William .... San Francisco, Cal. .... .1893
Geddes, Barbara Bel .... New York City 1922
Geddes, Norman Bel .... Adrian, Mich. 1893
George, Grace .... New York City 1879
Gershwin, Ira .... New York City 1896
Gielgud, Sir John .... London, England 1904
Gillmore, Margalo .... England 1901
Gilmore, Virginia .... El Monte, Cal. 1919
Gish, Dorothy .... Massillon, Ohio 1898
Gish, Lillian .... Springfield, Ohio 1896
Golden, John .... New York City 1874
Goodner, Carol .... New York City 1904
Gordon, Ruth .... Wollaston, Mass. 1896
Greaza, Walter .... St. Paul, Minn. 1900
Green, Martyn .... London, England 1899
Greenwood, Joan .... London, England 1921
Guinness, Alec .... London 1914
Gwenn, Edmund .... Glamorgan, Wales 1875

392 THE BEST PLAYS OF 1953-1954

Merman, Ethel ....Astoria, L. I. 1909
Middleton, Ray ....Chicago, Ill. 1907
Mielziner, Jo ....Paris, France 1901
Miller, Arthur ....New York City 1915
Miller, Gilbert ....New York City 1884
Mitchell, Thomas ....Elizabeth, N. J. 1892
Moore, Victor ....Hammonton, N. J. 1876
Moorehead, Agnes ....Clinton, Mass. 1906
Morgan, Claudia ....New York City 1912
Morley, Robert ....Semley, England 1908
Moss, Arnold ....Brooklyn, N. Y. 1910
Muni, Paul ....Lemberg, Austria 1895

Nagel, Conrad ....Keokuk, Iowa 1897
Natwick, Mildred ....Baltimore 1908
Neal, Patricia ....Packard, Ky. 1926
Nesbitt, Cathleen ....Cheshire, England 1889
Nugent, Elliott ....Dover, Ohio 1900

Odets, Clifford ....Philadelphia 1906
Oenslager, Donald ....Harrisburg, Pa. 1902
Olivier, Sir Laurence ....Dorking, Surrey, England 1907
Olsen, John Siguard (Ole) ... Peru, Ind. 1892
O'Malley, Rex ....London, England 1906
O'Neal, Frederick ....Brookville, Miss. 1905

Page, Geraldine ....Kirksville, Mo. 1925
Palmer, Lilli ....Posen, Austria 1914
Petina, Irra ....Leningrad, Russia 1900
Picon, Molly ....New York City 1898
Pinza, Ezio ....Rome, Italy 1895
Porter, Cole ....Peru, Ind. 1892
Price, Vincent ....St. Louis, Mo. 1914

Rains, Claude ....London, England 1889
Raitt, John ....Santa Ana, Cal. 1917
Rathbone, Basil ....Johannesburg 1892
Redman, Joyce ....Newcastle, Ireland 1918
Reed, Florence ....Philadelphia, Pa. 1883
Rennie, James ....Toronto, Canada 1890
Richardson, Sir Ralph ......Cheltenham, England 1902
Rice, Elmer ....New York City 1892
Roberts, Joan ....New York City 1918

Rodgers, Richard .... New York City 1902
Ross, Anthony .... New York City 1906
Royle, Selena .... New York City 1905

Sarnoff, Dorothy .... Brooklyn, N. Y. 1919
Saroyan, William .... Fresno, Cal. 1908
Scott, Martha .... Jamesport, Mo. 1914
Segal, Vivienne .... Philadelphia, Pa. 1897
Sherman, Hiram .... Boston, Mass. 1908
Sherwood, Robert Emmet .... New Rochelle, N. Y. 1896
Shumlin, Herman .... Atwood, Colo. 1898
Silvers, Phil .... Brooklyn, N. Y. 1911
Simms, Hilda .... Minneapolis, Minn. 1920
Skinner, Cornelia Otis ...... Chicago, Ill. 1902
Slezak, Walter .... Vienna, Austria 1902
Smith, Kent .... Smithfield, Me. 1910
Stapleton, Maureen .... Troy, N. Y. 1926
Starr, Frances .... Oneonta, N. Y. 1886
Stickney, Dorothy .... Dickinson, N. D. 1903
Stoddard, Haila .... Great Falls, Mont. 1914
Stone, Carol .... New York City 1917
Stone, Dorothy .... New York City 1905
Stone, Ezra .... New Bedford, Mass. 1918
Stone, Fred .... Denver, Colo. 1873
Straight, Beatrice .... Old Westbury, N. Y. 1918
Sullavan, Margaret .... Norfolk, Va. 1910
Sullivan, Francis L. .... London 1903

Tandy, Jessica .... London, England 1909
Tetzel, Joan .... New York City 1923
Thorndike, Sybil .... Gainsborough, England 1882
Tozere, Frederick .... Brookline, Mass. 1901
Tracy, Lee .... Atlanta, Ga. 1898
Truex, Ernest .... Red Hill, Mo. 1890

van Druten, John .... London, England 1902
Van Patten, Dick .... New York City 1929
Varden, Evelyn .... Venita, Okla. 1893

Walker, June .... New York City 1904
Walker, Nancy .... Philadelphia, Pa. 1922
Wallach, Eli .... Brooklyn, N. Y. 1915
Wanamaker, Sam .... Chicago, Ill. 1919

NECROLOGY

June 1, 1953—May 31, 1954

Adams, Maude, 80, actress. This "winsome, lonely dreamer of dreams" captivated audiences of three decades. Her career began at 9 months old during a performance of "The Lost Child" in Salt Lake City. When she was 16, she came under the management of Charles Frohman, with whom her career was thereafter closely identified. He staged and presented her plays from her first New York appearance in 1888 until his death on the *Lusitania* in 1915. She had been technically a star for 8 years before she opened at the Empire Theatre, and became world-famous, in James M. Barrie's "Peter Pan," November 6, 1905. Her Barrie roles came to be regarded as her most characteristic. She starred in "The Little Minister," "A Kiss for Cinderella," "Quality Street," "What Every Woman Knows" and "The Legend of Leonora." Other plays include "L'Aiglon," "Chantecler," "Twelfth Night" and "Romeo and Juliet." In 1931 she co-starred on tour with Otis Skinner in "The Merchant of Venice" but did not come to Broadway. She headed the drama department of Stephens College for five years, continuing as special adviser to the department after resigning as chairman in 1943. Born Salt Lake City; died Tannersville, N. Y., July 17, 1953.

Anderson, John Murray, 67, producer and director. Educated in Scotland, he came to the United States in 1910 as an antique dealer. Nine years later he entered show business by producing "The Greenwich Village Follies." It was a smash hit and he produced in all six editions of it. He created 34 musical comedies and revues (29 on Broadway and 5 in London), 7 circuses for Ringling Bros., 4 aquacades for Billy Rose, 11 pageants, 61 movie-house stage shows and 24 shows for night clubs; also the entire motion picture "The King of Jazz" and part of "Bathing Beauty." This is a grand total of 143 productions which employed over 11,000 performers. Some of the Broadway hits were "Life Begins at 8:40," "Ziegfeld Follies" of 1934, 1936, 1943, "Jumbo" and the last edition of "The Music Box Revue." His last production proved a hit—"John

397

Murray Anderson's Almanac." Born St. John's, Newfoundland; died New York, January 30, 1954.

Bailey, Frankie, 94, actress. Known as the girl with the "million dollar legs," she was a favorite Broadway showgirl of the '90s. She was 34 when she first wore tights and drew lasting attention. She appeared in most of the turn-of-the-century attractions at Weber & Fields' Music Hall, supporting such stars as Lillian Russell, Weber and Fields, and David Warfield. At 63 she went to Hollywood and played minor roles in several films. In 1936 she appeared in a revival of "The Black Crook" in Los Angeles. Born New Orleans; died Los Angeles, July 8, 1953.

Balderston, John, 64, playwright. Began his career as a newspaper man. He was a foreign correspondent for the *World* and served as war correspondent for the McClure Newspaper Syndicate 1914-1918. In collaboration with J. C. Squire he wrote "Berkeley Square"—produced in London in 1926 and on Broadway in 1929. He was also co-author of "Dracula," "Frankenstein" and "Farewell Performance." He wrote several original screen plays and adaptations including "Lives of a Bengal Lancer," "Prisoner of Zenda," "Gone with the Wind" and "Gaslight." Born Philadelphia; died Beverly Hills, Calif., March 8, 1954.

Bamberger, Theron, 59, stage producer. Began his career as a newspaper writer in Philadelphia. Came to New York and worked on the old New York *Globe* before becoming night city editor of the Evening *Post* in the late twenties. In 1935 he made his first Broadway production, "Fly Away Home"; in 1943, he produced "Tomorrow the World." For 13 years before his death he was managing director and producer of the Bucks County Playhouse, New Hope, Pa. Born Philadelphia; died New York, September 14, 1953.

Belmore, Bertha, 70, actress. Her long career, which embraced many roles on both sides of the Atlantic, began at the age of 8 in the children's pantomime "Robinson Crusoe" in Manchester, England. While still a child she toured with the John Tiller girls and for several seasons was Principal Boy in pantomimes; and for 7 years was one of the Belmore Sisters in British vaudeville. She came to the United States in 1911 with Ben Greet's Players and in 1912 made her Broadway debut with William Faversham in "Julius Caesar." During this early period she was also seen in the "Ziegfeld Follies." London did not see her until 1920 when she played there in "Irene." Among her other plays are "Johnny Belinda," "By Jupiter," "Antigone," "Caesar and Cleopatra" and "Gigi" with Audrey Hepburn.

Born Manchester, Eng.; died Barcelona, Spain, December 14, 1953.

Bernstein, Henri, 77, playwright. One of France's best-known playwrights, he was also one of the world's most successful—earning over $8,000,000. At his peak, before World War I, there was a Bernstein play acted somewhere every night for ten years and once there were 80 simultaneous performances of his plays. Among his many successes were "The Thief," "Samson," "Judith" and "Melo." Born Paris; died Paris, November 27, 1953.

Boardman, Lillian, 60, actress. For several years she appeared in Gus Edwards' revues and later was seen in such musicals as "Poor Mama," "Louisiana Lou" and "Canary Cottage." She retired some 20 years before her death. Born Bay City, Mich.; died New York, September 19, 1953.

Bruce, Nigel, 58, actor. Best known for his portrayals of Dr. Watson in film and radio dramatizations of "Sherlock Holmes," Mr. Bruce was also an accomplished stage performer. He made his first Broadway appearance in Noel Coward's "This Was a Man" in 1929 and is well remembered for his performance in "Springtime for Henry." Born Ensenada, Mexico; died Santa Monica, Calif., October 8, 1953.

Burry, Solen, 50, actor. During a 20-year career he played in vaudeville and stock as well as such Broadway plays as "Having Wonderful Time," "Native Son," "Barefoot Boy with Cheek" and "Death of a Salesman." Died Long Island City, N. Y., June 8, 1953.

Chalzel, Leo, 52, actor. He entered vaudeville at 16, then played stock on the road. He presented vaudeville acts with Al Lewis and Max Gordon and played the circuits in New York and London. Some of his better-known stage appearances include "My Sister Eileen," "My Dear Children" with John Barrymore, "Othello" with Walter Huston, "Here Come the Clowns" and "The Iceman Cometh." He also did considerable Summer stock and numerous films. Born Dayton, Ohio; died Westport, Conn., July 16, 1953.

Clark, Barrett Harper, 62, author and editor. After being an actor and an assistant stage manager for Mrs. Fiske he became an instructor in drama at Chautauqua, N. Y., and also taught at Columbia. From 1918 to 1936 he was literary editor for Samuel French. He was editor and co-editor of many books, and translator of many plays. He helped organize The Dramatists' Play Service and was long head of that organization. Born Toronto; died Briarcliff Manor, N. Y., August 5, 1953.

Cropper, Roy, 58, actor. He began his career as a boy soprano in the Cathedral Church of St. Paul at St. Paul. His first stage appearance was as a child on tour with William Faversham in "Herod" and his first Broadway appearance was in "Chu Chin Chow" in 1917. Since then New Yorkers have seen him in "Blossom Time," "Ziegfeld Follies of 1923," "The Student Prince," "Castles in the Air," The Milton Aborn Opera Company and The Civic Light Opera Company. Born Boston; died Miami, Fla., May 14, 1954.

Devereaux, Louise Drew, 72, actress. She made her New York stage debut in 1901, with her father, John Drew, in "Second in Command." She was also in "Iris," "Whitewashing Julia," "Strongheart," "Her Sister" and revivals of "Trelawney of the Wells" and "Alice Sit by the Fire." In the last three she supported her cousin, Ethel Barrymore. Her most important role was in 1914 in "It Pays to Advertise." Born New York; died New York, April 23, 1954.

Duncan, Augustin, 80, actor, producer, director. He made his Broadway acting debut in 1900 with Richard Mansfield in "Henry V." For the next twenty years he was on the New York stage. He both staged and played the lead in "John Ferguson," the play that established the Theatre Guild. He had a hand in the growth of the Provincetown Playhouse and the Greenwich Village Theatre as well as in the development of Actors' Equity. In the thirties he was with Maurice Evans in "Richard II" and "Hamlet." For the past twenty odd years he had been blind. His last Broadway appearance was in "Lute Song" with Mary Martin in 1946. He was the brother of Isadora Duncan. Born San Francisco; died Astoria, N. Y., February 20, 1954.

Edwards, Alan, 61, actor. After attending Rutgers and Princeton Universities, he took up acting and played leads opposite such stars as Leonore Ulric, Jane Cowl, Nora Bayes, Peggy Wood and Dorothy Stone. He began his motion picture career as early as 1912 and worked for nearly every major studio. Some of his films are "The White Sister," "Mr. District Attorney" and "Junior Miss." Born New York; died Los Angeles, May 8, 1954.

Ephriam, Lee, 76, producer. Mr. Ephriam emigrated to London in 1909 after losing a lucrative business in motors in the San Francisco earthquake. He traveled all over Europe before he began to produce plays in 1918, specializing in American hits for British audiences. His greatest venture of this kind was "Rose Marie" in 1925. Other American hits he brought to

London include "Sunny," "Desert Song," "Funny Face," "Rio Rita" and "On Your Toes." He also brought such London hits as "Sweet Aloes" and "Spring Meeting" to New York. Born Hopkinsville, Ky.; died London, September 26, 1953.

Fancourt, Darrell, 65, actor. Studied singing in England and Germany and in 1919 made his first stage appearance at Covent Garden, London, in "Prince Igor." The next year he joined the D'Oyly Carte Co., playing many Gilbert and Sullivan roles (he sang the title role of "The Mikado" over 3,000 times). With this company he came to New York in 1934, '36, '39, '47 and '51. Born London; died London, August 29, 1953.

Farnum, William, 76, actor. A professional actor for more than 50 years, he made his debut at the age of ten in a play with Edwin Booth. At 16 he joined a New Orleans stock company and later became a member of the Boston Amusement Stock Co. After 5 years in "Ben Hur" he formed his own repertory company. His first motion picture was "The Spoilers" which brought him fame and fortune and led to the making of many others. He was the highest-paid star of his era. In 1925, he returned to the stage in "The Buccaneer." He is said to have lost $2,000,000 in the 1929 stock market crash and shortly thereafter his fame declined and he was forced to play bit parts. In 1942 when "The Spoilers" was re-made he had a minor role. His brothers, Dustin and Marshall, were both well-known actors. Born Boston; died Hollywood, June 5, 1953.

Fortescue, Violet, 78, actress. She made her stage debut at five and later toured Australia and the English provinces. She supported Maxine Elliott and Mrs. Fiske and was in such plays as "Rebecca of Sunnybrook Farm," "Poor Little Rich Girl" and "The Heart of Paddy Whack." Born Columbus, Ga.; died New York, September 16, 1953.

Grant, Sydney, 80, actor. Active in the theatre for more than 60 years he began his career in 1890 in "Shore Acres." His last role was in the National Company of "Guys and Dolls." He was featured in "Madame Sherry" and "The Little Whopper" as well as a number of "Passing Shows." Died Santa Monica, Calif., July 12, 1953.

Grayson, Bette, 32, actress. The former wife of playwright Clifford Odets had appeared in revivals of "Night Music" and "Golden Boy." Died New York, February 22, 1954.

Greenstreet, Sydney Hughes, 74, actor. He began his career with the Ben Greet Players after a try at supervising a tea plantation in Ceylon and selling beer for a brewery in England. In 1904 he came to the United States with Ben Greet and for 5 years thereafter was a leading comedian in Shakespearean repertory. He knew more than 12,000 lines of Shakespeare. He appeared with Sir Herbert Beerbohm Tree, Julia Marlowe, Lou Tellegen, Margaret Anglin and the Lunts. He was with the latter for more than six years. His greatest recognition, however, came at 62 when he appeared in the motion picture "The Maltese Falcon" and from that time forward he was in constant demand by the picture companies. He played in such films as "Casablanca," "Across the Pacific," "The Velvet Touch," "Three Strangers" and many others. Born Sandwich, Kent; died Hollywood, January 18, 1954.

Hall, Porter, 65, actor. Well known on both stage and screen, he was early in his career a member of the Robert Mantell and Fritz Lieber Shakespeare Companies and later was prominent in Theatre Guild productions. He won special praise for his fine performances in "Night Hostess" and "The Dark Tower." Some of his pictures include "The Plainsman," "Dark Command" and "Double Indemnity." Died Los Angeles, October 6, 1953.

Harris, Leonore, age unrecorded, actress. Early in her career she was in "The Military Maid," "The Two Schools," "The Girl from Kay's" and "Idols." Later she was in such hits as "Our Betters" and "Dodsworth." Her last Broadway appearance was in Noel Coward's "Present Laughter." Died New York, September 27, 1953.

Herczeg, Geza, 65, playwright. Began his career as a war correspondent during the Balkan Wars and World War I, writing his first play in 1917. Before coming to the United States he was in the press department for the Hungarian Ministry of State. He collaborated with Alfred Gruenwald on the book for "Mr. Strauss Goes to Boston," and wrote scenarios for many films, including "Florian," "The Burning Bush" and "Zola." He wrote "Wonder Bar" for Al Jolson. Born Hungary; died Rome, February 28, 1954.

Horwin, C. Jerome, 49, author. He is perhaps best known for his screen plays—such as "Rose of Washington Square," "Stormy Weather" and "Gold Diggers." He also wrote the stage play "My Dear Children" which served John Barrymore as a vehicle for over two years. Born New York; died Hollywood, April 24, 1954.

Hymer, John B., 77, playwright. He co-authored many a Broadway success, the most successful being "East Is West" with

Samuel Shipman. He also wrote nearly 500 vaudeville sketches and many silent films for M.G.M. Born Nashville, Tenn.; died Los Angeles, June 16, 1953.

Kalman, Emmerich, 71, composer. As a young man he attended the Academy of Dramatic Arts and the Royal Academy of Music in Budapest. He became music critic on a Budapest paper and at 27 made a name for himself throughout Europe with his second operetta "Autumn Maneuvers." He was known at one time as one of the Big Three composers of Vienna, the others being Franz Lehar and Oskar Straus. In 1912 he composed "Sari" produced here in 1914. Among his other works produced in New York are "Her Soldier Boy," "The Riviera Girl," the very popular "Countess Maritza" and, in 1945, "Marinka." He was decorated with both Austrian and Hungarian government honors. Born Siofok, Hungary; died Paris, October 30, 1953.

Komisarjevsky, Theodore, 71, director. He studied architecture in Moscow but in 1906 joined his sister's theatre as managing director. During the next 12 years he directed many plays there and in his own theatre. In 1919 he went to England where he had a brilliant career directing a long list of plays. The Theatre Guild brought him to New York to direct its productions of "Peer Gynt" and "The Tidings Brought to Mary" in the season of 1922-23. In 1940 Broadway saw "Russian Bank," of which he was co-author as well as producer and director. In 1947 he did his last Broadway play when he presented "Crime and Punishment." Born Venice, Italy; died Darien, Conn., April 17, 1954.

Lait, Jack, 71, author. A prolific writer of the knock-down, drag-out school of journalism, Jacquin Leonard Lait started his career as a picture messenger for Chicago newspapers, eventually rising to be editor of the New York *Daily Mirror*. With Lee Mortimer he wrote the controversial "Confidential" books on New York, Chicago, Washington and the United States. In 1914 Oliver Morosco produced his first play "Help Wanted." He also wrote 17 motion pictures including "Broadway Melody" and "The Big House." Born New York; died Beverly Hills, Calif., April 1, 1954.

Laurie, Joe, Jr., 62, actor. By the time he was 16 he had held 80 jobs. He teamed with Aleen Bronson and trouped back and forth across the vaudeville stages of the United States. This was a forerunner of the "dumb blonde" act. He was in such Broadway successes as "Plain Jane," "If I Was Rich," "Weather Clear, Track Fast." He wrote over 100 sketches for vaudeville teams and for many years had a column in *Variety*. With Abel Green he wrote "Show Biz" and last year, "Vaudeville." Born New York; died New York, April 29, 1954.

Lonsdale, Frederick, 73, playwright. One of the world's most successful playwrights, he tried his hand at soldiering and was once a steward on an ocean liner. His first play was "The Early Worm" and King Edward VII told him it was "bad" but that in time he would write a good play if he took a little more trouble. He wrote lyrics for popular musicals, among them "Maid of the Mountains" and "The Balkan Princess." Writing in the tradition of Sheridan and Wilde he turned out one play after another. Among his best known are "On Approval," "Aren't We All?", "Spring Cleaning" and "The Last of Mrs. Cheyney." Many of his plays were made into motion pictures. Born on the channel island of Jersey; died London, April 4, 1954.

Lovell, Raymond, 53, actor. A familiar stage player in Britain since 1924, he made his only Broadway appearance in "Cry of the Peacock" in 1950 which ran only 2 performances. Made his stage debut in Dundalk, Ireland, in 1924 in "East Lynne." He was well known here for his many screen roles in such pictures as "Blackout," "The Young Mr. Pitt," "Quartet" and "Caesar and Cleopatra." He was also a theatre director and had his own repertory companies in Leeds and Southampton. Born Montreal; died London, October 1, 1953.

McKee, John, still an actor and director in his 80's. His career began with Joseph Jefferson in "Rip Van Winkle." In 1900 he was in New York in "Madame X." Among his other plays were "Excuse Me," "The Devil," "Libel," "Three Wise Fools," "Popsy," "The Big Knife" and—in 1951—"Romeo and Juliet." Born Belfast, Ireland; died New York, December 28, 1953.

MacMillan, Violet, 66, actress. Known as the Cinderella Girl after winning a contest to find a girl with small enough feet to wear a "Cinderella" golden slipper. She played the lead in the Broadway production of "The Time, the Place and the Girl." She supported Blanche Ring, Trixie Friganza and Julian Eltinge. Died Grand Rapids, Mich., December 28, 1953.

Mitchell, Esther, age unrecorded, actress. Made her stage debut in "The Blue Bird" in Sydney, Australia. Known for her "typical American" roles in Australia and South Africa, she came to the United States in 1922 and made her debut in "The Madras House" at the Neighborhood Playhouse. Since then she has appeared in many important Broadway roles in plays ranging from "The Cherry Orchard" and "Cyrano de Bergerac" to "The Corn Is Green" and "O Mistress Mine." She was in many Summer productions as well as radio and TV. Born Newcastle, New South Wales; died New York, November 26, 1953.

Mitchell, Millard, 48, actor. A leading Broadway character actor, he first appeared on the New York stage in 1925 in "The Holy Terror" and thereafter was in more than 50 productions including "Three Men on a Horse," "Boy Meets Girl" and "Mr. and Mrs. North." In recent years he alternated between stage and screen, playing in such pictures as "Strictly Dishonorable" and "My Six Convicts." He consistently refused star billing to avoid type casting. Born Havana, Cuba; died Santa Monica, Calif., October 13, 1953.

Moorhead, Jean, 39, actress. Began her career in the chorus of "Hellzapoppin' " in 1940 and remained with Olsen and Johnson musicals for five years, graduating to leading roles. She was recently talent director of the Miss America pageant. Born Ellisville, Miss.; died Linwood, N. J., November 1, 1953.

Morley, Victor, 82, actor. Made his first Broadway appearance with Grace George in "Pretty Peggy" in 1902. He was in such productions as "The Prince of Pilsen," "The Earl and the Girl," "The Student Prince" and "Blossom Time." Born Greenwich, Eng.; died New York, June 29, 1953.

Morris, Mrs. Felix, age not recorded, actress. As Florence Wood she made her stage debut in the Augustin Daly Stock Company in "The Lass O' Lowries." She retired after her marriage to comedian Felix Morris but resumed her career after his death appearing in such plays as "The Scarecrow," "Old Lady 31" and "One Night in Rome." Born Hannibal, Mo.; died Princeton, N. J., April 17, 1954.

Moscowitz, Jennie, 85, actress. This famous Jewish actress was noted for her mother roles. She celebrated her 55th year on the stage in 1943 when she appeared as Paul Muni's mother in "Counsellor-at-Law." She made her debut at 13 in Rumania as Nanine in "Camille." Sarah Bernhardt was the star and took such a liking to her that she guided her career for the next five years. She came to New York at 18 and supported such Yiddish actors as Jacob Adler and David Kessler. She learned English and thus achieved a role in "The Melting Pot" with Walker Whiteside. David Belasco engaged her to support David Warfield in "The Auctioneer" and thereafter she seldom lacked an engagement. She was seen in such plays as "Partners

Again," various editions of "Potash and Perlmutter" and "Kosher Kitty Kelly." Born Rumania; died New York, July 26, 1953.

O'Brien, Neil, 85, minstrel. While still a young man he joined a traveling minstrel company and later appeared with the Primrose and Dockstader Minstrel Co. During the early part of the century he was in many Broadway plays. In 1913, after playing for some time in vaudeville, he founded the Neil O'Brien Minstrel Co. and toured the country with it until 1925. Born Port Dickinson, N. Y.; died Mt. Vernon, N. Y., January 13, 1954.

O'Neill, Eugene Gladstone, 65, playwright. Generally regarded as America's foremost playwright, his prolific talents won him the Pulitzer Prize three times and he was the second United States citizen to win the Nobel Prize for Literature. In all he wrote some 38 plays. His father was James O'Neill, who starred for years in the "Count of Monte Cristo." For a time young Eugene was stage manager for his father. Later he shipped as an ordinary seaman on a freighter bound for Buenos Aires. This began his acquaintance with the forecastle that was to stand him in good dramatic stead later on. In 1912 he worked as a reporter on the New London *Telegraph*. His career as a newspaperman was cut short at the end of four months when he developed a mild case of tuberculosis and was sent to a sanitarium. It was during his stay there that he began to read Strindberg which, above all else, he once said, gave him a vision of what modern drama could be and first inspired him to write for the theatre. He then spent a year in George Baker's famous playwriting course at Harvard. In 1916 he went to live in Provincetown, Mass., and it was while here that the Wharf Theatre produced his one-act "Bound East for Cardiff." His first long play to be produced on Broadway was "Beyond the Horizon" in 1920. It was his first Pulitzer prize winner, and established him not only as a ranking playwright but also as a money-maker. The Theatre Guild began producing his plays in 1927 with "Marco Millions" and staged all of his plays thereafter. His other Pulitzer prize winners were "Anna Christie" and "Strange Interlude" but many feel that his greatest was "Mourning Becomes Electra" produced in 1931. Other plays include "All God's Chillun's Got Wings," "Desire Under the Elms," both of which caused considerable controversy, "The Hairy Ape," "The Emperor Jones," "The Iceman Cometh," and his one sentimental comedy "Ah, Wilderness!". Born New York; died, Boston, November 27, 1953.

Paige, Mabel, 74, actress. She began her career at an early age and for 30 years had her own stock company in the South. Her first motion picture, in 1924, was "Young and Willing" which was adapted from the Broadway play "Out of the Frying Pan" in which Miss Paige made a personal hit. She was also on Broadway in "Two Blind Mice." Some of her other pictures include "True to Life," "Dangerous Partners" and "Houdini." Born New York; died Van Nuys, Calif., February 8, 1954.

Payne, William (Lou), 80, actor. He played leading roles in such plays as "Eben Holden," "David Garrick" and "Mrs. Leffingwell's Boots." He was married to one of the most glamorous stars of her time, Mrs. Leslie Carter, and managed her business affairs until her death in 1937. He was also seen in several motion pictures. Born Elmira, N. Y.; died Hollywood, August 14, 1953.

Randolph, Louise, 83, actress. Made her stage debut in John Craig's Castle Square Stock Company in Boston. She was with Frances Starr in "The Easiest Way" and later toured extensively in stock. Mark Twain called her his favorite actress. Born Leavenworth, Kan.; died Port Chester, N. Y., November 2, 1953.

Rawlinson, Herbert, 67, actor. He came from England in 1910 as manager of the Belasco Stock Company of Los Angeles and later entered films, first as a leading man, then in character roles. His Hollywood career outshone his Broadway engagements which included "City Haul," "A Modern Virgin" and "When Ladies Meet." Born Brighton, Eng.; died Los Angeles, July 12, 1953.

Rennie, Hugh, 50, actor. Among the Broadway productions in which he appeared are "Joy to the World," "You Can't Take It with You," "Craig's Wife" and "Goodbye Again." He directed many Summer stock companies and was one of the best stage managers in the business. Born England; died New York, September 27, 1953.

Rice, Vernon, 46, drama editor. He was a graduate of the University of Oklahoma and the 47 Workshop of Prof. George Pierce Baker at Yale. He joined the *Post* in 1934 and served in several capacities before becoming drama editor. He also doubled as critic for a short time. He was a leading spokesman for a strong American theatre and particularly encouraged the development of the off-Broadway productions. He was elected presi-

dent of the Drama Desk in 1952 and served for one year. Born
St. Louis; died New York, May 5, 1954.

Richards, Donald, 34, actor. He made his debut with the St. Louis
Grand Opera Company. At 19 he won leading roles in "Faust"
and "Pagliacci." He was in "Winged Victory" and had Broadway leads in "Finian's Rainbow" and "Along Fifth Avenue."
He also appeared in radio and TV shows. Born New York;
died Ridgewood, N. J., September 26, 1953.

Ross, Robert, 52, actor. While taking a premedical course at the
University of California he became interested in the Little Theatre of Berkeley and turned to the stage. He got his professional training with the Daly Stock Co. and directed the Little
Theatre for a year. Rouben Mamoulian brought him east and
he served as assistant director at the Eastman Theatre in Roch-
ester. He made his Broadway debut in 1925 with Eva Le Gallienne's Civic Repertory Theatre. He was also in "The Farmer
Takes a Wife," "Mister Roberts" and "Point of No Return."
He was associate producer of "Dance Me a Song," was talent
scout for Warner Brothers and directed in St. Louis and Kansas
City. He was appearing with his wife, Margalo Gillmore, in
support of Mary Martin and Charles Boyer in "Kind Sir" when
he was taken ill and died. Born Port Colborne, Ont.; died
New York, February 23, 1954.

Scheff, Fritzi, 75, actress. She received her early training at Hoch's
Conservatoire in Frankfurt and made her stage debut in 1898
at the Royal Opera House in Munich in the title role of
"Martha." For the next few years she sang in various European theatres. In 1901 she made her first New York appearance at the Metropolitan as Musetta in "Bohème." Paderewski
called her "that little devil of the opera." In 1903 she went into
light opera, "Babette" being the first of many—"Fatinitza,"
"Girofle-Girofla," "The Prima Donna" and "The Duchess" were
others. But it was as Fifi in Charles Dillingham's production
of "Mlle. Modiste" that she had her greatest triumph and in
which she sang the song that became synonymous with her—
"Kiss Me Again." In late years she was seen in a few legitimate plays and made many radio, TV and night-club appearances. Born Vienna; died New York, April 8, 1954.

Shubert, Lee, 78, producer. With his brothers, Samuel and Jacob,
he started a theatrical career in his home town, and came to
New York in the first year of this century. They fought the
so-called "syndicate" of Klaw and Erlanger and soon had their
own circuit acquiring theatres throughout the country. At one

time while fighting the syndicate, it was Mr. Lee, as he was known, who boldly presented Sarah Bernhardt in halls, old theatres and even tents, because he was unable to get good bookings. Mr. Lee ruled the Shubert empire for over 50 years and had used the services of nearly every important performer since 1920 as well as virtually every successful playwright. They helped to fill the huge, but secret, Shubert coffers estimated at one time to hold in excess of $300,000,000. Mr. Lee was the chief sponsor of converting a play into the operetta "The Student Prince," still one of the most popular ever produced. He always resented the power of the critics. He admitted that they might be sincere but added "there's not a man living who can speak for the public in regard to the merits of a play." Born Syracuse, N. Y.; died, New York, December 25, 1953.

Silvers, Louis, 64, composer. He was well known on Broadway for his association with Gus Edwards' revues but achieved even greater fame as director of music for motion pictures, such as "The Jazz Singer" for Al Jolson. His song "April Showers" (sung by Jolson in "Bombo") drew 36 curtain calls on opening night. He served for 13 years as musical director for the Lux Radio Theatre. Born New York; died Hollywood, March 26, 1954.

Simmons, Ernest Romaine, in his late 80's, casting director and production assistant. Mr. Simmons had held only two positions in his life: one, for 15 years as accompanist and business manager for opera star Lillian Nordica; the other as dance director, casting director and production assistant for the Shuberts. Died New York, March 7, 1954.

Spooner, Edna May, 78, actress. She was a great favorite in Brooklyn stock companies from 1901 to World War I. Most of her appearances were with The Spooner Stock Co., managed by her mother, Mary Gibbs Spooner. She once operated the Fifth Avenue Theatre in New York. Died Sherman Oaks, Calif., July 14, 1953.

Stone, Lewis, 73, actor. Known and loved by three generations of entertainment seekers, Mr. Stone was perhaps best known for his portrayal of Judge Hardy in the pictures of the Hardy family. He was in silent pictures and in many Broadway productions. His first stage appearance was in "Sidetracked" in 1898; he also appeared in "The Bird of Paradise," "The Misleading Lady," "Inside the Lines," "The Brat" and "Where

Poppies Bloom." Born Worcester, Mass.; died Hollywood, September 12, 1953.

Straus, Oskar, 83, composer. He trained at the Vienna Conservatory and Vienna University and did graduate work at the Berlin School for Advanced Music. His first major success in the operetta field came in 1907 when "A Waltz Dream" was produced. "The Last Waltz" and "The Chocolate Soldier" followed. In all he had more than 50 light operas to his credit as well as many more serious works of music. He was among the last of the great Viennese waltz composers. Born Vienna; died Bad Ischl, Austria, January 11, 1954.

Strong, Jay, 57, actor, director, producer. For several years he was in stock and vaudeville (the latter with William Gaxton). He was a member of the original Washington Square Players and helped found the Metropolitan Players. His Broadway bow was in "Treasure Island" and he later appeared in "April," "Home Fires" and other Broadway productions. He directed the commercials for the TV "Show of Shows" and produced and wrote for TV as well. Died New York, December 1, 1953.

Tearle, Sir Godfrey, 68, actor. One of England's most distinguished actors, he made his debut in his father's (Osmond Tearle) company in "Richard III." His most notable roles included Hamlet, Comdr. Ferrers in "The Flashing Stream," and Antony to Katharine Cornell's Cleopatra. The listing of his roles takes up six columns in "Who's Who in the Theatre." His first picture role was as Romeo in 1906. He was the first president of British Actors' Equity, a post he held for 10 years. He was knighted in 1951. Born New York; died London, June 9, 1953.

Tilden, Bill, 60, tennis champion and actor. This great tennis star, always interested in drama and acting, made his stage debut in 1925 in "The Kid Himself." Subsequently he was in "Dracula," "They Got What They Wanted" and in Hollywood in his own play "The Nice Harmons." Born Germantown, Pa.; died Hollywood, June 4, 1953.

Vajda, Ernest, 67, playwright. He had five plays produced on Broadway: "Fata Morgana," "The Harem," "Grounds for Divorce," "Crown Prince" and "Confession." He also wrote such motion pictures as "The Love Parade" and "The Great Garrick." Success came early—Vajda's first play was produced while he was still an undergraduate at the University of Budapest. Before coming to the United States he was well known as a contributor to Budapest magazines and newspapers. Born Papa, Hungary; died Woodland Hills, Calif., April 3, 1954.

Wallace, Morgan, 72, actor. He started in stock and appeared for years with Lillian Russell. He also supported E. H. Sothern and Julia Marlowe. His more recent Broadway plays include "Women Go on Forever," "Ballyhoo" and "Loco." His pictures include "The Final Edition," "Mama Loves Papa" and "Thunder Mountain." He once had his own stock company in Bangor, Me. Born California; died Tarzana, Calif., December 12, 1953.

Wallis, Gladys, 80, actress. Before her marriage in 1899 to Samuel Insull, Sr., she was in a revival of "The Lady Slavey" in New York and appeared with William H. Crane's company. She returned to the stage briefly in 1926 heading her own company as Lady Teazle in "The School for Scandal." Born New York; died Chicago, September 23, 1953.

Walter, Edwin, 82, actor. He played the role of George Payne in "Tobacco Road" from 1933 to 1940. Started his career at 18 in Harlem's Comique Theatre. During 57 years on the stage he was seen in such productions as "The White Slave," "The Tavern," "Seven Keys to Baldpate," "Easy Come, Easy Go" and "She Means Business." Born Passaic, N. J.; died New York, November 23, 1953.

Wilde, Percival, 66, playwright. Graduated from Columbia in 1906, Mr. Wilde became one of the most prolific authors of plays, novels, short stories and textbooks on drama. His long list of plays includes: "The Aftermath," "The Reckoning," "Lady of Dreams" and (in collaboration) "The Woman in Room 13," "First Is Last" and "Crooked Gamblers." He is said to have had more plays produced in American "Little Theatres" than any other author. Perhaps his most important textbook is "The Craftmanship of the One-Act Play." He had served on the Advisory Board of the New York Theatre Guild, the Advisory Board of The Mystery Writers of America and had been Secretary and a Director of American Dramatists. Born New York; died New York, September 19, 1953.

Young, Roland, 65, actor. Educated to become an architect, he chose acting as a career. He made his first stage appearance in London in 1908 and his first appearance on Broadway in 1912. His numerous New York successes include "Beggar on Horseback," "The Last of Mrs. Cheyney," "The Queen's Husband," "Rollo's Wild Oat" and "Her Master's Voice." His pictures include: "The Guardsman," "Ruggles of Red Gap," "David Copperfield" and "Topper." Born London; died New York, June 5, 1953.

THE DECADES' TOLL

(Prominent Theatrical Figures Who Have Died in Recent Years)

	Born	Died
Adams, Maude	1872	1953
Anderson, John Murray	1886	1954
Arliss, George	1869	1946
Bennett, Richard	1873	1944
Bernstein, Henri	1876	1953
Carroll, Earl	1893	1948
Carte, Rupert D'Oyly	1876	1948
Christians, Mady	1900	1951
Cochran, Charles B.	1872	1951
Collier, Willie	1866	1943
Cowl, Jane	1884	1950
Craven, Frank	1890	1945
Crosman, Henrietta	1865	1944
Digges, Dudley	1879	1947
Duncan, Augustin	1872	1954
Errol, Leon	1881	1951
Fields, W. C.	1879	1946
Garfield, John	1913	1952
Gaige, Crosby	1883	1949
Hart, Lorenz	1895	1943
Hart, William S.	1870	1946
Hooker, Brian	1881	1947
Howard, Willie	1883	1949
Jolson, Al.	1886	1950
Jouvet, Louis	1887	1951
Kern, Jerome D.	1885	1945
Lawrence, Gertrude	1898	1952
Lehar, Franz	1870	1948
Loftus, Cecilia	1876	1943
Lord, Pauline	1890	1950
Mantle, Burns	1873	1948
Marlowe, Julia	1866	1950
Merivale, Philip	1886	1946

	Born	Died
Molnar, Ferenc	1878	1952
Moore, Grace	1901	1947
Nazimova, Alla	1879	1945
Nethersole, Olga	1870	1951
O'Neill, Eugene	1888	1953
Patterson, Joseph Medill	1879	1946
Perry, Antoinette	1888	1946
Powers, James T.	1862	1943
Reinhardt, Max	1873	1943
Romberg, Sigmund	1887	1951
Scheff, Fritzi	1879	1954
Selwyn, Edgar	1875	1944
Shaw, G. B.	1856	1950
Sheldon, Edward	1886	1946
Shubert, Lee	1875	1953
Tarkington, Booth	1869	1946
Tauber, Richard	1890	1948
Tyler, George C.	1867	1946
Ward, Fannie	1872	1952
Warfield, David	1866	1951
Webster, Ben	1864	1947
Whitty, Dame May	1865	1948
Woods, Al H.	1870	1951
Woollcott, Alexander	1887	1943
Youmans, Vincent	1899	1946

INDEX OF AUTHORS

415

INDEX OF PLAYS AND CASTS

**Bold face page numbers refer to pages on which
Cast of Characters may be found.**

420

INDEX OF PRODUCERS, DIRECTORS, DESIGNERS AND STAGE MANAGERS